THE CHRIST OF CATHOLICISM

THE CHRIST
OF CATHOLICISM

A MEDITATIVE STUDY

BY

DOM AELRED GRAHAM

MONK OF AMPLEFORTH

*"What Jesus Christ was yesterday, and is to-day,
He remains for ever."*
—Epistle to the Hebrews 13:8

LONGMANS, GREEN AND CO.

LONDON · NEW YORK · TORONTO

1947

LONGMANS, GREEN AND CO., INC.
55 FIFTH AVENUE, NEW YORK 3

LONGMANS, GREEN AND CO. LTD.
6 & 7 CLIFFORD STREET, LONDON, W. I.
NICOL ROAD, BOMBAY I
17 CHITTARANJAN AVENUE, CALCUTTA 13
36A MOUNT ROAD, MADRAS 2

LONGMANS, GREEN AND CO.
215 VICTORIA STREET, TORONTO I

PERMISSU SUPERIORUM
CONGREGATIONIS ANGLIAE
ORDINIS SANCTI BENEDICTI

•

NIHIL OBSTAT:
REGINALDUS PHILLIPS, S.T.L.
CENSOR DEPUTATUS

IMPRIMATUR:
E. MORROGH BERNARD
VICARIUS GENERALIS

WESTMONASTERII
7 MARTII 1947

THE CHRIST OF CATHOLICISM

Printed in the United States of America
VAN REES PRESS • NEW YORK

PREFACE

I believe ... in Jesus Christ, His only Son, our Lord....
What is the content of these familiar words of the Apostles'
Creed? This book is an attempt to answer that question.
Accordingly it does not aim at apologetic, that is, a defence
on merely rational grounds of the Catholic view of Christ;
except in so far as an explanation, here as elsewhere, is often
the most effective means of disarming hostile criticism. Curi-
ously enough, it seems that there is no single existing work, at
least in English, which covers the ground traversed in the following pages. The Catholic faithful are familiar, both with
the outlines of the Gospel story, and with the doctrine of the
Incarnation as this is summarily expressed in the Catechism.
At a deeper level, students have profited by an elucidation of
the New Testament in the light of recent research, as well
as by valuable theological treatises on the Incarnate Word.
We have also at our disposal a number of admirable "Lives"
of our Lord, some instructive expositions of the Gospel, in
addition to doctrinal and devotional studies of various aspects of his person and message. But we appear hitherto to
have lacked a synthesis of the scriptural testimony and the
dogmatic teaching of the Church on the most vital of all
questions: "What think you of Christ? Whose son is he?"

A number of reasons conspire to make such a work of co-
ordination perhaps especially timely. Pope Pius XII, in his
Encyclical *Divino afflante Spiritu*, has recalled the Catholic
world to the renewed study of Holy Scripture, making his
own the famous dictum of St Jerome: "To be ignorant of the
Scriptures is to be ignorant of Christ." We have lately bene-
fited by better and more intelligible translations of the New
Testament, both from the Latin Vulgate and from the original Greek,* so that there is now every opportunity for im-

* See Appendix, pp. 349–50.

v

plementing the wishes of the Pope. Among Catholics in general there is felt to be a need for focusing their lives ever more consciously upon him who is Life itself. And yet the all-embracing significance of Christ, to which the Church bears faithful witness, may by its very comprehensiveness have given some the excuse for remaining content with all too limited notions of what he stands for. For it is possible, while giving loyal assent to the Catholic Creeds, to harbour within the mind ideas which do little justice to their implications. Thus the gap which this book is an attempt to fill suggests the existence of one-sided views needing to be corrected by complementary aspects of the single truth. Let us consider one or two of them.

Even within the New Testament itself, one's mind may be so much in sympathy with what has been called, quite fallaciously, the "simple Gospel story" as to preclude an appreciation of St Paul's Epistles. Alternatively, we may be so attracted by the glorified and "mystical" Christ, with which these are chiefly concerned, as to take but little account of the concrete records of the Synoptic Gospels. Again, we can become so absorbed in the textual details of the Gospel narrative as to feel a certain embarrassment when confronted with its underlying theology. On the other hand, an exclusively theological approach can lead to an "intellectualist" treatment of the New Testament, to regarding it as little more than an armoury of dogmatic texts illustrative of a given thesis, and so to ignore the varieties and shades of meaning which go to form the complete picture. Worse still, we may yield to the temptation, within the acknowledged framework of Catholic doctrine, of devising an imaginative reconstruction of our Lord, using the Scripture texts as a starting-point for the elaboration of some personal fancy of our own. Such experiments are at best picturesque or sentimental, at worst unreal and even grotesque; either way they bring no lasting profit to devotion. A spiritual life not based on objective truth, so far as we are able to attain it, is built upon sand. Our task, therefore, is not to adapt the

Church's teaching on Jesus Christ to the limitations of our own minds, but to raise and expand the mind to grasping its essential purity.

Alas, this enterprise has only to be stated in words for us to see its impracticability. The Church alone is divinely commissioned to proclaim the complete view of Christ, with all that is involved in what St Augustine called the *Christus totus*. As individuals we can only approximate to so vast a conception. Hence the somewhat ambitious title of this book is at once modified by its sub-title, "a meditative study." This, not merely as indicating its devotional character, but as an acknowledgment that its author, despite himself, can hardly have escaped something of the subjectivity and one-sidedness which he deprecates. The most he can hope to achieve is an outline which is substantially faithful to its original, full enough to bring out its main features, not so laden with detail as to obscure the picture as a whole. To speak of the Christ of Catholicism is not, it need hardly be said, to reduce our subject to one of the many relative points of view still fashionable in certain quarters outside the Church—the Christ "of the Gospels," "of faith," "of history," and the rest; but to emphasize the fact that we are here concerned with a standpoint which is absolute and divinely authoritative. If the book may be said to argue any thesis, it is that all such partial viewpoints are invalidated by their very limitations; the Christ of Catholicism is the Christ of reality. What is aimed at is neither a formal treatise in theology nor a work exclusively of devotion, but an exposition acceptable to all who may be attracted by its title. It seemed needful to supply a preliminary chapter of some complexity, touching on matters of great importance to the theologian, as well as an "apparatus" for the benefit of the student; but these can be ignored without loss by those who feel no call to peruse them. The occasional introduction of phrases in Greek or Latin has proved unavoidable; in every case, however, they are either translated or paraphrased. Of the general reader no more is demanded than

viii   P R E F A C E

the attention and thoughtfulness inherent in any approach
to such a theme.

To those who are not, in the time-honoured phrase, "in
peace and communion with the Apostolic See," the work is
offered for their sympathetic consideration. Acknowledgment
is made, in a bibliographical note, of the works of non-
Catholic scholars which have been found suggestive in the
writing of this book. The use to which they have been put is
necessarily selective since, almost without exception, they
seem to the present writer to express an inadequate or incomplete Christology; though in this they give support to his conviction that whatever is of positive value in the whole field of
Christian scholarship finds its rightful place within the Catholic synthesis. However that may be, grateful tribute is due
to their learning and often profound insight, as well as to
their manifest devotion to him who is the Saviour of all men.
Even an occasional note of discord from a non-Christian
writer serves only to throw into relief the harmony of general
admiration. In a world without a vision by which to live,
noisy with the conflicting cries of "Christianity has failed"
and "Back to Christ," it should be of interest to know how
what is universally admitted to be the "great Church" of
Christendom understands her divine Founder—or, to be more
accurate, how a student cradled in the Catholic faith, enjoying the benefits of a *milieu* not unfavourable to meditating
on its content, ventures to present the treasure for which so
many of our contemporaries are searching in vain, "the unfathomable riches of Christ."

·   ·   ·

It remains to acknowledge the kindness of Messrs Thomas
Nelson and Sons for allowing use to be made of material
from a study by the author on "The Person and Teaching of
our Lord Jesus Christ," commissioned for the forthcoming
Catholic Commentary on Holy Scripture, and of Messrs
Burns Oates & Washbourne for similar permission with reference to an article entitled "The Church on Earth" for their
two-volume symposium, *The Teaching of the Catholic*

Church, together with the cordial acquiescence of the respective Editors of these publications. Sincere thanks are also due to the last-named publishers for agreeing to quotations being taken from Monsignor Ronald Knox's translation of the New Testament, and to Messrs Sheed & Ward for the like courtesy with reference to the American copyright of this work. To the Macmillan Company, New York, is owed an equal expression of thanks in connection with the late Very Reverend F. A. Spencer's translation of the New Testament from the Greek (edited by Charles J. Callan, O.P. and John A. McHugh, O.P.). With these must be coupled Messrs Browne & Nolan and Messrs Sands, for their co-operation with regard respectively to Dr. Edward J. Kissane's *Isaiah* (the author courteously consenting) and the *Psalter* newly translated from the Hebrew by the Reverend Cuthbert Lattey, S.J. for the Westminster Version of the Sacred Scriptures. A number of New Testament quotations appear from this version, thanks to the kindness of the General Editors, Fr John Murray, S.J. and, in particular, Fr Lattey, to whose friendly counsel in other respects also this book is indebted. Acknowledgment is due to Messrs William Heinemann for allowing two passages to be cited from Dr G. L. Prestige's *God in Patristic Thought,* with the author's kind consent, and to the Oxford University Press for similar permission with regard to Kierkegaard's *The Present Age* (translated by Alexander Dru and Walter Lowrie). Among other personal debts, mention must be made of Dom Ralph Russell and Dom Bernard Orchard of Downside Abbey, Fr Edmund F. Sutcliffe, S.J. of Heythrop College, and Dr R. C. Fuller of St Edmund's College, Ware, from whose criticism of portions of the material for this book much benefit has been derived. Not least among the obligations incurred are those to the Reverend J. H. Aveling for his collaboration in compiling two of the indexes and removing a number of blemishes from the text, and to Mr Laurence Eyres of Ampleforth College for invaluable help in correcting the proofs, as well as for his kind advice on not a few points of detail. Forgiveness is asked of any whose rights may have been inadvertently overlooked in this list of acknowledgments.

Finally, it seemed somehow inappropriate to attach any specific dedication to a book whose very title implies the intention of excluding none from its appeal. Had the author done so, it would have been to his own Abbot and Community at Ampleforth. By long-established precedent, such contribution as Benedictine monasticism has been able to make to Catholic Christianity has been corporate rather than individual in character. The present work is no exception to that rule. From the nature of the case, it can amount to little more than the sum total of the opportunities for study and reflection placed at its author's disposal by those whom it is his first duty to serve. One cannot, of course, evade in this way a personal responsibility for its defects; but whatever wisdom it may be found to contain is due, in largest measure, to those in whose company it was made so agreeable and easy to acquire it.

AELRED GRAHAM

Ampleforth Abbey, York
Feast of Saint Benedict
21 March 1947

CONTENTS

CHAPTER I

xi

CHAPTER IV

CHAPTER V

CHAPTER VI

CHAPTER VII

APPENDIX

INDEXES

NOTE

The use of initial capitals is always a difficulty when writing on the central Christian theme. Where almost everything is sacred, there is perhaps no need for the additional emphasis of any typographical device. Accordingly, the Biblical convention—a small initial letter for the pronominal form of the Divine Name—has been followed in the text.

A. G.

CHAPTER I

INTRODUCTION

§ 1. THE POINT OF VIEW OF THE CHURCH

COMMON experience has no clearer lesson to teach than that the strictly impartial judgement is among the rarest of human achievements. Strive as we may to form our opinions in the light of objective evidence, we find, if we are given to self-analysis, that our conclusions are conditioned, if not wholly determined, by alien factors. We see things, not as they are, but as we should like them to be, or alternatively, as coloured by our apprehension of what they might become; we project upon the situation our preconceived ideas and emotional states, our often unconscious sympathies and antipathies, and interpret it in the light of these. If this "pathetic fallacy" even obtrudes itself into such seemingly impersonal matters as science and philosophy, how much more manifold are the signs of it in our everyday human relationships! The heart undoubtedly has its reasons the mind knows nothing of; it can sometimes lead us to a truth beyond the reach of the detached processes of reasoning; but the depths of unreality into which men have been seduced in abandoning themselves to their instincts and intuitions give warning of the dangers involved in allowing free play to the irrational elements in our nature. If we are to arrive at a just opinion of our fellow-men at all, fundamentally we must do so by direct sense-observation and intellectual apprehension; the data thus provided must rigorously control all our subsequent reflections and psychological "insights"; they are not to be desiccated by an arid intellectualism on the one hand, or dissolved into the sensualist theories of psychoanalysis on the other.

These general observations are of some relevance to the meditation on which we are about to embark. So much depends upon the point of view, upon the frame of mind in which we approach our study. Historical enquiry, which should proceed in the light of evidence and a critical knowledge of human nature, can all too often be vitiated by unacknowledged prejudices and a naïve or superficial conception of the elements which make up man. No amount of comprehensive scholarship can compensate for these defects; the picture is falsified from the start. We are familiar with the "histories" which impose upon events the thesis-antithesis-synthesis of the Hegelian dialectic, with "biographies" whose subjects are coloured by the ideals, and even the personalities, of their authors. Most evidently do these personal factors betray themselves when men's deepest interests are engaged, when the answer that we give to our questioning is of vital importance to our own attitude and conduct. As soon as we enter the sphere of religion, above all, when we are concerned with the unique claims of Christianity, the inevitable question must present itself: What does this mean to me? We need not then be surprised at the abundance of "Lives" of Christ written "in the spirit of the age," as accommodations to the standpoint of the modern mind, or as ill-disguised essays in merely wishful thinking. They are often enough travesties of the New Testament records, without relevance to the earliest apostolical tradition, but they form an inverted tribute to the momentous significance of the subject with which they deal. Our western culture still retains sufficient of the Christian ethos for men to realize that they must make their reckoning with Christ our Lord, even if, with immeasurable pathos, they attempt to do so on their own terms rather than on his.

The confident boast of the biographer, *Je n'impose rien; je ne propose rien; j'expose,* could find no more complete refutation than in the Christological studies which have come to light during the past three centuries outside the Catholic Church. We have seen how the English Deists, rejecting the Gospel miracles, reduced the role of Jesus to that of a great prophet whose task it was to illuminate more profoundly the natural religion innate within the hearts of all men; how Voltaire and the eighteenth-century French rationalists followed this up by attacking the ethical code of the New Testament, as being a system devised by "artful priests" with a view to dominating and exploiting the masses; how Jean Jacques Rousseau was content to rank our Lord as a "sage hébreu," along with Socrates, a "sage grec." Nineteenth-century Germany saw the work of Strauss, Baur and the rise of the "Tübingen School"; here it was found convenient to ascribe whatever was unacceptable in the Gospel records to the "legend-creating faith" of the first Christians.

In 1863 appeared Renan's *La Vie de Jésus*—a historical novel, whose Hero is depicted as a philosopher-poet, a liberal with many of the characteristics of a French rationalist of the eighteen-sixties. The eschatological elements in our Lord's teaching absorbed the attention of Johannes Weiss, and still more notably, Albert Schweitzer, becoming for the latter all but the root-principle of explanation. According to this view, the moral code taught by Jesus is fundamentally an "interim-ethic," applicable only to the short intervening period between this present world and the world to come. Jesus himself was bound up almost entirely with the beliefs of his own people, time and country. For Harnack, on the other hand, he seems to rise so far above contemporary Judaism as to be practically untouched by it; he is in fact a modernist and philosopher, concerned to stress, on the highest humanitarian principles, the paramount importance of the Fatherhood of God. With Wellhausen the pendulum swings backwards once again: "Jesus was not a Christian; he was a Jew."

Thus the debate has continued down to our own day, the disputants having only this much ground in common: a concern to pursue their investigations in the light of reason alone and a rejection of any authoritative guidance, divine or otherwise. Viewed without prejudice, the various and mutually exclusive findings of modern scholarship do not inspire confidence in the capacity of the human mind to reach finality with regard to the significance of Jesus Christ. Is there any explanation, apart from the fallibility of even the most conscientious student, of the inconsistencies into which the private interpretation of Scripture has led the modern mind? Renan himself provides the clue; he propounds the dogma of rationalist unbelief, which has been accepted, consciously or unconsciously, by so many contemporary scholars. *Il n'y a pas de surnaturel;* the supernatural does not exist. Between the spiritual world and the world of nature there is no break in continuity; the one is as susceptible of scientific investigation as the other. Without in any way begging the question, it may be observed that an *a priori* denial of such a divine intervention into human affairs as is presupposed by the Catholic doctrine of the Incarnation is a crippling limitation to impose upon any mind intent on deciphering the New Testament. This is at length being realized even in circles hitherto most opposed to the ecclesiastical *magisterium* of Catholicism. The reaction towards the traditional Christology exemplified in such writers as Karl Barth and Emil Brunner, though raising difficulties of another order, is a striking demonstration of the failure of Liberal Protestantism to preserve, or to disclose anew, the essence of Christianity.

Is there then a point of view which, though accidentally modified according to the limitations of the individual intelligence, essentially transcends this ebb and flow of human opinion? The Catholic Church has always maintained that there is, and, moreover, that she has been divinely constituted for the express purpose of giving expression to it. With justifying this position we are not here directly concerned. Our task is the more modest one of explaining wherein the faithful believe it to consist. Of those who have been taught to regard such a claim as unwarranted presumption, we ask only that they should consider whether or not it be consistent with the deliverances of Scripture itself and the earliest Christian tradition. Further, they should reflect whether it was not antecedently probable that Christ, who on any showing attached vital importance to his teaching about himself, should have taken precautions to safeguard it from error; whether, finally, the scepticism and unbelief prevailing in the modern world, which have been fostered rather than dispelled by so much recent scholarship, do not imperatively demand some such authoritative guidance if complete shipwreck is not to be made of traditional Christianity.

The "faith that was handed down, once for all, to the saints" [1] was never, prior to the sixteenth century, conceived of as a mass of heterogeneous beliefs from which men could pick and choose according to their inclinations. It was an authoritative pattern of teaching, a "form of doctrine," to which, as St Paul reminded the Romans, the faithful had submitted themselves in obedience "from the heart." [2] The earliest believers were required, not to receive such of the Christian message as seemed to them most reasonable, but to concur in the "sound words of our Lord Jesus Christ" and in "that doctrine which is according to godliness." [3] Nothing could be more explicit than the following declaration in the second Johannine Epistle: "Whosoever revolteth and continueth not in the doctrine of Christ hath not God." [4] There is, from the beginning, a definite "confession" of faith to which we must "hold fast." [5] That this early apostolic confession was believed to be backed and supported by God's truth is clear from the words of our Lord himself: "I have still many things to say to you, but you cannot bear them now. But when he, the Spirit of truth, comes, he shall guide you into all the truth." [6] It is in the light of this assurance that we find the primitive Christian community speaking of itself as "the church of the living God, the pillar and ground of the truth." [7]

We know from the New Testament itself that Jesus gave further teaching to his disciples over and above what has come down to us in the four Gospels. St. Paul, when at

---

[1] Jude vs. 3.   [2] Rom. 6:17(R-D.).   [3] 1 Tim. 6:3.
[4] 2 John vs. 9(R.D.).   [5] Heb. 4:14.   [6] John 16:12–13(S.).
[7] 1 Tim. 3:15(R.D.).

Ephesus, recalls a well-remembered saying not recorded by the evangelists: ". . . the words spoken by the Lord Jesus himself, It is more blessed to give than to receive."[8] We have evidence also of additional instruction on the kingdom of God between the Resurrection and Ascension.[9] But at no point in our records do we find the conception of a definite doctrinal tradition, a formulated teaching transmitted from the apostles, to be lacking. The very title of what is perhaps the earliest Christian document we possess outside Scripture, the *Didache,* or "Teaching of the Twelve Apostles," composed between A.D. 90 and 100, testifies to it. St Polycarp, writing only a few years later to the Christians at Philippi, warns any who might be disposed to waver to "reject the vanity and false teaching of the many, and return to the doctrine which has been handed down from the beginning."[10] Long before the first Oecumenical Council at Nicaea, A.D. 325, we have abundant testimony to the existence of a *rule of faith* within the Church, a doctrinal norm or canon, conformity with which was demanded of the faithful. None of the ante-Nicene Fathers is more emphatic on this point than St Irenaeus, whose Christological teaching we shall later pass in review; writing before the end of the second century, he speaks of the "canon of the truth" which Christians accept at baptism,[11] and summarizes the content of faith "which the universal Church has received from the apostles and disciples."[12] At approximately the same date, about A.D. 200, Tertullian in appealing from heretical doctrine to "that rule, *regula,* which the Church has handed on from the apostles, the apostles from Christ, and Christ from God."[13] Almost identical language is to be found in a work written by Origen some thirty years later; he claims to be in continuity with the "apostolic preaching."[14] St Cyprian, whose dates are roughly A.D. 200-258, is no less clear;

---

[8] Acts 20:35.   [9] Cf. 1:3.
[10] *Epist. ad Philipp.* 7,1; *P.G.* 5, col. 1012.
[11] *Adversus haereses* 1,9,4; *P.G.* 7, col. 545.
[12] *Ibid.* 1,10,1; *P.G.* 7, col. 549-52.
[13] *De praescriptione haereticorum* 37; *P.L.* 2, col. 50.
[14] Περὶ ἀρχῶν 1, Praef., 4; *P.G.* 11, col. 117.

for him the final court of appeal is the "evangelical and apostolical tradition." [15]

What is implied in this "rule of faith," explicitly formulated in the Creeds or "Symbols," which are themselves developments of the primitive baptismal professions of belief required of the first converts to Christianity, is a living doctrinal Church tradition, *magisterium ecclesiasticum*, authorized to preserve intact, to hand on and explain, the original apostolic teaching. When we come to examine the proceedings of the Council of Nicaea, we find the principle of an ultimate ecclesiastical authority not only accepted but acted upon. The orthodox Fathers were at a loss to know how to counter the evasiveness of their Arian opponents with appropriate texts from Scripture; so they had recourse, admittedly with reluctance, to a non-scriptural word, ὁμοούσιον. Christ was *of the same substance* as the Father. The point at issue was not the words, but the *sense*, of Scripture, as Athanasius was at pains to point out.[16] Thus as long ago as the fourth century, in its first oecumenical assembly, the teaching Church showed itself aware of an authority to interpret decisively the deliverances of Scripture and unwritten Tradition, meeting new errors by new forms of doctrinal expression.

At the Council of Chalcedon, A.D. 451, the Catholic teaching on the Incarnation was finally formulated. Once more we are faced with a somewhat more elaborate terminology, accompanied by the avowal that those who employed it did so simply as the guardians and exponents of Tradition. The doctrine of the two natures in one divine person was defined, that Jesus Christ is "consubstantial [of the same substance] with the Father in respect of his deity, consubstantial with us in respect of his humanity . . . as the Lord himself taught and the symbol [Nicene] of the Fathers handed down to us." [17] The anxiety to be ever faithful to what had been laid

---

[15] *Epistola ad Magnum*, 3,69,3; *P.L.* 3, col. 1140.
[16] *De Decretis* 21 (Op. i. 178); *P.G.* 25, col. 453.
[17] Denzinger, *Enchiridion Symbolorum*, n. 148.

down from the beginning could not be made plainer than
in the statement read out, on behalf of the Papal legates, at
the Council's fourth session.[18] The "Rule of Faith" is referred to "as contained in the Creed of Nicaea, confirmed
by the Council of Constantinople, expounded at Ephesus
under Cyril, and set forth in the letter of Pope Leo when he
condemned the heresy of Nestorius and Eutyches. The present Synod holds this Faith; and can neither add thereto, nor
take therefrom." To this the assembled bishops replied with
shouts of assent: "So we all believe! So we were baptized! So
we baptize!" Over fifteen hundred years later, when the
Church's consciousness of her power to give authoritative
expression to the authentic Christian teaching has reached
its logical outcome in the claim to infallibility with reference
to it, we find the fundamental position unaltered; she remains the faithful guardian and exponent of Tradition,
wholly concentrated on what has been transmitted from
apostolic times. "All those things are to be believed by divine
and Catholic faith," declares the Vatican Council, "which
are contained in the word of God either written or handed
down—*quae in verbo Dei scripto vel tradito continentur*
—and which the Church proposes for our belief as being
divinely revealed, whether by a solemn definition (*judicium*)
or in her ordinary and universal *magisterium*." [19]

A question of some importance may here suggest itself to
the reflective reader. What assurance have we that the
dogmatic definitions of the Church, though intelligible
enough to those who lived at the time of the first Councils,
retain their identical validity to-day? Language tends to
change its meaning, philosophical systems grow out of date;
what then, if this be so, becomes of the Creeds and doctrinal
formulas expressed in terms now outmoded, presupposing a
philosophy no longer acceptable to the modern mind? These
were the questions raised by the Modernists. The only answer they could provide was tantamount to an abandonment

of traditional Christianity; they dissolved the age-long theological concepts of Catholicism into a residue of imagery and
symbolism. In striving to adapt the Christian message to the
mentality of their contemporaries, they succeeded only in
emptying it of vital significance. Thus the way was open to
the most insidious of all forms of scepticism: unbelief dis-
guised as a serious interest in religion. Modernism, effectively quashed within the Church, has not been without its
consequences outside the fold. Once Christian dogma is deprived of objective content, no limit can be placed to the
arbitrariness of the conclusions attained by individual research. The investigator, as we have seen, is left free to establish his chosen thesis. Traditional theology, dethroned from
its position as a normative science, may, it is true, be adapted
to humbler offices: to providing illustrative material for poets
and imaginative writers, to ministering to the fantasies of
the Jungian psychologists.

A detailed discussion of the problems just raised is clearly
outside the scope of the present work. It must suffice to recall
that the Church has taken full cognizance of them; Catholic
theologians have proved more than equal to the task of meeting these difficulties on grounds as rational and rigorously
critical as their opponents could desire.[20] Modernism, as is
now generally acknowledged, has its remote roots in the sev-
enteenth-century break with philosophical tradition represented by Descartes, "the father of modern philosophy." The
Cartesian "faux-pas" has been not unfairly described as "the
most disastrous moment in the history of Europe." [21] It con-

---

[20] The student may consult, for example: Gardeil, *Le Donné Révélé et
la Théologie;* Garrigou-Lagrange, *Le Sens Commun (La Philosophie de l'être
et les formules dogmatiques)*; Penido, *Le Rôle de l'Analogie en théologie
dogmatique.*

[21] William Temple, *Nature, Man and God,* Lecture iii, p. 57. Here one
may venture the opinion that the late Archbishop Temple, for all his intellectual distinction, did not wholly succeed in extricating himself from the
position which he criticizes so adversely. His acknowledged debt to Edward
Caird, himself deeply influenced by Hegel, suggests closer affinities with the
post- than with the pre-Cartesian school of thought. For a consistent critique
of Descartes, see Gilson, *Le Réalisme Méthodique* and *The Unity of Philosophical Experience,* pt. ii; also Maritain, *Le Songe de Descartes and Three
Reformers,* pt. ii.

sisted fundamentally in turning the philosopher's gaze from the observation of extra-mental reality to a preoccupation with the processes of his own mind. Stated crudely and in the most naïve terms, it lay in substituting subjectivism for objectivism. *Cogito, ergo sum—Je pense, donc je suis,* wrote Descartes in his famous *Discours de la Méthode:* "I think, therefore I am." Whence arose the primacy, not of *being,* which had been the chief concern of metaphysicians from Aristotle to St Thomas Aquinas, but of *thought.* To which the next step, proving irresistibly attractive to succeeding philosophers, is the supremacy of *my* thought. It cannot be denied that philosophical systems of vast range and ingenuity, notably those of Kant and Hegel, have arisen on this foundation. But once the connecting links between the knowing mind and objective evidence are broken, no force of intellectual power can avail to bridge the gap.

It was on the sandy bases of scepticism and a relativist conception of truth that the Christological theories which we have passed in review were built up. Small wonder that they have not endured. How manifestly is the work of so sincere and accomplished a scholar as Harnack vitiated by this underlying fallacy. Unprejudiced students of his monumental *History of Dogma* cannot fail to notice, notwithstanding its many invaluable pages, the gratuitousness of its basic assumption—that the transposition of the Gospel from its primitive Palestinian setting into the Graeco-Roman world carried with it the falsification of its original message. That the application of Greek philosophy to divine revelation—the "Hellenization of Christianity"—could have produced this result is clearly an arguable thesis; the history of the Gnostic and Arian heresies affords abundant proof of how real the danger was. That in fact it did not do so was due, humanly speaking, to the awareness of the early Fathers and theologians of what they were about. Men like Athanasius and Cyril of Alexandria may have lacked the historical and textual knowledge now available to us; but they were not less anxious, and were on the whole far better qualified, than

their twentieth-century critics to preserve the apostolic teaching from rationalistic perversion.

As has been well said,

> There is nothing particularly Hellenic, still less pagan, about
> rational method, except that the Greeks had the providential
> privilege of its discovery and development. In itself, it is part
> of the equipment with which human nature has been endowed
> by God who made mankind.[22]

The application to the revealed data of such terms as "nature," "substance" and "person," which now have their established place in the Church's theology, in no sense implied
a falsification of what has come down to us from Scripture
and Tradition. Within the New Testament itself, as Harnack
was obliged to admit, we can observe the influence of a terminology which has its parallels in Greek speculation. Hence
the primitive origin of this process renders the more difficult
and paradoxical the task of repudiating the validity of its
principles. As the writer just quoted has pointed out, this
manner of thinking

> permeated the very atmosphere mentally absorbed by Christians
> of the second and third centuries, even more completely than
> simplified biology and third-hand physics pervade the popular
> intellectual atmosphere of the twentieth century. Indeed, the
> ancient atmosphere was the more admirable, for it possessed,
> what the intellectual atmosphere of the modern populace does
> not possess, a really critical and philosophical basis. If people
> thought at all, they could only think in that kind of medium.
> No other rational method existed then, or exists now, but what
> has been derived ultimately from the great Greek philosophical
> schools.[23]

Not that this process of elucidation implied that Divine
Revelation was being reduced to the categories of Greek, or
of any other, philosophy. To demonstrate this point would
involve us in a discussion on metaphysics in general, and on

---

[22] G. L. Prestige, *God in Patristic Thought,* p. xiii.
[23] *Ibid.,* p. xvii.

the technicalities of what Catholic theologians understand by the *analogia entis*, the "analogy of being," in particular, which is outside our present scope.[24] Briefly it may be said that, for Catholicism, philosophy has always played an ancillary role in respect of its theology. In applying philosophical speculation to the truths of faith the object in view is not to "rationalize" these truths, to lower them, as it were, to the compass of the human mind, and so correlate them on the same plane with other departments of our knowledge. This is why the Church has, strictly speaking, no "philosophy of religion"; the subordination of religion to philosophy is a modern phenomenon, based precisely on the rejection of the ecclesiastical *magisterium*. The only "religious philosophy" that can be consistently adopted by a Catholic thinker derives from what is contained implicity in the "word of God, written or handed down." It is true that the Church has taken over a rational philosophy, a *philosophia perennis*, of

---

[24] Were we here engaged in a work of controversy, it would be profitable to discuss the *analogia entis* in detail. As is well known, it is the chief stumbling-block to the acceptance of the rational postulates of Catholicism by the Barthian theologians. "I regard the *analogia entis* as the invention of Antichrist, and think that because of it one can not become Catholic. Whereupon I at once allow myself to regard all other possible reasons for not becoming Catholic, as shortsighted and lacking in seriousness" (Karl Barth, *The Doctrine of the Word of God;* Edinburgh; T. & T. Clark, 1936. p. X). On this significant admission we can here offer but the briefest comment. Barth, in the work cited, makes a number of allusions to the *analogia entis* as upheld by the Thomists; but he does not give the impression that he understands it correctly. In this he may not always have been well served by his Catholic sources. He refers more than once to Fr Erich Przywara, who has discussed the *analogia entis* at length. (See *Polarity—A German Catholic's interpretation of religion*, trns. A. C. Bouquet; Oxford University Press, 1935). This essay was examined by the present writer in *Blackfriars*, Vol XVI, n. 187 (October 1935), where it was suggested that the concept of *analogy* there expounded was unsatisfactory. But in any case, the combination of Lutheran pessimism and anti-intellectual fideism which characterizes Barth must necessarily render him antipathetic to the idea in any form. His powerful mind has been wholly absorbed in what we may call the *prophetical* aspect of Christianity—the Word of God "striking vertically downwards." He gains in intensity, but loses in depth and comprehensiveness. Hence there are problems which fall outside the range of his discussion. "We do not say, How can man in general or how can man know the Word of God? We have already reminded ourselves that we are not concerned with man generally or with man universally; we are concerned concretely and definitely with man in the Church" (*op. cit.* pp. 215-16). To the Catholic theologian it seems that the nature of "man generally" and "man universally" is of some relevance to the condition of "man in the Church."

itself quite independent of theology, which reached its most comprehensive and elaborated form under the genius of St Thomas Aquinas; but its function, with respect to Catholic dogma, is to uplift the mind to the contemplation of the revealed truths, to provide the necessary rational substructure to the Faith, not to reduce the content of the Creeds to philosophical terms.

The legitimacy of this procedure is justified by the essential realism of the human mind. The ideas connoted by "nature" and "person," for example, are drawn from extramental reality; they are names applicable to things, universal in the sense that they can be applied to every case in which their definition is verified. That names, while being in themselves arbitrary symbols, really relate to things outside the mind on the one hand; and to ideas within it on the other, is the basis of all our thought. If this were not true, speech would be without significance, translation from one language to another an impossibility. We can truly apprehend reality and, within the limits of verbal usage, state its deliverances with accuracy. This is due to the essential objectivity of the intelligence which, through the medium of the senses, bears upon the world of facts and, as the ultimate ground of all individual things, upon what Aristotle and St Thomas call *being as such*.

It is true that the ideas of "nature" and "person" are derived from such embodiments of them as come within our own experience; hence they need to be "purified," that is, stripped of their individualizing elements, before they can be predicated of God himself. The ascribing of these terms to the Godhead does not involve us in anthropomorphism, a projection of our human limitations upon the Deity; for the notions they express, true as far as they go, have, by the process of intellectual abstraction, been deprived of the particularizing associations in which we found them, while being left rooted in the fundamental concept of *being*. From the latter concept, without which we cannot think at all, not even God himself can be excluded; though at once it must be affirmed that he infinitely transcends every mode of being known to us. It cannot even be said that the "absolute being" attained at the heights of metaphysical speculation is univocally applicable to him; for the theologian and philosopher, no less than for the rudest intelligence, God "dwells in unapproachable light." [25] To what end then does our philosophizing lead us?

Briefly the answer is this: we are enabled, by means of what has been called a "critically realist" philosophy, to form concepts about God, to think and speak of him truly, if inadequately, without detriment to the essential mystery in which he is enshrouded. Thus, when we apply the words "nature" and "person" to him, we are saying something of value; for the human mind is expressing its knowledge to itself in intelligible terms; while, at the same time, we are admitting the inadequacy of that knowledge. Having no "intuition" of God, we do not know the *mode* of being in which these concepts are realized in the Godhead. Or, to be more accurate, since God is *Being Itself, Ipsum esse subsistens,* we are acknowledging that "nature" and "person" are predicable of him only in that mode-less form of existence proper to the divine essence. In other words, our knowledge, valid within its limits because founded upon *being,* trails off, so to speak, into mystery when applied to God. When our minds contemplate revealed truth, and express it in language, the human intelligence is working at its highest attainable level, while still being immeasurably removed from the Object which is the source of our speculations. When the Church tells us that in Christ our Lord there are two natures in one divine person, and the theologians elaborate the concepts in which this teaching is formulated, we can understand the language employed, see for ourselves how it is but the rational expression of what is contained in Scripture and Tradition; but the "Mystery of Jesus" remains untouched. We have been provided with the mental equipment which enables us to concentrate our thoughts upon it, an intellectual

[25] 1 Tim. 6:16.

armoury to defend it against attack from any form or rationalistic philosophy, but we are no nearer to an adequate comprehension of the incarnate Word than we were before. The
mind of the most learned theologian, though possessed of a
deeper insight into the Church's doctrine, has not necessarily any surer grasp of the inner content of the Faith than
that of the simplest child. To both alike can be applied the
words spoken to St Peter: "It is not flesh and blood, it is
my Father in heaven that has revealed this to thee." [26]

From what has so far been said, it should be clear that the
widespread contemporary assumption that the inner essence
of Christianity will yield itself to research, or at least *modern*
research, embodies a radical departure from the standpoint
of the primitive Church. Those who study Christian origins
in this spirit are in reality begging the question; while supposing themselves to be freed from "credal considerations"
which determine their conclusions in advance, they betray a
far more flagrant *petitio principii* than can be charged
against the "older orthodoxy." What is taken for granted is
precisely the point at issue, namely, whether the significance
of Jesus Christ can be adequately estimated merely by historical investigation. To this crucial question much recent
study has assumed, without further discussion, that the answer is in the affirmative. The Catholic Church, on the other
hand, has never held that her teaching about Christ, as
formulated in the Nicene Creed and the definition of the
Council of Chalcedon, can be logically deduced from the
written Gospels in the same way as, for example, the character of Socrates may be inferred from the writings of Plato
and Xenophon. The Church's faith in Christ, though truly
if inadequately expressed in the "word of God, written or
handed down," has for its object the inner recesses of his
personality, far beyond the reach of human evidence, and
escaping rational analysis. Thus there is a sense in which it
is true to say that the Gospels are the results, and not the
cause, of Christian faith. This is a position by no means un-

[26] Matt. 16:17.

assailable on philosophical grounds, as Catholic theologians are well aware, but it is not touched by those who imagine that they can reconstruct the "historical Christ" solely on the basis of modern scholarship. The researches of the past century, fruitful as they have been in many respects, have conspicuously failed, and must of their nature fail, to reach finality as to the significance of Jesus.

In this connection it may be remarked that the attempt to discriminate the various strata in the sources of our existing Gospels by the process known as *Form-criticism* is but the latest example of the unbridled rationalism which has undermined the whole structure of traditional Christianity outside the Catholic Church. Once the scholar regards it as his task, not to harmonize the apparent inconsistencies among the evangelists on the basis of their substantial coherence, but to sift what is considered to be "history" from "legendary accretions," there can be no limits to the arbitrariness of the conclusions reached. "It seems, then, that the form of the earthly no less than of the heavenly Christ is for the most part hidden from us. For all the inestimable value of the Gospels, they yield us little more than a whisper of his voice; we trace in them but the outskirts of his ways." These words of a recent Bampton Lecturer are an interesting indication of what can become of the New Testament when submitted to this treatment. It is of course a commonplace among Catholic scholars that there are written sources behind our existing Gospel texts, and that each of the evangelists moulded his material to his own purposes. But to argue from these facts that their narratives on that account must be untrustworthy is to ignore the existence of an unwritten tradition by which they could be checked, as well as to dismiss the idea of a divine inspiration safeguarding their veracity as authentic records. That the Gospel writers enjoyed the assistance of the Spirit of Truth cannot be rationally demonstrated; but neither can it be disproved; and it further remains for the sceptics to account for the primitive Christian belief in its favour.

Happily, the aberrations of Form-criticism are at length being recognized at their true worth, even by the critics themselves. The following judgement of a scholar, by no means sympathetically disposed to Catholic orthodoxy, is worth recording:

In the case of the Gospels, however much the evangelists' idea of historical accuracy may have differed from our own, they would have defeated their own ends had they not at least intended and endeavoured to tell the story of the Lord's life truthfully according to their own literary standards. The clear distinction which Paul draws in 1 Cor. 7:10-12, 25, 40 (cf. 9:14) between the matrimonial and other regulations which he could quote as enjoined by Jesus himself, and those which he could not so quote, is an important indication of the weight which the early Church attached to the possession of an accurate record of his sayings.[27]

And again:

The characteristics of the Gospel-stories on which Form-criticism bases its classification of them are just as easily and naturally explained on the hypothesis that they are substantially truthful accounts of correctly-remembered incidents, as on the hypothesis that they were shaped—or perhaps created—by some contemporary literary habit. . . . The great Form-critics disagree widely with one another in their conclusions. Speaking generally, the result of Form-criticism is a heightened scepticism, which seems to be unreasonable—in some cases to the point of absurdity.[28]

These admissions, modest enough and unnecessarily restricted, may profitably be pondered by New Testament scholars in general. They should lead to a better appreciation of the Catholic Church's attitude towards our earliest Christian documents.

The scholastic theologians evolved an axiom which, though of universal validity, is especially relevant in our present context: *cognitum est in cognoscente secundum*

[27] C. J. Cadoux, "The Character of the Gospel Record," *Bulletin of the John Rylands Library Manchester*, Vol. 29, no. 2 (February 1946), p. 277. For a fully documented critique of Form-criticism, with special reference to the work of Dibelius and Bultmann, see Père Pierre Benoit, "Réflexions sur la 'Formgeschichtliche Methode,'" *Revue Biblique* (Octobre 1946), pp. 481–512.
[28] *Ibid.*, p. 279.

modum cognoscentis, "the object known is in the mind
that knows it according to the measure of that mind." As
we have aleady remarked, much depends upon the point of
view, upon the temper in which we approach our study. To
quote the words of a distinguished Anglican scholar:

> It should be needless to say that the Life of Christ can be
> written only by a believer. Renan had all the literary gifts—a *cu-
> riosa felicitas* of style, an aesthetic appreciation of his subject,
> and a saving common-sense which tempered his criticism; but
> even as literature his work is spoilt by self-consciousness and con-
> descension, and his science was not of the best.[29]

The same writer tells us that he knows of no *Life* which
possesses "such a balance and combination of qualities as
to rise quite to the level of a classic." And he adds signifi-
cantly: "What is wanted is a Newman, with science and
adequate knowledge."

Though the Church is committed to a certain view about
the person and life-work of our Lord, she is in no way opposed to the scientific investigation of Christian origins. On
the contrary, as the utterances of recent Popes go to show,[30]
she warmly encourages these researches, provided they be
conducted with due regard to the exigencies of their object.
Indeed, her consistent rejection of any "double standard"
of truth—whether it be the thirteenth-century contention
that what is true for theology need not necessarily be true
for philosophy, or the modernist opposition between the
"Christ of faith" and the "Christ of history"—implies a submission to historical evidence far more complete than can be
claimed by those critics who, bringing to their study preconceived theories and *a priori* categories, arrange their findings accordingly.

The historic revelation of Christianity can be considered
from two points of view. We may look at it from without,
as a series of facts and truths of peculiar interest, but nevertheless as no more than particular events in the general story

[29] Sanday, *Outlines of the Life of Christ,* p. 240.
[30] Cf. Pius XII, Encyclical Letter: *Divino afflante Spiritu,* 30th September
1943, *A.A.S.,* Vol. 35, no. 10, pp. 297–325.

of our race. Or, having received the gift of faith, we can study them from within, and see that they are realities of eternal significance. The Catholic scholar is free, should he so choose, to adopt the first line of approach—the science of Apologetics is in fact chiefly concerned with it—whereby he prescinds from, without abandoning, the act of faith. Furthermore the Church's insistence on the unity of all truth, the principle that a fact of revelation cannot conflict with a fact of history, precludes the manipulation of evidence to secure the desired conclusion. A strictly revealed dogma, so St Thomas teaches,[31] can no more be demonstrated by purely rational argument than can a truth accessible to reason be regarded as intrinsically an object of faith.

Though historical research and individual reflection may tell us much about Christ our Lord, may—and, as we hold, should—dispose the mind to the acceptance of the Church's faith concerning him, they cannot pronounce decisively either for or against the inner content of that faith. This is a revealed mystery of which the inherent possibility, let alone the fact, cannot be rationally established. Having spoken of the motives of credibility which lead up to belief in Christ, St Thomas adds these significant words:

But when a man, led on by these motives, makes the act of faith, then still can it be said that not in virtue of any of them does he believe: neither on account of the evidence of reason, nor through the witness of the law, nor as moved by what has come to him through preaching, but solely on account of the truth itself—*propter ipsam veritatem tantum.*[32]

In the last resort, it is the self-authenticating truth of Christ himself which wins the mind and heart of the believer.

As has already been noted, the Catholic belief in the person of our Lord received final formulation at the Council of Chalcedon. Here the doctrine of the two natures in one divine person was defined. Anyone who shares the convictions of the present writer must hold that a study of the New

31 *Summa Theologica* IIa IIae, q. 1, art. 5
32 *Comm. in Joan.*, cap. iv, lect. v, 2.

Testament will always lead "to a better appreciation of the Chalcedonian definition." [33] But whether or not this be accepted, it has yet to be shown that such a standpoint involves any distortion of the scriptural accounts. The Fathers of the Council maintained in the fifth century, as the Church maintains to-day, that they drew up an article of faith which did justice to the oral and written tradition about our Lord. They were concerned with nothing but this. Those who think that they erred may profitably enquire whether they themselves are not pre-judging the issue, though from different premises, by the same process with which they charge the orthodox theologians. To be prepossessed with the desire to accommodate Jesus to the grasp of the modern mind, or to rule out in advance the possibility of such a divine intervention into human affairs as the Catholic doctrine of the Incarnation implies, or to hold antecedently that miracles do not happen, or to think that antiquity means obscurantism and modernity enlightenment—all or any of these positions must, on the grounds of objectivity alone, have a gravely incapacitating effect upon a mind striving to understand the Gospels.

Of the Christological work performed at the early Church Councils, it has been well remarked: "The decisions in question were thus the outcome of a long evolution, every step in which was keenly debated by minds of great acumen and power, really far better equipped for such discussions than the average Anglo-American mind of to-day." [34] This judgement, which might also have included the average German mind, has gained rather than lost in force since it was first made. But it must not be thought that on this account the Catholic student is left free to ignore the positive results of recent scholarship. On the contrary, he owes it to himself to assimilate them; for unless the Church's dogmatic teaching on the incarnate Word is, as it were, filled in and illustrated by the New Testament narrative, he will be in danger

[33] Lowther Clarke, *Divine Humanity*, p. v.
[34] Sanday, *op. cit.*, p. 226.

of forming an abstract and impoverished notion of our Lord's personality. Thus, though the official Catholic doctrine has never failed to give full recognition to the complete humanity of Jesus, the same cannot be said of the conceptualizations and elaborations of that doctrine by certain theologians—and these have not been without influence on the minds of individual believers. The following criticism of Peter Lombard's Christology is interesting, not only for its own sake, but because it may suggest reflections of wider relevance:

His view illustrates the general tendency of later Greek theology, which he generally follows, to assign an excessive predominance to the Deity in Christ; a tendency resulting from an *a priori* method of reasoning in regard to the Incarnation, drawing conclusions not from the picture in the Gospels, but from the probable conditions under which an incarnation of Deity may be supposed to have occurred. [35]

The dogmatic formulas, precious though they be as affording an anchorage to the mind, do not exempt us from the task of re-thinking the New Testament for ourselves under the guidance of the Church. We have, in our own intelligence and imagination, to avoid each of the opposing departures from the central truth, into one or other of which men are bound to fall when they lose their balance on the knife-edge of orthodoxy. On the one hand is Docetism (of which Monophysitism is a form), which regards the Incarnation as a theophany, Christ's human nature as a mere apparition, or at best a veil to the divinity; for which in consequence Jesus is not truly man. On the other is Adoptionism (which lies at the root of Nestorianism), the prototype of humanitarian Christianity, which holds that Christ the man was in some way divinized, taken up into union with the Deity; whence it follows that Jesus is not truly God. We shall be preserved from both these errors in turning to the evangelical witness, and finding there disclosed to us the Christ of history, who is also the Christ of faith.

[35] R. L. Ottley, *The Doctrine of the Incarnation*, p. 521.

CHAPTER II

THE LIFE-WORK OF JESUS CHRIST

IN the sections which follow we shall not attempt to present the life of our Lord in any well-defined sequence of events. Indeed the Gospels themselves, except in broad outline, do not aim at any exact chronological order. Rather we shall concern ourselves with the most significant phases in the ministry of Jesus, as these throw light upon his person and message. Textual criticism, belonging more properly to a work of New Testament exegesis, falls outside our scope; the object in view is a doctrinal exposition which faithfully adheres to the meaning of the Scripture text. Accordingly, the generally accepted findings of Catholic scholars with regard to the sources behind the four Gospels, as well as the distinctive character of each, are assumed rather than discussed. We shall not hesitate to offer some reflections on the material before us, but any expression of personal views will be subordinated to the presentation of the Church's picture of Christ. That our study may foster some fruits of devotion is not the least among the motives which inspire it; but its appeal will be rather to the mind than to the heart, or more exactly, to the heart through the mind. Not that knowledge and love, mind and heart, can ever really be separated in matters of religion. "He that loveth not, knoweth not God, for God is love." [1] But just as love is born of knowledge, so must we have enlightened faith before we can reach the fulness of charity.

The life and teaching of Jesus is itself a dramatic illustration of this principle. He pleaded with men, not for their love, but for their faith; once this was achieved, once they

[1] 1 John 4:8(W.).

had surrendered themselves to him, love would be the inevitable issue. The tragedy of his rejection by his own people lay, not so much in the fact that they crucified the long-awaited Messiah, but in their antecedent failure to recognize him for what he was. "If thou also hadst known, and that in this thy day, the things that are to thy peace: but now they are hidden from thy eyes." [2] Time has taken nothing from the poignancy of these words spoken by Jesus, weeping over the doomed Jerusalem. What message have they for our contemporaries? Is there an undertone of hope amid the notes of foreboding? Or do they warn us that, as for ancient Jerusalem, so for the modern world, it is already too late?

[2] Luke 19:42(R-D.).

§ 2. OUR LORD'S INFANCY AND BOYHOOD

At Bethlehem, a small town in Judea five miles to the south of Jerusalem, "in the days of king Herod," [1] there took place the most significant event in the history of the world. Our Lord and Saviour Jesus Christ was born. The time, tradition tells us, was midwinter. St Matthew and St Luke recall the story ever afterwards to be enshrined in the Christmas Liturgy. Mary and Joseph had made the long journey from Nazareth for the enrolment decreed by the Emperor Augustus. Owing to the great number of people assembled for the registration, "there was no room for them in the inn." [2] So they found shelter in one of the caves outside the town which were sometimes utilized as a dwelling-place for man and a stable for beasts. They may have been there several days while Joseph waited his turn to be registered. At any rate, it was in this humblest of abodes that the Virgin Mother gave birth to her Child, wrapping him carefully in swaddling-clothes and laying him in a manger.

Not far distant some shepherds were guarding their flocks through the darkness of the night. Suddenly the light of

[1] Matt. 2:1.   [2] Luke 2:7.

heaven was all about them; they at least should be God's witnesses of the marvellous thing that had happened. Their fears were dispelled by the voice of an angel, telling them of "glad tidings of a great joy which shall be to all the people." [3] A Saviour had been born in the town of David: "Christ the Lord." [4] Thereupon, to signalize so wonderful a nativity, there appeared "a multitude of the heavenly host praising God and saying, Glory to God in the highest, and peace upon earth among men of his good pleasure." [5] These Judean shepherds were the first pilgrims to the cradle of the infant Jesus, the leaders of all those who to this day, touched by the memory of their visit, gather in faith and love before the Christmas crib. "Let us go, then, to Bethlehem and see this thing which is come to pass, which the Lord hath made known to us." [6]

> Poor world, said I, what wilt thou do
> To entertain this starry Stranger?
> Is this the best thou canst bestow—
> A cold and not too cleanly manger? [7]

The touching circumstances of our Lord's birth did not perhaps become widely known in the primitive Christian communities until many years after his Ascension. St Mark's Gospel, which concentrates on the public ministry, tells us nothing of them; they are not alluded to in the early apostolic preaching, as embodied in the Acts, nor in the Epistles of St Paul. Our Lady herself had been their chief witness; and it was characteristic of her, who "kept all these words, pondering them in her heart," [8] that she should have been reluctant to disclose a secret with associations at once so delicate and tender. St John, some have thought, hints at his knowledge of the virginal birth when he speaks of those who are born "not of blood, nor of the will of the flesh, nor of the will of man, but of God." [9] It is from the account of the

[3] Luke 2:10(W.).   [4] Vs. 11(R-D.).
[5] VV. 13–14(W.).   [6] Vs. 15(W.).
[7] Richard Crashaw, *Verses from the Shepherds' Hymn.*
[8] Vs. 19(R-D.); cf. vs. 51.   [9] John 1:13(R-D.).

Annunciation in St Luke,[10] which must have come originally from Mary's own lips, together with the explicit testimony of St Matthew,[11] that we learn of the birth of Jesus through the agency of the Holy Spirit, without the intermediary of a human father. St John, who was the "theologian" among the four evangelists, summarizes in a sentence, at the recital of which the faithful still kneel down in reverence, the tremendous implications of what had happened: "And the Word became flesh and dwelt among us (and we were beholders of his glory, such glory as that of the Only Begotten of the Father), full of grace and truth." [12]

This is the sum and substance of the Incarnation. God had set up his dwelling, had "tabernacled," among men. The eternal Word who, from the beginning, "was with God," who was in fact God himself,[13] had come down from heaven and "become flesh." For centuries the chosen people had known the "word of the Lord" only from the lips of their prophets and in the written Law, faint and imperfect symbols of the eloquence of God. Now the divine speech, in all its illumination and life-giving power, was embodied in manhood.[14] Not, however, in some glorious theophany, whose terror and strength might have impressed us with God's majesty, but left our hearts untouched. The happy hymns of Christmas celebrate no heavenly splendours; they tell of a Maiden-Mother and her Child, suckling him, like every mother, at the breast, amidst a poverty which only maternal love and Joseph's care could have redeemed from wretchedness. At Bethlehem the divine attribute of justice was submerged in those of love and mercy; God approaches man on a basis of equality, in a gesture of friendship which should evoke an answering sentiment in return. To those who were thus divinely favoured it brought peace; which means reconciliation with God and, in the mind of man, the ordered tranquillity uplifting him to a serener height above the stress and conflict in which, at lower levels, he may

---

10 1:26–38. See § 22, pp. 275 ff.   12 John 1:14(S.).
11 Matt. 1:18–20.   13 Vs. 1.
14 For fuller treatment of this point see § 14, pp. 167–74.

still be immersed. The destiny of this Infant was to be great indeed.

> For a child is born to us, and a son is given to us, and the government is upon his shoulder: and his name shall be called, Wonderful, Counsellor, God the Mighty, Father of the world to come, the Prince of Peace. His empire shall be multiplied, and there shall be no end of peace. He shall sit upon the throne of David, and upon his kingdom: to establish it and strengthen it with judgement, from henceforth and for ever.[15]

So the Church has applied to the Saviour the prophecy of Isaiah, a prophecy which will receive its complete fulfilment only when Christ's kingdom has attained its final triumph.[16]

On the eighth day the Child was circumcised and given the name of Jesus. It is a Greek form of the Hebrew name Joshua, and means "he shall save." After the prescribed forty days, Mary went up to the Temple at Jerusalem for her purification, "according to the law of Moses." [17] At the same time she presented her Child to God.[18] Not being able to afford the offering of a yearling lamb for a holocaust, she was allowed to substitute in its place two young pigeons.[19] In all this, with its Old Testament setting of obedience to the Jewish Law and reverent observance of the Temple ritual, it becomes clear to us how intimately connected is the Incarnation with the history of the chosen people. There is no revolutionary upheaval; everything is interwoven in the texture of an age-long ritualistic worship. The Child is circumcised, in remembrance of the divine covenant with Abraham; [20] Mary, already immaculate, submits to "purification"; she offers to God a first-born Son who is none other than the Son of God himself. How superfluous these external acts of dedication might seem, did we not realize that it is natural to man to translate the inner sentiments of the heart into visible signs and symbols!

St Luke tells us how the devout Simeon, a strict observer

---

[15] Isa. 9:6–7.
[16] See § 23, pp. 307–9.
[17] Luke 2:22; cf. Lev. 12.
[18] Cf. Exod. 13:2.
[19] Luke 2:24; cf. Lev. 12:8.
[20] Gen. 17:10.

of the Law and a man of deep personal piety, was watching in the Temple at this time, together with Anna, a "prophetess." They were the true representatives of that class who awaited in hope and holy fear the coming of "the consolation of Israel." [21] Simeon, under divine inspiration, recognized the Child as the long-expected Messiah and, taking him in his arms, uttered the *Nunc dimittis*:

> Now thou dost dismiss thy servant, O Master,
>   according to thy word, in peace;
> Because mine eyes have seen thy salvation,
>   which thou hast prepared before the face
>   of all the peoples:
> A light of revelation unto the gentiles,
>   and of glory for thy people Israel.[22]

He saw in him, not only the promised Saviour of Israel, but one whose redeeming mission would extend to the pagan world. In veiled language he foretold the future of the Child: his life's work would bring him no popular success; not all would accept him, though all would be affected by him. Men's response to his message would be the test of the sincerity of their own inmost thoughts. He would meet with opposition and contempt, and a sword of anguish would pierce his Mother's heart.

St Matthew now takes up the story with material peculiar to himself. He tells us of the visit of the "wise men from the east," [23] of their interview with Herod and their journey to Bethlehem, and of the act of homage paid there to the new-born Child.[24] Neither the identity of these mysterious visitors, nor their place of origin, is known with any certainty. They may have been astrologers from distant Persia who, interpreting the sudden appearance in the heavens of a new comet—if such it was—as heralding the birth of a great prince, had set out on a journey of investigation; more likely, perhaps, they came from Arabia. By this time Joseph had either found a more suitable dwelling for the Holy Family, or else

21 Luke 2:25(R-D.).   22 VV. 29-32(W.).
23 Matt. 2:1.   24 Vs. 11.

so transformed the cave at Bethlehem that it could be digni-
fied by the name now given to it—a "house." Thither the
wise men made their way and, entering within, "they saw
the child with Mary his mother, and falling down they worshipped him." Opening their treasures, they offered him
gifts: "gold and frankincense and myrrh." Symbolically, as
the minds of the faithful have interpreted these offerings,
the gold is a compliment to our Lord's kingship, the incense
a tribute to his Godhead, and the fragrant resin called myrrh
an omen of his burial.

The wise men, avoiding Jerusalem and Herod, "returned
to their own country by a different way." [25] On their departure, Joseph, warned by an angel in sleep, took the Child and
his Mother by night into Egypt. It was then that the murder-
ous decree of the crafty and suspicious Herod, fearing the
birth of some possible rival to his throne, was put into execution. All the male children up to two years of age in Bethlehem and its neighborhood were slaughtered. St Matthew
pictures the whole land aghast and grief-stricken at this atroc-
ity, which must have been one of the last acts of the already
dying monarch. We are to imagine the voice of Rachel, the
mother of Ephraim, who, it is said, was buried near Bethlehem, bewailing the loss of the Holy Innocents. Their memory
is recalled by the Church on the third day following Christmas; the altar and its ministers are vested in the purple of
mourning and no Alleluia is sung at Mass, in a perpetual
token of sympathy with the sorrowing mothers. A sign of
contradiction attends the cradle of the new-born King. Already, as we can now understand, a great paradox was becoming apparent; bloodshed and martyrdom, much sorrow
for the human heart, were to introduce the reign of the
Prince of Peace.

Meanwhile, Mary, Joseph and the Child had entered
Egypt. They may well have done no more than cross its
borders, since safety awaited them as soon as they had left
Judea. Nor need their sojourn there have been long, for

[25] Matt. 2:12.

the hostile Herod died shortly afterwards. Without delay
the Holy Family retraced their steps, not however to remain
in Judea, but to pass onwards to Galilee and Nazareth,
whence Mary and Joseph had journeyed to Bethlehem. It
is with this northern town that the name of Jesus was ever
afterwards to be associated. St Luke notices, like a good
physician, that the Child "grew and came to his strength,"
that he was "full of wisdom," [26] and that his mental and
physical development won him favour with God and man.[27]
In a word, he passed through the normal stages of boyhood
and youth in a way to delight all who came in contact with
him. From Joseph he would doubtless learn the carpenter's
trade, from Mary many of the domestic arts; but most of all
would his heart be in his sacred studies in the Synagogue at
Nazareth. There are some grounds for believing that, since
their return from the Babylonian exile and the growth of
the synagogue system, every Jewish community of any size
was provided with a school attached to its synagogue in which
all male children were taught the Law. In consequence the
level of popular education in the Judaism of our Lord's
time was, within its limits, intellectually, morally and spiritually higher than that of any other contemporary civilization.
Quite apart from the infused knowledge which belonged to
him as God's only begotten Son, we may suppose that Jesus
gained familiar acquaintance with the Old Testament scriptures by the normal process of studying and learning them
by heart. It is true that he did not attend the Rabbinical
schools; hence his hearers in later years, being unaware of
the real source of his message, were baffled at the extent of
his knowledge. They thought that he had "never studied." [28]

One incident in our Lord's boyhood is recorded by St
Luke. A Jewish boy became responsible for the discharge of
his religious duties, which as a circumcised Jew he was
bound to perform, at the age of twelve years. It was then
that he was admitted to the status of a "Son of the Law." So
we find Jesus, at the feast of Passover, at Jerusalem with

---

[26] Luke 2:40.   [27] Vs. 52.   [28] John 7:15.

Mary and Joseph. An oriental child of twelve is well able to
take care of himself; doubtless this knowledge, and perhaps
some confusion in the arrangements of the home-going cara-
van, caused his parents to lose contact with him for a time.
The rediscovery in the Temple presents a scene as significant
as it is charming. Save as an infant in arms, this was possibly
the first time our Lord had ever been within its walls, and
he was reluctant to depart. He recognized it as his Father's
house; [29] the consciousness of his unique status as Son of God,
which was always with him, is expressed in the first of his
recorded words.[30] We may note that in his role "in the midst
of the doctors," [31] Jesus may well have shown himself, in a
manner befitting his age, as the seeker after knowledge. It
seems that he must—with boyish modesty, as we may well
imagine—have raised some point of doctrine with these ex-
perts in Jerusalem. They in their turn appear to have en-
quired his reasons for asking, no doubt goodhumouredly
testing what he knew and weighing how much he deserved
to be taken seriously. For it is in his responses to these questions that he is seen as the youthful Doctor; they "were
in amazement at his quick understanding and at the answers
he gave." [32] The curtain now descends and is not raised again
for some eighteen years.

[29] Luke 2:49.
[31] Luke 2:46(R-D.).
[30] See § 22, p. 283.
[32] Vs. 47.

§ 3. THE BAPTISM

Possibly the autumn of A.D. 27 is the date indicated by St
Luke [1] when John, the son of Zachary and kinsman of Jesus,
was found baptizing and preaching repentance on the banks
of the Jordan not far from Jericho. Israel, which had lived
these hundreds of years by the written Law, without a
prophet to kindle their hearts to fervour,[2] once again heard
the voice of prophecy. John had assumed the famous garment
of camel's hair,[3] the official garb of the prophet,[4] which

[1] 3:1.
[3] Matt. 3:4; Mark 1:6.
[2] Ps. 73(74):9.
[4] Zach. 13:4.

perhaps no one living had seen before. His mission, as can
be gathered from Josephus [5] as well as from the Gospels,
created an immense popular stir. So far as outward and immediate effects were concerned, it may well have been more
impressive than that of Jesus himself. The burden of his
message, preached with great personal asceticism and fore-
bodings of an imminent revelation from God, was "Repent;
for the kingdom of heaven is at hand." [6] He demanded un-
compromisingly what the prophets before him had demanded—a change of heart, a more serious attention to what
his hearers knew to be their religious duty; but his teaching
does not seem to have implied any radical criticism of the
existing order, nor did it contain anything fundamentally
new. John knew himself to be the precursor of the Messiah;
but our Lord is in no real sense the continuator of his work.
He understood and appreciated John, while at the same time
insisting on the superiority of his own mission in its inspiration and vital significance.

Yet "Jesus came from Nazareth of Galilee and was baptized by John." [7] Sinless himself,[8] he nevertheless wished to
be identified with a sinful people. John demurred, conscious
at least of a holiness which made such a baptism incongru-
ous; but Jesus insists, for he needs must, in St Matthew's
characteristic phrase, "fulfil all righteousness." [9] God's will
is the supreme norm of what is righteous; John's mission
was a divine ordinance "from heaven," [10] and the Son's request for baptism was in accordance with the Father's will; [11]
hence it became them both that Christ's public mission
should begin with this act of humility, so setting the seal of
authenticity on the witness of the Baptist.

There are some differences of detail in the three Synoptic
accounts of the Baptism.[12] St Mark seems to suggest that the
Father's voice, together with the coming of the Holy Spirit,
was a consoling and strengthening experience for Jesus him-

5 *Antiquities*, XVIII, vii, 2.   6 Matt. 3:2(S.).
7 Mark 1:9(R-D.).   8 Acts 3:14; Heb. 4:15; 1 Pet. 2:22.
9 Matt. 3:15(S.).   10 21:25.   11 3:17.
12 Matt. 3:13-17; Mark 1:9-11; Luke 3:21-22.

self.[13] We may look upon this scene, the importance of which can hardly be exaggerated, as the external investiture of the Messianic King, the outward proclamation that this was the Lord's Anointed. It marks his public entry upon the saving mission he had come to perform. We recall how the apostles later looked back upon the days of their discipleship as "beginning from the baptism of John." [14] But there is nothing in the texts to show, as is sometimes alleged by non-Catholic critics, that it was not until this moment that our Lord became aware of his vocation as Israel's Messiah.[15] On the contrary, he had had before his mind, from its first awakening to consciousness, the destiny appointed him by God. As we have already seen, when still a boy of twelve, his thought was dominated by the paramount claims of his heavenly Father.[16]

St Luke adds a characteristic touch to his description of the Baptism; he tells us that Jesus was "praying." [17] This evangelist is careful to note that, at each of the successive crises of the public ministry, our Lord is to be found communing with God in prayer.[18] There could be no more moving testimony to his complete humanity, to his oneness with ourselves in the need for divine help and strength. It is as an answer to prayer that he saw the heavens "rent asunder," [19] heard the Father's voice, and experienced the descent of the Holy Spirit upon him. The words, "Thou art my beloved Son (i.e. the One who is uniquely loved, the "Only Begotten" [20]); in thee I am well pleased," [21] proclaimed that the time had come for Christ to begin his work of preaching the kingdom of God. They were an act of manifest recognition, an encouragement to him who was about to set out on a mission full of difficulty and danger. The Holy Spirit was present also, personifying God's power and love, telling us that a new regenerative force had come upon

[13] Mark 1:11.   [14] Acts 1:22(R-D.).
[15] For our Lord's role as the Messiah—for which "Christ" is the equivalent —see § 12, pp. 151–61.
[16] Luke 2:49.   [17] 3:21.
[18] 5:16; 6:12; 9:18, 28; 11:1; 22:41.   [19] Mark 1:10(S.).
[20] John 1:14, 18.   [21] Mark 1:11.

the world. Just as, at the first creation,[22] the Spirit of God
hovered like a bird over the waters, producing life and drawing order out of chaos, so likewise at this new creation the
Spirit was at hand to bring mankind to its second birth. For
this reason many theologians have seen here the decisive
moment in the institution of Christian Baptism by Jesus.
The earthly element of water was consecrated by its contact
with the sacred humanity, made ready, as it were, to become
a vehicle of grace for the souls of men.

Though St Mark implies that the theophany which accompanied the Baptism had an immense significance for our
Lord himself, the accounts of St Matthew and St Luke make
it clear that more was involved than a purely personal experience. It was the Father's proclamation that Jesus was
his only begotten Son and Israel's Messiah. John the Baptist
realized in some measure what was taking place,[23] though
he was later to suffer impatience at Jesus' seeming tardiness
in establishing his kingdom.[24] Christian tradition has seen in
the dove's flight above Jesus' head a visible sign of the
person of the Holy Spirit. There is thus signalized, at the
outset of our Lord's public ministry, the presence of the
Blessed Trinity, in whose name the apostles would receive
the parting commission to baptize all who were to believe
in him.[25] In the whole incident there is again disclosed to
us the continuity between the Old Testament and the New.
From the last of the prophets Christ received a baptism
which was no more than symbolic; by his life-giving death it
will become instinct with the power of the Holy Spirit. To
the eyes of faith it was indeed a manifestation, an *epiphany*,
of the Son of God—and it is so celebrated by the Church on
the octave-day of the Feast (13th January), being the counterpart of the first epiphany to the Magi. Nevertheless, if we
leave aside for the moment the fruits of subsequent reflection, there is no evidence that this theophany, striking as it
was, made any lasting impression upon whatever onlookers

22 Gen. 1:2.   23 John 1:32-33.
24 Matt. 11:3.   25 28:18-20.

were present at the Baptism. His unique status as Son of God now outwardly declared, our Lord "led by the Spirit" [26] undergoes temptation in the wilderness.

[26] Luke 4:1(R-D.).

§ 4. THE TEMPTATIONS

Standing like a prologue to the drama of our salvation we find the temptations of Jesus Christ. Strictly speaking they are a prelude to, rather than a part of, the public ministry. It would be a mistake to see in them merely a piece of divine play-acting, involving no inner struggle for our Lord himself. The fact that they took place when he was alone, and that presumably we should have heard nothing of them had he not thought fit to recount the experience to his disciples, suggests that they had a profound meaning for him, as well as for ourselves. The Epistle to the Hebrews shows that the early Church in no way accepted the view, to which every docetic form of Christianity is prone, that our Lord was not seriously assailed by temptation. "Wherefore, it behoved him in all things to be made like unto his brethren, that he might become a merciful and faithful high priest before God, that he might be a propitiation for the sins of the people. For in that wherein he himself hath suffered and been tempted he is able to succour them also that are tempted." [1] "And though he was a Son, he learned obedience from that which he suffered." [2]

At the same time Scripture nowhere suggests that Christ had to contend with that form of fleshly temptation to which the rest of humanity, the Blessed Virgin alone excepted, is subject. For, as the Church was later to make clear, this susceptibility is itself the result of sin, derived from our carnal descent from Adam. From this the second Adam, the new Head of the human race, was entirely immune. Nevertheless, to look upon the event as no more than a futile attempt to lead our Lord into sin is to miss its whole sig-

[1] Heb. 2:17–18(R-D.); cf. 4:15.   [2] 5:8(W.).

nificance. There is in fact a singular appropriateness in these particular temptations coming at this point. He had just heard the voice of the Father, and received an outpouring of strength from the Holy Spirit, both alike encouraging to his human nature—which, like our own, would be apt to shrink from a task so fraught with suffering and danger—to fulfil his predestined office of bringing salvation to Israel. Was it not to be expected that the forces of evil [3] should conspire together to oppose the projected work, if not by direct attack, then at least by infecting its motives and perverting its object? If the good deed was not to be frustrated, might not wickedness secure a more subtle triumph by ensuring that it should be misdirected? Satan was bent upon undoing what Jesus, the Lord's Anointed, had been called to carry through. It was not a random assault, an effort to exploit any discoverable human weakness; all the temptations converge upon one point; they aim at vitiating precisely what was most vital in the role of the Messiah. Our Lord, in the literal meaning of the phrase, was being tempted to play false to his vocation.

We may conjecture that Jesus, during these days of fasting and preparation in the desert, a kind of spiritual retreat, was passing in review the manner in which he had determined to accomplish the work to which he was about to set his hand. In the light of the knowledge which was his as the Son of God, everything, in a very real sense, would lie clearly before his mind; but he could still anticipate, with emotions which must surely have been mixed, a blending of exultation, sorrow and even fear, the experience which was yet to be his. In the midst of these reflections Satan comes to interpose his counsels. Ever since the proclamation of the coming of a Redeemer [4] he had waited and watched for his great opponent. There is no need to suppose that he recognized Christ's identity; this mystery had not been revealed to him; indeed one of the objects of the temptations was, if possible, to resolve it. The chief adversary—for that is the

[3] Cf. Eph. 6:12. [4] Gen. 3:15.

meaning of the Hebrew word "satan"—of man, having witnessed the striking scene at the Baptism, could not fail to
suspect that in Jesus of Nazareth had come the One whom
he had most cause to fear. Hence the temptations take the
form of a test, a putting to the question. We note also that
it is the Holy Spirit himself who brings the two protagonists face to face; [5] it is their first trial of strength. The
Devil must have heard the voice at the Baptism, with the
Father's felicitation to his "beloved Son"; so he strives to
induce Christ to take a step which would reveal the meaning
of these words. He puts a query in which the operative word
is *"if"*—"If thou art the Son of God . . ." [6]

We gather from St Mark [7] that the three recorded temptations come at the end, or perhaps comprise a summary, of a
long period of trial. The first of them consists in an invitation to our Lord to fulfil his own personal desires. He has
been fasting and is hungry—why not change these stones
into bread? [8] If he had the power, what could be more reasonable than that he should use it, and so achieve the double
purpose of satisfying his physical needs and disclosing himself for what he was? Some have seen in this suggestion a
symbolism of even wider significance. Jesus is being tempted
to use the Messianic office as a means of securing economic
relief for the poverty-stricken people, of whom there were
very many in Palestine, and so gain popularity and acceptance with them. However that may be, his reply—"Not in
bread alone doth man live, but in every word that proceedeth
from the mouth of God" [9]—gives no encouragement to any
conception of a Messiah to whom there could be applied the
materialistic test of temporal prosperity. Christ reveals the
deeper meaning of the Old Testament scripture which he
here quotes: [10] to do God's will is also man's meat.[11]

The second temptation is likewise an appeal to our Lord's
miracle-working powers. Surely, *if* he is Son of God, there
are no marvels he cannot perform! Let him make some

[5] Matt. 4:1. [6] Vv. 3 and 6. [7] Mark. 1:13.
[8] Matt. 4:3. [9] Matt. 4:4(R-D.). [10] Deut. 8:3.
[11] Cf. John 4:34.

spectacular display in proof of his complete confidence in the Father—for, after all, such things were just what would be expected of the Messiah—like jumping from the pinnacle of the Temple, and so win followers by gratifying their vulgar desire for excitement. Jesus, as we know, will work many miracles, but none of them in this spirit; he makes no concessions to those who seek the wonderful for its own sake,[12] and the reckless confidence which directly tempts God is to him an abomination. Again he appeals to Scripture: "Thou shalt not tempt the Lord thy God." [13] Finally, the Devil offers Jesus "all the kingdoms of the world" [14] on condition of his performing him an act of worship. A curious temptation, hard to understand, when we reflect on the protagonists engaged! Does it perhaps suggest a recourse to to political means, a response to the expectations of the fanatical Zealots, who looked to the Messiah to overthrow the Roman and Herodian power? In any case, our Lord had not come to secure for himself an earthly kingship; rather was it his mission to establish the kingdom of God, whereby Satan, the "prince of this world" [15] should be overthrown for ever. The tempter is dismissed with the invocation of the first and greatest commandment: "Thou shalt worship the Lord thy God, and serve none but him." [16]

After the temptations, we are told, "angels came and ministered to him." [17] Do the words with which St Luke concludes the scene—"the devil departed from him for a while" [18]—imply that our Lord was not put to the test in this way again throughout the course of the public ministry? This question cannot be answered with any certainty. Not until the hour of the Passion is approaching do we get any direct evidence of mental conflict and distress of soul; [19] and this could be sufficiently explained by Jesus' physical revulsion from the prospect of his sufferings, without the assumption of any satanic intervention. Then indeed "the

[12] Cf. Matt. 16:4.   [13] 4:7(R-D.); Deut. 6:16.
[14] Matt. 4:8.   [15] John 12:31; 14:30; 16:11.
[16] Matt. 4:10.   [17] Vs. 11.   [18] Luke 4:13(W.).
[19] John 12:27; Matt. 26:37–39; Mark 14:33–36; Luke 22:41–42.

prince of this world cometh"; yet "in me he hath not anything." [20] The truth is that the inmost significance of the
temptations is hidden from us; though they need be none
the less profitable for our meditation on that account. A
modern poet has put into the mouth of St Thomas of Canter-
bury the following remarkable words:

> The last temptation is the greatest treason:
> To do the right deed for the wrong reason. [21]

Do these verses perhaps disclose the essence of the trial from
which the Messiah triumphantly emerged?

There was nothing intrinsically blameworthy in turning
stones into bread, in employing supernatural gifts, or even in
securing political ascendancy, provided these things subserved the purpose of establishing God's kingdom. But what
if they ministered to self-love, to the assertion of one's own
personality, to lust for power? It is amazing, but surely deeply
consoling, for us to realize that our Lord could be tempted
precisely to this. We learn that self-conceit, vanity and pride,
are among the gravest infidelities to God. This is the lesson
impressed on us throughout the public ministry. The essence of sin is not in the flesh but in the spirit. Unbridled
sensuality is indeed an insurmountable obstacle to the beatific vision; [22] but this is so inasmuch as it is a form of self-
indulgence betokening a rebellion within the soul. When it
arises from human frailty, from influences of environment,
heredity or faulty upbringing, rather than deliberate malice,
then, as followers of Jesus Christ, we have no title to view it
with harshness. He who could openly console a woman of
the streets with the thought that her sins were forgiven on
account of her great love, [23] who warned the Jewish ecclesi-
astics that the tax-gatherers and harlots would enter God's
kingdom before them, [24] clearly comes before us as one whose
standard of moral values was not derived from any human
code of conventions. What is socially disreputable is not

---

[20] John 14:30(R-D.).
[21] T. S. Eliot, *Murder in the Cathedral,* p. 44.
[22] Matt. 5:8.   [23] Luke 7:47.   [24] Matt. 21:31.

necessarily most displeasing, nor what society approves most acceptable, in the eyes of God.

One lesson emerges from Christ's temptations as unmistakably clear—the condemnation of all self-interest, which not even the highest objective motives can redeem, and the absolute primacy of the divine will over every human desire. At the outset of his life's work, Jesus struggled in mortal combat with his most powerful enemy for the assertion of this principle. At his hands its triumphant vindication was complete; thereafter it dominates the Gospel. Thus, in the prologue to the great drama of salvation, its leading theme is enunciated by him who is its central Figure, is in fact embodied in his person. Human nature, whatever be the cost, must accept the mastery of God; men must surrender themselves to him in order to be saved. To this act of self-renunciation, reaching to the inmost depths of the soul, Christ's temptations invite us. Here, as in all else, he asks of his disciples no sacrifice which he has not offered himself, submits them to no experience of suffering and trial which he has not made his own. The temptations which come our way, often so unpromising in their material, are meant to be shaped and fashioned into God's praise. Our tempted Lord has shown us the way; he gives us the grace and strength to follow his example.

§ 5. THE SERMON ON THE MOUNT

The text of the Sermon on the Mount occupies three entire chapters in St Matthew's Gospel,[1] 111 verses in all; in St Luke, from whose account it is sometimes described as the "sermon on the plain," it is much shorter,[2] occupying only thirty-two verses. The apparent discrepancy of place can be accounted for by supposing that our Lord, having first ascended the mountain,[3] then chose, as a suitable spot

[1] Matt. 5–7.
[2] Luke 6:17–49; cf. 11:33–36; 14:34–35.
[3] Matt. 5:1.

for his discourse, one of the grassy terraces which are so numerous on the sides of the Galilean hills.[4] The points of similarity between Matthew and Luke outweigh the admittedly considerable differences, and the latter can be explained by their respective choice of materials. St Luke, bearing his Gentile readers in mind, was chiefly concerned with the new way of perfection summarized in the law of charity; hence he felt no need to emphasize the relation between our Lord's teaching and that of the Old Testament, which, for St Matthew, is fundamental to his whole plan. But if the latter gives us the fuller account, the former supplies the context; for while Matthew found it convenient to group together sayings and deeds of Jesus irrespective of their chronological sequence, Luke makes some attempt to set things out in the order in which they occurred.[5]

The point, however, need not detain us, since our present concern is less with exact chronology than with the doctrinal significance of what our Lord said and did. Nevertheless, considerable light is thrown precisely on this, when it is realized that the sermon was preached, not as an inaugural address, as one might gather from St Matthew, but at a later stage in the ministry. Jesus had given some preliminary teaching to the people;[6] this had led to a series of conflicts with the Pharisees[7] and, as a counter-measure, to the choosing of the twelve apostles;[8] through their co-operation his enemies would finally be defeated. It is primarily, though by no means exclusively, for the benefit of this select audience, an *élite* among the disciples, that the discourse was delivered.

Its theme, elaborated under a number of aspects, is the kingdom of God. The conditions of membership are here laid down in a solemn proclamation by the Messiah, in his office of Founder and Legislator of the new alliance between God and man. Our Lord's conception of morality is ex-

---

[4] Luke 6:17.

[5] 1:3.

[6] Mark 1:21-22, 39.

[7] Mark 2:1 ff.; 3:6 and parallels.

[8] Mark 3:13-19; Luke 6:12-16; cf. Matt. 10:1-4.

plained to us, a moral doctrine which reaches a deeper level than that of external conduct. Its practical realization lies beyond the range of the ethical virtues extolled by the pagan moralists; for it presupposes divine charity and all that is implied in Christian holiness. A meditation on the Sermon on the Mount is indispensable to our understanding of Jesus Christ. It both presents us with a faithful portrait of its Author's character—its teaching receives its unique embodiment in his own person—and throws light upon his relationship to the Jewish Law and the religious ideas of his contemporaries. The discourse is clearly based on a definite plan, though we must not expect to find the logical coherence of thought which is a characteristic of the cultivated Western, rather than the Eastern mind. By way of an exordium, in the Beatitudes, our Lord expounds the essential conditions for obtaining the right of citizenship in his kingdom.[9] He then goes on to indicate the duties and privileges of its subjects;[10] to conclude with an eloquent epilogue urging his hearers to put his precepts into practice.[11]

Both evangelists are at pains to bring out the solemnity of the occasion on which the sermon was preached. We know from St Luke that it followed upon the choosing of the apostles; he conveys to us also a scene of general enthusiasm and popular excitement, of which our Lord is the central figure:

a multitude of his disciples was there, and a great gathering of the people from all Judaea, and Jerusalem, and the sea-coast of Tyre and Sidon. These had come to listen to him, and to be healed of their diseases; and those who were troubled by unclean spirits were also cured; so that all the multitude was eager to touch him, because power went out from him, and healed them all.[12]

From St Matthew we gather that "he sat down"—a customary attitude with him, as with every Jewish Rabbi when speaking at length—and that "his disciples came about him."[13] It

9 Matt. 5:3–16; Luke 6:20–26.   10 Matt. 5:17; 7:23; Luke 6:27–46.
11 Matt. 7:24–27; Luke 6:47–49.   12 Luke 6:17–19.
13 Matt. 5:1.

was quite literally the "Divine Master" to whom they were now to listen. That this was indeed his role is emphasized by St Luke: "Then he lifted up his eyes towards his disciples" [14] —with what urgency and tenderness we can well imagine; as it is by St Matthew: "And opening his mouth, he taught them." [15] He begins with these words:

Blessed are the poor in spirit; for theirs is the kingdom of heaven.

Blessed are the meek; for they shall inherit the earth.

Blessed are the mourners; for they shall be comforted.

Blessed are they who hunger and thirst after righteousness; for they shall be filled.

Blessed are the merciful; for they shall obtain mercy.

Blessed are the pure in heart; for they shall see God.

Blessed are the peacemakers; for they shall be called children of God.

Blessed are they who suffer persecution for the sake of righteousness; for theirs is the kingdom of heaven. Blessed are you when men revile you and persecute you, and say everything evil against you falsely, for my sake. Be glad and rejoice, because your reward will be abundant in heaven; for so they persecuted the prophets who were before you.[16]

Blessed are the poor in spirit; for theirs is the kingdom of heaven.—Jesus begins by felicitating his hearers. Happy—for that is the meaning of the word "blessed"—are the poor, the meek, the mourners, those who hunger after righteousness! The new law is being proclaimed, not as amid the thunders of Mount Sinai, in awe-inspiring commandments, but as an invitation to holiness, enforced by the gracious presence of the Lawgiver himself and the persuasiveness of human speech. To our Lord's hearers, an oppressed and persecuted people, his words of benediction must have been deeply stirring. In the first Beatitude, as St Matthew makes clear, there is implied no condemnation of material possessions as such. Where one's heart is, there is one's treasure. What is commended is the "spirit" of poverty, that is, non-attachment to the things of the world, the recognition that what-

---

[14] Luke 6:20.   [15] Matt. 5:2(R-D.).   [16] VV. 3–12(S.).

ever we have is given us in trust from God, to be withdrawn
at his pleasure. It must be recognized, however, that the
whole tenour of Christ's teaching [17] shows how conscious he
was that the well-to-do classes are all but inevitably tainted
with worldliness and irreligion. Actual poverty is one of the
most potent means of bringing home to us our state of utter
dependence on God; when so accepted it can lead to the
"perfect joy" experienced by St Francis of Assisi. Abundance
of possessions, on the other hand, can all too easily induce
blindness and arrogance of mind, that unreality and false
sense of values against which we are warned in the Apocalypse: ". . . thou sayest: I am rich and made wealthy and have
need of nothing: and knowest not that thou art wretched
and miserable and poor and blind and naked. . . ." [18]

Blessed are the meek; for they shall inherit the earth.—
Here our Lord praises a quality of soul which was so manifestly his own that he can point to it as an invitation to his
hearers to accept his teaching: "Take my yoke upon yourselves and learn from me; I am gentle and humble of
heart." [19] So memorably attractive had it made him that St
Paul could later exhort the Corinthians "by the gentleness
and the courtesy of Christ." [20] In this, as in all the Beatitudes,
he recalls the best teaching of the Old Testament: "But the
meek shall inherit the land, and shall delight in the abundance of peace." [21] By contrast with the self-assertive methods
by which people normally stake out their claims to land, this
inheritance belongs to those who know how to bear and
forbear. It goes without saying that Christ's gentleness lacked
nothing of strength and firm resolve; to confuse it with
weakness or lack of moral energy would be a complete mistake. The endurance of trial with unresisting tranquillity is
often a more searching test of courage than to meet opposition by direct assault. The Christian is pledged to observe
justice and charity, even in the height of conflict; he may
ride rough-shod over none. It is the supreme ideal; and yet

[17] Mark 10:25 and parallels.   [18] Apoc. 3:17(R-D.).
[19] Matt. 11:29.   [20] 2 Cor. 10:1.   [21] Ps. 36(37):11.

how much worldly, as well as heavenly, wisdom is contained in our Lord's counsel to gentleness and courtesy! We know that fidelity to a principle is not seldom best served by being maintained in a conciliatory temper. Provided nothing essential is compromised, we gain more by knowing how to yield, to treat gently with an opponent, than by an attitude of intransigence. Only the weak or stupid man is incapable of giving way. When the cause at stake clearly permits of no concessions being made, then at least "the gentleness and the courtesy of Christ" should preserve our defence of it from being marred by motives of self-esteem and personal prestige.

Blessed are the mourners; for they shall be comforted.— Words of divine consolation for the afflicted and sorrowful! Whether the occasion for grief be our sense of sin or some bereavement, we need not perhaps enquire. Though our Lord doubtless had first in mind the pitiable plight of many among his original hearers, in a deeper and more universal sense he is surely counselling us to become aware simply of our human predicament. He would have us penetrate the artificial mask under which we attempt to hide, from ourselves as well as others, the essential pathos of even the least troubled of lives. Comparatively few, and they not the most fortunate, fail to find enough of frustration and suffering in day-to-day existence to convince them that it is idle to look for anything approaching permanent happiness here on earth. Unfortunately we are all too often unwilling to acknowledge this abject state of things; we seek to be rid of its seriousness by such escapes and evasions as will distract us from the contemplation of ourselves as we are. Man cannot long endure facing reality; hence he takes refuge in the levity and irresponsibility which enable him, for a time, to forget both himself and God. Of this the inevitable result is sin. Among the safeguards against such betrayal is our sense of the doom of mortality upon everything in the world. *Sunt lacrimae rerum et mentem mortalia tangunt.*

There can be no real depth of character where a man has

grown to maturity with his heart untouched by "the still, sad music of humanity." If we remain insensible to the true state of affairs, precariously set as we are among all manner of evil, if we have no eyes for the vast burden of distress which weighs insupportably upon countless millions of our fellow-men, it follows that we can feel no need for liberation and release. Our Lord would indeed uplift us even now from being immersed in earthly sorrow, impart to us something of the joy which radiates from the "good news" he came to bring; but he gives no countenance to the light-hearted optimism of those who profess themselves satisfied with the world as they find it. In their present state of well-being such people have already received their reward; accordingly they have no call to turn for relief to the God of all consolation. Not to them are addressed the words of the Apocalypse, which have brought solace to the anguished soul of so many believers:

Lo, the dwelling-place of God is with men, and he shall dwell with them, and they shall be his peoples, and God himself shall be with them. And he shall wipe away every tear from their eyes; and death shall be no more, nor shall grief nor wailing nor pain be any more; for the former things are passed away.[22]

Blessed are they who hunger and thirst after righteousness; for they shall be filled.—Only those who suffer a divine discontent can hope to find their satisfaction in God. What they seek is more than can be expressed by the word "justice"; it is the state of being *right* with God. The imagery, familiar and deeply significant to every Jew, had been used by the prophet Amos: "Behold the days come, saith the Lord, and I will send forth a famine into the land: not a famine of bread, nor a thirst of water, but of hearing the word of the Lord." [23] "I shall be satisfied," writes the Psalmist, "when thy glory shall appear." [24] Christ alone can appease this hunger and thirst: "Labour not for the food that perishes, but for the food that endures to eternal life, which the Son

[22] Apoc. 21:3-4(S.).   [23] Amos 8:11.   [24] Ps. 16(17):15.

of Man will give you"; [25] "but the water that I shall give him shall become in him a fountain of water leaping up into everlasting life." [26] The righteousness of which our Lord speaks is the state of grace and holiness. It means more than the confomity of our actions to a divinely appointed standard; what is implied is both man's fidelity to the will of God and the completion of God's gracious purpose in man himself. It is in this consummation that those who are dissatisfied with themselves, and oppressed with the difficulties of life, will find the fulfilment of their heart's desire.

Blessed are the merciful; for they shall obtain mercy.—If we are to obtain God's mercy, we must be merciful to others. No principle is more characteristic of the teaching of Jesus than this. Again he takes up, and places in a new context, doctrine well known to his hearers.

Forgive thy neighbour if he hath hurt thee: and then shall thy sins be forgiven to thee when thou prayest. Man to man reserveth anger: And doth he seek remedy of God? He hath no mercy on a man like himself: And doth he entreat for his own sins? He that is but flesh nourisheth anger: And doth he ask forgiveness of God? Who shall obtain pardon for his sins? [27]

It is the theme of the parable of the Unmerciful Servant [28] and is embodied in the Lord's Prayer.[29] "And when you stand to pray, forgive if you have aught against any man: that your Father also, who is in heaven, may forgive you your sins." [30] The indispensable condition of our obtaining forgiveness is that we should forgive the offences done to us. Nor is this based simply on equity, a sort of *quid pro quo,* God's pardon being a reward for our pardoning others. It reaches a much deeper level. An unforgiving spirit of itself imposes a barrier upon God's merciful action towards us; we shut him out, as it were, behind the wall of our own self-righteousness.

[25] John 6:27(S.). [26] 4:14(S.); cf. 7:37–38; Apoc. 22:17.
[27] Ecclus. 28:2–5. [28] Matt. 18:23–35.
[29] Matt. 6:12; cf. vv. 14, 15; 7:2; Mark 4:24; Luke 6:38; 17:3.
[30] Mark 11:25(R-D.).

Unless we know how to overcome evil by good, we lack any effective insight into Christ's scheme of things, of which the secret is that we must learn to look upon men with the merciful eyes of God himself. This can lead us to understand the offender, even to sympathize with him; better still, we may learn to disregard the offence altogether. How many seeming affronts have reality only in the imagination of the wounded party! To be merciful means more than an attitude of good-humoured indulgence towards others; it differs from the "magnanimity" praised by the pagan moralist—for there can be an element of patronage about this. We must take account of our own shortcomings, realize that we have defects of character that are a source of provocation to those about us. "And why seest thou the mote that is in thy brother's eye; and seest not the beam that is in thy own eye?" [31] Here we have the New Testament version of what modern psychologists describe as *projection*: we thrust upon another the unresolved conflicts of which we are the unconscious victims, and resist as an external irritant what exists largely within ourselves. Acquiescence in this unpalatable truth should help us to be slow to take offence, to avoid being "hurt" and unduly "sensitive" when our own interests are touched. Not that our Lord's counsel of mercy is reducible to a merely humanitarian philosophy of live-and-let-live. Even the worldly-wise know how to accept one another's weaknesses and come together in mutual tolerance. What is called for is the creative power of divine charity, which supplies for every defect, ignores all antagonism with the long-suffering of one who knows how precious is the least attractive of his fellow-creatures in God's sight, and overwhelms opposition with the positive forces of generosity and love.[32]

Blessed are the pure in heart; for they shall see God.— Something more was required of the Jews than the ritual cleansing needful for those who take part in the Temple

---

[31] Matt. 7:3(R-D.).
[32] See St. Paul's great hymn in praise of charity, 1 Cor. 13.

ritual. Here, as elsewhere in Scripture, the "heart" is the seat of deliberative thought and purpose.[33] The "pure in heart" are they who seek God from unmixed motives and with simplicity of intention.[34] The emphasis is upon God's holiness and man's need for detachment from all that is earthly in order to approach him. The prophet Isaiah, who considered himself "a man of unclean lips," had seen the six-winged seraphim before the Throne and heard them crying to one another: "Holy, Holy, Holy, the Lord God of hosts, all the earth is full of his glory." [35] In our Lord's day men's minds were in fact overburdened with the thought of God's inaccessibility. They conceived of his rule too much in terms of earthly kingship and the unapproachableness of the typical despotic monarchs of the East; [36] the divine transcendence dominated Israel's religion. The Jews had yet to learn the secret of Jesus Christ: that God wishes to admit men to an intimate communion with himself. But for this there is an indispensable condition—the abandonment of everything that is opposed to God, a despoilment of self, the shedding of all impurity and worldliness. Thus the Fathers and theologians were right in seeing in this Beatitude a warning against fleshy sin; the beatific vision is reserved for those who are pure enough to be able to gaze upon it.[37] It is not necessary for carnal indulgence to be directly punished by our being deprived of the sight of God; of its nature it tends to close the eyes of the soul so that they no longer see.

Blessed are the peacemakers; for they shall be called children of God.—The detachment from the world achieved by dedication to God produces within the soul that tranquillity of order which is peace. These ideals are in fact closely allied: "Pursue peace with all, and the holiness without which no one shall see the Lord." [38] The peacemaker

[33] Cf. Matt. 9:4; 15:19; Ps. 23(24):4.
[34] Cf. Matt. 6:21–22; Wisd. 1:1–2; Jas 4:8.
[35] Isa. 6:1–7.   [36] Cf. 3 Kings 10:8; Esther 1:14.
[37] Cf. St Augustine, *De videndo Deo, P.L.* 33, col. 596-622.
[38] Heb. 12:14(S.).

is more than the non-resister of evil; he is a positive force of harmony and reconciliation in others. When we survey the world about us, we may well despair of removing dissensions from among men; but it should be remembered that the peace in question is *God's* peace. He is truly the "God of peace," [39] just as Jesus Christ is "our peace" [40] and "the Lord of peace." [41] To reconcile the world with God is the supreme act of pacification; no earthly peace is possible on any other basis than this. We are peacemakers by entering into God's providential plan, sharing his work of healing and unification, gathering all together in the arms of love. It is thus that we become "children of God"; he is our Father and every man our brother; we see the distracted and divided human race as the seed of one great family, which can be unified only in him who is the source of all unity. With Jesus we pray "that they should all be one, as we are one, ... and so they may be perfectly made one." [42]

Blessed are they who suffer persecution for the sake of righteousness; for theirs is the kingdom of heaven. Blessed are you when men revile you and persecute you, and say everything evil against you falsely, for my sake. Be glad and rejoice, because your reward will be abundant in heaven; for so they persecuted the prophets who were before you.— The Beatitudes end with a note of warning—there is a price to be paid before the promised felicity can be enjoyed. The discerning among Christ's hearers could perhaps appreciate how poverty of spirit, gentleness and moral purity were the prerequisites of the state of blessedness; but that it had also as its condition positive suffering was a harder lesson to learn. It was especially hard for the Jews, who had an all but ineradicable tendency to interpret God's favours in terms of temporal prosperity. Although, or perhaps because, the greatest of their prophets had been victims of persecution, they looked for a Messiah who would be immune precisely from this. The Messianic age, so they thought, was

[39] Rom. 15:33(R-D.); 16:20.   [40] Eph. 2:14(R-D.).
[41] 2 Thess. 3:16.   [42] John 17:22–23.

to put an end to earthly misery. That the event apparently proved to be the reverse of this was, as St Paul clearly saw, the "stumbling-block" [43] that led to Christ's rejection by his own people. And yet here, in his first great discourse, we find him putting the issue unmistakably before his disciples—neither he nor his followers can expect any fate different from that of the prophets. Already he was identifying their destiny with his, as he would later remind them: "Do not forget what I said to you, No servant can be greater than his master. They will persecute you just as they have persecuted me; they will pay the same attention to your words as to mine." [44]

The shadow of the Cross lies across the first pages of the Gospel. God's witnesses are not to expect popular acceptance with the world; rather will they meet with hostility and rejection.

> Truth for ever on the scaffold,
> Wrong for ever on the throne.

So it must be until earthly power makes its submission to the rule of God. It was no tragic accident, a fortuitous and unrepeatable set of circumstances, which led to the Crucifixion. There is no reason to believe that the forces of evil which brought it about are less potent in our own day than they were in first-century Palestine. Whether they be aligned in open persecution of the Church, or take the more insidious form of undermining religion from within by reducing its divine values to the level of a secularist humanitarianism, the underlying motive is the same—a rejection of God's absolute claims on man's service. It is in the nature of things that the impact of unqualified goodness upon the stony human heart must strike fire, either of love or hatred. If, in a perverse attempt to safeguard our self-esteem, we refuse to yield to this invasion of our world, then inevitably we rebel. Man's pride cannot endure to gaze upon the selflessness of Christ; so disturbing an object of self-reproach must be removed from the line of vision. Men are willing to pay tribute

[43] 1 Cor. 1:23.   [44] John 15:20.

to virtue, the more so when it does not affect their interests or can be utilized for their own purposes; but when it is embodied in such a form as to demand their personal surrender to it, then all is changed. The Satanic *"I will not serve,"* which is the motto of unregenerate human nature, has for its logical issue the final repudiation: *"Crucify him! Crucify him!"* As with the Master, so with the disciples; they will be persecuted until the end of the world.

The followers of Jesus are to find joy in the fact that they are ill spoken of—provided it be "falsely"; provided also that it is "for my sake." Hence certain conditions need to be fulfilled before we may claim the consolations of this Beatitude. We must be sure that those who oppose and speak against us have no grounds for their complaint. We should beware of readily thinking ourselves "misunderstood" and undeservedly unpopular. Occasionally we may be right; but normally, when such things happen, we have largely ourselves to blame. Before ranging ourselves among the martyrs —and it is wiser to leave that honour to be conferred on us by others!—let us be sure that it is for God's truth we are being persecuted. Our Lord insists also on purity of motive; it must be for *his* sake. Then indeed his witnesses are made one with him; well may they rejoice, for their reward in heaven is great. Even on earth, as the death of the martyrs and the saints' lives go to prove, there can be a mysterious marriage between happiness and suffering. The pain of self-detachment from the world, though it may be violently imposed by persecution, merges into the joy of being wholly fulfilled in God.

Before passing on to a brief summary of the remainder of the sermon, it is well for us to understand the immense significance of the Beatitudes. They set the key for the whole of our Lord's teaching on the kingdom of God. And his conception of the "kingdom," from the standpoint of the Synoptic Gospels, is the sum and substance of his message. He makes clear at the outset that man is destined for happiness; for that, as we have seen, is what is meant by being "blessed." The religion of Jesus is therefore, in the language of philosophy, eudaemonist; its effect is to make us happy. At the same time, it is expressed in a number of paradoxes which constitute a radical criticism of the commonly accepted notions of happiness. There is a reversal of all human values: the poor, the meek, the persecuted are in reality the happy ones. But if it is true that Christ aimed at reconciling the unfortunate to their lot by fixing their hearts on the state of final blessedness, he showed both in word and deed that he gave no countenance to human misery for its own sake. His thesis was that later formulated by St Paul: "For I reckon that the sufferings of the present time are not worthy to be compared with the glory to be revealed in us." [45]

We notice also that there is, so to say, an organic development between man's present state, as it is acknowledged by Jesus, and the issue to which it leads. The promised rewards are the direct consequence of the conditions attaching to them: the poor, by their very poverty, lay claim to the kingdom; to be merciful to others calls down God's mercy upon ourselves; purity of heart is itself a medium for seeing God. Thus the New Law, which is now supplanting the Old, is not a code of commandments expressed in the imperative mood, "Thou shalt"—"Thou shalt not." We are not being driven from behind, but led forward in the light of a vision of what is noblest and best; our eyes are opened to the ideal of Christian morality. Jesus invited his disciples to good will and the right direction of their thoughts; once this was achieved, conformity to their new obligations would follow as a matter of course. He wished men to understand the nature of the kingdom of God and consciously to long for its coming. With their minds so enlightened and their hearts on fire with charity, they would not fail to act as befitted its members.

You are the salt of the earth; but if the salt becomes insipid, with what shall it be salted? It is no longer good for anything but to be thrown out and trodden under foot by men.

[45] Rom. 8:18(W.).

You are the light of the world. A city set on a hill cannot be hid. Nor do men light a lamp and place it under the corn-measure, but upon the lampstand; and it gives light to all that are in the house. In the same way let your light shine before men, so that they may see your good works and give glory to your Father who is in heaven.[46]

The ideal of the Christian life must be made known to all the world; those charged with this task, the disciples, are like strongly flavoured salt, which seasons everything with which it comes in contact. But if the salt becomes insipid, that is, if fervour and devotion are lost, the seasoning process ceases and the material becomes useless for its purpose. Now as at the beginning of the world the divine command goes forth: "Let there be light." [47] Just as at the first creation God's characteristic activity is the giving of light, so is it likewise with his spiritual re-creation. The Light which is Christ [48] was to be reflected in his disciples; they too are "the light of the world." Their good works would shine out before men and cause them to give praise to God. How searching are the familiar thoughts! If we are to be true followers of Christ men must taste something of his savour in all that we are and do, a measure of his saving and enlightening power must go out from us.

"Do not think that I am come to destroy the law or the prophets. I am not come to destroy but to fulfil." [49] Here the important question arises concerning our Lord's attitude to the Jewish Law. Did this new teaching conflict with the old? For his hearers the Law was something sacred and inviolable; even the appearance of tampering with it would have alienated their sympathy at once. Jesus reassures them; the Law and the prophets, the time-honoured instruments of God's revelation, remain. They were not to be abrogated, but fulfilled, that is, brought to perfection. If the new Christian law was now being promulgated, it was not yet put into force. St Paul would explain how, with the Crucifixion, the

46 Matt. 5:13–16(S.).
48 John 9:5.
47 Gen. 1:3.
49 Matt. 5:17(R-D.).

old dispensation had come to an end.[50] Until then, however, it still held. Jesus himself well knew that he was infusing a new spirit into the Law, from which would result its eventual disappearance. He pointed out the inevitable consequences of attempting to patch an old garment with new cloth, to pour freshly fermenting wine into old wine-skins; the garment would be torn and the wine-skins burst asunder.[51] It would become clear that the divinely given Old Testament Law was a preparation for the Messiah's coming, a "tutor unto Christ," [52] whereby those who were as yet children were led up to him. But Israel must first grow to maturity before it could make an end of "childish ways." [53]

Nevertheless, our Lord's attitude to the Law was, and has remained, a source of scandal and bewilderment to the literal-minded Jews. We find him affirming its eternal validity; no detail—not "one jot or one tittle"—of it should cease to be operative "till all be fulfilled." [54] And yet, though he is himself a strict observer, his actions reveal a sovereign freedom with reference to it which those who repudiated his authority did not hesitate to interpret as an infringement of the Law. His teaching on the subject of sacrifices,[55] fasting,[56] the observance of the Sabbath [57]—where his own conduct was a particular occasion for grievance with his enemies—and ritual ablutions [58] show him lifting the whole matter of legal obligation on to a plane which could only be reached by those who accepted him as their Master. He is in fact preparing the way for the abrogation of the Law, as this was recognized and proclaimed by St Paul. Jesus criticizes, not the Law itself (this he never does), but the spirit of those who claimed to reverence it and the manner in which its precepts had been amplified by the man-made traditions of the scribes. This criticism is best understood in the light of such a passage as Mark, chapter 7, verses 6–13. Rabbinical casuistry was in fact making a barren mockery of the Mosaic code.

---

50 See pp. 337–41.   51 Mark 2:21–22 and parallels.
52 Gal. 3:24.   53 1 Cor. 13:11.   54 Matt. 5:18(R-D.).
55 Mark 12:33.   56 Matt. 9:14–15.   57 12:3–8.
58 Mark 7:1–23.

Our Lord charges the scribes with stultifying the Law by their interpretations of it; it is they, not he, who are "making void the word of God." [59] He brings to light the true meaning of the Law: it is an instrument for conforming men to his Father's will; this was God's ultimate purpose in framing it.

We can gain much insight both into Jesus' view of the Law, and the whole character of his ministry, from the following verses in St Luke:

And here one of the lawyers answered him; Master, he said, in speaking thus thou art bringing us too into contempt. And he said, Woe upon you too, you lawyers, for loading men with packs too heavy to be borne, packs that you yourselves will not touch with one finger. Woe upon you, for building up the tombs of the prophets, the same prophets who were murdered by your fathers; sure witness that you approve what your fathers did, since you build tombs for the men they murdered. Whereupon the wisdom of God warns you, I will send my prophets and my apostles to them, and there will be some they will kill and persecute; so they will be answerable for all the blood of the prophets that has been shed since the beginning of the world, from the blood of Abel to the blood of Zacharias, who was killed between the altar and the temple; yes, I tell you, this generation will be held answerable for it. Woe upon you, you lawyers, for taking away with you the key of knowledge; you have neither entered yourselves, nor let others enter when they would.[60]

The accusation against the scribes—the Jewish doctors of the Law—is that they are laying upon men too heavy a burden, while themselves not raising a finger to help those who find it insupportable. Be it noted that our Lord does not here tax them with failing to practise what they preached, with evading the obligations they imposed on others. That is not the point. The charge is that they lacked fellow-feeling for those who could not keep faith with the Law. To such of the weaker brethren the legal-minded scribes had nothing to say, except that they were "sinners"—that is, non-observers. Now it was

[59] Mark 7:13.   [60] Luke 11:45-52.

just here that Jesus parted company with them. Not that he
denied the Law's binding force, still less that he claimed any
exemption from it, but that his heart was moved to compassion at the spectacle of those who were unable to keep it.
He was "a friend of publicans and sinners." [61] These were
just the people, the tax-gatherers and non-observers, most
obnoxious to the scribes and Pharisees, and, by his sympathy
with their lot, our Lord incurred the stigma attaching to
them. Clearly there was something radically wrong in a
religious system so pitiless in its practical application; it
was an intolerable state of things that God's children should
be estranged from him in their very attempts to keep his
Law. Jesus exposes the hollowness of the situation by an
appeal to the prophets. And in so doing he provoked the
greater enmity of the official teachers of his day; for the
Rabbis placed the Law above the prophets.

There is no more revealing clue to our Lord's interpretation of the Law, and to the nature of his clash with contemporary Judaism, than in his use of Old Testament scripture. Of the ninety-four quotations in the Synoptic Gospels,
forty-six are from the prophetic books, twenty-three are
from the Psalms and Daniel; only twenty-four are from the
Law. The suggestion, borne out by the general teaching of
Jesus, that the Law was to be interpreted in the light of the
prophetical writings, discloses a quite different emphasis
from that of the scribes. For them the Law was supreme;
it could be confirmed, but not reformed, by prophecy. We
know that this principle had endangered the inclusion of
the Book of Ezekiel in the Hebrew canon, since it was
thought to be at variance with the Law. The official view
was that the living voice of prophecy had no relevance to the
written code. The ancient prophets might be revered, but
their message had little bearing upon the present; they were
dead, and the scribes were well content that they should
remain so. This was the substance of our Lord's reproach to
them. Persecution had been the lot of every claimant to be

61 Matt. 11:19.

the mouthpiece of God; and this rule still held, as the fate of John the Baptist, and of Jesus himself, was to show. Himself the greatest of the prophets, the living Word of God, he shed upon Judaism the light of prophecy, infused with the dazzling rays of the Godhead. So great an illumination could not be endured. "And the light shines in darkness, a darkness which was not able to master it." [62]

The Sermon on the Mount now passes from general principles to their particular application.[63] Entry into God's kingdom is not to be gained by a mechanical obedience to the written tradition as taught by the scribes and Pharisees. A change of heart, a new spirit, reaching a deeper level than merely external observance, was required. Our Lord illustrates this by an incisive commentary on six precepts of the Old Law.[64] He explains them in the light of the new, showing how the former is perfected and spiritualized by the latter, so raising man's religious and social obligations on to a plane unattainable by the Mosaic legislation. The Decalogue forbade murder, an act of violence abhorrent to God and punishable as a legal offence; to the Christian is proscribed that of which no earthly tribunal can take account—the motives prompting such a crime, hatred and contempt. Even the knowledge that we have given grievance to another excludes us from approaching God; we must first seek reconciliation before presuming to offer our sacrifice. It is the same with the sin of adultery; the inner dispositions which lead to it—unbridled desire, the wandering eye—are also wrong. The Old Testament allowed divorce; Jesus forbids it. His teaching here is based, not on an interpretation of the Mosaic code, but on an appeal beyond it, to God's original purpose in instituting marriage:

It was to suit your hard hearts that Moses wrote such a command as that; God, from the first days of creation, made them man and woman. A man, therefore, will leave his father and mother and will cling to his wife, and the two will become one

62 John 1:5. 63 Matt. 5:20 ff.
64 5:21-47; cf. Luke 6:27-35.

flesh. Why then, since they are no longer two, but one flesh, what God has joined, let not man put asunder.[65]

On the question of vows and oaths, and the sin of perjury, the Old Testament had much to say,[66] to which rabbinical casuistry had added an elaborate code of what was, and what was not, permissible. Once more Jesus lays bare the underlying principle. The essential requirement is a disposition to tell the truth. Granted this, oath-taking in any form becomes superfluous. "Let your word be Yes for Yes, and No for No." [67] The simple "yes" or "no" of an honest man is more trustworthy than the protestations of a liar, however solemnly affirmed. The famous law of retaliation, *lex talionis* —"an eye for an eye and a tooth for a tooth"—next comes under review.[68] It should be remembered that this law, when first instituted, was itself an advance on existing custom. It put an end to the interminable vendetta and the repaying of injuries with interest. But it falls far below the standard demanded by Christ. We have to think, not of revenge, but of how to overcome evil by good. The practical instances of the way ill usage should be met aim at inculcating an inward spirit rather than laying down precise rules of conduct. In conformity with the teaching method of the Jewish Rabbis, Jesus indulges in a form of verbal exaggeration well understood by his hearers,[69] in order to heighten the emphasis and drive the lesson home. This is obvious, for example, in the counsel to the man whose outer garment has been stolen to let the thief have his shirt as well.[70] Taken literally, the issue of this advice would be nudity; which is sufficient reason for seeking another explanation.

The point of our Lord's teaching here is that we should not resent personal slights and injuries; there must be no vindictiveness. He does not require of us non-resistance to evil. His own challenge to the scribes and Pharisees shows

[65] Mark 10:5–9; cf. Gen. 2:24.
[66] Exod. 20:7; Lev. 19:12; Deut. 5:11.
[67] Matt. 5:37; cf. Jas 5:12.   [68] Exod. 21:22–25; Lev. 24:19.
[69] E.g. Matt. 5:29–30.   [70] Luke 6:29.

that there is such a thing as righteous indignation; no one was more courageous and outspoken than he in calling evil things by their true names. He could even question a direct injustice to himself on a point of procedure at his trial.[71] What he would remove from us is the wish to retaliate when roughly dealt with; we must bear no malice. It is a heroic ideal, human nature being what it is. But heroism is of the essence of Christianity; its aim is to uplift the natural man, so that he becomes something more than merely human. With Christ's all-conquering love, in which we are meant to share, we have to win over our enemies as well as embrace our friends. It is thus that we become the sons of our Father in heaven, "who makes his sun rise on the evil and equally on the good, his rain fall on the just and equally on the unjust." [72]

Our Lord demands that we show charity to others besides our neighbour. Or rather, as we learn from the parable of the Good Samaritan,[73] he extends the definition of "neighbour" to include all. There the lawyer had asked for a clear definition of this term, so that he might know how far his obligations went. Jesus brushes such considerations aside. The lesson of the parable is that we do not need to know where to draw the line between neighbour and non-neighbour. If we have love in our heart, we shall recognize at once who our neighbour is. And Christ intends our good will to be such that it will include our enemies. Christian charity implies far more than the normal courtesies of life: loving those who love us, saluting those who salute us. "Will not the very heathen do as much?" [74] It means being well disposed towards all, those who offend no less than those who please, because that is the way God himself acts. "You are to be perfect, as your heavenly Father is perfect." [75]

Jesus now lays down a principle which must govern all our religious duties: well-doing should be from the highest motive, for God's sake; there must be nothing ostentatious

71 John 18:23. 72 Matt. 5:45. 73 Luke 10:29–37.
74 Matt. 5:47. 75 5:48.

or hypocritical about it. "Be sure you do not perform your
acts of piety before men, for them to watch; if you do that,
you have no title to a reward from your Father who is in
heaven." [76] This principle is then applied to three practices
of religion: almsgiving, prayer and fasting. Those who give
alms with an eye to the public may do a good deed; but
"they have their reward already." [77] They get what they pay
for, namely, the onlookers' admiration. With that the trans-
action—for this is what the hypocrite's "charity" amounts
to—is closed; from God they get nothing. Not so with the
true disciples of Christ. The proof of a worthy motive is that
the almsgiving will be done secretly. It is not enough to
relieve the necessities of others; we must take care how we
do it. Respect and a sense of delicacy for those we wish to
help are constituent parts of Christian charity. Which means
that, in all such matters, we shall behave as unobtrusively
as possible. The public knows nothing about it, but the
Father, "who sees what is done in secret," [78] will show his
approval.

It is the same with prayer.[79] Our Lord's teaching at this
point begins with the negative advice—how not to pray—
leading on to a positive example, which is the pattern of all
prayer, the Our Father. The hypocrite parades his sham
piety by praying in a conspicuous place. "But when thou art
praying, go into thy inner room and shut the door upon
thyself, and so pray to thy Father in secret." [80] Jesus, it
need hardly be said, is not disparaging common prayer in
public. We know that he, and his disciples after him, took
part in the congregational worship of both Temple and
Synagogue. His point is that private devotion should be
private; we must pray alone and unobserved, so that the
whole man may be concentrated on God, with no eye for
possible spectators or to gaining a reputation for piety. The
saying about "do not use many phrases" [81] when at prayer
refers to the superstitious custom of the heathen in calling

[76] Matt. 6:1–2.   [77] Vs. 3.   [78] Vs. 4.
[79] Matt. 6:5–15.   [80] Vs. 6.   [81] Vs. 7.

upon their gods by many names lest, if they failed to hit upon the right one, their prayer should prove ineffectual. Christ's disciples, knowing well the God to whom they pray, need not indulge in such expedients as these. That we have every encouragement to pray persistently is shown, for example, by the parable of the Importunate Friend.[82] It is enforced by Jesus' own practice of devoting long periods to prayer,[83] and by his often-repeated petitions during the agony in Gethsemane.

The Our Father is not only the supreme prayer; it is a complete summary of what, in the mind of Jesus Christ, is meant by the Fatherhood of God. As we believe, so do we pray—*lex credendi est lex orandi;* prayer both directs our thoughts to God and reveals what kind of God we hold him to be. The Lord's prayer, though characteristically Jewish in its separate phrases, bears the unique stamp of its Author, alike in the selection and arrangement of its petitions and in the brevity and completeness of the composition as a whole. The text in St Matthew,[84] which is the one familiar to us from the Church's Liturgy, appears in a slightly different form in St Luke,[85] where our Lord is found repeating it to his disciples at their own request—that he should teach them how to pray. The prayer falls into two main divisions, each of them concerned with God's providence, first as this extends to all the world, and then in its bearing on the daily needs of the individual. The loving and almighty Father, whose wisdom "reacheth from end to end mightily and ordereth all things sweetly," [86] is the same God who forgets not a single sparrow and has numbered the very hairs of our head.[87]

We say "*Our* Father" because, even when praying alone, we approach him as one of his children, united in mind and heart with the great family who together acknowledge his Fatherhood. "*Hallowed be thy name.*" The Jews scarcely distinguished between the name and what it signified; to

---

[82] Luke 11:5 ff.   [83] See p. 32.   [84] Matt. 6:9–13.
[85] Luke 11:2–4.   [86] Wisd. 8:1.   [87] Luke 12:6–7.

honour God's name is to honour him. We desire both that he should manifest his glory by his mighty acts and that men, in recognizing them, should give him praise and conform their lives to his will. This wish is expressed in another form in the petition *"Thy kingdom come."* What is asked for is that God's empire and rule should be established for ever—the coming of the kingdom "with power." [88] We shall see that, in a real sense, the kingdom of God has already come; [89] but we still await the final issue of its coming, when Christ "hands over the kingdom to God and the Father." [90] With the early Christians we can still pray: "Come, Lord Jesus." [91] *"Thy will be done, on earth as it is in heaven."* This is how the great coming is prepared for, by *our* doing God's will. *"Give us this day our daily bread."* The request is neither for riches nor for lasting material security, but for sufficient provisions to meet day to day needs, so that our services of God may not be hindered by harassing cares and actual physical want. *"And forgive us our trespasses, as we forgive them that trespass against us."* Our Lord's characteristic teaching is here brought out: our plea for forgiveness must be grounded on our own forgiveness of others. *"And lead us not into temptation, but deliver us from evil. Amen."* "Temptation" means both the seduction of sin and the trial of persecution—the latter a very terrible reality to the early Church, with its accompanying danger of apostasy, than which there could be no greater betrayal. God never, of course, directly tempts us to evil; but, without his care, we find ourselves in situations in which it cannot be withstood. From these we ask to be delivered.

Having taught us how to pray, Jesus now speaks of fasting.[92] In addition to such solemn public fasts as the Day of Atonement and New Year the pious Jew kept many private fasts. We know that these were observed by the disciples of John the Baptist and by the Pharisees.[93] The latter had the

[88] Mark 9:1.
[90] 1 Cor. 15:24(S.).
[92] Matt. 6:16–18.

[89] See p. 297.
[91] Apoc. 22:20.
[93] Mark 2:18; Luke 18:12.

custom of keeping them on Monday and Thursday; the primitive Christians, to distinguish themselves, chose Wednesday and Friday. Praiseworthy as is this asceticism, when prompted by sincere motives, it can be a pitfall to its devotees. When advertised to the world, it brings its reward in terms of a reputation for piety; there is admiration for the self-discipline revealed in emaciated looks and austerity of life. Many of the Pharisees, when fasting, proclaimed the fact by not washing or anointing and strewing the head with ashes. Our Lord will have nothing of this. "But do thou, at thy times of fasting, anoint thy head and wash thy face, so that thy fast may not be known to men, but to thy Father who dwells in secret; and then thy Father, who sees what is done in secret, will reward thee." [94]

Riches and worldly cares come next under review.[95] "Do not lay up for yourselves treasures upon the earth ...; but lay up for yourselves treasures in heaven.... For where thy treasure is, there will thy heart be also." [96] The test of the thing we most prize is what claims our undivided attention; if this be given to the amassing of wealth, then we shall be caught up in the busy world of commerce and affairs and lose interest in what lies beyond. The only way to heaven, says Cardinal Newman, is the desire for heaven. It is a fitting comment on our Lord's teaching here. "The lamp of thy body is thine eye. If, therefore thine eye is sound, thy whole body shall be illuminated; but if thine eye is blind, thy whole body shall be in darkness. If, therefore the light within thee is darkness, how great is the darkness!" [97] If we have a sound eye, we see things as they are, we are truly facing the facts; if the eye is blind, we are lost in unreality—of which the result is sure and certain disaster for ourselves and all who are influenced by us. It will lead us into hopeless compromises, the vain attempt to serve "two masters." Only the

[94] Matt. 6:17–18.
[95] Matt. 6:19–34; cf. Luke 12:33–34; 11:34–36; 16:13; 12:22–31, being the parallels to Matthew.
[96] Matt. 6:19–21(S.).   [97] VV. 22–23(S.).

clear, the "single," eye can realize the tremendous *either/or* of the Gospel. "You cannot serve God and mammon." [98]

"Do not be anxious" is the theme of the counsels that follow.[99] The Our Father has taught us that there is a hierarchy of values which we must make our own. We have to say, and mean, *"Thy kingdom come; thy will be done"* before we pray, *"Give us this day our daily bread."* Jesus does not urge us to be improvident, but to trust in God; we may take prudent forethought for our temporal needs, yet not so anxiously as to lose confidence in the Father's care. "Behold the birds of the air, for they neither sow, nor do they reap nor gather into barns: and your heavenly Father feedeth them. Are not you of much more value than they?" [100] Undue preoccupation with the problems of food and clothing, besides being a poor tribute to God's providence, is pointless also. We cannot increase our height—or prolong our life (for that may be the meaning of Matthew, chapter 6, verse 27)—by becoming agitated about it. In words of touching eloquence and beauty our Lord enforces the point:

And for raiment why are you solicitous? Consider the lilies of the field, how they grow: they labour not, neither do they spin. But I say to you that not even Solomon in all his glory was arrayed as one of these. And if the grass of the field, which is to-day and to-morrow is cast into the oven, God doth so clothe: how much more you, O ye of little faith? Be not solicitous therefore, saying, What shall we eat: or, What shall we drink: or, Wherewith shall we be clothed? For after all these things do the heathens seek. For your Father knoweth that you have need of all these things.[101]

Such solicitude may be expected of unbelievers; it should have no part in the life of Christ's disciples. If anxieties press in upon us, let them at least be present ones, confined to to-day. To-morrow's will be different from what we anticipate; they can be left to take care of themselves, and to God. Best of all, we should find their solution in fixing our gaze

[98] Matt. 6:24(R-D.).
[99] VV. 25–34(R-D.).
[100] Vs. 26(R-D.).
[101] VV. 28–32(R-D.).

on the only thing that matters: "Seek ye therefore the kingdom of God and his justice: and all these things shall be
added unto you." [102]

The sayings of our Lord in Matthew, chapter 7, are but
loosely connected with each other. They begin with a warning: "Judge not, that you may not be judged." [103] It is not
our business to sit in judgement on anyone. This does not
abolish the judicial investigation of crime, which is necessary for the protection of society, or the use of moral insight
to determine what is objectively right and wrong; but it
rules out the imputation of motives. Only God can truly
read men's hearts; we must not usurp his prerogative. We
should beware also of reading our own defects into other
people, being prompted by the beam in our own eye to
discover the mote in our neighbour's. A fault-finding and
censorious attitude towards those about us is fatal to our
relations with God; it shuts out his forgiveness and invites'
his stern judgement upon us. A generous and forgiving spirit
is our only assurance that God will deal in like manner with
ourselves.

Condemn not: and you shall not be condemned. Forgive: and
you shall be forgiven. Give: and it shall be given to you: good
measure and pressed down and shaken together and running over
shall they give into your bosom. For with the same measure that
you shall mete withal, it shall be measured to you again.[104]

But if there are no bounds to be put to Christian charity,
we should still be circumspect in our administration of what
is sacred. "You must not give that which is holy to dogs. Do
not cast your pearls before swine." [105] We must risk no prof-
anation of God's treasure. Our Lord himself, as we shall see
presently, acts on this principle in his preaching by parables.
So the Church has followed his example in her careful guardi-
anship of the sacred mysteries, especially the Eucharist,
against desecration by unbelievers. Neither Christian prudence, nor the practice of forgiveness and charity, nor indeed

[102] Matt. 6:33.
[104] Luke 6:37–38(R-D.).
[103] Matt. 7:1(R-D.).
[105] Matt. 7:6.

any of the foregoing precepts are easy for human nature.
Without the divine help we cannot hope to keep faithful.
But Jesus assures us that the needful grace will be forthcoming, if only we persevere in prayer. If a human father, despite
his natural shortcomings, is such that his children can turn
confidently to him in times of trouble, how much more true
must this be in our relations with God! The good things that
come to us are not the result of chance, or of the processes
of nature, or of inevitable "progress"; they are the Father's
gifts, all the more generously given because we pay him the
tribute of asking for them. "Every god gift and every perfect endowment is from above, coming down from the Father
of lights." [106] Therefore: "Ask, and it shall be given you:
seek, and you shall find: knock, and it shall be opened to
you. For everyone that asketh, receiveth: and he that seeketh,
findeth: and to him that knocketh, it shall be opened." [107]

.Now comes the Golden Rule, in which our Lord sums up
"the law and the prophets": "All things therefore whatsoever
you would that men should do to you, do you also to
them." [108] It is the positive form of a principle familiar to
the Jews: "See thou never do to another what thou wouldst
hate to have done to thee by another." [109] More is demanded
of us than the passive and colourless role of not giving offence; we must take the initiative dictated by charity and
engage in active well-doing, showing to others the concern
and kindliness we ourselves should appreciate were we in
their place. A modern unbeliever, with misplaced humour,
has criticized the wisdom of this precept, on the grounds
that "tastes differ": it is dangerous to assume that other
people's wants are the same as our own. The comment is
cynical enough, but it points to the need of seeing the Golden
Rule in its true context. Christ presupposes in his hearers
the acceptance of his teaching as so far given; taking for
granted their faith and love, he gives them a practical rule
of thumb as to how to act when in doubt: Do as you would

[106] Jas. 1:17(S.).   [107] Matt. 7:7–8(R-D.).   [108] Vs. 12(R-D.).
[109] Tob. 4:16(15); cf. Ecclus. 31:18(15).

be done by. What is called for is the reverse of imposing our own wishes upon others—the failing of the "charitable" busybody!—rather we are being asked to acquire the Christian "sensibility." Seeing those around us in the light of faith and having boundless good will towards them, we put ourselves in their place, at the same time trying to take full account of their differences from ourselves. Much tact and fellow-feeling are required; but, granted the insight which comes from genuine charity, there is no safer guide in treating with others than our awareness of what we personally should like were the positions reversed.

Our Lord ends the great sermon with words of admonition to his hearers; he would impress upon them the terrible urgency of his message. Christianity is not merely a doctrine, it is a way of life; belief must issue in corresponding deeds. The yoke of Christ is easy to those who have submitted to it; but the surrender is hard. Most men prefer the seductions of the world, its wealth and power, its pleasure and success, to entering the "narrow gate . . . that leadeth to life." [110] Let them not say that they were not warned. We must beware also of "false prophets," [111] religious sophists, who, it may be, can discourse eloquently on the beauties of mysticism and the good life, but are without credentials. The test of all such is their own conduct. "By their fruits you shall know them." [112] Do these betoken the followers of Christ? "A good tree cannot produce bad fruit, nor can a decayed tree produce good fruit. Every tree not producing good fruit is cut down and thrown on the fire." [113]

To conclude, there comes a final warning about the futility of all merely verbal professions of belief.[114] The context shows our Lord pointing to his office as Judge of all mankind.[115] It will be idle for the disciples if they can only protest that they prophesied and worked miracles in his name, idle no doubt for us simply to be able to say that we were "Christians" and "Catholics." Lip-service and what has been called

[110] Matt. 7:14(R-D.).   [111] Vs. 15.   [112] Vs. 16(R-D.).
[113] VV. 18–19(S.).   [114] VV. 21–27.   [115] Cf. Luke 13:22–30.

the "knee-drill" of the Church will not pass scrutiny then; the dispositions of our hearts, the dominating motives of our lives, will be the subject for examination. If they have not been good, we shall pass unrecognized; unless the kingdom, the rule, of God has taken possession of us, so that our will is at one with his, we shall hear from Christ the awful sentence: "I never knew you; depart from me, you workers of iniquity." [116] He who is a disciple only in name, whose loyalty consists in nothing more than words, builds his life upon sand; at the first onset of wind and weather it will collapse. But whoever "heareth these my words and doth them, he shall be like to a wise man who built his house upon a rock. And the rain fell, and the torrents came, and the winds blew and beat against that house, and it fell not, for it was founded upon the rock." [117]

So ends this greatest of all sermons. St Matthew tells us that "when Jesus had brought these words to a close, the multitudes were astounded at his teaching." [118] Well they might have been. Their own doctors of the Law, with their pedantic appeals to tradition and precedent, could never have so moved them. There was nothing academic or bookish about our Lord's method of preaching; it had the vital spontaneity of one whose doctrine was his own. "For he was teaching them as one having authority, and not as their scribes." What he said was the issue of an incomparable insight into the true meaning of man's relationship with God. The Beatitudes, the interpretation of the Law in the light of love, the insistence on forgiving injuries, on the primacy of deeds over words, the unceasing note of moral earnestness—these are what lay bare the heart of religion. It is this, or it is nothing. How could it have been otherwise? The message of Jesus is embodied in his own person. The Sermon on the Mount is more than a summary of doctrine; it depicts the character of him who preached it, the flawless perfection of one in whom there was no discrepancy between what he was and what he taught. The discourse does not contain the full

---

[116] Matt. 7:23(R-D.).   [117] VV. 24–25(W.).   [118] VV. 28–29(W.).

mystery of Jesus Christ; we must turn to other parts of the
New Testament, especially to St John, to explore the depths
within depths of his personality; but it portrays him in his
great role as our Divine Master, whose teaching men must
either accept or perish. Only when it has begun to mould
our lives shall we gain a real understanding of him; for to
live by his words is to perceive their life-giving power, to
know that they come from God the Father, of whom Christ
is the complete revelation. "My teaching is not mine, but his
who sent me. If anyone willeth to do his will, he shall know
of my teaching whether it cometh from God, or whether I
speak from myself." [119]

[119] John 7:16–17 (W.).

§ 6. THE PREACHING IN PARABLES

If it were possible to sum up in a phrase the burden of our
Lord's message, it would be his doctrine of the kingdom of
God. We shall examine on a later page something of what
is implied in his conception of the kingdom.[1] Here it must
suffice to note that its fundamental idea is the rule or dominion of God, and the absolute primacy of the divine will
which this involves, God and man being respectively what
they are. The Sermon on the Mount puts before us the
conditions of entry into, and the obligations of membership
of, the kingdom. But throughout his ministry the thought of
it dominates Jesus' mind; he is concerned with impressing
upon his hearers its imperative claims. Yet we must note
an important change in his method of teaching, a change
which throws light upon his message and, in so doing, gives
us a deeper insight into his redeeming mission. He begins
to teach in parables. This was not the customary practice of
the Rabbis, and the disciples were puzzled by it: "Why dost
thou speak to them in parables?" [2] The Sermon, though containing many figures of speech which might be described as

[1] See § 23.   [2] Matt. 13:10.

parables (notably Matthew, chapter 7, verses 24–27), was for the most part straightforward popular teaching; sublime as were its implications, its main drift could be readily grasped by anyone who chose to think about it. This is in fact true also of the parables; but there is an element of complexity here which cannot pass unnoticed.

The term *parable* means "a placing of one thing beside another" with a view to comparison. This definition is so wide as to make it difficult to determine the precise number of our Lord's parables. The usual estimate of New Testament scholars is between thirty and thirty-five, two-thirds of which are preserved by St Luke; but if all the short parabolic sayings were included the total would be much larger. We shall not here be concerned with examining the parables in any detail, but rather with enquiring what was their general significance. The parable of the Sower [3] appears to mark the turning-point between the popular and parabolic teaching; for it is in this context that St Mark notes that Jesus was now preaching the word only in parables, with the added qualification that he did so "according as they were able to listen to it." [4] While they have many lessons to impart, the parables are most of all concerned with "the mystery of the kingdom of God"; [5] though the allusion is clearer in some than in others. The more explicit ones open with the formula, "The kingdom of heaven [or 'of God'] is like to . . ." Such are the parables of the Tares,[6] of the Mustard Seed,[7] of the Leaven [8] and of the Hidden Treasure.[9]

The use of parables, whose simplicity is often more apparent than real, gives rise to two important questions. How are they to be interpreted? And what was their purpose? Our Lord is acknowledged on all hands to be the supreme master of the art of inculcating doctrine by happy illustrations drawn from everyday life. But it is a mistake to regard his parables simply as a pedagogical device, an adaptation of

3 Mark 4:2 ff. and parallels.   4 4:33(S.).
5 Vs. 11(R-D.).   6 Matt. 13:24 ff.   7 VV. 31 ff.
8 VV. 33 ff.   9 VV. 44 ff.; cf. Mark 4:26.

his teaching, by means of homely similes and metaphors, to his hearers' mentality. The truth is that imagery and figurative language do not always make for clarity of exposition; that Jesus, ever supremely conscious of what he was about, should make use of them shows that he had a further object in view. No one knew better than he how to call a spade a spade; he could be directness itself, far too direct for many of those who listened to him. That he was now quite deliberately veiling his thought is clear from the fact that, though his parables were often not understood, he reserved an explanation—at least of those which have the "kingdom" for their theme—to the intimate circle of his followers—"privately he explained everything to his disciples." [10]

As a preliminary to the solution of this problem, let us first consider how the parables are to be interpreted. When we read these remarkable instances and strikingly beautiful stories with which our Lord clothed his message, are we to look for a definite meaning in each of their details? Or may we take them as being in the main illustrations of one particular point which he wished to impress upon his hearers? The latter seems the safer principle to follow. It is now generally admitted that the allegorical treatment to which the parables were submitted by some of the Church Fathers was not seldom arbitrary and unconvincing. It consisted in taking every term in the story as a cryptogram for an idea, and so decoding the whole term by term.[11] This method gave scope to much ingenuity, and was even justifiable as a vehicle for the exposition of doctrine valid enough on other grounds, but it gives little help when we are concerned to elucidate the literal meaning of the text. It must be borne in mind, however, that the borderline between a strict parable, a story told to illustrate a single main lesson, and an allegory, containing many significant features, is not always clear-cut. This is evident from those cases in which we have

---

[10] Mark 4:34(S.).

[11] For a typical example from St Augustine, see his *Quaestiones Evangeliorum*, II, 19; paraphrased by C. H. Dodd, *The Parables of the Kingdom*, pp. 11–12.

our Lord's own interpretations—see the Sower [12] and the
Tares [13]—where many of their several features are explained.
Nevertheless, it is probable that the typical parable, whether
it be a simple metaphor or a more elaborate similitude or a
full-length story, presents one single point of comparison;
its details are not intended to have independent significance.
Thus, in the parable of the Importunate Friend, [14] we are
not meant to ask who is represented by the friend arriving
from a journey or by the children in bed; these and other
details serve merely to build up the picture of a sudden
critical need, calling for an urgency otherwise untimely and
out of place. Even in the Sower the incidental features would
seem in the first place to be no more than the setting for a
single main picture—that of the vast amount of wasted labour
the farmer must face, so throwing into relief the satisfaction
brought by the harvest in spite of all.

The remarkable realism and vividness of the parables,
their faithfulness to nature, the fact that they are not far-
fetched and artificial analogies, is due to the affinity which
does in truth exist between the natural order and the spiritual order. The kingdom of God is, in many respects, intrinsically *like* the processes of nature and the daily life of
men. We may note also, as illustrative of our Lord's teaching
method, that the parable has the character of an argument,
in that it entices the hearer to a judgement upon the situation depicted, and then challenges him, directly or by im-
plication, to apply the judgement to the matter in hand. A
famous example of this is the Old Testament account of
Nathan's story to David about the poor man's ewe lamb
which was stolen by the rich man—with its dramatic conclusion, "Thou art the man." [15] So was it with the parables of
Jesus; always there is an underlying question, explicit or
implicit. "What man among you who has a hundred
sheep. . . . ?" [16] "Which of these three, dost thou think,

[12] Matt. 13:18 ff.   [13] VV. 36 ff.   [14] Luke 11:5–8.
[15] 2 Kings(Samuel) 12:1 ff.   [16] Luke 15:4(S.).

proved neighbour to him who fell among the robbers?" [17]
We are invited to a judgement on the imagined situation and
so to grasp, by a process of active assimilation, the lesson intended.[18] All of which brings us back to the question: What
was our Lord's motive in teaching by parables?

The foregoing remarks have already suggested a partial
answer. Jesus, a master of pedagogy, wished to persuade his
hearers by evoking an assent based on their own reflections.
"Take heed, therefore, *how* you hear." [19] Each of the parables contains a truth embodied in a tale; the earnest and attentive listener would discover it there. This is the context
of our Lord's saying: "The measure in which you give is the
measure in which you will be repaid, and more will be given
you besides." [20] The effort we make to comprehend will be
rewarded by a proportionate insight; we shall in fact find
more than we seek. A sympathetic concentration upon the
Gospel enriches us with the discernment of its true meaning; where this is lacking, the mind becomes impoverished
and we begin to lose even such grip as we have upon the
realities of the Christian life. Such are the implications of
the apparent paradox: "If a man is rich, gifts will be made
to him; if he is poor, even the little he has will be taken
away from him." [21] Thus, though it will be lost on the in-
attentive, there is nothing esoteric about our Lord's teaching. "Is the lamp brought in to be placed under the corn-
measure or under the bed? Is it not in order to be set upon
the lampstand? For there is nothing secret but that it should
be made known, nor has anything been concealed but in
order that it might come to light." [22] If he had held colloquy
privately with his disciples, it was only so that they might
presently proclaim his message abroad. "What is veiled will
all be revealed, what is hidden will all be known; what you
have said in darkness, will be repeated in the light of day,

[17] Luke 10:36(S.).　　[18] Cf. Dodd, *op. cit.*, pp. 22–24.
[19] Luke 8:18(R-D.).　　[20] Mark 4:24.　　　[21] Vs. 25.
[22] Mark 4:21–22(S.); cf. Luke 8:16–17; John 18:20.

what you have whispered in secret chambers, will be proclaimed on the housetops." [23]

At the same time, the parabolic teaching shows that our
Lord was now concentrating upon the formation of an *élite,*
a band of faithful followers who would continue his work
after he was gone. It was not his intention to fulfil his mission single-handed; there must be a company of elect souls
to whom it could be entrusted; these would be won over by
the parables. Hence his selection of the apostles; they, with
their appointed leader, were to be the foundation of the
Church.[24] Under the Master's tuition the deeper aspects of
the kingdom would become increasingly manifest to them,
in proportion to their fidelity and willingness to understand.
As yet the kingdom was hardly to be discerned; its future
lay in the hands of a "little flock"; [25] but, as the three parables of the kingdom go to prove,[26] its influence will gradually extend through human society until all mankind is given
the opportunity of being conformed to the divine ideal.

All this is closely connected with one of the themes in our
Lord's teaching which shows the unity of his thought with
that of the Hebrew prophets. When first he begins to preach
in parables, Jesus adapts to his own purpose a passage from
Isaiah,[27] which concerns what is known to Old Testament
scholars as the "Doctrine of the Remnant." The prophets
bore the burden of the heart-rending truth that, among all
those to whom they preached, no more than a minority
would be converted—only a remnant could be saved. It is as
an echo of this message that our Lord utters the dark saying:
"To you hath been imparted the mystery of the kingdom of
God, but to them that are without, all things are treated in
parables, that seeing they may see and not perceive, and

---

23 Luke 12:2–3.   24 Cf. Eph. 2:20.   25 Luke 12:32.
26 Mark 4:26–29; vv. 30–32 and parallels; Matt. 13:33.
27 "Ye shall hear indeed, but ye shall not understand; and ye shall see
indeed, but ye shall not perceive. For the heart of this people has become
gross, and their ears are dull of hearing, and their eyes have they closed;
lest they should see with their eyes, and hear with their ears, and understand with their heart, and be converted, and I shall hear them."—Isa. 6:9–10
(LXX).

hearing they may hear and not understand, lest perchance they return again and be forgiven." [28] Here it should be observed that the Semitic idiom, of which the Gospel Greek is the expression, finds no place for the distinction, familiar to the Church Fathers and theologians, between what God positively wills and what he permits. To the Jewish mind everything happened because God had so decided, so decreed. But the economy of mercy, which is the Gospel's chief characteristic, as well as the light subsequently thrown on the matter by the theologians,[29] rules out the possibility of a divine predestining to sin and damnation.

Christ recognized man's freedom to determine his fate by his own choice. Though he tells us explicitly that "No man can come to me, except the Father, who hath sent me, draw him," [30] the conclusion of this same discourse shows that, in responding to such a call, we exercise our liberty. An alternative is offered to us: "Would you, too, go away?" [31] Nor are we justified in concluding that Jesus shared the pessimistic view of the prophets concerning the fewness of those who would ultimately be saved. The immediate circle of his disciples might be few—a "remnant"—but through them he would bring salvation to "many." This is in fact the message to be found in the latter part of Isaiah, a prophecy of which our Lord's own mission was to be the fulfilment.

> And Jahweh [32] was pleased to crush him with suffering;
> Though his own life be made a sin-offering,
> He shall see a seed that shall have length of days,
> And the purpose of Jahweh shall prosper in his hand.

[28] Mark 4:11–12(W.); cf. Matt. 13:10–17; Luke 8:9–10. On this, and the whole question of the parables, see D. Buzy, *Introduction aux Paraboles Évangéliques,* in particular, pp. 233–86.
[29] See St Augustine, *Tractatus 53 in Joannem, P.L.* 35, col. 1774 *et seq.;* St Thomas, *Expositio in Joannem,* cap. xii, lectio 7 (Parma edition, X, 519).
[30] John 6:44(R-D.). [31] Vs. 68.
[32] A transliteration of the *tetragrammaton,* i.e., the Hebrew form of the sacred name, translated in the Catholic Bible by *"the Lord."* Its most familiar version is *Jehovah,* though it is more frequently rendered by modern scholars as *Yahweh.*

Because of his soul's sorrow he shall see it,
Through his sufferings he shall be filled;
A righteous one, My servant, shall make many righteous
And their iniquities he shall bear;
Therefore will I give him a portion with the mighty,
And with the powerful shall he divide the spoil;
Because he shall have poured out his soul to death,
And been numbered with the rebellious,
So shall he take away the sins of many,
And make intercession for the rebellious.[33]

Though Christ's life-work would end in apparent failure, the final success of his mission was assured. In being raised upon the Cross he would draw all men to himself.[34] His death would both redeem his own nation and "bring together into one all God's children, scattered far and wide." [35]

Thus history will prove that Israel's apostasy, culminating in the rejection of her Messiah, tragic as have been its consequences for the Jewish people, was not irrevocable. There is a sense in which they still remain the chosen of God, one day to enjoy his salvation. Such is St Paul's teaching in the eleventh chapter of the Epistle to the Romans, which constitutes an inspired and annihilating condemnation of that most unhappy phenomenon—Christian anti-Semitism.[36] In connection with the parables themselves, there are grounds for supposing the people's unresponsiveness was not always due to malice and bad faith. As Grandmaison shrewdly remarks:

With many of those who heard Jesus, it was less a case of grave sin against the light than an attitude suggested to them and almost forced upon them by the prestige of the scribes and doctors, who were enemies of the Gospel. It was a temporary attitude, a heaviness which the evangelical leaven could eventually lighten. For such men (and they were legion) this teaching, given in parable and metaphor, whose enigmatic nature did not

[33] Isa. 53:10–12.—Dr Kissane's translations from the Hebrew, with verses relevant to present context italicized.
[34] John 12:32.   [35] 11:52; cf. Eph. 1:10.
[36] For a brief exposition by the present writer of the Pauline doctrine on Israel's rejection, see *Blackfriars,* Vol. XXV, no. 287 (February 1944), pp. 58–62.

demand—as a clearly expressed instruction would have demanded—the immediate decisions of which they were as yet incapable, though apparently a punishment, was in reality a great act of mercy. They were sent back to await a more favourable season, and were not excluded from the kingdom of God. Meanwhile the idea of the kingdom was kept before them, and its character explained to them "according as they were capable of understanding." [37]

In this there is disclosed to us a divine forbearance in the ministry of him who would not break the bruised reed or extinguish the wick that scarcely burns.[38] Nevertheless, we cannot overlook the fact that there is such a thing as the "hardening of the heart," a sinning against the light, which brings with it the penalty of God's withdrawal of grace. Among "those without" who listened to the parables there were certainly proud and self-interested men determined to resist Jesus at all costs. They could be won over by nothing; therefore their doom was pronounced. Whatever the possibility of a last-minute repentance for individuals, the final consequences of such a general attitude are inescapable; and our Lord was concerned to impress upon his hearers the fearful urgency of his message, not to make allowances for those who rejected it. Set for the fall and the rise of many in Israel, he embodied in his own person the most tremendous *crisis* with which mankind could be presented. Following the method of the Jewish Rabbis, he put it before the people in those strong contrasting phrases which alone could give expression to it. Moreover, the synoptic writers, confronted with the patent results of widespread rejection, had good reason for throwing the words of Jesus into the sharpest relief. St John also, in his powerful epilogue to the public ministry, records the fulfilment of Isaiah's predictions concerning the blinding of the eyes and the hardening of the heart.[39] It was the darker obverse side of the Gospel picture, the dread alternative to the experience of believers: "Blessed

[37] Léonce de Grandmaison, *Jésus Christ*, I, 334–35 (E.T. II, 41).
[38] Matt. 12:20; Isa. 42:3.   [39] John 12:37–41.

are your eyes, because they see; and your ears, because they
hear! For, indeed, I tell you that many prophets and just men
longed to see the things that you see, and did not see them,
and to hear the things that you hear, and did not hear
them." [40]

[40] Matt. 13:16–17(S.).

§ 7. THE MIRACLES

Here it will be in place to consider briefly the miracles or
"signs" which our records show Jesus to have worked habitually throughout his public life. A discussion on the miraculous as such is outside our present scope; [1] nor, since we
are not engaged in a work of apologetic, shall we do more
than allude to the sense in which the miracles may be regarded as "proofs" of the validity of Christ's claims. Rather
shall we confine ourselves to taking account of the miraculous
elements in our Lord's ministry, as these throw further light
on his person and message. By way of preliminary it must be
observed that the miracles form an integral part of the evangelists' story; they have nothing of the character of decorative
embellishments; were they eliminated, the whole narrative
would have to be recast on different lines—a consequence
which has been clearly seen and boldly acted upon by many
of the modern critics. [2] This notwithstanding, the judgement
still remains true that:

we cannot construct a consistent picture of the life of Jesus
Christ from the Gospels, if we do not take account of his miraculous powers, however those "miraculous" powers are to be explained; ... the whole history is grounded in them and presupposes them.... We cannot contrive any theory by which we
may entirely eliminate the miraculous, and yet save the histo-
ricity, in any intelligible sense, of those wonderful narratives. [3]

[1] The student may consult Grandmaison, op. cit., II, 225–55, 313–68
(E.T. III, 3–23, 97–154); Michel, D.T.C., Vol. X, pt. 2, 1798–1859; De
Tonquédec, D.A.F.C., III, 517–78.
[2] For an acute critique of recent attempts to explain away the New Testament miracles, see Allo, Le Scandale de Jésus, pp. 57–100.
[3] Bernard, "Miracle," H.D.B., Vol. III, p. 389b.

The miracles have often been classified as "miracles of
healing" and "cosmic" miracles—a division which, though
roughly applicable, is not wholly satisfactory. Whether all
our Lord's cures are to be ranked technically as "miracles"
depends upon our definition of that term and, in particular,
upon the account we give of demoniacal possession, with
which so many of them were concerned.[4] Among this class
we find the cures of the demoniacs,[5] of the impotent man at
the pool of Bethesda,[6] of the man with a withered hand,[7]
of the woman with a spirit of infirmity,[8] of the dumb man
with a devil [9] and of the man "possessed with a devil, blind and
dumb." [10] Perhaps even more striking than these, when their
circumstances are closely examined, are the cases of the centurion's servant,[11] of the palsied man,[12] of the deaf and dumb
man,[13] of the blind,[14] and the very remarkable instance,
which occasioned such a stir at the time, of the healing of
the man "blind from birth." [15] Here we may also note the
cures of the dropsical man,[16] of the fever patient healed with
a touch,[17] of the woman with a haemorrhage,[18] of the
lepers [19] and of the servant Malchus.[20] Most arresting of all
are the three instances of the restoration of life: to Jairus's
daughter,[21] to the widow of Nain's son,[22] and to Lazarus.[23]

The "cosmic" miracles, that is, those worked on nature as
distinct from man, include the first "sign" of all, the transformation of water into wine at the marriage feast,[24] the
stilling of the storm [25] and the walking upon the waters,[26] the
feeding of the five thousand,[27] and of the four thousand,[28]
and the blasting of the fig tree.[29] In addition, there are the

[4] See Grandmaison, op. cit., II, 341–68 (E.T. III, 128–40).
[5] Mark 1:23 ff.; Matt. 8:28 ff.; 15:21 ff.; 17:14 ff.
[6] John 5:2 ff.   [7] Matt. 12:10 ff.   [8] Luke 13:11 ff.
[9] Matt. 9:32 ff.   [10] 12:22 ff.   [11] 8:5 ff.
[12] 9:2 ff.   [13] Mark 7:32 ff.
[14] 8:22 ff. Matt. 9:27 ff.; 20:30 ff.   [15] John 9:1 ff.
[16] Luke 14:2 ff.   [17] Matt. 8:14 ff.   [18] 9:20 ff.
[19] 8:2 ff.; Luke 17:11 ff.   [20] Luke 22:50; John 18:10.
[21] Mark 5:21 ff.   [22] Luke 7:11 ff.   [23] John 11:43 ff.
[24] 2:1 ff.   [25] Matt. 8:26.   [26] 14:25 ff.
[27] 14:18 ff.   [28] Mark 8:1 ff.   [29] Matt. 21:19.

remarkable "coincidences" of the great draught of fishes [30] and the finding of a silver coin in the fish's mouth.[31] Finally, in a class apart and transcending all others, is the Resurrection of Jesus himself. This was the credential to which the Church continually appealed.[32] Over and above the explicit testimony of the evangelists,[33] the Resurrection is presupposed in all the apostolic Epistles; it is likewise the burden of the apostolic preaching in the Acts.[34] It would be hard to surpass the circumstantiality of St Paul's account of it in the First Epistle to the Corinthians, chapter 15, verses 3–8.[35] So confident is he, that he can appeal to the fact of the Lord's resurrection as a *reductio ad absurdum* of those who would deny that we too shall rise again.[36] It is from the actual historical event that he draws forth its spiritual and symbolic meaning: "that, as Christ rose from the dead in the glory of the Father, thus we also might walk in newness of life." [37]

Our Lord was not, it need hardly be said, a wonder-worker, a thaumaturge, in any ordinary sense. This role, precisely the one which the Devil had tempted him to assume,[38] he had explicitly rejected.[39] If there was to come a time when, in a last vain attempt to win over the incredulous, he would point to his wonderful deeds as proof that he came from God—"let my actions convince you where I cannot" [40]—he did not parade them in this light, as being, so to say, ocular demonstrations of divinity. Proofs and evidences to the well-disposed they certainly were, and have always been so regarded by the Church; but their probative force is not compelling. Human pride is impervious to the appeal of miracles; in such an atmosphere they can even oc-

[30] Luke 5:1 ff.; John 21:6.   [31] Matt. 17:24 ff.
[32] Rom. 1:4; 4:24; 1 Pet. 1:21.   [33] See § 11.
[34] Acts 2:32; 3:15; 10:40; 13:34; 17:3, 31; 26:23.
[35] Cf. Rom. 8:34; 14:9; 2 Cor. 5:15; 1 Thess. 4:13 (14).
[36] 1 Cor. 15:13 ff.
[37] Rom. 6:4(S.); Cf. Phil. 3:10; col. 3:1.
[38] Matt. 4:3–7.   [39] Mark 8:11–13; Matt. 16:4.
[40] John 10:38.

casion disbelief. That the miraculous element in the Gospels is nowadays sometimes looked upon as an obstacle rather than an aid to faith is no peculiarly modern phenomenon. It was the experience of Jesus himself. His enemies, who could not gainsay the facts, were anxious to ascribe them to the agency of Satan.[41] The Galilean prophet might well have cured a man blind from birth; but what of that? The point to consider was that he had offended by doing so on the Sabbath![24] Of what use are miracles to this temper of mind?

The truth is that the miracles are as much, and more, manifestations of God's love than demonstrations of his power. Power in subordination to love, love declaring itself in power—is the key to the understanding of the miracles. The preternatural works of Jesus were almost without exception beneficent deeds—to alleviate human misery or to further the interests of the kingdom. They were not arbitrary interferences with the course of nature, a show of divine might, without reference to the needs of the situation or the saving character of Christ's mission. On the contrary, they were outpourings of God's favour, wholly of a piece with the mercy and loving-kindness which received their supreme embodiment in the person of Jesus. For this reason he himself seems almost to make light of his miraculous healings, or to desire at least to keep them secret.[43] There was a moment when the people would have acclaimed him as the mighty wonder-working Messiah of their earthly expectations, only to find him wholly unresponsive.[44] During the early days in Galilee, when he had met with some temporary success, the popular demand would have changed the character of his mission—for the primary work of preaching the kingdom of God to become simply a ministry of healing; and he openly rebuked the crowds for seeing in his miracles no more than the alleviation of material necessities.[45] Our Lord's

41 Matt. 12:24.   42 John 9:16.   43 Mark 7:36; 8:26.
44 John 6:14-15.   45 Vs. 26.

wonderful works were thus the symbols of God's goodness, and only good will could rightly respond to them. Considered as mere evidences, they were not sufficient to produce belief; there was needed also the inward enlightenment of the mind and heart for which they were the occasion. For all the persuasive power of the miracles of Jesus, they would not of themselves have sufficed to make refusal to accept him inexcusable, had they not been accompanied for the unbelievers by an interior grace of illumination which revealed their true significance.[46]

From the point of view of Christian apologetics, it should be remembered that the supreme motive of credibility is not the miracles, but the character of him who worked them. This was the influence which could subjugate all hearts, a light irresistibly alluring to those who did not voluntarily close their eyes. The charm and majesty of the mere presence of Jesus, his unblemished holiness, the serenity which distinguished him from the Old Testament prophets, the manifest good will, at once so accessible and so resourceful, the incomparable teaching, proclaimed with such divine assurance, in a manner so different from that of the Jewish Rabbis —these are what constituted the most impressive "miracle" of all. Even had there been no miracles, men ought still to have believed in Jesus Christ; for he both personified, and could bring to bear upon the soul, the appeal and illumination of ultimate Truth, loved instinctively by every creature. To resist this inward impulson is suicide for the intelligence, a sin only to be explained by perversity of heart. That our Lord chose to corroborate his message with miracles only made the enormity of those who rejected him the greater. "If I had not come and spoken to them, they would not have sin; but now they have no excuse for their sin.... If I had not done among them the works that no other hath done, they would not have sin; but now they have seen and they have hated both me and my Father." [47]

46 S. Thom., *Expos. in Joan.*, XV, v, 4. Parma ed. X, 573.
47 John 15:22, 24(W.).

§ 8. THE FOUNDING OF THE CHURCH

No complete view of Christ our Lord is possible without considering his relationship to the Church. We shall see later that there is a sense in which the Church is actually included in the "whole Christ"—the *Christus totus* of St Augustine.[1] It will also be our task to consider in what measure this organized society of believers coincides with the kingdom of God.[2] In this section, however, our thoughts will be centred upon Christ's work of establishing the Church and the role he assigned to it. We know that he gathered about him a group of disciples, men who acknowledged him as the "Master," [3] and were willing to be taught by him how best they might serve God. They were of mixed quality: some, like Nicodemus and Joseph of Arimathea, could not bring themselves to make public profession of their loyalty; others seem only to have been occasional followers; [4] others again were half-hearted and proved to be deserters.[5] Only a few were prepared to give an unqualified allegiance, so embracing a way of life which involved the severing of family ties,[6] together with the acceptance of the hardships and privations endured by our Lord himself.[7] It was from men such as these last that he chose the select company of twelve who were to be the foundations of his Church.

It will be remembered how this inner circle of disciples were the favoured audience for the Sermon on the Mount. Likewise it was they who could be relied on to discern the inner meaning of the parables. St Mark makes clear how deliberate the choice had been; Jesus "called to him those whom it pleased him to call." [8] The twelve were not self-appointed volunteers; they had been the object of a special election on the part of the Master himself, as he was later to remind them. "It was not you that chose me, it was I that

---

[1] *Enarr, in Ps.* XVII, 51 and XC, 2,1; *P.L.* 36, col. 154 and *P.L.* 37, col. 1159.
[2] See pp. 304 ff.   [3] Matt. 8:19; cf. Luke 9:57.
[4] Matt. 15:32, cf. Mark 8:2.   [5] John 6:66.
[6] Matt. 8:22.   [7] VV. 19–20.   [8] Mark 3:13.

chose you. The task I have appointed you is to go out and bear fruit, fruit which will endure." [9] To St Luke we owe the details that the momentous choice had been preceded by a night spent in prayer, and that it was our Lord himself who gave to the selected twelve the official title of "apostles." [10] The frequent use of the phrase "the twelve" [11] shows that this group was quite distinct from the rest of the disciples; they formed a "college" united to one another by the common bond of their calling and the work committed to their charge. In closest contact with the Master, they were especially trained by him; they heard his discourses, received from him private instructions, witnessed his miracles; in a word, they were the repositories of "the mystery of the kingdom of God." [12] As Christ himself was God's Ambassador—not a servant but the Son; [13] not one of the prophets but the Messianic Son of God,[14] and in this sense the "apostle" *par excellence* [15]—so in his turn he appointed these disciples his own ambassadors. During his lifetime they enjoyed but a limited commission,[16] as shepherds of the lost sheep and workers in the Lord's vineyard.[17] After his death they would enter with full rights upon their ministry, as authorized representatives of Christ.

As the Lord had received his mission from the Father, so did he hand on the same to his apostles. "He that receiveth you receiveth me: and he that receiveth me receiveth him that sent me." [18] It is interesting to note that, after speaking words which show his decision to pass on to others his own intimate knowledge of the Father,[19] Christ then adds the invitation: "Come to me, all you who labour and are heavy-laden, and I will give you rest." [20] His "easy yoke and light burden" [21] denote the obligations of the members of his

9 John 15:16; cf. vs. 19.   10 Luke 6:12–13.
11 For a conspectus of the N.T. uses of this phrase, as also of "the eleven" and "the ten," see Dieckmann, *De Ecclesia*, I, 208.
12 Mark 4:11(R-D.).   13 Matt. 21:33 ff.
14 16:13 ff.; cf. Heb. 1:1-3.   15 3:1.
16 Mark 6:7–13; Luke 9:1–6.
17 Matt. 9:35-38.   18 10:40(R-D.); cf. Luke 10:16.
19 Matt. 11:27.   20 Vs. 28(S.).   21 Vs. 30.

kingdom, to which he is summoning all men even as he calls them to himself. This gathering in of mankind, a harvesting, was committed to the apostles: "I have sent you to reap that in which you did not labour." [22] The theme is repeated at the Last Supper: "Thou [Father] hast sent me into the world on thy errand, and I have sent them [the twelve] into the world on thy errand." [23] All of which was ratified after the Resurrection, when Jesus passed on his own mission to the faithful eleven—"I came upon an errand from my Father, and now I am sending you out in my turn" [24]—thus making them apostles in the fullest sense of the term.

Here we must note that to one of the twelve, Simon son of Jonah, had been given the headship of the apostolic college. So it was promised, on a memorable occasion near Caesarea Philippi, when he had brought joy to the heart of his Master with his great confession of faith—

Thou art the Christ [i.e. the Messiah], the Son of the living God.[25]

Let us recall the words of this most significant text:

And Jesus answered him, blessed art thou, Simon son of Jona; it is not flesh and blood, it is my Father in heaven that has revealed this to thee. And I tell thee this in my turn, that thou art Peter, and it is upon this rock that I will build my church; and the gates of heaven shall not prevail against it; and I will give to thee the keys of the kingdom of heaven; and whatever thou shalt bind on earth shall be bound in heaven, and whatever thou shalt loose on earth shall be loosed in heaven.[26]

---

[22] John 4:38(R-D.).   [23] 17:18.   [24] 20:21.
[25] Matt. 16:16; cf. Mark 8:29; Luke 9:20; John 6:68–69.
[26] Matt. 16:17–19. The Greek rendering, "Thou art Peter [Πέτρος] and upon this rock [μέτρα] "—which has to change a feminine to a masculine termination in order to make the word the name of a man—lacks the force of the original Aramaic used by Christ: "Thou art *Kepha* (Cephas—rock) and upon this *Kepha* ...," thus clearly identifying the "rock" with "Peter." In English this significance is lost; though it is happily preserved in French: "Tu es Pierre, et sur cette pierre je bâtirai mon église." That Simon was known as Cephas in the primitive Church is clear from such texts as Gal. 1:18; 2:9; 1 Cor. 9:5.

This is the only instance in the New Testament where Christ's own lips pronounce an individual "blessed." It is his answering felicitation to Simon.

Because thou hast said to me, "Thou art the Christ..." I in turn say to thee, not in words vain and ineffectual, but I say to thee, because for me to have said a thing is to have made it so.[27]

In this passage Jesus makes known his will in a series of three metaphors, whose meaning, clear enough to us, would be still clearer to listeners familiar both with the Old Testament writings and the teaching methods of the Rabbis. He first compares his Church to a building of which Peter is to be the foundation; he next employs the comparison suggested by "the keys," which will be handed to Peter as a sign of his power over Christ's house; finally comes the reference to "binding and loosing," a symbol of the moral nature of the office, which is furthermore backed by a divine sanction.

The comparison of the Church to a *house*—that is, *of Israel*—is derived from the Old Testament and occurs frequently in the New. [28] Equally scriptural is the idea of a *foundation* to the building.[29] To the firmness of that upon which it is based the house owes its stability, enabling it to withstand rain, wind and floods, "for it was founded upon the rock." [30] Similarly, it is from its foundation that the unity of the house arises, the walls, roof and the whole structure being bound together in one edifice in virtue of the rock upon which it is based. All this illustrates the function of Peter in the Church. He who was Simon is made the rock-foundation to the building erected by Christ. By Peter the new house of Israel is to be unified and stabilized so that nothing, not even "the gates of hell"—symbol of death and

---

[27] St Jerome, *ad. loc.; P.L.* 26, col. 117.

[28] The Greek word for "church" (ἐκκλησία) is the LXX rendering of the Hebrew *qahal,* the assembly of Israel (cf. Num. 20:4; Deut. 23:2–3). In Matt. 16:18 it stands for the new "Israel of God" (Gal. 6:16), the Messianic kingdom as referred to in vs. 19 (cf. 18:17). See also Acts 2:36; 7:42; 1 Tim. 3:15; Heb. 3:6.

[29] See especially Eph. 2:19 ff.; cf. 3:17; Col. 1:23; 1 Cor. 3:10.

[30] Matt. 7:25(W.)—in which Christ himself uses "rock" in the same sense as in 16:18.

destruction, and hence, of all that is opposed to Christ's kingdom—can prevail against it. For the Church, as constituted by Christ, is to endure "until the consummation of the world." [31]

The "keys"—attributed in the New Testament only to Christ [32] and to Peter—are the symbols of supreme power and authority.[33] Hence Peter's primacy is one not merely of honour but of jurisdiction; his power is plenary ("whatsoever"), being subordinated to no earthly authority, since the judgements which he passes "on earth" are forthwith ratified "in heaven." The character of the power bestowed is indicated in the words "bind" and "loose." The terminology is that of the Rabbinical schools. What was prohibited was said to be "bound"; what was ruled to be lawful was said to be "loosed." In both cases an obligation in conscience was implied. Thus Peter was to hold authority before God over the members of Christ's Church. Of this our Lord, foreseeing the coming denial, was to remind him at the Last Supper: "Simon, Simon, behold Satan hath desired to have *you* [plural], that he may sift *you* as wheat. But I have prayed for *thee* [singular], that thy faith fail not; and thou, being once converted, confirm thy brethren." [34]

Through the self-knowledge gained by his denial and subsequent repentance, with his faith wholly revived by the Resurrection, Simon Peter returned to his Master, to atone for his fault by his thrice-spoken profession of love. It was then that he received the threefold commission: "Feed my lambs.... Shepherd my sheep.... Feed my sheep." [35] So the promised primacy was conferred in the words of the risen Christ. He who had spoken of himself as the "good shepherd," [36] who desired that there should be "one flock and one shepherd," [37] was handing over the sheepfold to Peter's

---

[31] Matt. 28:20.   [32] Apoc. 1:18; cf. 3:7.   [33] Cf. Isa. 22:22.
[34] Luke 22:31–32(R-D.). We may note the parallels: Satan hath desired you —the gates of hell; I have prayed for thee—I will build upon this rock; confirm thy brethren—Peter the stabilizing force in the apostolic college. See p. 112.
[35] John 21:15–17(W.).   [36] John 10:11.   [37] Vs. 16(W.); cf. 11:52.

care; for he himself was to ascend to the Father.[38] True, our Lord himself was only withdrawing his visible presence; just as he remained, in support of Peter, the Church's principal "corner-stone," [39] so would he still take care of his own as their "Chief Shepherd." [40] Hence the phrasing of his commission: "Feed *my* sheep." But the characteristic visibility of the Church, which belonged to it as the Body of Christ, would have been lacking in default of a visible head. Thus Peter had become the shepherd of Christ's flock; he can now act as the Lord's representative, his "vicar," and he, together with the rest of the apostles under his supervision,[41] is the true pastor of the Christian flock. Nor can it be supposed that this pastoral office was to terminate with Peter's death. For God's kingdom on earth was to endure until the end of ages.[42] Accordingly, unless the gates of hell were to prevail, there could never come a time when, before the eyes of men, Christ's sheepfold would be deprived of its shepherd, his Church of its rock-foundation.

It would be out of place in our present context to examine in any detail the organized constitution of Christ's Church, though certain aspects of it emerge from what has already been said. We have seen that it enjoys a hierarchic form of government, under the apostles, with Peter at their head; on this foundation the Church was to endure "until the consummation of the world." [43] The content of the apostolic commission was doctrinal: all nations were to be made the disciples of Jesus Christ.[44] But the same text shows that more than this was involved; the apostles were to be the ministers of the sacraments, as well as of the word of God—"baptizing . . . in the name of the Father, and of the Son, and of the Holy Ghost." The religion of Jesus is above all a worship of God "in spirit and truth," [45] but he knew too well the needs of sense-bound human nature to leave his followers without

[38] John 20:17.   [39] Eph. 2:20.   [40] 1 Pet. 5:4(S.).
[41] Matt. 18:18.   [42] 28:18–20; cf. 13:38, 49.
[43] Matt. 28:20.   [44] 28:19.   [45] John 4:24.

the aid of an external cultus. The clear evidence in the Gospels for the institution of Baptism [46] and the Eucharist,[47] as also of the sacrament of Penance,[48] indicates that he willed these ordinances to be the indispensable channels of the Christian life.

Within the limits of the New Testament we can discover three successive states of Christ's Church. First, the preparatory stage which we have just considered; this took place during our Lord's public ministry. Until his death on the Cross the Church did not properly speaking exist; the disciples were still under the Jewish Law and the Old Testament theocracy. But the ground-plan of the newly formed kingdom of God on earth had already been drawn up by Christ himself. So long as he was preaching within a restricted territory—for he had "been sent only to the lost sheep of the house of Israel" [49]—both the law and the Gospel were in force together. But by his death on Calvary he abrogated the Law, with its precepts and decrees,[50] and nailed the handwriting of the Old Testament to the Cross,[51] establishing the New Covenant in his own blood, which he shed for the whole human race. "At that moment," says St Leo the Great, "there came about so evident a transition from the Law to the Gospel, from the Synagogue to the Church, from the multitude of sacrifices to the one Victim, that when the Lord gave up the ghost, the mystic veil, interposed to hide the inner parts of the Temple and the secret sanctuary, was rent with sudden violence from top to bottom." [52]

The Church took its rise from Christ's atoning sacrifice on Calvary. It was thus that the Mosaic dispensation was superseded and the Messianic kingdom on earth came into being. The mystical Body of Christ—which is but another name for the Church—was brought to birth, like another Eve, from

[46] Matt. 28:19; Mark. 16:16; John 3:5.
[47] Matt. 26:26–28; Mark 14:22–24; Luke 22:19–20; cf. 1 Cor. 11:23–25.
[48] John 20:22–23.   [49] Matt. 15:24(R-D.).
[50] Eph. 2:15.   [51] Col. 2:14.
[52] S. Leo, *Serm.* LXVIII, 3; *P.L.* 54, col. 374.

the side of the dying Saviour: to become the new "mother of all the living." [53] Finally, the Church was confirmed in its newness of life with the coming of the Holy Spirit at Pentecost; [54] thereby Christ infused each of the organs of his Body with his own power, endowing the whole with inexhaustible vitality and fruitfulness. Just as the Father had sent the Spirit upon his Son to manifest his Messiahship at the beginning of his public ministry, so the Son in his turn sent the same Spirit upon his apostles to declare them before the world as his own, to strengthen them in their ministry, and to reveal that in the Church his mission from the Father was being fulfilled.

We shall have occasion later to examine how intimate is the union between Jesus Christ and his Church. It is the realization on earth of the kingdom of God; [55] in it the incarnation of the Word achieves its completion.[56] The Church is the Body of which Christ is the Head; [57] without it he would remain unfulfilled, a Bridegroom severed from his Bride.[58] Gradually, as we learn from the parables of the Mustard Seed [59] and the Leaven,[60] the Church would grow to its full stature, become in fact what it was by right, a universal, a *Catholic*,[61] Church. This catholicity, far from arising through an accident of history, was part of the divine plan from the beginning. The whole scheme of the Redemption demands it; all divisions of nation against nation, master against slave, are to be transcended. "There can be neither Jew nor Greek, there can be neither slave nor freeman, there can be no male and female; for you all are one in Christ Jesus." [62] To this objective the apostles had been directed at the outset of their ministry: "Go out all over the world,

[53] Gen. 3:20.   [54] Acts 2:1–4.   [55] See pp. 301 ff.
[56] See pp. 310 ff.   [57] Col. 1:18; 2:19; Eph. 4:15–16.
[58] Apoc. 21:2, 9; 22:17.   [59] Matt. 13:31–32.   [60] Vs. 33.
[61] The phrase *"Catholic Church"* appears in Christian literature within the lifetime of those who knew the apostles; its use is significant: "wheresoever Christ Jesus is, there is the Catholic Church."—St Ignatius of Antioch, *Epistle to the Smyrnaeans*, viii, 2; *P.G.* 5, col. 713. (St Ignatius was martyred not later than 117 A.D.)
[62] Gal. 3:28(S.).

and preach the gospel to the whole of creation." [63] And forthwith they set their hands to its achievement: "they went out
and preached everywhere, the Lord aiding them, and attest-
ing his word by the miracles that went with them." [64]

[63] Mark 16:15.   [64] Vs. 20.

§ 9. THE TRANSFIGURATION AND AFTER

Much of the doctrine just considered has carried us far
beyond the limits of our Lord's public ministry. How closely
the one is bound up with the other will emerge from the
chapters which follow. For the present, however, we must
return to the perspective of the earthly life of the Son of
God. The events which immediately precede the Transfiguration, and the intervening period between it and the last
days at Jerusalem, are of peculiar significance in the life-
work of Jesus Christ. It is now that the issue of his saving
ministry becomes clearly defined. The mission in Galilee
has, for the most part, failed and Jesus for the first time discloses to the disciples the meaning of his Messianic office.
Contrary to all expectations, it involves no popular triumph,
but rejection, suffering and death. Victory will come in the
end, but only after the Resurrection. The present prospect
is dark with foreboding, though relieved for a brief moment
by the glory of the Transfiguration. "And now the time was
drawing near for his taking away from the earth, and he
turned his eyes steadfastly towards the way that led to Jerusalem." [1]

St Mark tells us that, following Peter's great profession
of faith in his Master as the Messiah, which we have seen to
be the occasion of his being promised the headship of Christ's
Church, "he began to teach them that the Son of man must
suffer many things and be rejected by the ancients and by
the high priests and the scribes: and be killed and after
three days rise again." [2]

[1] Luke 9:51.
[2] Mark 8:31(R-D.); cf. Matt. 16:21; Luke 9:22.

This is the Lord's first unmistakable prediction of his Passion. We note also that the term "Son of Man" is here clearly used as a Messianic title.[3] The journey to Jerusalem is to be no triumphal progress; it will end in the Messiah's death. To Peter the thought that things were to turn out thus was unendurable. With characteristic boldness and impetuosity, he began to reproach his Master;—only to receive words of reproof as telling as had been those of felicitation shortly before: "Back, Satan...these thoughts of thine are man's, not God's."[4] Peter is unwittingly playing the role of the tempter, proving himself a stumbling-block in Jesus' path, one who would lead him to offend against the divine will. Far from being deterred or withdrawing from what he has said, Jesus goes on to declare that his followers must likewise be prepared to share his fate: "If any one desires to come after me, let him deny himself, take up his cross and follow me."[5] These words must have had a fearful meaning for his listeners. The Romans had taught this hideous punishment to the Jews, having crucified them in their thousands in order to quell revolt. In Judea, and still more so in Galilee, everyone knew what it meant to carry the cross; and when Jesus told his disciples to take up their cross, they must have seen in imagination the unhappy groups of the condemned, numbering among them, perhaps, many of their own neighbours and friends.

In the light of Calvary and the Resurrection we can now see the glory of the Cross. Looking forward to it, the disciples must have been filled with dread. But for us, as for them, there is an inescapable lesson. "Whoever wishes to save his life shall lose it; but whoever loses his life for my sake and the gospel's shall save it."[6] We are saved, not by following our instinct for self-preservation, but by losing ourselves in Christ's cause, surrendering our lives to God with all that we are and have. It is thus that we truly find ourselves, by becoming disentangled from the world and gaining posses-

3 See pp. 154 ff.   4 Mark 8:33.
5 Vs. 34(S.).   6 Mark 8:35(S.).

sion of our souls. "He who loves his life will lose it: he who is an enemy to his own life in this world will keep it, so as to live eternally." [7] We need the sense of ultimate values, to see that earthly power and riches must crumble to dust, and we with them, if ever they become the goal of our endeavour. "For what shall it profit a man, if he gain the whole world and suffer the loss of his soul? Or what shall a man give in exchange for his soul?" [8] Relentlessly the lesson is brought home: men must not be ashamed to acknowledge Christ for what he is and to take sides with him; if they are, then he in his turn will disown them "when he shall come in the glory of his Father with the holy angels." [9]

Small wonder that the disciples were plunged in dejection at the tragic prospect opening out before them! It was all so different from what they had anticipated. Was it for this that they had left their homes and families, to throw in their lot with the Messiah? Or was he the Messiah after all? At least his role was proving very unlike the one which, in their dreams, they had assigned to him. Such were the doubts and misgivings which must have filled the minds of the three favourite disciples, when "six days afterwards, Jesus took Peter and James and John with him, and led them up to a high mountain where they were alone by themselves." [10] St Luke, the evangelist of the praying Christ, tells us that he went up the mountain side "to pray." "And even as he prayed, the fashion of his face was altered, and his garments became white and dazzling; and two men appeared conversing with him, Moses and Elias, seen now in glory; and they spoke of the death which he was to achieve at Jerusalem." [11] Moses stood for the law and Elias for the prophets. "In this scene all that was most sacred in Israel's past does homage to the new prophet, and upholds what he has foretold about the scandal of his death." [12] The splendour of Christ's appearance at the Transfiguration was not due, as

[7] John 12:25.   [8] Mark 8:36–37(R-D.).   [9] Vs. 38(R-D.).
[10] Mark 9:2.   [11] Luke 9:29–31.
[12] M.-J. Lagrange, *L'Évangile de Jésus-Christ*, p. 257 (E.T. I, 269).

is sometimes said, to a direct disclosure of divinity through
the medium of his human nature; for the majesty of the
Godhead must always remain inaccessible to sense perception. More exactly, as St Thomas explains,[13] it was a mo-
mentary revelation of his glorified body as it would be after
the Resurrection. To this state of glory, a refulgence from a
human soul substantially united to the Divinity, our Lord
was entitled from the beginning; but it was held, so to say,
in suspense until after his Passion and death, so that he
might carry out his saving mission as a man among men.
Indeed it had been ordained that he should *merit* the glorified state—"Ought not the Christ to have suffered these
things, and thus enter into his glory?"[14]—since he was to be
the leader of all those who are one day to share it. "He will
form this humbled body of ours anew, moulding it into the
image of his glorified body, so effective in his power to make
all things obey him."[15] Here, on the mount of Transfiguration, he gives the disciples in his own person a brief vision
of the state of glory.

The effect upon the three witnesses, Peter most of all,
was deep and lasting—a blend of enthusiasm and awe. "Master, it is well that we should be here ...; he did not know
what to say, for they were overcome with fear."[16] A lu-
minous cloud—the *Shekinah,* age-long symbol of the Divine
Presence—overshadows them all, while the voice of the Father
is heard acknowledging the person and confirming the mission of his Son, the one uniquely beloved. The minds of
the disciples would again be overclouded, but how memorable this experience had been in confirming their belief in
Jesus Christ is shown by the way in which it was subsequently
recalled:

We were not crediting fables of man's invention, when we
preached to you about the power of our Lord Jesus Christ, and
about his coming; we had been eyewitnesses of his exaltation.
Such honour, such glory was bestowed on him by God the Father,

[13] III, q. 45, art. 2.   [14] Luke 24:26(W.).
[15] Phil. 3:21.   [16] Mark 9:4–6.

that a voice came to him out of the splendour which dazzles human eyes; This, it said, is my beloved Son, in whom I am well pleased; to him, then, listen. We, his companions on the holy mountain, heard the voice coming from heaven, and now the word of the prophets gives us more confidence than ever.[17]

On their way down from the mountain, Jesus enjoins his disciples to silence concerning what they have witnessed. The time has not yet come for his Messiahship to be proclaimed openly to the world. In answer to their puzzled questioning about the teaching of Scripture, he gives them to understand that Elias has already come in the person of John the Baptist.[18] Following upon a cure of an epileptic boy, we find our Lord returning to the theme of his coming Passion and Resurrection.[19] He reminds the disciples that he who would be great among them must be the servant of all.[20] This is the guiding principle for every Christian in the exercise of authority. Such power and influence as we have over others must be used for their benefit, not for our own. Before God we should preserve the simplicity, the teachableness, of children. "Whoever, therefore, humbles himself as this little child, he is the greatest in the kingdom of heaven." [21] Nor is true discipleship compatible with any narrow party spirit; let us not presume to repudiate anyone who does a good deed in the name of Jesus. "The man who is not against you is on your side. Why, if anyone gives you a cup of water to drink, because you are Christ's, I promise you, he shall not miss his reward." [22]

On no point is our Lord's teaching more uncompromising than in the matter of giving scandal, that is, hurting the conscience of others by anything in the nature of equivocal conduct. Most of all is this an offence when we give bad example to children, who are too impressionable not to be put off when they see those to whom they look for guidance betraying the cause. "But he that shall scandalize one of the little ones that believe in me, it were better for him that

[17] 2 Pet. 1:16–19. [18] Matt. 17:10–13. [19] Mark 9:30–31.
[20] Vs. 34–35. [21] Matt. 18:4(S.). [22] Mark 9:39–40.

a millstone should be hanged about his neck and that he should be drowned in the depth of the sea. Woe to the world because of scandals. For it must needs be that scandals come: but nevertheless woe to that man by whom the scandal cometh." [23] It is perhaps shortly after this that Jesus makes clear how fraternal correction is to be practised among the disciples, with the final invoking of the Church's authority.[24] He is brought back by a question from Peter to his favourite doctrine of mutual forgiveness, strikingly illustrated by the parable of the Unmerciful Servant: "It is thus that my heavenly Father will deal with you, if brother does not forgive brother with all his heart." [25]

The Galilean ministry has come to an end, by all human standards a tragic failure. Jesus laments the fate of the cities of the lakeside, Capharnaum, Chorazin, Bethsaida, where he has preached and worked his miracles in vain, and sets out for Jerusalem. We find him there for the feast of Tabernacles.[26] His teaching in the Temple precincts is the occasion of a plot to arrest him.[27] Presently he cures the man blind from birth by sending him to wash in the pool of Siloam, a miracle in keeping with his character as "the light of the world." [28] Then there comes the touching self-disclosure: "I am the good shepherd, and I know my own, and my own know me, as the Father knows me, and I know the Father; and I lay down my life for my sheep. And other sheep I have which are not of this fold; those also I must bring, and they will hear my voice, and there shall be one flock under one shepherd." [29]

Much of what took place on the journey to Jerusalem, as this is seen by St Luke [30]—for one of the dominating themes of the third Gospel is that of the pilgrim Jesus, moving forward to the foreseen consummation of his death—can perhaps be placed after St John's account of the feast of Tabernacles. Here we find our Lord dealing with aspirants

---

[23] Matt. 18:6–7(R.-D.).   [24] VV. 15–17.   [25] Vs. 35.
[26] John 7:10 ff.   [27] VV. 30–32.   [28] 9:5.
[29] 10:14–16(S.).   [30] Luke 9:51, 18:14.

to discipleship [31] and with the mission of the seventy-two.[32] There comes the moment when, in the joy of the Holy Spirit, he gives thanks to the Father; despite appearances, his message is even now being received by those whom he has chosen as his own.

I give praise to thee, O Father, lord of heaven and earth, because, having hidden these things from the wise and clever, thou hast revealed them to little ones. Even so, Father; for so it is well pleasing in thy sight. All things have been delivered to me by my Father; and no one knows who the Son is except the Father, and who the Father is except the Son, and he to whom it is the pleasure of the Son to reveal him.[33]

There follows what is perhaps the greatest of the parables, that of the Good Samaritan.[34] The story illustrates Christ's teaching on the duty of loving our neighbour as ourselves. One of the scribes wished to know where to draw the line between neighbour and non-neighbour. All ancient civilizations drew the line somewhere, whether between Roman citizen and foreigner, Greek and barbarian, Jew and Gentile. How then, in the opinion of Jesus, was "neighbour" to be defined? No definition emerges from the parable; and for an excellent reason. The question presupposes an entirely wrong approach. The love which is charity does not begin by first delimiting its sphere; rather it invests everything it sees with its own light and warmth. Our failure to observe the great commandment arises not from lack of information about how it is to be applied. The lesson of the Good Samaritan is that, if we have love in our hearts, we shall not need to be told who our neighbour is.

St Luke next records the charming encounter with the two sisters, Martha and Mary,[35] which the Church Fathers have allegorized as the type of the "two lives"—that of action and that of contemplation. The disciples are again taught what is to be the formula of their prayer.[36] Two further

---

[31] Luke 9:57–62.
[33] 10:21–22(S.); Matt. 11:25–27.
[35] Luke 10:38–42.

[32] 10:1–12, 16.
[34] Luke 10:30–37.
[36] Luke 11:1–4.

cures are followed by the odious charge of his enemies, so effectively refuted, that Jesus performs his miracles with the aid of black magic. This gross slander, to be urged from the Jewish side for centuries,[37] testifies to the ever-increasing hostility of the Pharisees. In their culpable blindness they are sinning against the light. Abandoning the attempt to win over the Pharisaic party, our Lord instructs his disciples on how they are to preach the Gospel, promising them the help of the Holy Spirit.[38] He emphasizes the supreme value of the human soul [39] and the need for being ever on the watch.[40] His gaze is fixed more and more upon the future, on the Passion, the baptism with which he is to be baptized; [41] and the urgency of the Gospel dominates his thought.

The healing of the deformed woman on the Sabbath [42] serves only to deepen the gulf between Jesus and official Judaism. He is again at Jerusalem for the winter feast of the Dedication; [43] this was the last great festivity prior to the fateful Passover of the following spring. He now speaks of himself openly as the Son of God, uniquely one with the Father; only to meet with hostility and rejection.[44] Thereafter he withdraws into Perea, east of Jordan. In his teaching he speaks of the condemnation which awaits those who have refused to accept him, and of their place in the kingdom being taken by many "from the east and the west, the north and the south." [45] Undeterred by a warning from Herod,[46] Jesus proceeds on his healing mission until the appointed hour at Jerusalem. He still dines with certain of the Pharisees, still insists without compromise on the claims of the kingdom, while bidding men think what they do before counting themselves his disciples.[47] Yet his message is softened by a wonderful revelation of divine mercy, illustrated by the parables of the Lost Sheep and the Prodigal Son.[48]

[37] Klausner, *Jesus of Nazareth*, pp. 18–54.
[38] Mark 13:10–11.   [39] 8:35–36.
[40] 13:33–37. For the eschatological teaching of Christ see pp. 298 ff.
[41] Luke 12:50.   [42] 13:10–17.   [43] John 10:22 ff.
[44] VV. 30 ff.   [45] Luke 13:29.   [46] VV. 31–33.
[47] 14:25–33.   [48] Luke 15.

It may well be that our Lord's teaching on the subject of riches and the right treatment of the poor,[49] as well as the reminder that even the most faithful of his disciples must acknowledge that they have nothing in which to glory,[50] was delivered shortly before the final approach to Jerusalem.[51] On his way he heals the ten lepers, he teaches the people that God's kingdom has already come,[52] warns them of the advent of the Son of Man in judgement,[53] and urges them to keep faith with him.[54] The story of the Pharisee and the publican,[55] the teaching on marriage and divorce,[56] Jesus' touching welcome to the little children,[57] the illustration of the entire gratuitousness of God's gifts by the parable of the labourers in the vineyard,[58] are what precede the raising of Lazarus at Bethany.[59] This miracle is the occasion for Caiaphas, with the leaders of the Sanhedrin, to resolve to do away with him—"it is best for us if one man is put to death for the sake of the people." [60] Political expediency demands his removal. Jesus is now an outlaw to his own nation, virtually under sentence of death.

Yet once more does our Lord forewarn his disciples of what lies in store for him, while encouraging them with the prediction that he will rise from the dead; [61] but they, fearful and perplexed, fail to grasp his meaning. He lingers awhile on the northern outskirts of the city, preaching and teaching, before going up to Jerusalem to celebrate the momentous Passover. He has still to rebuke James and John for their worldly ambition and to remind his followers that precedence in God's kingdom goes, not with earthly prestige, but in the measure of their willingness to serve others and to suffer with him. Let them weigh the implications of the fact that "the Son of Man himself came not to be served but to serve, and to give his life a ransom for many." [62] Near Jericho

49 Luke 16:19–31.   50 17:7–10.   51 Vs. 11.
52 VV. 12–21.   53 Matt. 25:31–46.   54 Luke 18:1–8.
55 Luke 18:9–14.   56 Mark 10:2–12; Matt. 19:3–12.
57 Mark 10:13–16.   58 Matt. 20:1–16.
59 John 11:1–44.   60 Vs. 50.
61 Matt. 20:17–19; Mark 10:32–34; Luke 18:31–34.
62 Mark 10:45(S.).

he cures the blind Bartimaeus in dramatic circumstances.[63] In the town itself we have the vivid, attractive, half-humorous scene of the Lord's visit to the house of the tax-gatherer, Zacchaeus.[64] Here, in an atmosphere heavy with expectation of the imminent coming of the kingdom,—did not Jesus' advance upon Jerusalem suggest some political *coup d'état?*—he tells his commercial-minded audience the parable of the pounds; [65] his outward triumph is not yet, but let his enemies beware of what is involved in their rejection of him. There remains only the anointing at Bethany,[66] where the Master's defence of Mary's seeming extravagance brings to a head Judas's resolve to betray him, before the Messianic entry into Jerusalem on Palm Sunday.[67] As he draws near he weeps over the city, now about to precipitate its doom.

It is at this point, appropriately enough, that the Lord's words take on an unsurpassed grandeur and poignancy; [68] even the Gentiles within the Temple courts are seeking him out. The events of Holy Week include the cursing of the barren fig tree (an acted parable, symbolizing God's anger with Israel, whose religion flourishes outwardly but bears no genuine fruit) [69] and the claim before the agents of the Sanhedrin to derive his authority from the same source as John the Baptist.[70] His teaching has for its chief theme the Jews' rejection of their Messiah; it comprises the parables of the two sons,[71] the wicked husbandman (partly an allegory),[72] the eschatological parable of the wise and foolish virgins,[73] as well as the two discourses on the destruction of the Temple and the coming of the Son of Man "with power." [74] He defends the resurrection of the dead against the Sadducees, and counters, with vigour and great dialectical skill, the polemic of the Sanhedrin representatives, to the confusion of his enemies and the enthusiastic admira-

63 Luke 18:35-43.   64 19:1-10.   65 Luke 19:11-28.
66 Matt. 26:6-13; Mark 14:3-9; John 12:1-11.
67 Matt. 21:1-11, 14-16 and parallels.
68 Cf. John 12:20-36.   69 Matt. 21:18-22.
70 Mark 11:27-33 and parallels.   71 Matt. 21:28-32.
72 VV. 33-46 and parallels.   73 25:1-13.
74 Mark 13:1 ff.

tion of his friends.[75] He is not to be caught in the dilemma between the rival claims of God and Caesar.[76] Presently he again proves himself more than a match for his questioners; he challenges them to explain how it is that the Christ is at the same time David's Son and David's Lord.[77] Nor does his argumentative mastery fail to make its impression; with at least one member of his learned audience he is able to lift the controversy to the highest level of religion.[78] Undaunted to the last, he denounces in their own citadel of Jerusalem the hypocrisy of the scribes and Pharisees,[79] commenting pointedly on the value of the widow's mite cast into the Temple treasury.[80]

The climax is at hand. On the Wednesday of Holy Week Judas Iscariot agrees with the high-priestly faction to betray his Master for money.[81] The public ministry of our Lord Jesus Christ has come to an end, frustrated by the unyielding obduracy of his enemies and the perfidy of a friend. The solemn events we are about to contemplate will show his power to draw good out of evil, turning defeat into glorious triumph. But such considerations should not be allowed to hide from view the tragedy of what had happened. The long-awaited Messiah had been rejected by those whom most of all he would have saved, a rejection which brought in its train irreparable disaster for them and heart-piercing sorrow to him. Looking back upon it, in our enjoyment of the fruits of Calvary and the Resurrection, we may be almost tempted to make light of it, supposing the outcome to have been in some way inevitable. But it was not so. The forces opposed to Christ were set in motion by the free play of the human will, the will of men in no way essentially different from ourselves. Malice, culpable stupidity and bad faith were at the root of the opposition; but then, as now, these evil things could so blind their victims as to produce a perverted sincerity. So in fact our Lord was to warn his disciples: "The

---

[75] Matt. 22:23–33 and parallels.   [76] Matt. 22:16–22 and parallels.
[77] VV. 41–46 and parallels; cf. Ps. 109 (110):1.
[78] Mark 12:28 ff.   [79] VV. 38–40 and parallels.
[80] VV. 41–44.   [81] 14:10–11 and parallels.

hour cometh when anyone that killeth you shall think to
be offering worship to God." [82]

It is not then enough for us to refrain from passing
harsh judgment upon the scribes, the Pharisees and Sadducees. Here, as always, the final verdict rests with God.
More profitable is it for us to ask ourselves, on what side
we should have taken our stand had we been witnesses to the
conflict between them and Jesus. There is much in human
nature which impels us, in religion as in every other sphere,
to take refuge in tradition and the accepted conventions,
rather than face the ultimate personal challenge to our own
integrity; we prefer the unexamined life to the scrutiny of
ourselves as we are. No such escape was possible to the Jews
of first-century Palestine. They were confronted with an in-
eluctable *either/or*. What grounds have we for supposing
that the choice for the men of the modern world is less per-
emptory? Courage, simplicity, an open and lowly heart were
the conditions for making the right response. They have
not changed. With them we find ourselves in the company
of Martha and Mary, of Peter, James and John. Without
them—where? The Sermon on the Mount has overthrown
in advance a merely nominal Christianity: "Not everyone
that saith to me, Lord, Lord, shall enter into the kingdom
of heaven...." [83] The crucial test—in the literal meaning of
that phrase—is the love of truth. "Whoever belongs to the
truth listens to my voice." [84] Failing that, we may not so
much as hear it.

[82] John 16:2(W.).   [83] Matt. 7:21(R-D.).   [84] John 18:37.

§ 10. THE LAST SUPPER AND CALVARY

On the Thursday of Holy Week Jesus took his last meal
with the disciples.[1] When all were gathered at table, he said

[1] On the difficult question of the precise date of the Last Supper, and the
reconciliation of the Synoptic accounts with St John, see Lagrange, *op. cit.*,
pp. 494–99 (E.T. II, 191–96); also Lebreton, *Life and Teaching of Jesus
Christ*, II, 213–20; J. P. Arendzen, *Men and Manners in the Days of Christ*,
pp. 11–25.

to them: "Earnestly have I desired to eat this passover with you before I suffer; for I tell you, that I will eat it no more, until it is fulfilled in the kingdom of God." [2] The order of the feast, which was the most joyful of the Jewish year, would follow the simple ritual laid down in the twelfth chapter of the Book of Exodus, with doubtless the slight elaborations which had been introduced in the course of centuries. At least four cups of wine would be drunk; for food there was unleavened bread, bitter herbs and the paschal lamb itself. While those at table conversed freely together, the religious character of the meal was kept in mind throughout. Commemoration was made of the mercies of God and, in particular, of Israel's deliverance, which was the reason for celebrating the rite. A blessing preceded the drinking of the wine, the fourth cup being followed by the hymn *Hallel,* which was composed of Psalms 115–18.[3] Here would occur the words, so expressive of the Messianic hope, alluded to by our Lord only a few days before: "Believe me, you shall see nothing of me hence-forward, until the time when you will be saying, *Blessed is he that comes in the name of the Lord.*" [4]

None of the evangelists is concerned with the details of the Last Supper in their Old Testament significance. The three synoptic writers see it as the framework for the institution of the New Covenant in Christ's blood; for St John it is the occasion of our Lord's great lesson in humility and his sublimest and most intimate teaching. For instance, no mention is made of the traditional paschal lamb, and St Luke groups together the blessing of the first cup,[5] with which the meal began, and the cup of "the new covenant in my blood," [6] which came at the end. In the words "I shall not drink of the fruit of the vine again, till the kingdom of God has come," [7] Jesus tells his disciples that this is the last Passover of his mortal life. He is about to die; with his resur-

---

[2] Luke 22:15–16(S.).
[3] Heb. Psalt.; Vulg. Ps. 113:9–18, 114–17.
[4] Matt. 23:39.   [5] Luke 22:17.
[6] Vs. 20(W.).   [7] Vs. 18.

rection and ascension into heaven God's kingdom will be
established on earth. St John discloses the inner meaning
of what was taking place:

Before the paschal feast began, Jesus already knew that the
time had come for his passage from this world to the Father. He
still loved those who were his own, whom he was leaving in the
world, and he would give them the uttermost proof of his love.
... Jesus knew well that the Father had left everything in his
hands; knew it was from God that he came, and to God that he
went.[8]

But even now, when the time is so short, the disciples are
not at one with their Master. There is a sinister note which
disturbs the harmony of those gathered at the supper-table—
"the devil had already put it into the heart of Judas, son
of Simon, the Iscariot, to betray him." [9] Among the rest
there is an all too human spirit of rivalry and dissension.
They felt the greatness of the occasion and perhaps fell to
quarrelling over their order of precedence. Which of them
would not wish to be placed nearest the Master on a night
so momentous? Gently he reminds them that such jealousy
and ambition befit, not his chosen ones, but the Gentiles.
"With you it is not to be so; no difference is to be made,
among you, between the greatest and the youngest of all,
between him who commands and him who serves." [10] Is not
he, their Lord, who reclines at table, greater than them all?
And yet, "I am here among you as your servant." [11] Suiting
the action to his words, "rising from supper, he laid his
garments aside, took a towel, and put it about him; and then
he poured water into the basin, and began to wash the feet
of his disciples, wiping them with the towel that girded
him." [12]

The twelve were discomfited at this scene; and it may
well be that we share their embarrassment. It is fitting that
we should pay service to God; but not surely that we should
allow him to serve us. So at least thought Simon Peter:

[8] John 13:1, 3.   [9] John 13:2.   [10] Luke 22:26.
[11] Vs. 27.   [12] John 13:4-5.

"Lord, is it for thee to wash my feet?" [13] We learn that there can be a wrong, as well as a right, form of self-reliance. It is always wrong as an attitude towards God. He mercifully accepts our pitiful attempts to serve him, even though we can give him no honour which is not already his. In reality it is he who serves us, ministering to each of our needs. Peter, made aware of the Master's disapproval, now goes to the other extreme. "Then, Lord, wash my hands and my head too, not only my feet." [14] It is well meant, but still there is self-will; he would have it done in his, not Jesus', way. In truth there was no need for further cleansing; to Peter and the rest, save one, the Lord could say: "You, through the message I have preached to you, are clean already." [15] Judas with treachery in his heart, had submitted to the feet-washing in silence. But Jesus knew.

Nor does he fail to point the moral of his acted parable:

Do you understand what it is I have done to you? You hail me as the Master, and the Lord; and you are right, it is what I am. Why then, if I have washed your feet, I who am the Master and the Lord, you in your turn ought to wash each other's feet; I have been setting you an example, which will teach you in your turn to do what I have done for you.[16]

Jesus has taught us that we are beggars before God, needing his service. We need that of others also;—which is a harder lesson to learn. How much easier it is for the zealous Christian to do good to his neighbour than to allow it to be done to himself! The desire "not to be beholden to anyone" is deeply rooted in the hearts of most of us. It is one of the commonest forms of human pride. We must know how to receive favours, as well as bestow them. Only then perhaps can we rightly play the part of benefactor, with no touch of superiority or patronage. Here we are told of the lowly service we must be ready to give to others. We would willingly wash the feet of our Divine Master, welcoming so great an honour. But he nowhere asks that of us.

13 John 13:6.   14 Vs. 9.
15 15:3.   16 13:12–15.

It is our neighbour's feet that we should be prepared to wash. St John constantly returns to this fundamental theme of Christ's teaching. The real test of our love and devotion to God is our love and devotion to those around us. "Beloved, if God has shown such love to us, we too must love one another." [17] "If a man boasts of loving God, while he hates his own brother, he is a liar." [18]

The Host at the supper-table is troubled in spirit; there is one present who no longer believes in him. "After saying so much, Jesus bore witness to the distress he felt in his heart; Believe me, he said, believe me, one of you is to betray me." [19] He had borne unruffled the taunts of his enemies, the scribes and Pharisees, but the thought of a traitor among his intimate friends is all but insupportable. Consternation falls upon the disciples. They know their Master too well to repudiate his suggestion; their self-distrust is sufficient to make them doubt their own constancy. "They were full of sorrow, and began to say, one after another, Lord, Is it I?" [20] Among the questioners was Judas. Boldly, so as not to lose countenance before the rest, he put the query: "Master, is it I?" Softly, lest his identity should be revealed to all, came the answer: "Thy own lips have said it." [21] The whispered exchange of confidences between Jesus and John, the beloved disciple, could not have been heard by the others. The latter, we may well believe, returned no answer to Peter's question, "Who is it he means?" [22] John would be content to await his Master's lead; but it is hard to think of the impulsive Peter resting silent and inactive, had he known the traitor's name. Meanwhile the others remain unenlightened: "Thereupon they fell to surmising among themselves, which of them it was that would do this." [23] The tension is unrelieved by the solemn words of Jesus, a final appeal to Judas to weigh well the consequences of what he is about to do: "The Son of Man goes on his

[17] 1 John 4:11.   [18] Vs. 20.   [19] John 13:21.
[20] Matt. 26:22.   [21] Vs. 25.
[22] John 13:24.   [23] Luke 22:23.

way, as the scripture foretells of him; but woe upon that man
by whom the Son of Man is to be betrayed; better for that
man if he had never been born." [24]

Our Lord and the disciples were reclining on cushions
or low couches at the table, Eastern fashion, with their feet
at the farthest distance from it. They would be resting on
the left elbow, leaving the right hand free to take food. We
do not know the exact position of each in relation to their
Host; but John held a place of honour next to him, for he
could easily turn half back and rest his head on the Lord's
breast, so being able to speak to him unheard by the others.
Peter must have been close to John. Judas, treasurer and
steward of the company, was doubtless next to Jesus on the
other side. He would thus be available for receiving and
carrying out orders. They were still at the earlier part of
the meal, where the Master of the house and those at table
with him ate the herbs dipped in sauce.[25] It was customary
for a host to show special honour to one of his guests by
himself dipping a choice morsel of food in the dish and
handing it to him. Jesus selected the betrayer for this act
of favour. It was his last appeal. He had known from the
beginning the character of those he had called to discipleship, Judas among them. "I know who are the men I have
chosen." [26] There had been promise in Judas; the hardness
of his nature would perhaps yield to the pressure of divine
love. Jesus foresaw that it would turn out otherwise; this
knowledge was what led him to warn the disciples of the
coming betrayal, lest the scandal of it should afterwards
overwhelm them. He quoted a verse from the Psalms, "Even
mine own friend, in whom I trusted, who ate my bread,
hath freely used his heel against me"; [27] and he added, "I
am telling you this now, before it happens, so that when it
happens you may believe it was written of me." [28] But the

[24] Mark 14:21.
[25] Mishnah, *Pesahim*, X, 3.   [26] John 13:18.
[27] Ps. 40(41):10(Fr Lattey's translation from the Hebrew).
[28] John 13:19.

Lord's charity knows no defeat; even Judas might still be won. He handed him the morsel.

The gesture was unavailing. The traitor's face grew dark. "Satan entered into him." [29] All hope of reconciliation at an end, Jesus was anxious only that the inevitable should come without delay. The whole situation, with the presence of Judas at this banquet of love, had become intolerable. Peremptorily came the order: "What thou art bent upon, do quickly." [30] Still the disciples were unaware of what was happening; they supposed instruction to have been given for some almsgiving or necessary purchase. Judas was allowed to go out under the protecting silence of Jesus. That silence, humanly speaking, sealed his fate. One word of denunciation, and the faithful eleven, who were not unwilling to use violent measures,[31] would have rendered the traitor powerless to do harm. He who could have summoned to his aid "more than twelve legions of angels" [32] lifted no finger to save himself. From the presence of the Light of the World [33] Judas withdrew, of his own will, into the outer darkness. There are no more pregnant words in all literature than those with which St John signalizes that unhappy exit: "And it was night." [34]

With the departure of Judas all was changed. The tension was relaxed and the company at last wholly at one with the Master. Now he could give them his most cherished gift, unburden his heart to them as never before. The dejection which had lain heavily on the disciples was banished as they were uplifted by Jesus' words of exultation: "Now is the Son of Man glorified, and God is glorified in him." [35] The moment had come for him to institute the Sacrament of his body and blood. He took bread and, following the sacred custom, blessed it, broke it, and gave it to the disciples with the words: "Take ye, this is my body." [36] This was the last act of the supper; for he next took the cup of wine, the

29 John 13:27.
30 Vs. 27(S.).
31 Cf. Luke 22:38, 49-50.
32 Matt. 26:53.
33 John 9:5.
34 13:30(R-D.).
35 Vs. 31(R-D.).
36 Mark 14:22(R-D.).

third according to the Jewish ritual, which was appointed
to be drunk in thanksgiving for the Passover meal.[37] He
handed it to them, so that all might drink from the same
cup, saying: "This is my blood of the covenant, which is
poured out for many." [38]

In view of the adequate account given by the three synoptists [39] and by St Paul,[40] it would have been superfluous for
St John to record the institution of the Eucharist. He is
chiefly concerned with our Lord's discourse, to whose sublime heights perhaps his mind alone among the evangelists
was capable of rising. He could the more afford to omit
it, as he had, at an earlier stage, recalled our Lord's teaching
on the Bread of Life and the promise so faithfully fulfilled
on the night before he died.

I am the living bread come down from heaven. If any one eat
of this bread, he shall live for ever; and the bread which I will
give is my flesh, for the life of the world. . . . Amen, amen, I say
to you, unless ye eat the flesh of the Son of Man and drink his
blood, ye have not life in you. He that eateth my flesh and drinketh my blood hath everlasting life; and I will raise him up on
the last day. For my flesh is food indeed, and my blood is drink
indeed. He that eateth my flesh and drinketh my blood abideth
in me, and I in him. As the living Father hath sent me, and as I
live because of the Father, so he that eateth me, he also shall
live because of me. This is the bread come down from heaven:
not as the fathers ate and died: he that eateth this bread shall
live for ever.[41]

We learn from St John that Christ's teaching on the Eucharist is the climax of his doctrine of faith. Even when
he first calls himself "the bread of life," [42] it would seem
from the context that he is referring to men's acceptance of
him by the mind, rather than explicitly to his Eucharistic
presence. And so it cannot but be: unless we are already
united to Jesus through faith, the Blessed Sacrament can

[37] Luke 22:20; 1 Cor. 11:25.   [38] Mark 14:24(S.).
[39] Matt. 26:26–28; Mark 14:22–24; Luke 22:19–20.
[40] 1 Cor. 11:23–25.   [41] John 6:51, 53–58(W.).
[42] Vs. 35.

have little meaning for us. Not that the Real Presence depends on faith; not that it is any less real because some
choose to disbelieve it; but because our supernatural life is
rooted and grounded in faith, it follows that the quickening of that life, which the Eucharist brings, presupposes faith.
Thus the belief in Christ which will make us truly apprecia-
tive of the Eucharist must be akin to the faith of the first
disciples. They did not simply accept with their minds certain statements *about* Christ; it was he himself who counted
for everything; there was nothing and nobody else. "Lord to
whom shall we go? Thou hast the words of everlasting
life." [43] Believing in Jesus, we partake of his body and blood.
So nourished, our faith becomes a thing of light and the
spirit within takes fire.

How real the Presence was is shown by the words of institution. They can be understood only in the literal sense.
"This is my body.... This cup is the new covenant in my
blood." [44] Sacramentally our Lord makes present his body
and blood under the appearances of bread and wine. We can
gather from St Luke how this act looks forward to, is in some
sense one thing with, the supreme sacrifice of the morrow:
Christ's body is here and now *"given for you,"* his blood
"poured out for you." St Matthew adds: *"for the remission
of sins."* [45] Thus the first eucharistic sacrifice—the "Mass,"
as it was later to be called—was celebrated by Christ himself. In a symbolism which made real what it signified he
enacted his sacrificial death, destined to be a historic fact but
a few hours afterwards. Through this alone could man's redemption be achieved; only thus could he be "sanctified
through the offering of the body of Jesus Christ once for
all." [46] But here, on this solemn night, was its sacramental
counterpart. The separate consecration, first of the bread
into the body, then of the wine into the blood, was the ritual
foreshadowing of that act whereby the body and blood of
the Victim would indeed be rent violently asunder. In this

43 John 6:68(W.).   44 Luke 22:19–20(S.).
45 Matt. 26:28.   46 Heb. 10:10(S.).

immolation Christ, the true Paschal Lamb,[47] was sacrificed, and all man's sacrifice save this for ever made void.

But the unique offering on Calvary was to endure, a living memory, throughout the ages. The commission had been given to the apostles: "Do this in remembrance of me." [48] With these words the Lord made them priests, giving them a share in his own priesthood. The eleven and those they would appoint were to be the guardians of the New Covenant which, now being anticipated in a sacramental form, was to reach its consummation on the Cross. So the Catholic Church has understood from the beginning: "It is the Lord's death that you are heralding, whenever you eat this bread and drink this cup, until he comes." [49] *Until he comes*— this is why the Mass has always been, and will remain, the vital centre of the Church's worship. It is her most sacred trust; faithfully it will be discharged as a pledge of the remission of sins, of propitiation, thanksgiving and worship, until "the end," when Christ "hands over the kingdom to God and the Father, when he abolishes all other sovereignty, authority and power." [50]

Enshrining the sacrament and sacrifice of the Eucharist we find our Lord's most intimate teaching. To receive Christ's body fosters our love for God and our neighbour; but it also presupposes that love. So he reminds us in heart-searching words: "I have a new commandment to give you, that you are to love one another; that your love for one another is to be like the love I have borne you." [51] This is the essence, the "religious philosophy," of the Gospel. The injunction to mutual love is no novelty; but that our love for one another should be "like the love I have borne you"—that is unique. True, Jesus had said it before in other contexts, but never so expressly or so movingly. We have to imitate the love of a Saviour who came to win sinners to himself,[52] a love destitute of all self-righteousness, full of exquisite compassion

---

[47] 1 Cor. 5:7.
[48] Luke 22:19(S.); 1 Cor. 11:24.
[49] 1 Cor. 11:26.
[50] 15:24(S.).
[51] John 13:34.
[52] Cf. Mark 2:17.

for the weak and the feeble. For us it must be a *fraternal* charity, based upon equality and fellowship, without tincture of patronage or paternalism. We recall the lesson of the Sermon on the Mount: "All things therefore whatsoever you would that men should do to you, do you also to them. For this is the law and the prophets." [53] Mercifulness is supreme among God's attributes; in bidding us aim at the perfection of his heavenly Father,[54] our Lord is in fact inviting us to imitate his mercy: "Be compassionate, therefore, as your Father is compassionate." [55]

Following the order of St Luke and St John, we are still in the supper-room when Jesus foretells the dispersion of the apostles and Peter's denial. With what is to come clearly before his mind, he tries to fortify the disciples against the scandal of his Passion by warning them in advance of its effect upon them, adding once more the promise of the Resurrection: "You will all be scandalized in my regard this night. For it is written, I will strike the shepherd, and the sheep shall be dispersed. But after I shall be risen again, I will go before you into Galilee." [56] Upon Peter especially, the chief of the apostles, he would impress the fact of their coming desertion: "Simon, Simon, behold Satan hath desired to have you, that he may sift you as wheat." [57] Peter will be allowed to fall, that he may gain self-knowledge, to rise to greater heights in the strength of his repentance; for the Lord knows that a lasting failure on Peter's part would bring irreparable disaster to the rest. That they would lose faith in him he does not suggest, but it remains that the privilege of unfailing faith is guaranteed only to Peter, the rock-foundation of the Church.[58] It is assured him by the protecting and infallibly efficacious prayer of Jesus: "But I have prayed for thee, that thy faith fail not: and thou, being once converted, confirm thy brethren." [59] Peter's self-assur-

[53] Matt. 7:12(R-D.).   [54] Cf. 5:48.   [55] Luke 6:36(S.).
[56] Mark 14:27–28(R-D.).   [57] Luke 22:31(R-D.).   [58] Matt. 16:18–19.
[59] Luke 22:32(R-D.); cf. p. 87. The exact sense of the obscure second part of this verse is perhaps better rendered by Monsignor Knox: "When, after a while, thou hast come back to me, it is for thee to be the support of thy brethren."

ance has yet to be shaken; he, like the rest of us, has to learn that it does not lie within man's own power to keep loyal to God. It is vain for him to protest, in the warmth of his emotion, that he will never disown, that he is prepared to die for, the Master. "Thou art ready, answered Jesus, to lay down thy life for my sake? Believe me, by cock-crow thou wilt thrice disown me." [60]

Jesus breaks in upon the pathetic avowals of loyalty from Peter and the rest, to recall them to the realities of the new situation. There had been a time back in Galilee, in the first fervour of popular enthusiasm, when they had been listened to with sympathy and hospitably received. Then they could travel light, "without purse, or wallet, or shoes," [61] and be sure of obtaining food and lodging. Now all that was changed; the hostility they must expect would be such that their elementary needs would have to be extorted virtually at the sword-point. So does our Lord heighten the picture of what lies in store for those who will afterwards claim fellowship with him who was "counted among the malefactors." [62] The disciples, literal-minded Galileans, not unused to reinforcing words with blows, were undismayed; they had even brought two weapons with them in case of emergency. Later, reflecting on the words spoken to Peter, they would grow more wise. "Put thy sword back into its place; all those who take up the sword will perish by the sword." [63] For the moment Jesus does not see fit to quench their ardour. To their boast of already being prepared with "two swords," he observes with the gentlest irony—"smilingly" as St Cyril of Alexandria suggests—"That is enough." [64]

By this time more than sufficient had happened at the supper-table to throw the disciples into a state of uneasy depression. They had been given the priceless gift of Christ's body and blood, though as yet perhaps they hardly realized its full significance. But the Master's words about his betrayal and their forthcoming desertion of him, crowned by the warning of the unpopularity awaiting themselves, had

[60] John 13:38.   [61] Luke 22:35.   [62] Vs. 37.
[63] Matt. 26:52.   [64] Luke 22:38.

had their effect. A moment of forced enthusiasm is no more than a cover for their underlying anxiety. In a self-disclosure of boundless consolation Jesus takes them into his confidence: "Do not let your heart be distressed; as you have faith in God, have faith in me." [65] If he is leaving them on a journey, it is only as a friend who goes forward to prepare a lodging for his companions; soon they will be reunited. For a brief visit, at the Resurrection, he will come back to reassure them; then he will gather them to himself with the Father. Let not Thomas say that the journey's end, or the way thither, is unknown. "Jesus said to him, I am the way, the truth and the life; no one comes to the Father but by me." [66] Let not Philip demand a clearer revelation of the Father. What he asks for is before his eyes. "Have I been so long a time with you, and you do not know me? Philip, he who has seen me has seen the Father; how canst thou say, Show us the Father? Dost thou not believe that I am in the Father, and the Father is in me?" [67]

Again comes the insistence on faith, and the promise that goes therewith. "He who believes in me shall himself do the works that I do—and greater than these shall he do." [68] This pledge has not been left unfulfilled. Jesus himself had confined his mission to Israel; but the apostles, at his bidding, would carry it to the Gentiles and the pagan world. The "works" of Christ include his miracles certainly; and these have had their counterpart throughout the Church's history. But the greatest of all his works was his charity, the generous creative love of God and all mankind. For his followers also this must hold the first place, as St Paul teaches.[69] There are more spectacular gifts, like prophecy and speaking with tongues; but charity is "yet a more excellent way." [70] The life of the Church, which is the Body of Christ, so productive of good in its manifold activities, has testified to the works "greater than these" which were to be accomplished by his power.

[65] John 14:1.   [66] Vs. 6(S.).   [67] VV. 9–10(S.).
[68] Vs. 12(S.).   [69] 1 Cor. 13.   [70] 12:31(R-D.).

The disciples must pray. So complete is the Son's union with the almighty Father that prayer in his name will always be answered—and by the Son himself, who is of co-equal power: "Whatever you shall ask in my name, that I will do." [71] But we must not overlook the condition of this prayer —"that the Father may be glorified in the Son." There may be many objects of our petition, but if it lacks this underlying motive, it is not the prayer alluded to by Christ. Now he returns to the greatest theme of all, the love of God: "If anyone loves me, he will keep my word; and my Father will love him, and we will come to him and make our abode with him. . . . He who has my commandments and observes them, he it is who loves me; and he who loves me shall be loved by my Father, and I will love him, and will manifest myself to him." [72] It is an interchange of love between the disciples, on the one hand, and Father and the Son on the other—a love of which "the Spirit of Truth" [73] is to be the pledge Love and truth go together, the first being conditioned by the second; and the Paraclete, the Comforter, personifies them both. "The Holy Ghost, whom the Father will send in my name, He will teach you all things, and will remind you of all I have told you." [74] Thus the divine guidance is promised to the apostles and their successors, that they may the better understand, and preserve from error, God's revelation. With what gratitude do Catholic Christians look back to this assurance in their vindication of their claim to belong, however unworthily, to "the church of the living God, the pillar and ground of the truth." [75]

"I will not leave you orphans; I will come to you. A little while longer, and the world shall see me no more; but you shall see me, because I live, and you shall live." [76] The disciples are puzzled at the mysterious intimacy of our Lord's words. Still their anticipations are too short-sighted; they think in terms of the Messiah's visible manifestation to the world in glory. In reality, as we now see, what is disclosed

---

[71] John 14:13(S.).   [72] VV. 23, 21(S.).   [73] Vs. 17(S.).
[74] Vs. 26(S.).   [75] 1 Tim. 3:15(R-D.).   [76] John 14:18-19(S.).

is the presence of the Blessed Trinity within the human spirit, to give countenance to that quasi-experimental knowledge of God which is the reward of the life of charity. We note how the evangelical mysticism is to be distinguished from its numerous counterfeits, ranging from philosophical neo-Platonism, through aestheticism and the various forms of "nature mysticism," down to the eccentricities of the theosophists. Jesus has laid down the condition for the aspirant to such a grace; he must "keep my word." Here, as at every stage of his ministry, he is terribly in earnest; for all his tenderness, he is uncompromising in the demand for sincerity and truth as manifested in practical conduct. He can admit to discipleship the sinner and moral weakling, but not the poseur and religious dilettante.

Jesus repeats his words of encouragement: "Do not let your heart be distressed, or play the coward." [77] There is little time left now for further converse with them; "the world," the scheme of things opposed to God, is about to have its way. The Lord will submit to it, even though Satan, the world's ruler, has no hold at all over him. He is on his way to the Father, to give the final proof of his love. For the Father, with whom the Son of God is equal in dignity, is greater than he according to his human nature; and it is as man that he is to pay the tribute of sacrifice. "The world must be convinced that I love the Father, and act only as the Father has commanded me to act." [78] He has a parting gift for the disciples—"*peace.*" To wish peace to another was a conventional greeting among the Jews, often no more than a form of words. With Jesus it was different: "I do not give peace as the world gives it." It was *his* peace. Even at this moment, in the toils of the traitor, compassed by his enemies, and with the dread prospect of his suffering before him, his tranquillity is undisturbed; he is at one with himself and the Father—"the peace which I give you is mine to give." [79] So he meant it to be for his followers: "For the kingdom of God is not food and drink, but righteousness and peace and

[77] John 14:27.   [78] Vs. 31.   [79] Vs. 27.

gladness in the Holy Spirit." [80] The time has come for them to leave the supper-room. "Rise up, we must be going on our way." [81]

* * *

It may well be that, before departing, our Lord uttered the prayer of praise to God, and entreaty for his disciples, recorded in the seventeenth chapter of St John. It would come most appropriately then. But it is difficult to imagine that the discourse, to be found in the fifteenth and sixteenth chapters, continued as the company was making its way through the crowded streets of Jerusalem. We may perhaps follow the suggestion of certain Catholic scholars in supposing that these two chapters contain further recollections of St John, which he embodied in the text after completing the main outline of his Gospel.[82] Certainly there would be nothing easier than for him to associate the Master's teaching on the True Vine [83] with that memorable walk through the city's darkened streets. They would have to cross the Temple court and, in doing so, would catch sight of the great golden vine that trailed over the porch. Before their eyes, glistening in the full light of the paschal moon, was the type of the life of Israel entwined about the sanctuary of God. Its rich symbolism would not be lost upon them. The Psalmist had written of the vine brought out of Egypt, now growing upon the land whence the nations had been driven out, and spreading its branches so that "the mountains were covered with its shadow." [84] They would recall the words of Isaiah:

I will sing of my friend
The song of his love for his vineyard:
My friend had a vineyard
On a fertile hill; ...
What more should I have done to my vineyard,
That I have not done to it?

[80] Rom. 14:17(S.).　　　　　[81] John 14:31.
[82] Cf. Lebreton, *op. cit.*, II, 268.　　[83] John 15:1–10.
[84] Ps. 79(80):11(Fr Lattey's translation).

> Wherefore, when I expected that it should yield grapes,
> Has it yielded sour grapes? . . .
> For the vineyard of Jahweh of hosts is the house of
> Israel
> And the men of Judah his beloved planting;
> And he expected justice, and behold bloodshed,
> And righteousness, and behold oppression.[85]

Jesus speaks: "I am the true vine, and my Father is the vine-dresser." [86] What follows, in the form of an allegory, is the theology of grace; it is the Johannine source, though in somewhat different imagery, of the Church's teaching on the mystical Body of Christ.[87] The supernatural life of the disciples has its origin in our Lord himself; they are the branches, drawing sap from the parent vine. If they yield no fruit (and they are free not to do so), they become withered and useless; then the Father, who tends the vine, will cut them away. The fruitful branch he will prune further, though the process be painful, so that it may bloom with yet more abundant life. Thereby the Father's name will be glorified and the disciples prove their worth. The divine vitality is already theirs; to preserve it they have only to keep faithful. "Abide in me, and I will abide in you." [88] If they lose faith and love they at once become impotent—"apart from me you can produce nothing." [89]

Grace and charity are merged together. "I have bestowed my love upon you, just as my Father has bestowed his love upon me; live on, then, in my love." [90] True lovers have no secrets from each other. So it is with Jesus and his chosen ones; they are no longer in a state of servitude but friendship. "I no longer call you servants, for the servant is ignorant of what his master does; but I have called you friends, because everything that I heard from my Father I have made known to you." [91] They will show their loyalty by observing

---

[85] Isa. 5:1, 4, 7(Dr Kissane's translation from the Hebrew).
[86] John 15:1(S.).   [87] See § 24; in particular, pp. 311, 325.
[88] Vs. 4(S.).   [89] Vs. 5(S.).
[90] Vs. 9.   [91] Vs. 15(S.).

their Lord's commands; he will give proof of his in a manner none can gainsay. "This is the greatest love a man can
show, that he should lay down his life for his friends." [92] But
this parting, tinged as it is with sadness, should not leave
them sorrowful. It is the loveless, self-centred man who knows
no joy. With the disciples it must be wholly otherwise. "All
this I have told you, so that my joy may be yours, and the
measure of your joy may be filled up." [93] The allegory of the
True Vine must be translated into action: "The task I have
appointed you is to go out and bear fruit, fruit which will
endure." [94] We are brought back to the precept of mutual
charity, in which all is summed up: "These are the directions
I give you, that you should love one another." [95] In this way
the living branches of the vine will show their common
origin from a single stock. *Abide in me—Love one another;*
each of these themes calls for its counterpart; where one is
lacking, the harmony is broken.

But if the disciples are united in love with Jesus Christ,
simultaneously they must incur the world's hatred: "Do not
forget what I said to you, No servant can be greater than his
master. They will persecute you just as they have persecuted
me; they will pay the same attention to your words as to
mine." [96] The direct reference here is to the active antagonism the infant Church will experience at the hands of the
men who have rejected the Messiah.[97] Our Lord's words,
however, have a universal application. Of our three chief
enemies, the world, the flesh and the devil, the first is the
most insidious in its attack. Nowadays, in a civilized country,
where at least lip-service is paid to the Christian tradition,
we have some support against the flesh and the devil. Nor
are we always persecuted for being Christians; it is even
possible to come to a working compromise with the world.
Here precisely lies the danger. To be hated is no proof that
we are followers of Christ; nevertheless, those who follow
him in earnest will always be hated. They may escape physi-

[92] John 15:13.   [93] Vs. 11.   [94] Vs. 16.
[95] Vs. 17.   [96] Vs. 20.   [97] Cf. 16:2.

cal violence, but not unpopularity and contempt. The world loves its own and hates those whom a higher allegiance keeps aloof. If we are acceptable to all, welcome companions to the irreligious and the worldlings, then we have cause to fear: "Woe upon you, when all men speak well of you." [98]

The peculiar heinousness of those who rejected Christ lay in their opposition to self-evident Goodness. Men do not in fact love the highest when they see it, unless their own dispositions are such that they can appreciate its true worth. Had not Jesus come before them, his enemies might have been pardoned their blindness. As it is they have no excuse. "If I had not done among them the works that no other hath done, they would not have sin; but now they have seen and they have hated both me and my Father." [99] It will be the same for his disciples: "They will treat you thus because you bear my name; they have no knowledge of him who sent me." [100] If he had not broken this news to them before, it was because he was still in their midst; now he forewarns them, so that when it happens, they may not be taken unawares. But when their time of trial comes, they will not be left without light and strength. Jesus will send as his witness the truth-giving Spirit, who proceeds from the Father. Under his inspiration the little company, which had kept faithful to the Lord from the beginning, would in their turn be his witnesses. But as yet they are not ready. The sense of mystery and foreboding, and the prospect of his departure, have left them speechless with sorrow. They cannot even ask him, as Peter had done earlier: [101] "Where is it thou art going?" [102] Yet, after all, it is better for them that Jesus should go. For then he will send the Spirit—the Comforter of his friends, the Advocate of his cause—who will prove his enemies wrong, him and his disciples right. Our Lord now explains what is to be the function of the Holy Spirit.[103] He

98 Luke 6:26.   99 John 15:24(W.).
100 Vs. 21.   101 Cf. 13:36.   102 16:5.
103 For a commentary on John 16:12–15, see § 21, p. 270.

will convict the world of error on three counts: "about sin, and about rightness of heart, and about judging." [104]

The sin in question is men's rejection of Christ. Many of those who are about to assist at his judicial murder will no doubt call themselves sincere,[105] say that they are acting according to their lights. But their lights are false lights. They may know no better now; but that is precisely their sin; they *should* have known. It is not enough for men to follow their conscience, if this be not awake to their real responsibilities, but dulled and insensitive to the truth. Evil deeds produce a faulty moral judgement, so that we come to think right what is in fact wrong, and thus set in train the whole course of sin. This is the sense in which the enemies of Jesus were guilty. "Rejection lies in this, that when the light came into the world men preferred darkness to light; preferred it, because their doings were evil." [106] The Holy Spirit's coming would convince the world of their guilt, vindicating Christ's claims and making glorious his Church.

The Spirit would also show that official Judaism was wrong about the nature of righteousness. Our Lord had taught that rightness of heart lay, not in the minutiae of the Law and the observance of scribal traditions, but in the love of God and one's neighbour, to which all else was subordinate. Instead of accepting him as the Master, the God-sent interpreter of the Law, they repudiated him as a revolutionary innovator, a false Messiah worthy of death. They thought that, in disposing of him, there would be an end of the matter; they would be left masters of the situation and free to continue as before. In this they were tragically wrong. They might think that they were sending him to a criminal's death on the gibbet; in truth he was returning to the Father whom they claimed to serve. "I am going back to my Father." [107] Nor would he suffer anything from them against his will. "This my Father loves in me, that I am laying down my life, to take it up again afterwards. Nobody

104 John 16:8.
106 3:19.
105 Cf. vs. 2.
107 16:10.

can rob me of it; I lay it down of my own accord. I am free
to lay it down, free to take it up again; that is the charge
which my Father has given me." [108] All this the Holy Spirit
would make clear. "To those who court their own ruin, the
message of the cross is but folly; to us, who are on the way to
salvation, it is the evidence of God's power." [109] What to the
Jewish leaders was the final ignominy, justly merited by a
blaspheming impostor, the Spirit would reveal in its true
light. "Therefore let us also, since we are encompassed by
so great a cloud of witnesses, throw aside every encumbrance
and the sin which so closely clings to us, and run with
perseverance the race set before us, looking towards Jesus
the author and perfecter of our faith; who for the joy set before him endured the cross, despising shame, and is seated at
the right hand of the throne of God." [110]

Finally, the Holy Spirit would prove the world wrong in
its judgement. When the High Priest tore his garments, and
"they all adjudged him to be deserving of death," [111] had
they but known it, it was themselves, not Jesus, they were
condemning. In this they were the ministers of Satan, "he
who rules this world," [112] and so incurred the sentence long
since passed on him.

Yes, I know you are of Abraham's breed; yet you design to
kill me, because my word does not find any place in you....
You belong to your father, that is, the devil, and are eager to
gratify the appetites which are your father's. He, from the first,
was a murderer; and as for truth, he has never taken his stand
upon that; there is no truth in him. When he utters falsehood,
he is only uttering what is natural to him; he is all false, and it
was he who gave falsehood its birth.[113]

Soon the reproach for this false judgement would be brought
home by the Holy Spirit through the mouthpiece of Peter:

This man you have put to death; by God's fixed design and foreknowledge, he was betrayed to you, and you, through the hands
of sinful men, have cruelly murdered him.... God, then, has

---

108 John 10:17–18.   109 1 Cor. 1:18.   110 Heb. 12:1–2(S.).
111 Mark 14:64(S.).   112 John 16:11.   113 8:37, 44.

raised up this man, Jesus, from the dead; we are all witnesses of it. And now, exalted at God's right hand, he has claimed from his Father his promise to bestow the Holy Spirit; and he has poured out that Spirit, as you can see and hear for yourselves.[114]

But these times of triumph were as yet in the future; at the moment the disciples are in need of comfort. It is at once forthcoming; the Lord assures them that, even though he is returning to the Father, they will see him again—"after a little while."[115] He still seems to them to be talking in riddles; they do not understand the allusion to his presence among them after the Resurrection. He explains that their case is like that of a woman in labour; she is full of distress now, but her anguish is forgotten in the joy that comes with the birth of her child. So it will be with them when, to the growing pains of faith, there succeeds the vision of the risen Christ. "I will see you again and your hearts shall rejoice. And your joy no man shall take from you."[116] Then they can make their petitions to the Father, sure of an answer and fulfilment. Let them forget their old manner of prayer, and pray in the name of Jesus: "Hitherto, you have not asked anything in my name. Ask, and you shall receive; that your joy may be full."[117] They will be heard for the reason that "the Father himself loves you, because you have loved me, and have believed that I came forth from God."[118]

Our Lord reads the unexpressed wish of the apostles, that he should speak more plainly. He has been clothing his thought in metaphors and similes; now he gives them a plain declaration: "It was from the Father I came out, when I entered the world, and now I am leaving the world, and going on my way to the Father."[119] At last, so they think, they have understood. "Why, now thou art speaking openly enough...; this gives us faith that thou wast sent by God."[120] Jesus knows that they have not fully grasped the

114 Acts 2:23, 32–33.   115 John 16:16.   116 Vs. 22(R-D.).
117 Vs. 24(R-D.).   118 Vs. 27(S.).   119 Vs. 28.
120 VV. 29–30. NOTE: In vs. 28 Christ says that he came into the world "from beside the Father" (παρὰ τοῦ πατρός) thus implying both his own pre-existence with, and procession from, the Father. In vs. 30 the disciples

implications of his words, at least not so strongly as to fortify them against the approaching scandal. "You have faith now? ... Behold, the time is coming, nay, has already come, when you are to be scattered, each of you taking his own path, and to leave me alone." [121] His hour of dereliction is near; in what he is about to undergo he will find no human support. He will be sustained only by his union with the Father. It is enough. He asks nothing from his disciples; rather it is he who gives to them. He renews the promise which accompanied the first mention of the Comforter; [122] he bequeaths them his "peace." [123] In the world, which knows no peace, they cannot find it. "But take courage, I have overcome the world." It is as a conqueror that he moves forward to death; in the moment of utter defeat, when raised upon the Cross, the victory will lie with him. "Sentence is now being passed on this world; now is the time when the prince of this world is to be cast out. Yes, if only I am lifted up from the earth, I will attract all men to myself." [124]

Having spoken his last words to the disciples, Jesus raises his eyes to heaven and prays. We may be spared all but the briefest comment upon what is surely the most sacred passage to be found in the New Testament. Our Mediator and great High Priest communes aloud with the Father, to whom he has dedicated himself in sacrifice: "Give glory now to thy Son, that thy Son may give glory to thee." [125] Such exaltation is indeed his by right; for he has been appointed ruler of all mankind, the bearer of everlasting life to his chosen ones. "Eternal life is knowing thee, who art the only true God, and Jesus Christ, whom thou hast sent." [126] The only immortality that matters is to be united in knowledge and love to God and his sole-begotten Son. Christ prays for his disciples, commending them to the Father's care:

---

acknowledge no more than that he comes "from God" (ἀπὸ Θεοῦ). They have not risen to the heights of his thought.

121 John 16:32.   122 14:26–27.   123 16:33.
124 12:31–32.   125 17:1.   126 Vs. 3.

I have made thy name known to the men whom thou hast entrusted to me, chosen out of the world. They belonged to thee, and have become mine through thy gift, and they have kept true to thy word. Now they have learned to recognize all the gifts thou gavest me as coming from thee; I have given them the message which thou gavest to me, and they, receiving it, recognized it for truth that I came from thee, and found faith to believe that it was thou who didst send me. It is for these I pray; I am not praying for the world, but for those whom thou hast entrusted to me; they belong to thee, as all I have is thine, and all thou hast is mine; and in them my glory is achieved.

I am remaining in the world no longer, but they remain in the world, while I am on my way to thee. Holy Father, keep them true to thy name, thy gift to me, that they may be one, as we are one. As long as I was with them, it was for me to keep them true to thy name; and I have watched over them, so that only one has been lost, he whom perdition claims for its own, in fulfilment of the scripture. But now I am coming to thee; and while I am still in the world I am telling them this, so that my joy may be theirs, and reach its full measure in them. I have given them thy message, and the world has nothing but hatred for them, because they do not belong to the world, as I, too, do not belong to the world. I am not asking that thou shouldst take them out of the world, but that thou shouldst keep them clear of what is evil. They do not belong to the world, as I, too, do not belong to the world; keep them holy, then, through the truth; it is thy word that is truth. Thou hast sent me into the world on thy errand, and I have sent them into the world on my errand; and I dedicate myself for their sakes, that they too may be dedicated through the truth.[127]

He prays for unity among his followers, a unity to be achieved in his Church through the work of the apostles, guided by the truth-giving Spirit:

It is not only for them that I pray; I pray for those who are to find faith in me through their word; that they may all be one; that they too may be one in us, as thou Father, art in me, and I in thee; so that the world may come to believe that it is thou who hast sent me. And I have given them the privilege which thou gavest to me, that they should all be one, as we are one;

127 John 17:6–19.

that while thou art in me, I may be in them, and so they may be perfectly made one. So let the world know that it is thou who hast sent me, and that thou hast bestowed thy love upon them, as thou hast bestowed it upon me. This, Father, is my desire, that all those whom thou hast entrusted to me may be with me where I am, so as to see my glory, thy gift made to me, in that love which thou didst bestow upon me before the foundation of the world.[128]

In this is fulfilment, the Reality which is the soul's food; without it, the delusion and misery of being confined within the afflicting bonds of selfhood. To bring us release from this last Christ goes forward to his appointed task. He proclaims the Father's justice, glad at heart to have borne him witness before the world, grateful to have won a like testimony from the disciples, and pledging himself to increase in them the knowledge of God and his love:

Father, thou art just; the world has never acknowledged thee, but I have acknowledged thee, and these men have acknowledged that thou hast sent me. I have revealed, and will reveal, thy name to them; so that the love thou hast bestowed upon me may dwell in them, and I, too, may dwell in them.[129]

*   *   *

"When Jesus had spoken these words, he went out with his disciples across the brook Kedron, where there was a garden, into which he entered with his disciples." [130] They had reached Gethsemane. He ordered those with him to be seated, while he withdrew from them—to pray. It is he who is in need of comfort now; the mood of exultation has passed and he is all but overwhelmed with sadness. Taking with him his favourite disciples, Peter, James and John—the same three who had been witnesses of a very different scene on the mount of Transfiguration—he advances a little from the group. "My soul, he said to them, is ready to die with sorrow; do you abide here, and keep watch." [131] At a stone's throw he fell prostrate on the ground and cried aloud in

---

[128] John 17:20–24.   [129] VV. 25–26.
[130] John 18:1(S.); cf. Matt. 26:30; Mark 14:26; Luke 22:39.
[131] Mark 14:34.

anguish: "Abba, Father, all things are possible to thee; take away this chalice from before me." [132] An angel comes from heaven to support him; but the sweat of fear pours from his body like drops of blood.[133] He is at one with us now in all the weakness of our humanity. Yet deep within his spirit remains the inflexible purpose: utter conformity to the wishes of the Father—"only as thy will is, not as mine is." [134] He is quite alone; those to whom he might have looked for encouragement have fallen asleep. A second and a third time he returns and gently reproaches them: "The spirit indeed is willing, but the flesh is weak." [135] Had they but observed his command—"Watch and pray"—they might not have cut such sorry figures in what followed. But now it is too late. "Enough; the time has come; behold, the Son of Man is to be betrayed into the hands of sinners. Rise up, let us go on our way; already, he that is to betray me is close at hand." [136]

Judas had agreed with the Temple guard to reveal the identity of the one they were to arrest by going up and saluting him with a kiss. He was as good as his word. "Jesus said to him, Judas, wouldst thou betray the Son of Man with a kiss?" [137] This loving reproach should have struck sorrow into the traitor's heart; instead—for his pride would suffer no reclamation—it was the beginning of his despair. Our Lord stood face to face with his assailants; so great was the impression of his dignity that they stumbled backwards, momentarily overawed.[138] Having acknowledged that he is the man they seek, Jesus of Nazareth, he asked that his disciples might be allowed to go free. But Peter, with impulsive courage, seeing them lay hands on him, drew his sword and cut off the ear of Malchus, the high priest's servant. The Lord gave no approval to such resistance; he touched the wound and healed it.[139] Recourse to violence, in the face of such odds, will only bring disaster on the chosen company and their Master's cause. Besides, that was not to be the way

[132] Mark 14:36.
[135] Vs. 38(R-D.).
[138] John 18:6.
[133] Luke 22:43–44.
[136] VV. 41–42.
[139] Luke 22:51.
[134] Mark 14:36.
[137] Luke 22:48.

of it; the chalice, from which he had prayed to be delivered, was still before him. "Am I not to drink that cup which my Father himself has appointed for me?" [140]

There was something grotesque in this military display, at the arrest of a prisoner from whom they could have anticipated no resistance, whose only crime had been to preach God's message to the people. "Then Jesus said to them aloud, You have come out to my arrest with swords and clubs, as if I were a robber; and yet I used to teach in the temple close to you, day after day, and you never laid hands on me." [141] He was alone, at the mercy of his enemies. The moment he had foretold, when he would be deserted by his friends, had come. "And now all his disciples abandoned him, and fled." [142]

Jesus was led bound before Annas, and thence to his son-in-law, Caiaphas the high priest. It was he who had advised the Sanhedrin as to the expediency of disposing of this new prophet.[143] We find him now engaged on an informal enquiry, with a view to obtaining evidence which would incriminate the prisoner at the official trial on the morrow. What he wished to establish was the charge of sedition; for he knew that only this would be likely to induce Pilate to pronounce the death sentence. So he asked Jesus about his followers and what he taught them.[144] It might be that the Galilean would welcome the opportunity of opening his mind before an audience so distinguished as the high priest and his closest associates. But Jesus had nothing to say to them. He, who had come for the express purpose of preaching God's kingdom to all who would listen, was content to clear himself of the charge of conspiracy. He had taught nothing in secret; his disciples could testify that what he had said to them in the supper-room was all of a piece with what he had proclaimed publicly.[145] The whole procedure before Caiaphas was illegal; witnesses should have been called, for the defence as well as for the prosecution, in place of this

140 John 18:11.   141 Mark 14:48–49.   142 Vs. 50.
143 John 11:49–50.   144 John 18:19.   145 Vs. 20.

attempt to convict the prisoner out of his own mouth. Jesus showed Caiaphas that he knew him to be exceeding his rights,[146] to the latter's discomfiture. For it was no doubt the high priest's obvious irritation which emboldened one of the court policemen, anxious to curry favour, to slap our Lord across the face. This, again, on a point of legality was inexcusable. Calmly Jesus points it out: "If there was harm in what I said, tell us what is harmful in it; if not, why dost thou strike me?" [147] Caiaphas saw that his ends were not to be so easily gained and adjourned the proceedings until the morning.

It was during this interrogation before the high priest that Simon Peter's courage gave way. While warming himself at the fire in the hall near by, he had been questioned and had denied knowledge of his Master. As with Judas, it was a betrayal of the cause; but how different in its circumstances and still more so in its effects upon the sinner! Simon had the heart of a penitent. "Then Peter remembered the word of Jesus, how he had said, Before the cock crows, thou wilt thrice disown me; and he went out, and wept bitterly." [148] Meanwhile our Lord, their prisoner for the night, is submitted to outrage and insult at the hands of the Jewish court officials. Was this then the Messiah, with no signs of royal dignity and no one to support him? "Then some of them fell to spitting upon him, and covering his face while they buffeted him and bade him prophesy; the servants, too, caught him blows on the cheek." [149]

Early the next morning the Sanhedrin, with the high priest presiding, met in full assembly. Jesus was brought before them. Caiaphas, grown wiser from the previous night's interview, had suborned certain witnesses. But their conflicting testimony was of little value; even the court lawyers were dissatisfied.[150] There was a vague remembrance that Jesus had spoken of the destruction of the Temple, but no agreement as to the significance of his words. The high priest,

146 John 18:21.   147 Vs. 23.   148 Matt. 26:75.
149 Mark 14:65.   150 Vs. 59.

impatient of delay, repeated the attempt to elicit a compromising confession from the prisoner: "Hast thou no answer
to make to the accusations these men bring against thee?" [151]
Jesus had none. But Caiaphas now put the crucial question,
which he knew our Lord would not refuse to answer: "Art
thou the Christ, the Son of the Blessed One?" [152] In a word,
did Jesus claim to be the Messiah? Silence was impossible for
a pious Jew before a question which he was adjured on
solemn oath [153] to answer. To this question it was on any
grounds impossible. The reply "No" would be the denial
of his life's work; to answer "Yes" would be self-condemna-
tion. Jesus said to him: "I am"; to which he added: "And
you shall see the Son of Man seated at the right hand of
Power, and coming with the clouds of heaven." [154] It was
enough; Caiaphas had gained his objective. "The high priest
thereupon tore his robes, exclaiming, What further need
have we of witnesses? You have heard the blasphemy. What
is your opinion? And they all adjudged him to be deserving
of death." [155]

[151] Matt. 26:62.   [152] Mark 14:61(S.).
[153] Matt. 26:63.   [154] Mark 14:62(S.).
[155] VV. 63–64(S.). The following passage from the Book of Deuteronomy
(13:1–5), was, in the eyes of official Judaism, the legal sanction for their
condemnation of Jesus:
"If there rise in the midst of thee a prophet or one that saith he hath
dreamed a dream, and he foretell a sign and a wonder.
"And that come to pass which he spoke, and he say to thee: Let us go and
follow strange gods, which thou knowest not, and let us serve them,
"Thou shalt not hear the words of that prophet or dreamer: for the
Lord your God trieth you, that it may appear whether you love him with
all your heart, and with all your soul, or not.
"Follow the Lord your God, and fear him, and keep his commandments,
and hear his voice: him you shall serve, and to him you shall cleave.
"*And that prophet or forger of dreams shall be slain*: because he spoke
to draw you away from the Lord your God, who brought you out of the
land of Egypt, and redeemed you from the house of bondage: to make thee
go out of the way, which the Lord thy God commanded thee: *and thou
shalt take away the evil out of the midst of thee.*" Though here it should be
noted that it was our Lord's claim to be the "Son of God" (Luke 22:70–71;
John 19:7), rather than the assertion of his Messiahship, which constituted
the "blasphemy" for which he was condemned (cf. John 5:18; 10:36). Ready
to hand lay the text from the Book of Leviticus (24:16): "And he that blasphemeth the name of the Lord, dying let him die. All the multitude shall
stone him, whether he be a native or a stranger. He that blasphemeth the
name of the Lord, dying let him die."
These were the statutes which Caiaphas and his friends thought fit to apply

He was to die for claiming to be what he was. In saving the world, Jesus Christ was a martyr—which means a witness—to the Truth.

It is at this point, as his former Master was being led from the high priest's court to the praetorium of the Roman Procurator, that we learn of the remorse of the unhappy Judas.[156] "I have sinned," he told the men with whom he had made his compact, "in betraying the blood of an innocent man." [157] Had Judas's self-reproaches turned to genuine sorrow, our Lord would have forgiven him with a look, as he had done with Peter; but the traitor's heart was hardened against such surrender and he chose another course. Seeing that his confession was of no interest to the court, "he left them, throwing down the pieces of silver there in the temple, and went and hanged himself." [158]

Meanwhile Jesus had been brought into the presence of Pontius Pilate; for it was only by his express order that the sentence of the Sanhedrin could be put into execution. The Roman Procurator was extremely loth to be involved in the religious affairs of the Jews; but the spokesmen in the crowd were astute enough to be prepared for this. They employed the age-long device of charging a witness to God's truth with being an offender against the State. The human conscience, even at its basest, rebels against persecution on purely religious grounds; some other pretext must be found. "We have discovered, they said, that this man is subverting the loyalty of our people, forbids the payment of tribute to Caesar, and calls himself Christ the king." [159]

What has the prisoner to say to this charge? Pilate puts the question directly: "Art thou the king of the Jews?" [160]

---

to the case of Jesus of Nazareth! Israel's sin, as we have already seen (John 15:22–25), was not that of knowingly rejecting her Messiah, but of not knowing him when he came. In virtue of his manifest authority and self-evident goodness, Jesus carried with him his own authenticity; the Jews should have revised both their conception of the Law and their anticipations of the Messianic office under his direction. In refusing to do this, the Law recoiled upon themselves to their destruction.

[156] Matt. 27:3–10; cf. Acts 1:15–20.   [157] Matt. 27:4.
[158] Vs. 5.   [159] Luke 23:2.   [160] John 18:33.

Our Lord, as so often, withholds a direct answer; he would first elicit the reason for this query. Was his questioner himself interested in the point? Or was it a mere official enquiry based on hearsay? A Roman procurator could hardly take kindly to the suggestion that the details of this absurd squabble were his personal concern. He doubtless knew little, and cared less, about the religious traditions of the despised Jews. "Am *I* a Jew?" [161] he asked contemptuously. It was not he, but Jesus' own people, who were making the charge; what had he done? Our Lord answers by explaining the significance of his kingship. He claims no political dominion; if he did, then it would have to be established like every earthly kingdom, by armed conquest. But with Christ nothing is won by violence. The rule of truth and love is indeed absolute in its demands; but it does not coerce; its only subjects are those who have submitted willingly to its sway. Pilate can make little of a kingdom which "does not belong to this world." [162] Puzzled, he asks, "Thou art a king, then?" [163]

Jesus does not return a direct affirmative to this. He is indeed a king, but not in any sense his questioner would understand. So he leaves Pilate with his question—"It is thy own lips that have called me a king"—and then declares his meaning. He says in effect: I am charged with aiming at kingship, but here is the real situation—"What I was born for, what I came into the world for is to bear witness of the truth. Whoever belongs to the truth, listens to my voice." [164] This is the clearest single statement in the Gospels of our Lord's mission and the nature of the kingdom of God. All kingdoms which "belong to this world" are based in some measure upon falsehood; the power which holds them in being is, in the last resort, force. Their claim to be a real community of people is largely a legal fiction, a façade beneath which lie the elements of compulsion sustaining their unity. It is a fact that earthly kingdoms are also upheld

[161] John 18:35.   [162] Vs. 36.
[163] Vs. 37.   [164] Vs. 37.

by sentiments of kinship and good will among their members. This sense of solidarity may reach as far as the well-being of the nation; but that it does not extend further, that its limits are precisely what give rise to many kingdoms, existing side by side in mutual rivalry or self-interested alliance, is itself a proof that they do not rest on ultimate truth. What Christ came to bear witness to was quite otherwise—"my kingdom does not take its origin here." [165] His rulership was based on the real constitution of the universe in its relation to God; this was the *Truth*—to be realized progressively as mankind, listening to Christ's voice, joined with him in common brotherhood under the Father. "There can be neither Jew nor Greek, there can be neither slave nor freeman, there can be no male and female, for you all are one in Christ Jesus." [166]

" 'What is truth?' [167] said jesting Pilate and would not wait for an answer." [168] It would have been better had he waited. The answer, did he but know it, was before him. "I am the truth." [169] But if the practical-minded Pilate could fathom nothing of this, he could at least see that no danger to the State lay in a harmless Jewish visionary. "I can find no fault in him," [170] he told the crowd. At this the shouts of denunciation increased.[171] Hearing that Jesus was a Galilean, Pilate, hoping thus to rid himself of an unpleasant affair, sent him under escort to Herod Antipas, who had come to Jerusalem for the Passover. The superstitious Herod was delighted at the prospect of an interview with so famous a wonder-worker. "He asked him many questions, but could get no answer from him, although the chief priests and scribes stood there, loudly accusing him." [172] So, having put the prisoner to public mockery, he sent him back to Pilate. "That day, Herod and Pilate, who had hitherto been at enmity with one another, became friends." [173]

[165] John 18:36. [166] Gal. 3:28(S.). [167] John 18:38.
[168] Francis Bacon, *Of Truth*. [169] John 14:6.
[170] 18:38. [171] Luke 23:5.
[172] Luke 23:9–10. [173] Vs. 12.

Pilate, for his part, had gained nothing. But another way of escape from the painful business suggested itself. It was the custom for the Jews to have a prisoner released to them at the Passover festival. Perhaps he could dispose of Jesus that way. True, he had there in gaol a notorious character named Barabbas—"a man who had been thrown into prison for raising a revolt in the city, and for murder" [174]—but the crowd was unlikely to prefer him to this inoffensive Galilean. "So, when they gathered about him, Pilate asked them, Whom shall I release? Barabbas, or Jesus who is called the Christ?" [175] "But the chief priests and elders had persuaded the multitude to ask for Barabbas and have Jesus put to death." [176] Pilate was powerless to quell the popular clamour. The cry went up: "Not this man, but Barabbas." [177] What then was he to do with Jesus, who had done no wrong? They said: "Let him be crucified." [178] The leaders of the Jewish nation had made their choice. "Barabbas," St John tells us, "was a robber." [179]

"Then Pilate took Jesus and scourged him. And the soldiers put on his head a crown which they had woven out of thorns, and dressed him in a scarlet cloak; they would come up to him and say, Hail, king of the Jews, and then strike him on the face." [180] Christians throughout the ages were to look back on this scene with pity and horror. Many of the saints have told us that our divine Saviour endured the scourging in atonement for our sins of the flesh! How unanswerable a rebuke to all earthly glory is the thought that the only crown ever worn by him who is "the King of kings and the Lord of lords" [181] was a wreath of thorns battered upon his head as a mark of ridicule! Even Pilate felt a twinge of contemptuous pity at the sight of a prisoner in whom he could find no fault reduced to this abject spectacle. He brought him out before the people, hoping to move them

174 Luke 23:19.   175 Matt. 27:17.   176 Vs. 20.
177 John 18:40(R-D.).   178 Matt. 27:22.   179 John 18:40.
180 19:1–3.   181 Apoc. 19:16.

to mercy, and said: "Behold the man." [182] He was greeted
with shouts of "Crucify him, crucify him." [183]

It was idle for Pilate to try to force responsibility for the
crucifixion on the Jews themselves; they appealed to their
own Law, which he, as the Roman Procurator, was pledged
to respect. Pilate himself must order the execution, for Jesus
was guilty of "pretending to be the Son of God." [184] *"Son
of God!"*—Pilate's superstitious fears were aroused at this.
"Whence hast thou come?" [185] he asked. Impatient at receiving no reply, he reminded Jesus that the power of life
and death lay in his hands. Calmly the answer came: "Thou
wouldst not have any power over me at all, if it had not been
given thee from above. That is why the man who gave me
up to thee is more guilty yet." [186] Such delegated authority
as Pilate had came to him in the last resort, not from Caesar,
but from God. Here, for all his bluster and moral cowardice,
he was acting merely as the executive of the law; the malice
of Judas and Caiaphas was the driving force behind the
crime.

The prisoner's quiet assessment of motives, his appeal to
God's authority, his ability to act as judge in his own case,
were only the more convincing proofs to Pilate of his innocence. He "was for releasing him." [187] But the Jewish
leaders made their final thrust; if he did so, he was "no
friend to Caesar . . . ; the man who pretends to be a king is
Caesar's rival." They had succeeded; Pilate could not suffer
even the appearance of disloyalty to Rome. He sat down on
the seat of judgement. The message of his wife's dream might
shake, but it could not deter him now.[188] The theatrical gesture of washing his hands of innocent blood would be understood by the Jews; [189] it could hardly have appeased them.
Nor could it render him who performed it guiltless of condemning a just man. But, with terrible irony, the responsi-

[182] John 19:5(R-D.).   [183] Vs. 6.   [184] Vs. 7.
[185] Vs. 9.   [186] Vs. 11.   [187] Vs. 12.
[188] Matt. 27:19.   [189] Cf. Deut. 21:6.

bility was claimed by those to whom it belonged: "And the whole people answered, His blood be upon us, and upon our children." [190] Jesus was sentenced to crucifixion. The day was that of the preparation for the Passover; the time, about six hours after sunrise, twelve o'clock noon.

Jesus dragged his own cross after him, "to a place called Golgotha, which means, The place of a skull." [191] Too weak to go on alone, he was helped by Simon of Cyrene. Seeing a group of women who mourned for him, our Lord turned to them and said: "It is not for me that you should weep, daughters of Jerusalem; you should weep for yourselves and your children. Behold, a time is coming when men will say, It is well for the barren, for the wombs that never bore children, and the breasts that never suckled them. It is then that they will begin to say to the mountains, Fall on us, and to the hills, Cover us." [192] Having arrived at the place of execution, he was offered a draught of wine mixed with gall. Jesus moistened his lips, but would not drink; this was not the chalice appointed him by the Father. Then they crucified him. And with him two thieves, "one on the right and the other on his left, so fulfilling the words of scripture, And he was counted among the wrong-doers." [193] Above his head was nailed a placard bearing the inscription, in Greek, Latin and Hebrew, "Jesus of Nazareth, the king of the Jews." [194] Beneath the Cross the soldiers shared out his garments among them, and not wishing to cut up his seamless robe, cast lots for it. As the Victim's agony went on, he was derided by passers-by, by the chief priests, the scribes and elders, and by the Roman soldiers. Was not this a fitting end for a deluded visionary who had claimed to be the Messiah? "The chief priests, with the scribes and elders, mocked him in the same way. He saved others, they said, he cannot save himself. If he is the king of Israel, he has but to come down from the cross, here and now, and we will believe in him.

[190] Matt. 27:25.   [191] Mark 15:22.   [192] Luke 23:28–30.
[193] Mark 15:27–28; Isa. 53:12.   [194] John 19:19.

He trusted in God; let God, if he favours him, succour him now; he told us, I am the Son of God." [195]

Jesus had spoken from the Cross: "Father, forgive them, for they know not what they do." [196] He who had so often taught that men must forgive their enemies, now gives us the most eloquent lesson of all—the sermon of the dying Christ. At the foot of the Cross was standing Mary his Mother, and near by the beloved disciple, John. "Woman, this is thy son," Jesus said to her; and to him: "This is thy mother." [197] St John was young enough then to be our Lady's son; at that moment all Christendom stood with him. It was not for himself alone that "from that hour the disciple took her into his own keeping." Even the thieves, who had been crucified with Christ, joined in the common mockery; [198] but one of them, touched by the grace of faith, at length turned to him and said: "Lord, remember me when thou comest into thy kingdom." [199] He was rewarded with words of consolation and hope: "I promise thee, this day thou shalt be with me in Paradise." [200] Then the whole sky grew dark, a symbol of the clouding of the mind of Jesus. It seemed that his Father, for whose honour he had lived and come to die, was now deserting him. His words bear witness to the dereliction of the Son of Man: "Eloi, Eloi, lama sabachthani? which means, My God, my God, why hast thou forsaken me?" [201] It was the dark night of the soul, from which so many Christian mystics, who were later to share his experience, would draw their strength. The words were those of a Hebrew Psalm, spoken by our Lord in Aramaic:

> My God, my God, why hast thou forsaken me,
>   Being far from my cry, and from the words I roar?
> My God, I call by day, but thou answerest not:
>   And by night, but I find no respite.[202]

The Psalm ends with sentiments of gratitude for God's triumph:

[195] Matt. 27:41–43.   [196] Luke 23:34(R-D.).   [197] John 19:26–27.
[198] Luke 23:39.   [199] Luke 23:42.   [200] Vs. 43.
[201] Mark 15:34.   [202] Ps. 21(22):1–2.

All the ends of the earth shall remember,
And shall return unto Jehovah,
And all the clans of the nations
Shall worship before him. . . .
They shall tell of my Lord
To the generation which is to come:
They shall declare his justness
To a people which shall be born,
Even that so Jehovah wrought.[203]

But the opening verses held a terrible reality for Jesus. In truth, as St Paul was to write: "Christ ransomed us from the curse of the law by becoming a curse for us; for it is written, Cursed is anyone hanging upon a tree." [204]

The end was near. Our Lord's parched lips were murmuring: "I thirst." [205] Again the context is that of the Psalms, which tell of the suffering of the just man:

Thyself knowest my reproach and my shame and my confusion:
All mine adversaries are in thy sight.
Reproach hath broken my heart,
And I am sore sick.
And I looked for one to console me, but there was none,
And for comforters, but I found not.
And they put poison into my food,
And in my thirst they gave me vinegar to drink.[206]

A sponge dipped in vinegar was offered him, and he drank. He had accomplished the work his Father had given him to do.[207] Testifying to its complete achievement, he uttered the words: "It is finished." [208] "Crowned, now, with glory and honour," [209] he could return to the Father, whence he had come. "And Jesus said, crying with a loud voice, Father, into thy hands I commend my spirit; and yielded up his spirit as he said it." [210] When he had shown by this strong cry that he freely surrendered himself to death, Jesus died. At the

203 Ps. 21(22):28, 31–32(Psalm in Fr. Lattey's version).
204 Gal. 3:13(S.). Cf. Deut. 21:23.   205 John 19:28(R-D.).
206 Ps. 68(69):20–22(Fr. Lattey's version).
207 John 17:4.   208 19:30(W.).
209 Heb. 2:9.   210 Luke 23:46.

moment when the Jews were preparing to keep the ancient Passover—"the shadow of those blessings which were still to come"[211]—the true Paschal Lamb was sacrificed. The Temple ritual, which now presaged nothing, had become no more than empty pageantry. As if to symbolize the passing of its glory, "behold, the curtain of the temple was rent in two from top to bottom."[212]

Presently the soldiers came, and finding that our Lord was already dead, one of them "opened his side with a spear; and immediately blood and water flowed out."[213]

After this Joseph of Arimathea, who was a disciple of Jesus, but in secret, for fear of the Jews, asked Pilate to let him take away the body of Jesus. Pilate gave him leave; so he came and took Jesus' body away; and with him was Nicodemus, the same who made his first visit to Jesus by night; he brought with him a mixture of myrrh and aloes, of about a hundred pounds' weight. They took Jesus' body, then, and wrapped it in winding-cloths with the spices; that is how the Jews prepare a body for burial. In the same quarter where he was crucified there was a garden, with a new tomb in it, one in which no man had ever yet been buried. Here, since the tomb was close at hand, they laid Jesus, because of the Jewish feast on the morrow.[214]

* * *

After his death on the Cross the Son of God, with the human soul he had assumed, went down into Hades. It was fitting that he, who had died for the salvation of all men, should so present himself to the souls of the Patriarchs, and of all those who had confidently awaited, but had not lived to see, his coming. By descending to the depths and then ascending to the highest heaven Christ has claimed the whole universe as his rightful possession.[215] Our Lord's soul was present substantially only in the limbo where dwelt the righteous of Old Testament times; though the power which radiated from him extended to all the inhabitants of

211 Heb. 10:1. 212 Matt. 27:51(S.). 213 John 19:34.
214 VV. 38–42. 215 Cf. Eph. 4:7–10.

Hades.[216] To the redeemed souls he brought the long-looked-for liberation; even though he had not yet ascended into heaven, he shed upon them the light of glory.[217] Thus his promise to the good thief was fulfilled: "This day thou shalt be with me in Paradise." [218] To those who could not otherwise have heard it, he now declared the message of salvation he had proclaimed on earth. "In his mortal nature he was done to death, but endowed with fresh life in his spirit, and it was in his spirit that he went and preached to the spirits who lay in prison." [219] But Christ's soul could not long remain in Hades, since to him applied the words which David addressed to God: "Thou wilt not leave my soul to the abode of the dead, nor wilt thou suffer thy holy one to see corruption." [220] Hence it was that "God raised him up again, releasing him from the pangs of death; it was impossible that death should have the mastery over him." [221]

[216] St Thomas, III, q. 52, art. 2.   [217] Ibid., art. 5.
[218] Luke 23:43.   [219] 1 Pet. 3:18–19.
[220] Acts 2:27(S.).   [221] Vs. 24.

§ 11. THE RESURRECTION

We cannot be quite certain of the precise order of events on Easter Sunday morning.[1] But if there is some obscurity in regard to details, there is none at all about the main picture. We know that, "at very early dawn on the first day of

[1] As the scope of the present work is doctrinal rather than exegetical and historical, we shall not attempt a critical examination of the evangelists' accounts of what led up to, and followed upon, the discovery of the empty tomb. Materials are lacking for a wholly satisfactory reconstruction of what happened; though, as Lagrange remarks, "The four evangelists relate, each in his own way, how the tomb of Jesus was found empty, to the great astonishment of Christ's friends. St Matthew and St Mark are the most alike. St Luke is usually closer to St Mark. As for St John, he goes his own way, but is in agreement with St Luke concerning the search made by Peter. The difficulty of harmonizing the four accounts has been greatly exaggerated. Nothing is more simple, provided we do not stick at unimportant details, provided also we pay attention to the way in which each Gospel was composed."—Op. cit., p. 582 (E.T. II, 283). For details cf. pp. 581–605 (282–305) with the same scholar's Synopsis Evangelica, nn. 306–320.

the week" [2] Mary Magdalen and the devout women made their way to the tomb where they had seen their Lord buried and, arriving there, found it empty. The significance of this discovery was revealed to them by the angelic message: "Why are you seeking one who is alive, here among the dead? He is not here, he has risen again; remember how he told you, while he was still in Galilee, The Son of Man is to be given up into the hands of sinners, and to be crucified, and to rise again the third day." [3] The report that the tomb was empty was brought at once to the eleven, as well as to the other disciples, and was verified without delay by Peter and John. Even the "beloved disciple," who had been given the deepest insight into his Master's teaching, had still to realize that Calvary was but the prelude to the Resurrection. "Then the other disciple, who had reached the tomb first, also went in, and saw this, and learned to believe. They had not yet mastered what was written of him, that he was to rise from the dead." [4]

"But he had risen again, at dawn on the first day of the week, and showed himself first of all to Mary Magdalen." [5] She heard someone, whom she took to be a gardener, saying to her: "Why art thou weeping? For whom art thou searching?" [6] Only a moment before she had been explaining to the angels the reason for her tears—"Because they have carried away my Lord, she said, and I cannot tell where they have taken him." [7] Not until Jesus calls her by her name does she recognize him—"Mary." Throwing herself at his feet, she answered, "Rabboni (which is the Hebrew for Master)." [8] But this was not the time for penitence and the old familiar expressions of devotion; a new and more spiritual relationship had come into being. Besides, the great tidings of the Resurrection must be brought to the faithful before Jesus ascended into heaven. As yet he was still on earth; Mary had no need to handle to make sure that it was

[2] Luke 24:1.
[3] VV. 5–7; cf. Mark 16:6–7; Matt. 28:5–6.
[4] John 20:8–9.   [5] Mark 16:9.   [6] John 20;15.
[7] Vs. 13.   [8] Vs. 16.

he: "Do not hold me, for I have not yet ascended to my
Father; but go to my brethren, and say to them, I ascend to
my Father and your Father, to my God and your God." [9]

On the afternoon of Easter Sunday our Lord appeared to
the two disciples on the road to Emmaus. They too did not
at first know who it was who had joined them on their
journey. The events of the past days, and the scandal of the
Cross, weighed heavy upon them. Even when he expounded
their true meaning, that the Messiah's sufferings were what
had been foretold of him by the prophets, their eyes remained closed. They could see no point in his question:
"Ought not the Christ to have suffered these things, and
thus enter into his glory?" [10] It was at their evening meal together, on seeing his characteristic way of blessing and break-
ing bread, that at length they knew him. "And they said
to one another, Were not our hearts burning within us when
he spoke to us on the road, and when he made the scriptures
plain to us?" [11]

So the news was brought to the apostolic company: "The
Lord has indeed risen, and has appeared to Simon. And
they told the story of their encounter in the road, and how
they recognized him when he broke bread." [12] They had not
long to wait for the fullest confirmation: "And now it was
evening on the same day, the first day of the week; for fear
of the Jews, the disciples had locked the doors of the room
in which they had assembled; and Jesus came, and stood in
their midst. Peace be unto you, he said." [13] It was his well-
known greeting. But they were still incredulous, thinking
that they were victims of hallucination, or that they saw a
spirit; they needed his reassurance.

What, he said to them, are you dismayed? Whence come these
surmises in your hearts? Look at my hands and my feet, to be
assured that it is myself; touch me, and look; a spirit has not
flesh and bones, as you see that I have. And as he spoke thus, he
showed them his hands and his feet. Then, while they were still
doubtful, and bewildered with joy, he asked them, Have you any-

[9] John 20:17(S.).   [10] Luke 24:26(W.).   [11] Vs. 32.
[12] Vs. 34-35.   [13] John 20:19; cf. Luke 24:36-37.

thing here to eat? So they put before him a piece of roast fish, and a honeycomb; and he took these and ate in their presence.[14]

Having satisfied the apostles' desire for concrete evidence, the Lord again wished them "Peace," and told them of the work which he was presently to entrust to them: "I came upon an errand from my Father, and now I am sending you out in my turn."[15] What follows shows that this commission had to do with spiritual authority and the care of souls. Having breathed on them, he said: "Receive the Holy Ghost; whose sins you forgive they are forgiven them; and whose sins you retain they are retained."[16] With these words the apostles were endued with power, in God's name, to give pardon to the repentant sinner, or to withhold it from the unrepentant;—an act of spiritual jurisdiction which demands knowledge of the individual's state of soul and therefore implies the confession of sins. It was thus, on the evening of the first Easter Sunday, that our Lord instituted the sacrament of Penance.

The apostle Thomas, loyal and courageous but distrustful of mere hearsay, was absent from this appearance of the risen Christ. Nothing would induce him to credit it. "Until I have seen the mark of the nails on his hands, until I have put my finger into the mark of the nails, and put my hand into his side, you will never make me believe."[17] Jesus is very tender with this doubting but much loved disciple. Eight days later he appeared again, when Thomas was present. "Then he said to Thomas, Let me have thy finger; see here are my hands. Let me have thy hand; put it into my side. Cease thy doubting, and believe."[18] We are more than compensated for this moment of scepticism. In the post-resurrection faith of the doubting Thomas the New Testament records the authentic expression of the Church's belief in the person of Jesus Christ: "My Lord and my God."[19] Nevertheless, it remained faith and was not vision; since what Thomas saw was the risen humanity of Jesus, but what he believed in was his divinity. Still, he had been at fault;

[14] Luke 24:38–43. [15] John 20:21. [16] VV. 22–23(S.).
[17] Vs. 25. [18] Vs. 27. [19] Vs. 28.

for he should have accepted this, as millions were to receive it afterwards, on the testimony of accredited witnesses. This is what Christ impresses upon him, in words of forgiveness and gentle reproach: "Thou hast learned to believe, Thomas, because thou hast seen me. Blessed are those who have not seen, and yet have learned to believe." [20] "He calls Thomas, and through him every unbelieving soul, to open his own heart and to receive the full assurance of the Resurrection." [21]

But it was not only at Jerusalem that the disciples were to see their risen Master. He had made an appointment with them in their native Galilee, where they had first met together and would be most at ease in finding him. On the morning of Easter Day, to the holy women at the empty tomb, the angel had said: "Go and tell Peter and the rest of his disciples that he is going before you into Galilee. There you shall have sight of him, as he promised you." [22] As always, he is faithful to his word. Most fittingly he chose an occasion which would bring back memories of those early happy days when he had called them to his company. He came to them on the shores of the Lake of Galilee. Simon Peter, Thomas, Nathanael, the sons of Zebedee, and two others were there. They were fishing as of old, earning a livelihood, until the Holy Spirit should come as the Lord had promised, giving them power to become fishers of men.[23] John was the first to recognize him, standing there on the bank. "It is the Lord," [24] he said to Peter. Jesus had made a fire and, having told them to bring some of their great haul of fishes, he invited them to break their fast with him. They watched in awe-struck silence, as he broke bread in the way they knew so well and handed it to them.

It was after this meal that Jesus drew from Peter his threefold profession of love in answer to the thrice-repeated question: "Simon, son of John, dost thou love me?" [25] Taught wisdom as well as penitence by his denials, Peter had lost

[20] John 20:28.
[21] Origen, *In Canticum Canticorum (Pericopiana)* 5. *P.G.* 13, col. 205.
[22] Mark 16:7–8.   [23] Cf. Matt. 4:19.
[24] John 21:7.   [25] VV. 15–17(S.).

his impetuous self-confidence. He relied now, not on the force of his own protestations, but on his Master's knowledge of men's hearts: "Lord, thou knowest all things; thou knowest that I love thee." [26] He was rewarded by being entrusted with the care of Christ's flock. Peter was appointed shepherd over the sheep for whom Christ had laid down his life.[27] The perpetuity of his office, as the visible Head of Christ's Church, had been made known after his profession of faith at Caesarea Philippi; he was the "rock," [28] as durable as the Church itself, co-extensive with its life, "until the consummation of the world." [29] Here, in response to his profession of love, was given him the universality of the pastoral charge. There would always be sheep of the Christian flock; different sheep, as age succeeded age; so there would ever be a Peter, a shepherd to tend the flock until "the Chief Shepherd makes his appearance," to reward every true pastor with "the unfading wreath of glory." [30]

The New Testament makes it clear that our Lord appeared to the disciples on occasions of which we have no explicit record in the Gospels. St Luke, for example, tells us that, "he had shown them by many proofs that he was still alive, after his passion; throughout the course of forty days he had been appearing to them, and telling them about the kingdom of God." [31] We gather also from St Paul "that he was seen by Cephas, then by the eleven apostles, and afterwards by more than five hundred of the brethren at once, most of whom are alive at this day, though some have gone to their rest." [32] The striking manifestation here mentioned must almost certainly have been in Galilee; for only there would so great a number of believers be available at call. At all events, a Galilean mountain side was the scene of his appearance to the eleven, where he gave them their final instructions: "All authority in heaven and on earth, he said, has been given to me; you, therefore, must go out, making disciples of all nations, and baptizing them in the name of

[26] John 21:17.   [27] Cf. 10:15.   [28] Matt. 16:18.
[29] 28:20.   [30] 1 Pet. 5:4(S.).   [31] Acts 1:3.
[32] 1 Cor. 15:5–6; see vv. 7–8.

the Father, and of the Son, and of the Holy Ghost, teaching them to observe all the commandments which I have given you." [33] To which he added the promise of his abiding presence throughout all time.

Allusion has just been made to St Paul's witness to the Resurrection. His account is in fact our earliest written record of that great event; for the First Epistle to the Corinthians was composed perhaps as much as twenty years before the existing text of the Synoptic Gospels. Broadly speaking, it may be said that, while the evangelists concentrate upon chronicling the best-remembered appearances of the risen Lord from Easter Day to the Ascension, St Paul is concerned with the significance of Christ's triumph over death as it affects the lives of all Christians. He sees in the Cross the decisive conquest of sin, in the Resurrection the new life of innocence which we are meant to share. The faithful were to learn "that Christ, having risen from the dead, dies no more. Death has no more dominion over him. For in dying he died to sin once for all; but in living he lives to God. Thus must you also regard yourselves as dead to sin, but as living to God in Christ Jesus." [34]

The Resurrection is the divine witness to man's immortality, the pledge that death is not the end, but rather the prelude to everlasting life. "If we have a hope in Christ only for this life, we are of all men most pitiable. But, in fact, Christ has risen from the dead, the first-fruits of those who sleep. For since by a man came death, by a man also came the resurrection of the dead; for as in Adam all die, so also in the Christ shall all be made alive." [35] Christ's headship of his mystical Body, the Church, is closely connected with the fact of the Resurrection. "He too is that head whose body is the Church; it begins with him, since his was the first birth out of death; thus in every way the primacy was to become his." [36] St John, in the Apocalypse, bears the same witness to the achievement of our risen Lord: "Jesus Christ, the faithful witness, first-born of the risen

33 Matt. 28:18–20.
35 1 Cor. 15:19–22(S.).
34 Rom. 6:9–11(S.).
36 Col. 1:18.

dead, who rules over all earthly kings. He has proved his love for us, by washing us clean from our sins in his own blood, and made us a royal race of priests, to serve God, his Father; glory and power be his through endless ages, Amen." [37]

Above all, it is in the Resurrection that we find the crown and fulfillment of Calvary. By his death on the Cross our Lord had accomplished our redemption; such was the significance of his dying words—"It is finished." [38] But his rising again put the seal of completion on that work; he was "handed over to death for our sins, and raised to life for our justification." [39] So the sacrament of regeneration, Christian Baptism, symbolizes our passage through the tomb with Jesus, to be born again with a new kind of existence. "We were buried therefore with him by baptism into death; so that, as Christ rose from the dead in the glory of the Father, thus we also might walk in newness of life." [40] And this rebirth, when brought to full fruition, embraces the body as well as the soul. Christ at his final coming "will form this humbled body of ours anew, moulding it into the image of his glorified body, so effective is his power to make all things obey him." [41] Thus his rising from the grave forms an integral part of his redeeming work; Good Friday cannot be thought of without its complement on Easter Sunday. The Atonement, achieved through our Lord's Passion and death, was consummated in the Resurrection. These three phases taken together are what fulfil the prophecies concerning the Messiah, as he himself was to remind the apostles at his last meeting with them in Jerusalem. "Then he opened their minds to understand the scriptures. Thus it is written, he told them, that the Christ should suffer, and rise again from the dead on the third day." [42]

It was in accordance with God's plan that the final scene should have Jerusalem for its setting. "For from Sion shall go forth teaching, and the word of Jahweh from Jerusalem." [43] Our Lord's appearance to James, as mentioned

[37] Apoc. 1:5–6. [38] John 19:30(W.). [39] Rom. 4:25.
[40] 6:4(S.). [41] Phil. 3:21. [42] Luke 24:45–46(S.).
[43] Isa. 2:3(Kissane); cf. Mich. 4:1–2.

by St Paul,[44] and then to all the apostles, was doubtless identical with that recorded by St Luke.[45] It took place at Jerusalem, whither he must have required his disciples to return, there to await the coming of the Holy Spirit. Only then would they be empowered to begin their work of preaching the Gospel. Appearing in their midst, Christ told them how "repentance and remission of sins should be preached in his name to all the nations, beginning at Jerusalem." [46] Of these good tidings they were to be the witnesses; though, for the present, they must remain in the city, awaiting "the gift which was promised by my Father," when they would be "clothed with power from on high." [47]

With these parting instructions our Lord takes leave of his disciples. The time had come for him to ascend to the Father. "When he had led them out as far as Bethany, he lifted up his hands and blessed them; and even as he blessed them he parted from them, and was carried up into heaven." [48] "And so the Lord Jesus, when he had finished speaking to them, was taken up to heaven, and is seated now at the right hand of God." [49] Thus did he reach the summit of his exaltation in glory. His being seated symbolizes the heavenly peace to which he has attained; for us it is the pledge of that rest from labour which awaits our toiling humanity. His place at God's right hand signifies his sharing in the Father's royalty and judicial power.[50] He is now the ever glorious Son of God, a "Son whom he appointed heir of all things, and through whom he made the worlds. He being the effulgence of God's glory and the very image of his substance upholds the universe by God's powerful mandate. After effecting purification from sins, he seated himself at the right hand of the Majesty on high, having been made as much superior to the angels as he had inherited a more distinguished name than they." [51] There, as our great High Priest, "he is able for all time to save

44 1 Cor. 15:7.   45 Luke 24:44–49.   46 Vs. 47.
47 Vs. 48.   48 Vs. 50–51.   49 Mark 16:19.
50 Cf. Eph. 1:18–23.   51 Heb. 1:2–4(S.).

those who come to God through him, since he is always living to intercede for them." [52]

Meanwhile the disciples, having bowed down in worship before their ascending Lord, "went back full of joy to Jerusalem, where they spent the time continually in the temple, praising and blessing God." [53] Now they had only a few days to wait for that ever memorable Whit Sunday. Assurance came to them amid "a sound from heaven like that of a strong wind blowing" [54] and the Pentecostal fire. Then Peter, the shepherd of the Christian flock, inspired with the fearless eloquence of the Holy Spirit, rose to defend the life-work of his Master:

Men of Israel, listen to this. Jesus of Nazareth was a man duly accredited to you from God; such were the miracles and wonders and signs which God did through him in your midst, as you yourselves well know. This man you have put to death; by God's fixed design and foreknowledge, he was betrayed to you, and you through the hands of sinful men have cruelly murdered him. But God raised him up again, releasing him from the pangs of death; it was impossible that death should have the mastery over him. . . . God, then, has raised up this man, Jesus, from the dead; we are all witnesses of it. And now, exalted at God's right hand, he has claimed from his Father his promise to bestow the Holy Spirit; and he has poured out that Spirit, as you can see and hear for yourselves. . . . Let it be known, then, beyond doubt, to all the house of Israel, that God has made him Master and Christ, this Jesus whom you crucified.[55]

[52] Heb. 7:25(S.).
[54] Acts 2:2.
[53] Luke 24:52–53.
[55] VV. 22–24, 32–33, 36.

CHAPTER III

THE PERSONALITY OF JESUS

HAVING seen, in broad outline, the significance of our Lord's
life-work, we must now attempt to enter more deeply into
the mystery of his personality. What precise answer are we
to give to the question: Who is Jesus Christ? The Greek
word Χριστός does not, of course, correspond to a surname;
it designates an office, being an exact rendering of the Hebrew word which scholars transliterate as *mâshiah* (in
Aramaic, *meshiḥa*). Thus, when we add to the name "Jesus"
that of "Christ," we implicitly acknowledge that he is the
fulfilment of the Jewish prophecies concerning the Messiah.
This is the point made by St Matthew, at the end of his
genealogy of our Lord, when he tells us that "Jacob begot
Joseph, the husband of Mary, of whom was born Jesus,
who is called Christ." [1] It is likewise this which made St
Peter's confession of faith at Caesarea Philippi so striking:
"Thou art the Christ." [2] For he was then giving his Master
a title, the laying claim to which brought about his death,
since the Jews held, and still hold, that he was no more
than a pretender to the Messianic office. It should be clear,
then, that the whole drama of the acceptance and rejection
of Jesus hinges upon the meaning of *Messiah*. The title by
which he is most familiar to us, viz., "the Lord"—*our* Lord—
was originally closely linked with his Messiahship. We shall
see that the revealed doctrine concerning Christ, more particularly with reference to his being the *Son of God,* transcends even the loftiest conceptions of Jewish Messianism;
but it is indispensable to our right understanding of him
to realize what was implied in his claim to be Israel's
Messiah.

[1] Matt. 1:16(R-D.).   [2] Mark 8:29; cf. Matt. 16:16.

§ 12. THE MESSIAH

It was a commonplace of Jewish thought that their national God, Yahweh,[1] was to be attended by an Anointed One—for that is the meaning of the word "Messiah"—to whom he would delegate all or a part of his executive functions. In the coronation ceremony of an Israelite king the essential feature was not the crowning, but the anointing.[2] This was regarded as a special grace conferred upon his chosen servant by Yahweh. There was also a sense in which the nation itself was considered to be anointed, and so to bear a Messianic character. In this connection there can be little doubt that the famous fifty-third chapter of Isaiah, which the New Testament shows to have been a prophecy of the passion of Christ, had little significance for the Jewish teachers of our Lord's day.[3] The Rabbis, their minds filled with the anticipated splendours of the kingdom, shut their eyes to those texts which predicted the sufferings of the Lord's Anointed. It was not until the latter half of the second century A.D. that they realized that Isaiah had foretold them; though even then they were interpreted as applying to a personification, either of Israel as a whole, or of the dynasty of David. This incomprehension is what explains, more than any other single factor, why a "crucified Christ" was "a stumbling-block to the Jews." [4] It has remained so to this day.

Quite apart from considerations of Catholic dogma, no serious student of the New Testament can doubt that Jesus both thought of, and finally proclaimed himself to be, the long-awaited Messiah. Commenting on the one-time fashionable assumption that our Lord never looked upon himself as the Messiah, and only after his death was acclaimed as such by his disciples, a distinguished Jewish scholar shrewdly

---

[1] We adopt this, the more common, spelling; except when citing translations from the Hebrew where another is used; see p. 75 n.

[2] Cf. 3 Kings(1 Kings) 19:16.

[3] For the identity of the *Servant of Yahweh* in Isaiah 52:13—53:12, see Dr E. J. Kissane's *The Book of Isaiah*, Vol. 2, pp. 175–191.

[4] 1 Cor. 1:23(S.).

remarks, "... had this been true it would never have occurred to his disciples (simple-minded Jews) that one who had suffered crucifixion ("a curse of God is he that is hanged") could be the Messiah; and the Messianic idea meant nothing whatever to the Gentile converts. *Ex nihilo nihil fit:* when we see that Jesus' Messianic claims became a fundamental principle of Christianity soon after his crucifixion, this is standing proof that even in his lifetime Jesus regarded himself as the Messiah." [5]

According to the Johannine account, Jesus was recognized as the Messiah, the one "Moses wrote of in his law, and the prophets too," [6] from the early days of his ministry. He does not, however, appear to have wished to divulge his Messianic character to the people at large. "Then he strictly forbade them to tell any man that he, Jesus, was the Christ; [7] "and he strictly charged them not to tell anyone about him." [8] Consistently with this, he never unequivocally ascribed to himself, in the hearing of the Jewish crowds, one of the common names of the Messiah. He knew that such a disclosure would give rise to the popular demand that he should fulfil the role generally assigned to his office. After one of his exorcisms, St Luke tells us that "he rebuked them and would not have them speak, because they knew that he was the Christ." [9] His self-effacement was such that he would conceal his own identity, rather than allow a premature revelation of it to prejudice his mission of convincing men of the paramount claims of his heavenly Father and the dire need of their own souls.

But the simple folk could not refrain from ascribing to him the most popular of all the Messianic titles: "Is not this the Son of David?" [10] So, in effect, the act of recognition had come, from the woman of Samaria,[11] from the Canaanite woman,[12] above all in Peter's great confession.[13] Jesus responded by a miracle to the prayer of the blind men at Jericho, with its salutation to the "Son of David." [14] The

[5] Klausner, *Jesus of Nazareth*, pp. 255–56.
[6] John 1:45.   [7] Matt. 16:20.   [8] Mark 8:30.
[9] Luke 4:41.   [10] Matt. 12:23(R-D.).   [11] John 4:29.
[12] Matt. 15:22.   [13] Mark 8:29.   [14] Matt. 20:30.

THEOLOGY

Salisbury, William S. Religion in A
Stanley, David M. The apostolic ch
240.302/S78a
Schnackenburg, Rudolf. God's rule
Cooke, Bernard J. Christian sacrame
241.236/C77c

Mussner, Franz. Christ and the end
Dame, 1965. 24L.469/:497wE
Monden, Louis. Sin, liberty, and La
24L.751/A74vE
Fuchs, Josef. The natural law. Shee
Spirituality in church and world. p
Godin, Andre. The pastor as counsel
242.933/G54F

acclamations which burst forth at the triumphal entry into Jerusalem were expressly Messianic. To the protesting Pharisees Jesus replied: "I tell you, that if they were to hold their peace, the stones would cry aloud." [15] That he knew himself to be the Messianic Son of David clearly emerges from the difficulty he propounds to the Pharisees over Psalm 109 (110): "How come the scribes to say that the Christ is the Son of David?" [16] Finally, at his trial, our Lord returned to an explicit question from the high priest a no less explicit answer: "Art thou the Christ, the Son of the Blessed One?" And he said to him, "I am." [17] This was the "blasphemy" for which "they all adjudged him to be worthy of death." [18]

It should be borne in mind, however, that when the people hailed our Lord as "Son of David," they could do so quite consistently with their limited conceptions of who the Messiah was to be. The house of David was associated in their minds with the restoration of the chosen people and the full realization, *on this earth,* of the promises made by Yahweh to their ancestors. "In that day I will raise up the tabernacle of David, that is fallen: and I will close up the breaches of the walls thereof and repair what was fallen: and I will rebuild it as in the days of old." [19] "And after this the children of Israel shall return and shall seek the Lord their God and David their king." [20] It was in conformity with these ideas, literally interpreted, that a group of enthusiasts would have acclaimed Jesus as the Davidic king. "Knowing, then, that they meant to come and carry him off, so as to make a king of him, Jesus once again withdrew on to the hill side all alone." [21]

In all four Gospels—most frequently in Matthew, Luke and John, but also in Mark—Jesus is referred to as "the Lord." Often it may well be no more than a courtesy title; as perhaps in its use by the Syrophenician woman.[22] But of its meaning on the lips of Jesus himself in such a passage

15 Luke 19:40(S.).   16 Mark 12:35(S.).   17 Mark 14:61–62(S.).
18 Vs. 64(S.).   19 Amos 9:11.   20 Hosea 3:5.
21 John 6:15.   22 Mark 7:28.

as the following there can be no doubt: "Tell him, the Lord has need of it [viz., the colt]"[23] The context is Messianic and the title must be so too. The Lord (Maran, Κύριος) is, in the usual court language of Syro-Greek royalties, the reigning monarch. Here it signifies the Messianic King, as his disciples must have been clearly aware. But as the ideas associated with Messianism, though of fundamental importance for the understanding of Jesus, meant very little to the non-Jewish world, it was but natural that the appellation "Lord" should take on its more extended meaning as Christianity spread through the early Hellenistic communities. Jesus is the supreme Lord, *Dominus,* in the same sense as God is; he is "Lord of lords and King of kings."[24]

The most significant title of all, however, since it is the one most frequently applied by our Lord to himself, is "the Son of Man." This designation appears sixty-nine times in the Synoptic Gospels alone and is employed probably on forty distinct occasions.[25] In Hebrew "son of man" means simply "man"; as in the Book of Numbers,[26] where it first appears in the Old Testament, and in Ezekiel, where it occurs over ninety times, always with reference to the prophet. But in Aramaic, the language spoken by our Lord, the phrase is often no more than the idiomatic equivalent for *I, myself.*[27] Nevertheless there are passages where the familiar expression assumes on the lips of Jesus a suggestion of mysteriousness. "Who do men say the Son of Man is?"[28] In the comparison between the Son of Man and John the Baptist,[29] we get an impression of a reserved meaning which cannot be exactly expressed. The formula even points to a being of superhuman grandeur when it is hinted that there can be such a thing as "blasphemy" against the Son of Man."[30] In certain contexts the meaning seems to pass from being an emphatic *"I"* to that of a personal appella-

[23] Mark 11:3; cf. 12:36.   [24] Apoc. 17:14(R-D.).
[25] Cf. Driver, *H.D.B.*, IV, 579.   [26] Num. 23:19.
[27] Cf. Matt. 8:20; 11:19; Luke 6:22; 7:34, etc.; in John 6:26 ff. Jesus uses both "I" and "Son of Man" in turn.
[28] Matt. 16:13.   [29] Matt. 11:18–19; Luke 7:33–34.
[30] Luke 12:10.

tion; while designating Jesus, it simultaneously manifests the powers with which he knows himself to be invested and the mission which he claims as his.[31] In other words, "the Son of Man" has become a Messianic title.[32]

The most significant context in which the expression occurs is at our Lord's trial, where he says to his judges, following upon the explicit admission of his Messiahship: "And you shall see the Son of Man seated at the right hand of Power [i.e. Yahweh, God], and coming with the clouds of heaven." [33] This was tantamount to identifying the role of "the Son of Man" with that assigned to him in the Book of Daniel, which is our first record of it in Aramaic literature: "I beheld therefore in the vision of the night, and lo, one like the son of man came with the clouds of heaven. And he came even to the ancient of days; and they presented him before him." [34] The "Son of Man" in question may here mean no more than a *man,* but he is clearly a heavenly personage; and when this passage is read in connection with the apocalyptic writings—notably the *Enoch* and *Ezra* Apocalypses—with which the Jews of our Lord's day were familiar, the passage becomes highly significant. For there the *Son of Man* is identified with the Messiah; he is a supernatural being, virtually a *Son of God,* existing in heaven before time began, and destined to appear on earth at his appointed hour.[35] There was thus a conception of a Messiah as one who stands in the closest possible relationship to God. He comes from on high, and has pre-existed before the creation of the world. His nature is divine and, as such, worship is offered to him. On the other hand, as Son of Man, his nature is human. He is the Chosen One of God, acting in all things in accordance with God's will. He is endowed with divine wisdom, and righteousness is his outstanding characteristic. In divine-human power he will come as Judge of both angels

[31] Luke 5:24; 6:5; 11:30; 19:10; Matt. 13:37.
[32] Mark 14:62; Matt. 26:64; Luke 22:69.
[33] Mark 14:62(S.); Luke 22:69 has "the power of God."
[34] Dan. 7:13.
[35] For references, see Index under "Son of Man" and "Son of God" in Charles's *The Apocrypha and Pseudepigrapha of the Old Testament,* II, 867.

and men, and will annihilate the powers of evil.[36] Hence, at
his trial, our Lord not only declared his Messiahship, but
revealed what kind of Messiah he conceived himself to be.

But to understand the full import of Jesus' conception
of the Messianic *Son of Man,* and the point where his teaching departed from that commonly held by his contemporaries, we must go back to an earlier stage in his ministry.
Following upon St Peter's acknowledgment of his Master as
the Messiah, we find the following significant passage in St
Marks' Gospel: "And he began to teach them that the Son
of Man must suffer many things and be rejected by the
ancients and by the high priests and the scribes: and be
killed and after three days rise again." [37] The same solemn
note is struck again after the Transfiguration: "He spent
the time teaching his disciples, The Son of Man, he
said, is to be given up into the hands of men. They will put
him to death, and he will rise again on the third day." [38]
It is finally repeated while on the road, near Jericho:
"Now, we are going up to Jerusalem; and there the Son
of Man will be given up into the hands of the chief priests
and scribes, who will condemn him to death; and these will
give him up into the hands of the gentiles, who will mock
him, and spit upon him, and scourge him, and kill him;
but on the third day he will rise again." [39]

All this was new teaching. In two respects our Lord
showed an insight into the meaning of the Messianic office
so far in advance of the Rabbis as to appear to them a
complete transformation of Messianism. The less disturbing
of these emerges from his controversy with the Pharisees,
where he propounds the question: How can the Messiah,
who is David's son, nevertheless be David's Lord? [40] The
answer, implied rather than explicitly given by Jesus, lies
in his conception of the role of the Son of Man noted above.
The Messiah was David's Lord because, unlike any earthly

---

[36] Cf. Oesterley, *The Jews and Judaism during the Greek Period,* pp. 152–159.
[37] Mark 8:31(R-D.).   [38] 9:31.
[39] 10:33-34.   [40] 12:35-37.

king, he was the Son of Man seated at the right hand of God himself. But if contemporary Judaism could perhaps have been persuaded to rise to this exalted view of their Messiah, it was a very different matter when it came to accepting the obverse side of the picture: *The Son of man must suffer.*

How difficult the doctrine was is shown by the disciples' first reaction to it: "Whereupon Peter, drawing him to his side, began remonstrating with him; Never, Lord, he said; no such thing shall befall thee." [41] Despite his insistence on the point, "they could not understand his meaning, and were afraid to ask him." [42] Their attitude of incomprehension never changed: "They could make nothing of all this; his meaning was hidden from them, so that they could not understand what he said." [43] It was only in the triumphant light of the Resurrection that they understood. Not until then could the two disciples who were journeying to Emmaus realize the astounding truth: "And they said to one another, Were not our hearts burning within us when he spoke to us on the road, and when he made the scriptures plain to us?" [44] It was the same with the apostles themselves:

This is what I told you, he said, while I still walked in your company; how all that was written of me in the law of Moses, and in the prophets, and in the psalms must be fulfilled. Then he enlightened their minds to make them understand the scriptures; So it was written, he told them, and so it was fitting that Christ should suffer, and should rise again from the dead on the third day. [45]

From this we learn that for our Lord his sufferings had a Messianic significance. He did not see them merely as the inevitable outcome of the conflict between good and evil in which he was engaged; they belonged precisely to his role as Messiah. The Son of Man *must* suffer. Jesus looked upon his Passion and death as the fulfilment of what had been written by Isaiah about the Suffering Servant:

[41] Matt. 16:22; cf. Mark 8:32.   [42] Mark 9:32.
[43] Luke 18:34.   [44] 24:32.   [45] Vv. 44–46.

He was despised and aloof from men,
  A man of pains and familiar with suffering,
As one who hid his face from us
  He was despised and we esteemed him not.
But it was our sufferings that he bore,
  Our pains that he endured;
And we accounted him stricken,
  Smitten by God and afflicted,
But he was wounded for our rebellions,
  He was bruised for our sin;
Upon him was the chastisement which made us whole,
  And by his stripes we were healed.[46]

That our Lord *must* suffer does not mean that he saw himself as the victim of some blind and ruthless destiny. Rather it was that he knew his suffering to be bound up with his office as the Saviour, with the work summed up in his own words: "That is what the Son of Man has come for, to search out and save what was lost." [47] To save was also the function of Isaiah's Suffering Servant. Therefore the Son of Man *must* be the redemptively suffering Servant of God if he is to be true to his vocation, namely that of Saviour.

"For the Son of Man himself came not to be served, but to serve, and to give his life a ransom for many." [48] These words of Jesus again show him fusing the role of the Son of Man with Isaiah's Servant of God. The Son of Man was traditionally conceived by the Jews as a personage, majestic and kindly indeed, but by no means a humble ministering figure. Such a lowly ministry of service belonged to the Servant of God; it was to reach its climax in a voluntary self-surrender to death. "To give his life *a ransom for many*." Nothing could make clearer than this the allusion to the fifty-third chapter of Isaiah:

A righteous one, My servant *shall make many righteous,*
  And their iniquities he shall bear....
Because he shall have poured out his soul to death,
  And been numbered with the rebellious,

[46] Isa. 53:3-5(Kissane).   [47] Luke 19:10.   [48] Mark 10:45(S.).

So shall he take away the sins of many,
And make intercession for the rebellious.[49]

But if the Messianic significance of Isaiah's message was but slowly realized by our Lord's disciples, it became embedded indelibly in the mind of the early Church. In the Acts we find that the passage of Scripture explained by Philip to his convert eunuch was the following: "He was led as a sheep to the slaughter; and as a lamb before its shearer is dumb, so he opened not his mouth."[50] "The chief message I handed on to you, as it was handed on to me," writes St Paul to the Corinthians, "was that Christ, as the scriptures had foretold, died for our sins."[51] St Peter's thought likewise is coloured by that of Isaiah:

Christ also suffered for you, leaving you an example to follow in his footsteps, who committed no sin, nor was deceit found in his mouth; who, when reviled, reviled not in return; who suffering, threatened not, but committed his cause to him who judges justly; who himself bore our sins in his own body upon the tree, in order that having died away from sins, we might live to righteousness; by whose wounds you are healed. For you were wandering like sheep, but have now returned to the shepherd and bishop of your souls.[52]

So also with St John: "You know well enough that when God revealed himself, it was to take away our sins; there is no sinfulness in him."[53] Why then was the Messianic import of Isaiah's prophecy lost upon the Jews as a whole? St Paul, with this very doctrine in mind, provides the answer: "There are some who have not obeyed the call of the gospel; so Isaias says, Lord, who has given us a faithful hearing?"[54]

The fault of the Jewish teachers, notably the Pharisees and the scribes, was not their incapacity to see for themselves all that was involved in the Messianic office, but that, despite his unassailable credentials, they would not accept

[49] Isa. 53:11, 12(Kissane).
[50] Acts 8:32(S.).   [51] 1 Cor. 15:3.   [52] 1 Pet. 2:21–25(S.).
[53] 1 John 3:5.   [54] Rom. 10:16.

Jesus as a prophet sent by God.[55] "Neither can they [the Jewish nation] regard him as a prophet: he lacks the prophet's political perception and the prophet's spirit of national consolation in the political-national sense" [56] (!) Thus, down to our own day, the words of our Lord are verified: "Believe me, no prophet finds acceptance in his own country." [57] In consequence of this, official Judaism denied him the authority, which belongs to every prophet, to throw a new light upon the Mosaic Law, to disclose a revelation from God which went beyond its own received dogmas and scribal traditions. Indeed, what won the admiration of the common people, namely, his spontaneous originality of method born of true vision—that Jesus "taught them, not like their scribes and Pharisees, but like one who had authority" [58]—was just what incensed their accepted teachers, whose defective insight confined them almost exclusively to a pedantic commentary upon the Law. Hence, as a class they could not share the enthusiasm of those who said: "Beyond doubt this is the prophet." [59] Their eyes were closed; and it is for this blindness that our Lord chiefly reproaches them: "If I had not come and spoken to them, they would not have sin; but now they have no excuse for their sin." [60]

But if Jesus had the unquestionable right to denounce the culpable blindness of his enemies, in not recognizing him as their Messiah, we Christians should remember that we do not share his divine insight for reading men's hearts. We may record the facts; but it would be pharisaical on our part to pass self-righteous judgment on the motives of those who refused to accept him. As we are the inheritors of nineteen centuries of Christian belief, it is easy for us to see the situation in its true light; but it was not easy for those who were first confronted with it in all its urgency. More profitable is it for us to ask ourselves what our own choice would have been, had we been faced with their dilemma. What assurance have we that our place would have been

---

[55] See § 18, pp. 224–30.
[57] Luke 4:24.
[59] John 7:40; cf. Deut. 18:15.

[56] Klausner, op. cit., p. 414.
[58] Matt. 7:29.
[60] 15:22(R-D.).

with the first disciples, rather than on the side of the scribes and Pharisees? If Christianity itself has become for us merely a matter of routine, an external observance which leaves untouched our inner inconsistencies, our mental narrowness and unconscious prejudices, we have none at all. Unless our hearts are open to God, loving the truth for its own sake,[61] we cannot make the right response to Christ. Only on condition that we surrender to him, not in some imaginative reconstruction adapted to our tastes, but as the challenging, soul-searching Figure who comes before us in the Gospels, can we rejoice gratefully in his felicitation: "Blessed are the eyes that see what you see." [62]

[61] Cf. John 18:37.   [62] Luke 10:24.

§ 13. THE SON OF GOD

It is illuminating to bear in mind that, when we profess our belief in Jesus Christ as the unique *Son of God,* we do more than recognize his Messiahship. The Jews would naturally have thought of their Messiah as being a "Son of God," but this was not a title especially reserved to him as, for example, was that of the "Son of David." It is this fact which lends added significance to St Peter's momentous confession at Caesarea Philippi. When he added the words, "the Son of the living God," to his declaration, "Thou art the Christ," [1] he was making an assertion which, like the statement it amplified, contained implications deeper than Peter could have learned from any human source. He was acknowledging more than he could have acquired from contemporary Jewish teaching about the Messiah, or from the commonly accepted interpretation of Old Testament prophecy, more even than Jesus' self-manifestation up to that point had warranted. This was why he received from our Lord such warm felicitation, and had addressed to him the significant words: "It is not flesh and blood, it is my Father in heaven that has revealed this to thee." [2] On Peter's lips the phrase, "Son of God," had broken the bounds of

[1] Matt. 16:16.   [2] Vs. 17.

metaphor and taken on its natural connotation; his Master was divine, the Son of God by nature.

Although the Old Testament discloses a belief in the heavenly excellence of the future Redeemer, it is only in the light of the New that we can infer that his sonship was literally divine. In none of the pre-Christian Jewish literature does the formula "Son of God" appear as a distinctively Messianic title. There it was generally understood to mean one singled out for God's paternal love, by an act comparable to the adoption of a child. So God loved Israel,[3] and favoured its royal representative;[4] in a similar, though not identical, sense the just man also is the "son of God."[5] To the expected Davidic king Yahweh says: "Thou art my son, this day have I begotten thee";[6] but in this phrase the Jews saw no more than an outstanding expression of divine affection. As Origen was obliged to point out, in his refutation of Celsus: "A Jew, however, would not admit that any prophet used the expression, 'The Son of God will come'; for the term which they employ is 'The Christ of God will come.'"[7] In what sense, then, does the Christian Revelation show our Lord to be the Son of God?

It is well known that the Fourth Gospel was composed for the express purpose of making this point clear. "So much has been written down, that you may learn to believe Jesus is the Christ, the Son of God, and so believing find life through his name."[8] For St John, as for the Catholic Church, our Lord is God's "only begotten Son, who abides in the bosom of the Father."[9] It is worth while, however, to examine first how the same doctrine emerges from the Synoptic Gospels, which were written with no such preoccupation. For the indirect and implicit statement of a truth is often more interesting to reflect upon than its direct affirmation. Consider, for example, the not immediately significant text: "Where two or three are gathered together in my name, I

3 Deut. 14:1 ff.   4 2 Kings(Samuel) 7:14.
5 Wisd. 2:13.   6 Ps. 2:7.
7 Origen, *Contra Celsum*, i, 49; *P.G.* 11, col. 753.
8 John 20:31.   9 1:18.

am there in the midst of them." [10] In this connection we may recall a saying of the Rabbi Hananiah ben Tradyon (about A.D. 135): "Where two are seated together, intent upon the Torah, glory (Yahweh) is in the midst of them." There is thus suggested, in St Matthew, a parallel between the presence of Jesus and the presence of Yahweh. When we ponder such sayings as: "I tell you one greater than the temple is here" [11] and "the Son of Man is lord of the sabbath," [12] we cannot escape the conclusion that Jesus is asserting of himself a dignity and power equivalent to that of Yahweh, the God of the Old Testament, Lord of the Temple and the Sabbath. No one less than Yahweh could have dared to say to an audience of Jews: "I am sending prophets and wise men and men of learning to preach to you"; [13] or to his disciples: "I will give you such eloquence and such wisdom as all your adversaries shall not be able to withstand, or to confute." [14] Who but the Author of the Old Covenant could have replaced it with—"the new covenant in my blood"? [15]

For all his self-effacement, Jesus requires of his followers the uncompromising devotion demanded by Yahweh himself: "Hear, O Israel: the Lord thy God is one God. And thou shalt love the Lord thy God with thy whole heart and with thy whole soul and with thy whole mind and with thy whole strength." [16] This precept must always hold good; and yet our Lord can say: "He who loves father or mother more than me is not worthy of me; and he who loves son or daughter more than me is not worthy of me; and he who does not take his cross and follow me is not worthy of me." [17] Just as his own miracles showed him to possess the divine omnipotence, so he is able to make his disciples instruments of this power: "Heal the sick, raise the dead, cleanse the lepers, cast out devils: give as you have received the gift, without payment." [18] After the mission of the seventy-two, they returned rejoicing: "Lord, they said, even

[10] Matt. 18:20. [11] 12:6(S.). [12] Vs. 8(S.).
[13] 23:34. [14] Luke 21:15. [15] 22:20(W.).
[16] Mark 12:29–30(R-D.); Deut. 6:5.
[17] Matt. 10:37–38(S.). [18] Vs. 8.

the devils are made subject to us through *thy* name." [19] The
power to forgive sins which the scribes knew to be the prerogative of God [20] Jesus claimed for himself—"the Son of
Man possesses authority upon earth to forgive sins." [21] At the
Last Day, it is he who, as the Judge to whom men's hidden
thoughts and secret desires lie open, will appoint each to
everlasting life or eternal damnation.[22]

It should be noted that our Lord nowhere asserts his
divinity in such an unequivocal phrase as "I am God." Language of this kind would have been regarded as rank blasphemy by the Jews, whose uncontaminated monotheism
was their proudest boast. Thus, when St John records him
to have affirmed "I and the Father are one," [23] his hearers,
correctly enough, interpreted him in a literal sense, and
would have stoned him on the spot; [24] even though he goes
on to explain how he would be understood—"I am the Son
of God." [25] What he is concerned to make clear is his unique
Sonship in virtue of which he is co-equal with God his
Father. In other words, he steadfastly maintains the traditional monotheism, while elucidating this in the light
of an added revelation concerning a distinction of persons within the Godhead. He is the Second Person of
the Blessed Trinity, as the Church was soon to realize.
For him to have manifested his divinity in any other
way than he did would have both left this sublime mystery undisclosed, and been a direct affront to the mon-
otheistic dogma of Judaism. The earliest Gospel records
show Jesus as the natural son and heir of Yahweh, who
is the Lord of the vineyard of Israel.[26] Into that vineyard Christ was sent by the Father, to meet with repudiation
at the hands of the evil vine-dressers. God's messengers, the
prophets, had come before him on a like errand; but to no
purpose. "He had still one messenger left, his own well-
beloved son; him he sent to them last of all; They will have
reverence, he said, for my son. But the vine-dressers said

[19] Luke 10:17.   [20] Matt. 9:3.   [21] Vs. 6(S.).
[22] Matt. 7:21–23; 13:41–43; 25:31–46.
[23] John 10:30(R-D.)   [24] Vs. 31.
[25] Vs. 36.   [26] Isa. 5:1 ff.

among themselves, This is the heir, come, let us kill him, and then his inheritance will be ours. So they took him and killed him, and cast him out of the vineyard." [27]

Christ would have his disciples think of themselves as children of his heavenly Father, but he nowhere places their sonship on a level with his own. He teaches them to pray *"Our* Father"; with Jesus himself it is invariably *"My* Father." When the Son of Man appears in glory, he will welcome the just with "a blessing from my Father"; [28] he is to keep high festival with his own "in the kingdom of my Father"; [29] the Holy Spirit's light and strength, which will fortify them at Pentecost, is "the gift which was promised by my Father." [30] It had always been the same, from his first recorded words as a boy of twelve in the Temple: "Could you not tell that I must needs be in the place which belongs to my Father?" [31] Nor is all this merely a matter of words, an expression of intense personal devotion. It has its roots in his consciousness of God's omnipotence and infinite knowledge, in which he knows himself, as the Son, to have an equal share: "All things have been delivered to me by my Father; and no one knows the Son except the Father, and no one knows the Father except the Son, and he to whom it is the pleasure of the Son to reveal him." [32]

"Thou art my beloved Son; in thee I am well pleased." [33] So our Lord was acknowledged publicly by his Father at the Baptism. Likewise, at the Transfiguration, from out of the cloud there came a voice: "This is my beloved Son; to him, then, listen." [34] From quite another source and at a wholly different scene, the same act of recognition was to come. Not even at the hour of his dereliction on the Cross could Christ's divinity be hidden from a Gentile who was willing to believe it: "No doubt but this was the Son of God." [35]

But it is from St John, who was also present on Calvary, that we gain the deepest insight into the mystery of our

[27] Mark. 12:6–7.   [28] Matt. 25:34.   [29] 26:29.
[30] Luke 24:49.   [31] 2:49.   [32] Matt. 11:27(S.).
[33] Mark 1:11.   [34] 9:7.   [35] 15:39.

Lord's personality. In his colloquy with Nicodemus we find the following:

Amen, amen, I say to thee that we speak what we know, and we testify what we have seen; and you receive not our testimony. If I have spoken to you earthly things, and you believe not: how will you believe, if I shall speak to you heavenly things? And no man hath ascended into heaven, but he that descended from heaven, the Son of Man. . . .[36]

Here we find, in veiled and designedly thought-provoking language, the full doctrine of the Incarnation—affirmed, not as might have been expected, of the Son of God, but of the Son of Man. It is personally he who "descended from heaven"; and we learn of the continuing presence—"in the bosom of the Father" [37]—of the Son of God, who, as Son of Man, is living on earth.

Our Lord dramatically illustrates his claim to equality with the Father in his Sabbath-day cure at the pool of Bethesda.[38] Nor did his enemies fail to draw the correct inference from his saying, "My Father is working until now, and I also work." [39] St John adds: "The Jews therefore wanted all the more to kill him, for the reason that he not only broke the Sabbath, but also called God his own Father, making himself equal to God." [40] In the verses which follow, Jesus implicitly accepts the charge; while derogating nothing from the profound submission which he in his human nature owes to God, he at the same time acknowledges the unique relation to God in which the Son is placed by the Incarnation.

Jesus Christ did not rely merely on words to establish his claim to a natural sonship with the Father; he appealed to his deeds as being an irrefutable proof. "If you find that I do not act like the son of my Father, then put no trust in me; but if I do, then let my actions convince you where I cannot; so you will recognize and learn to believe that the Father is in me, and I in him." [41] Even with the disciples,

---

[36] John 3:11–13(R-D.).   [37] 1:18.   [38] 5:1 ff.
[39] Vs. 17(S.).   [40] Vs. 18(S.).   [41] 10:37–38.

who cannot fully realize that in their Master they have the living embodiment of the Father,[42] he uses the same argument: "The words I speak to you are not my words; and the Father, who dwells continually in me, achieves in me his own acts of power." [43] The omnipotence of the Father, as Lord of life and death, belongs also to the Son: "Just as the Father bids the dead rise up and gives them life, so the Son gives life to whomsoever he will." [44] The faith which is owed to God alone Jesus invites men to give to himself: "Do not let your hearts be distressed; as you have faith in God, have faith in me." [45] He gathers us together, as it were, in the communion of divine charity proper to himself and the Father: "I have bestowed my love upon you, just as my Father has bestowed his love upon me; live on, then, in my love." [46] So united is he with the Father, in knowledge and power, that any petition made in his name will be answered by Jesus himself: "Whatever you shall ask in my name, that I will do." [47] This he could say because the very source of his being was in the Father: "It was from God I took my origin, from him I have come"; [48] "all that belongs to the Father belongs to me." [49] Hence it is that all judgement, and with it the worship due to the supreme Judge, is vested in Jesus Christ. "So it is with judgement; the Father, instead of passing judgement on any man himself, has left all judgement to the Son, so that all may reverence the Son just as they reverence the Father; to deny reverence to the Son is to deny reverence to the Father who has sent him." [50]

---

[42] John 14:8-9.   [43] Vs. 10.   [44] 5:21.
[45] 14:1.   [46] 15:9.   [47] 14:13(S.).
[48] 8:42.   [49] 16:15.   [50] 5:22-23.

§14. THE INCARNATE WORD

The New Testament synthesis of God's revelation on the personality of Jesus is given us in the Prologue to St John's Gospel.[1] We find there the most comprehensive statement

[1] 1:1-18.

of the doctrine of the Incarnation: "And the Word became
flesh, and dwelt among us (and we were beholders of his
glory, such glory as that of the Only Begotten of the Father)
full of grace and truth." [2] Here the question at once arises:
what meaning did St John attach to the Greek term Logos,
which we translate by "Word"? Much scholarly research
has been given to this subject. Some have thought that the
author of the Fourth Gospel borrowed the Logos from the
Alexandrine Jew, Philo, for whom it seems to have been some
vague and indeterminate divine principle, mediating between the transcendent Deity and the natural universe. Logos
was in fact one of the key-words in the form of Platonism in
vogue in the Hellenistic world at the beginning of the
Christian era. That St John should use it was claimed to
lend support to the thesis of such historians of dogma as
Ritschl and Harnack that primitive Christianity was, at an
early stage, adulterated by Greek influences, with a view to
making it more acceptable in a non-Jewish, semi-philosophical
milieu.[3]

More recently, affinities have been traced between the
Christian Logos and mythological ideas in popular Gnosticism and the "Redeemer" mysteries of the Hermetic type.
To these Greek and Egyptian sources further elements have
been added from Mesopotamia and Persia, comprising a mysterious triad of Manichaean, Mandaean and Iranian influences. It has even been said with reference to the doctrine
of the "Word" that "Christianity has not contributed any
original element to this, it has only (!) added one point: it
has applied it in all its fulness and variety to the Person of
Jesus Christ." [4] Viewed from the merely human point of
view, that is, from the standpoint of historical research, this
judgement may or may not be true. Indeed, we need take
no exception to it, provided it be seen in the light of God's
redeeming plan, as summarized by St Paul: "For he made
known to us the mystery of his will, the free design which
he had determined to carry out in the fulness of times,

[2] 1:14(S.).   [3] On this see § 1, p. 10 ff.
[4] Bousset, *Kyrios Christos*, p. 316.

namely, to bring back all things both in the heavens and on the earth under the headship of the Christ." [5]

The truth is, as has often been pointed out, that the notion of the Logos was as common in St John's day as is the idea of Evolution in our own. Accordingly, it had different meanings for different people; in each case it was coloured by the thought and mental associations of the one who used it. Now if Logos expressed one of the leading ideas in the Greek philosophy of religion, it was also the term used in the Septuagint [6] to translate the Hebrew *dabar,* which means "word." And this is itself a fundamental concept in Old Testament scripture. The prophets speak of "the *word* of the Lord" *coming* to them. Whether St John ever read Philo, or what other contemporary factors had influenced him in the selection of the term, we shall never know; but what we do know is that his Gospel is impregnated with Hebrew thought. For the prophets God's "word" was his revealing activity. The Jews also thought of his creative power as being the divine *speech,* a giving utterance to a "word." "And God *said,* Let there be light; and there was light." [7] "By his *word* the heavens were made, and all the host thereof by the *breath of his mouth";* [8] "For he *spoke,* and it came to be: he *commanded,* and it stood." [9]

In the Wisdom literature of the Old Testament we can discover the same line of thought; "wisdom" corresponds to "word." "When he [God] prepared the heavens, I [Wisdom] was present: ... when he balanced the foundations of the earth, I was with him forming all things...." [10] Wisdom itself is "a vapour of the power of God and a certain pure emanation of the glory of the almighty God." [11] It is true that St John does not use the word "wisdom" (σοφία), either in the Prologue or elsewhere, to designate the Son of God. He is concerned with the doctrine of the "Word" (λόγος),

---

[5] Eph. 1:9–10(S.).

[6] The Greek version of the Old Testament, said to have been made about 270 B.C. by seventy translators. It was familiar to, and is often quoted by, the writers of the New Testament.

[7] Gen. 1:3.   [8] Ps. 32(33):6(Lattey).   [9] Vs. 9.

[10] Prov. 8:27, 29–30.   [11] Wisd. 7:25.

who "in the beginning ... was with God," who in fact "was God," through whom "all things came into existence," [12] who finally "became flesh and dwelt among us." [13] But we shall see that there is a close connection between the theology of the λόγος and the Old Testament Wisdom teaching. At the time of the writing of the Fourth Gospel, the Son of God had already been endowed by St Paul with the properties pertaining to Wisdom. Christ is "the power of God and the wisdom of God." [14] Being the Wisdom of God, he is also his true image antecedent to creation, "the image of the invisible God, the first-born of all creation"; [15] "for in him were created all things in the heavens and on earth." [16] Here we have the doctrine mentioned above in Proverbs and the Book of Wisdom, where God's creative act is associated with "wisdom." [17]

Moreover the idea of "image" can be ascribed to Christ as illuminator; [18] and this is also the office of "wisdom." [19] Now for St Paul, all things came into existence *through* Christ (δι' αὐτοῦ) ; [20] not that Christ can be regarded as an instrumental cause in creation, since he is also its end—all things exist *for* him" (εἰς αὐτόν)[21]—but the phrase is employed in order to distinguish him from the invisible God whose image he is. In the Epistle to the Hebrews the description of the Son of God, as "the effulgence of God's glory and the very image of his substance" [22] reproduces the Old Testament Wisdom language.[23] Thus St Paul, in declaring all things to have been created through Christ and at the same time describing him as God's image, implicitly identifies him both with the divine wisdom and with the Artificer of the universe.[24]

But if Christ had a special part in the creation of the world, we already know that, according to the Old Testament, God created all things *by his word*. From this it follows that to Christ, the medium of creation, the name Logos

12 John 1:1–3(S.).   13 Vs. 14(S.).   14 1 Cor. 1:24(R-D.).
15 Col. 1:15(S.).   16 Vs. 16(S.).   17 Wisd. 7:26–27.
18 2 Cor. 4:4.   19 Wisd. 7:22.   20 1 Cor. 8:6.
21 Col. 1:16.   22 Heb. 1:3(S.).   23 Wisd. 7:26–27.
24 VV. 26–27 and 21–22.

would be as applicable as that of Wisdom. In other words, in our present context, λόγος and σοφία could be considered as equivalent terms. That they were so regarded by St John is confirmed by his first statement concerning the function of the Word: "All things came into existence through him (δι' αὐτοῦ)." [25] The thought being once expressed by the name Logos, it might well appear from many points of view a more suitable one; it is both masculine in gender and could signify with less obscurity than σοφία a distinct hypostasis; for speech implies activity and, with reference to God, is more easily distinguishable as proceeding from a divine source than as being simply one of God's attributes. Furthermore, speech was not necessarily an act of God having a term outside himself; for the Greeks had fully grasped the idea of a dialogue within the mind itself. In God the Logos was an interior Word; but for man it was "Light." To describe God revealing himself and speaking to man, the Jewish Rabbis would speak of "the word" (Aramaic: *memra*). To express the divine person, Christ, the fount of all light and revelation, what term could be more fitting than "the Word"?

But the incarnate Word (or Wisdom) has another role in the teaching of St John. He is *Light* and *Life,* particularly the latter. St Matthew tells us that "the people that abode in darkness has seen a great light"; [26] for St Luke Jesus is "a light of revelation unto the gentiles." [27] The full exposition of this sublime theme, however, was left to St John. "I am the light of the world; he who follows me shall never walk in darkness, but shall have the light of life." [28] "While I am in the world I am the light of the world." [29] Jesus, the incarnate Word, is the Light because he is the Truth, illuminating the minds of those who accept him.[30] "I have come into the world as a light, so that all those who believe in me may continue no longer in darkness." [31] He who is the Light of men is likewise their Life.[32] The "life eternal" which, in the

---

[25] John 1:3(S.).
[27] Luke 2:32(W.).
[30] 14:6; 18:37.

[26] Matt. 4:16; cf. Isa. 9:1-2.
[28] John 8:12(S.).   [29] 9:5(S.).
[31] 12:46.   [32] Cf. 1:4.

synoptists, is synonymous with the kingdom of God [33] becomes in the Fourth Gospel one of the chief attributes of
Christ. "And as Moses lifted up the [brazen] serpent in the
desert, so must the Son of Man be lifted up [on the Cross],
in order that whoever believes in him may possess eternal
life. For God so loved the world that he gave his only-
begotten Son, in order that whoever believes in him should
not perish, but possess eternal life." [34]

As we have already remarked, it was with the object of
proclaiming the life-giving faith in Christ that St John's
Gospel was written. For the fourth evangelist, the bestowal
of life was the dominating aspect of Jesus' teaching. In this
again he is at one with the thought of the Old Testament.
The God of Israel was a *living* God, and in him was the
source of life: "For with thee is the fountain of life; in thy
light do we see light." [35] If the Israelites were concerned for
the most part with the happy life as a state of temporal and
earthly well-being, Isaiah can yet speak in terms reminiscent
of St John himself: "And Jahweh shall guide thee continually, and satisfy thy soul in dry places, and make strong thy
bones; and thou shalt be like a well-watered garden, and
like a spring whose waters fail not." [36] Among the Hebrews,
faith in a blessed immortality seems to have had as its basis
the desire of never being separated from their God: "Thou
wilt not abandon me to the netherworld, nor suffer thy pious
one to see the pit," writes the Psalmist.[37] "The path of life
goeth upwards for the wise, that he may depart from the
lowest hell." [38]

St John records the enlightening of these shadowy intimations of the Old Covenant with the enheartening assurance of the New: "Yes, this is the will of him who sent me,
that all those who believe in the Son when they see him
should enjoy eternal life; I am to raise them up at the last
day." [39] This was the message which was to fulfil the hopes
of an abiding life expressed in the later writings of the Old

33 Mark 9:43; Matt. 19:16.   34 John 3:14–16(S.).
35 Ps. 35(36):10.   36 Isa. 58:11(Kissane); cf. John 4:14.
37 Ps. 15(16):10(Lattey).   38 Prov. 15:24.   39 John 6:40.

Testament.[40] Yet it was not merely the promise of an unceasing beatitude to be enjoyed in the world to come; a new life was beginning at once for those who believed; they already *have* eternal life: "Believe me when I tell you this, the man who listens to my words, and puts his trust in him who sent me, enjoys eternal life." [41] "He that eateth my flesh and drinketh my blood hath everlasting life, and I will raise him up on the last day." [42] To accept the incarnate Word is to receive the pledge and first beginnings of eternal life.

It should be noted that the revelation of Christ as the "Life" transcends the limits of Jewish Messianism. What St John wishes to impress upon us is that in Jesus is embodied the very life of the Godhead. The quickening power which belongs to the Father is possessed also by the Son.[43] The Eucharistic discourse [44] carries us far beyond purely Messianic conceptions. Our Lord here speaks of himself according to his human nature, richly endowed with the Father's gifts, but at the same time in the character of *Son*. "As I live because of the Father, the living Father who has sent me, so he who eats me will live, in his turn, because of me." [45] In this context, the *I* and the *me* can refer only to the person of the Son, conscious of an equality in nature with the Father.

If we consider again St John's Prologue, we find that the Gospel's central theme—namely, the identification of Christ with "life eternal"—is there closely connected with the doctrine of the "Word"—who is "the Word of God." [46] The union of these two ideas is never absent from the evangelist's mind, as can be seen from what he writes elsewhere: "Our message concerns that Word, who is life; what he was from the first, what we have heard about him, what our own eyes have seen of him; what it was that met our gaze, and the touch of our hands. Yes, life dawned; and it is as eyewitnesses that we give you news of that life, that eternal life, which ever abode with the Father and has dawned, now, on us." [47]

---

40 Cf. 2 Mach. 7:9.   41 John 5:24.   42 6:54(R-D.),
43 5:21.   44 6:35 ff.   45 6:57.
46 Apoc. 19:13.   47 1 John 1:1-2.

The Prologue starts from the pre-existence of the Word with God, passing thence to speak of the part played by the Word in the creation of the world, to rest finally on the thought that the Word has become incarnate in Jesus Christ. The familiar *light* and *life* motif is enunciated: "the life was the light of men." [48] Christ is then introduced as closely linked with the historical witness of the Baptist,[49] implicitly as the Word,[50] explicitly as the Light "which enlightens every man." [51] The "grace and truth," which come from the Word's being made flesh, signify humanity's participation in light and life.

Through the Incarnation, the Word of God ceased to be expressed in literature or in prophecy, and became embodied in human flesh. Thus it was that the Old Testament was fulfilled. "God, having spoken of old to our forefathers through the prophets, by many degrees and in many ways, has at last in these days spoken to us by his Son, whom he appointed heir of all things, and through whom he made the worlds." [52] The *finality* of Christ, the fact that he is the unique revealer of the secrets of the Godhead, is the real conclusion of the Prologue; it is the central truth of the Gospel. "No man hath seen God at any time; the only begotten Son, who is in the bosom of the Father, he hath declared him." [53] This was the tremendous import of the "Messianic secret" which Jesus, with the incomparable pedagogical skill of the Master, gradually made known to his disciples, until it bore fruit in the post-Resurrection faith of the reluctant Thomas: "My Lord and my God." [54] From that day to this these words have summarized the authentic confession of Catholic Christianity to the person of Jesus Christ.

[48] John 1:4.   [49] Vv. 6–8.   [50] Vs. 14.
[51] Vs. 9.   [52] Heb. 1:1–2(S.).   [53] John 1:18(R-D.).
[54] 20:28.

§ 15. THE GOD-MAN

The Gospels portray in Jesus Christ "a person who, despite his obvious humanity, impresses us throughout as being at home in two worlds." [1] He was a man of his age, a pure Jew, with all the ardour and intensity of his race. He was not a "superman," nor yet, as some have thought, an apparition from some higher realm clothed in human flesh. Everything points to his being a sharer in our common clay. He was tired and hungry, could rejoice familiarly with his friends and weep with them in sorrow; when he chose, he could speak out vehemently against his enemies, yet be prostrated in anguished apprehension at the prospect of his torments. We know that he had a Mother and near relatives; in early life he had plied a trade; there is nothing remote or inaccessible about him. On no reading of his character could he be described as a shadowy and colourless figure; so remarkable was the impression of vitality upon his contemporaries, that they were moved either to worshipping admiration or passionate hatred. In a word, if the colloquialism may be allowed, he was one of ourselves: "consubstantial [i.e. of the same substance] with us according to humanity (ὁμοούσιον ἡμῖν τὸν αὐτὸν κατὰ τὴν ἀνθρωπότητα)." [2]

But along with all this he was immeasurably more. Notwithstanding his approachableness, the disciples, save when they forgot themselves, looked upon him with something akin to awe. There was about his person the fascination of the numinous; the All Holy was present within him—"Leave me, Lord, for I am a sinful man." [3] Christ knew and declared himself to be more than a prophet, which was the highest ideal of manhood in his day; for the prophetic formula, "Thus saith the Lord," he substituted the ultimately authoritative "*I* say unto you." Nor does he show the least trace of having scaled to this sublime level, as it were from below; in this sense he is no "hero" who has raised himself, or been raised in the common estimation, above his fellows by a series of outstanding exploits. The divine quality within him is not the result of an achievement; it is something already given, a fact. The marvellous deeds, their mastery of per-

[1] Illingworth, *Divine Immanence*, p. 50.
[2] *Conciliar Definition at Chalcedon*, A.D. 451; Denz., 148.
[3] Luke 5:8(S.).

formance, the incomparable sayings, though embodied in the texture of human life, issue from a source that is more than human; the deep underlying serenity, undisturbed by surface turmoil and conflict, points rather to the Godhead's "striking downwards" than to a human individual's aspiring to the heights. Our Lord acts and speaks as one for whom heaven is his native element, the Deity a personal possession: "consubstantial with the Father according to divinity (ὁμοούσιον τῷ πατρὶ κατὰ τὴν θεότητα)."

Yet there is no suggestion that divinity and humanity are anything but harmoniously united. Deeds and words, and the whole conduct of the public ministry, hold together with flawless consistency; never was a life led with such complete unity of purpose. Jesus could experience both depression and elation, but of a "split personality" there is not a trace. He is equally poised, at one with himself, when being acclaimed by the multitudes and when standing as a prisoner before Pilate; the personal "I" comes as naturally to his lips in the familiar instructions to the disciples as when united in prayer to his heavenly Father; there is one sole *ego*, in whatever heights or depths it may be said to dwell. How is this duality in oneness to be put into words? "One *person*, two *natures*," such is the traditional Catholic formula, attempting to express the inexpressible. (The reader may find it helpful to bear in mind, throughout this and the following section, that the distinction between *nature* and *person* is well illustrated by the two quite different answers demanded by the questions *"What* am I?" and *"Who* am I?" The reply to the first will be in terms of *nature*, to the second in terms of *person*. For a simple and attractive exposition of this point with reference to the Incarnation, see Dr J. P. Arendzen's *Whom do You say—?*, p. 59 ff.) It is inevitably inadequate to what it represents; nor can an analysis of its terms yield the fulness of the knowledge of Jesus available only in the inspired scriptural texts. The statement is in no sense offered as the conclusion of a demonstration of the truth of the Incarnation; for, as has already been said, this is a mystery of faith not susceptible of rational proof. But it was believed by those responsible for its formulation, as it is held by the vast majority of Christians to-day, to be a proposition in comprehensible language which does least injustice to the evidence of Scripture.

It cannot be said that recent attempts, outside the Catholic Church, to suggest an alternative phraseology have given any grounds for supposing that the modern mind has fundamentally a better understanding of our Lord than the Fathers at Chalcedon. The orthodox formula can be assailed, but, from the nature of the case, it cannot be refuted. The "Mystery of Jesus" remains—a subject more proper for adoring contemplation than theological disputation. It is the supreme glory of the Church to have made full allowance for this mystery; at one and the same time guarding the inner secrets of the Lord's personality from the desecrating hands of rationalists and unbelievers, and presenting to the world in intelligible terms the Truth by which alone it may hope to live: "Eternal life is knowing thee, who art the only true God, and Jesus Christ, whom thou hast sent." [4]

On a later page we shall consider further the character of our Lord as portrayed in the Gospels; [5] here, however, the point has been reached when we must examine in closer detail—as briefly and simply as the subject-matter permits—the theology of the Incarnation. For it carries us into the mystery of his personality, the right understanding of which, so far as we can achieve it, is the hall-mark of Catholic orthodoxy. Put in the form of a question, the great Christological problem is this: How can he who is one divine person be said at the same time to be truly God and truly man? In what sense is the unity of the two natures in Christ to be understood?

This was the debate which engaged the ablest minds in the Church throughout the first four centuries of the Christian era. It was finally settled, as has just been recalled, at the oecumenical Council of Chalcedon in A.D. 451. We need not here trace the history of the preceding controversies; it must suffice to note that, subsequently to the Nicene Council

[4] John 17:3.   [5] § 21, pp. 262 ff.

(A.D. 325)—where our Lord had been proclaimed to be "of
one substance with the Father (ὁμοούσιον τῷ πατρί) [6]—there
arose two heresies, Nestorianism and Monophysitism, which,
though mutually opposed, alike departed from the central
truth. Both agreed with the Church in acknowledging
Christ's divinity and humanity, but they disagreed in their
account of the manner in which the two natures were united.
Nestorianism dissolved the unity of his person, and, by im-
plication, made Christ less than God. Monophysitism confused the two natures in one, merging the human into the
divine, and thus, in its anxiety to make him more than man,
actually made him something quite different from man. We
shall now see how the Catholic position, which is the "golden
mean" between these two opposing errors, harmonizes with
all that the New Testament has told us about our Lord.

The first thing to be remembered is that when we say
anything about Jesus Christ, whether as referring to his
Godhead or to his human nature, our speech applies to the
one individual who is both God and man. Thus, in calling
him the "Son of God" or the "Son of the Virgin Mary,"
we are not referring to his divine nature in the first case
and his humanity in the second; we have in mind simply
the *person* of our Lord himself. This seems obvious enough,
though it was just the point that Nestorius failed to see. St
Paul, however, is quite clear about it; he makes no distinction between the Father's only-begotten Son and him who
was born at Bethlehem. "God sent his Son, made from a
woman, made under the law, in order that he might redeem
those under the law, in order that we might receive our
adoption as sons." [7] It was not, for example, merely Jesus
"as man" or "according to his human nature" who was crucified, but "the Lord of glory." [8] The Godhead cannot die,
but he who was God could and did; "you killed," not
"Christ the man," but "the Author of life." [9] "Christ" in
whom "resides bodily all the complete fulness of the Godhead," he, and no other, not simply his "body" nor his "hu-

[6] *Nicene Creed;* Denz., 54.   [7] Gal. 4:4–5(S.).
[8] 1 Cor. 2:8(R-D.).   [9] Acts 3:15.

man nature," was the one whom "God raised from the dead." [10]

There is nothing merely theoretical and academic in being careful of our phraseology on these points; any looseness of terms, as the Church's history shows, may betray the central fact of Christianity, that Jesus Christ is God incarnate. Let us attempt to come to closer grips with what is involved. When St John tells us that "the Word became flesh," [11] the subject of this proposition, namely "the Word," is he who "was God." [12] "Flesh," in the language of Scripture, signifies human nature.[13] In saying, then, that "the Word became flesh," the meaning cannot be that the eternal Word underwent change; for that would be opposed to God's attribute of immutability. What we are told is that the Word had become man without ceasing to be God; he assumed a human nature into unity with himself, in a union so close that the distinctive personality of the Word is what distinguishes the human nature of Christ from that of every other man. But the individual resulting from this union is still the Word, now become "flesh," whose "glory" St John had seen, "such glory as that of the Only Begotten of the Father, full of grace and truth."

Through the Incarnation a change had occurred, though one which is without parallel in the whole universe. Every change of which we have experience involves, if not something coming into existence for the first time, then at least the modification of what already exists, either in respect of that substance itself, or as touching its accidental qualities. But here nothing of this took place. We can truly speak of a before and after with reference to the Incarnation; it is an event, the decisive event, in world history; it happened in "the fulness of time." [14] We may even say that human nature was changed by it; to make possible such a transformation for humanity in general—namely, that men should be able to become "children of God" [15]—was indeed its whole

10 Col. 2:8–9, 12(S.).   11 John 1:14(S.).   12 Vs. 1.
13 Cf. Gen. 6:12; Isa. 58:7; Jer. 17:5.
14 Gal. 4:4.   15 John 1:12.

purpose. But what we cannot say is that Christ's individual human nature underwent a change as a result of it; for the reason that his human nature never existed for an instant without being united to the Word. At the very moment of its coming into existence, it was taken up into the incommunicable personality of God's unchanging Word, so as to constitute one divine person with him.

This is the heart of the mystery known as the *Hypostatic Union*. Here it must be emphasized that an understanding of the terms in which this is expressed is indispensable, if we are to grasp anything more than the rudiments of the Catholic doctrine on the Incarnation. The Greek word *hypostasis* (ὑπόστασις) is found in Scripture;[16] but, in the Christological controversies of the early Church, its meaning fluctuated between the closely related ideas of "essence," "substance" and "person." It was through the persuasive powers of St Athanasius, the great Doctor of the Incarnation, that confusion was finally eliminated by both East and West agreeing to equate the Greek ὑπόστασις with the Latin *persona*. The latter word remotely derives from "mask"—with special reference to the disguise worn by play-actors in their impersonations of famous men—but, under the influence of the Roman Law, it soon came to have a more precise meaning. St Augustine, however, writing early in the fifth century, cannot yet use it with any sureness of touch in his discussions on the Trinity. But by the sixth century "person" was practically stabilized in the famous definition of Boethius: "an individual substance of a rational nature."[17] This was the conception later taken over by the scholastic theologians, in their tractates on the Trinity and the Incarnation, though they showed themselves fully conscious of the latent anthropomorphism in the term as defined by Boethius.

There is nothing in the *Summa Theologica* more characteristic of St Thomas's genius than his treatment *Of the Divine Persons*.[18] He pierces to the metaphysical essence of

16 Heb. 1:3.
17 Boethius, *De persona et duabus naturis; P.L.* 64, col. 1337–1354.
18 I, q. 29, art. 1–4.

persona, stripping it of all elements which would render it inapplicable to God:

> *Person* signifies what is most perfect in all nature—that is, a subsistent individual of a rational nature. Hence, since everything that is perfect must be attributed to God, forasmuch as his essence contains every perfection, this name *person* is fittingly applied to God; not, however, as it is applied to creatures, but in a more excellent way; as other names also, which, while giving them to creatures, we attribute to God.[19]

> It may be said that God has a rational *nature*, if rationality be taken to mean, not discursive thought, but in a general sense, an intelligent nature. But God cannot be called an *individual*, in the sense that his individuality comes from matter; but only in the sense which implies incommunicability. *Substance* can be applied to God in the sense of signifying self-subsistence. There are some, however, who say that the definition of Boethius, quoted above, is not a definition of *person* in the sense we use when speaking of the persons in God. Therefore Richard of St Victor amends this definition, by adding that *person* in God is *the incommunicable existence of the divine nature*.[20]

Later theologians have further refined upon the concepts of "person" and "personality"; [21] but this is not the place to pursue their discussions. We may defer the consideration of the more psychological aspects of these ideas until the next section. For the moment, we are sufficiently well equipped to understand the theology of the Incarnation if, following St Thomas, we bear in mind that, from the metaphysical point of view, what constitutes "personality" is *the ultimately distinctive and incommunicable element in nature* [22]—both in man's and, all qualifications being made, in God's.

After this necessary digression, we can now return to closer contact with our sources. Before St John wrote his Gospel, St Paul, speaking of "Christ Jesus," had written as follows to the Philippians:

---

[19] *Ibid.*, art. 3.   [20] Ad. 4.
[21] Cf. Garrigou-Lagrange, *Le Sauveur et son amour pour nous*, pp. 108–116.
[22] It should further be understood that "the ultimately distinctive and incommunicable element in nature" is not something super-added to nature itself. It is what makes an individual nature *per se* or *sui juris*; somewhat in the way that the points which terminate a line drawn on paper make that particular line *per se*, without being able to be separated from it.

Though he was divine by nature (ἐν μορφῇ Θεοῦ), he did not consider his being on an equality with God a thing to be grasped; but on the contrary he emptied himself, took the nature of a slave (μορφὴν δούλου), and was made like to men. Then, having come in human form (ὡς ἄνθρωπος), he humbled himself, becoming obedient unto death, even the death of the cross.[23]

Here again, it is one and the same "He," who was "divine by nature," who "emptied himself . . . and was made like to men." He who was formerly God remains God; for Christ shares the same nature with the Father, "with whom there can be no variation, nor a trace of change." [24] But he took "the nature of a slave"; that is, he assumed our human nature. St Paul's doctrine is thus quite incompatible with any form of adoptionist Christianity; to wit, the notion that Christ was a man who in some way subsequently became divine; it refuted Nestorianism in advance. Our Lord was not a man who was adopted by God the Father as his Son. This would have implied not his self-emptying and humiliation but his exaltation, which is the reverse of what Scripture teaches us at this point. Rather it was that Christ, having pre-existed as God, subsequently underwent the humiliation of coming to us "in human form" through the Incarnation. "You do not need to be reminded how gracious our Lord Jesus Christ was; how he impoverished himself for your sakes, when he was so rich, so that you might become rich through his poverty." [25]

We may note, in passing, that these texts from St Paul have given rise to a departure from Catholic Christology known as the *Kenotic theory* of the Incarnation. (For an able discussion of some recent varieties of this aberration, see E. L. Mascall, *Christ, the Christian, and the Church*, pp. 25 ff.) Its name is derived from the Greek words, ἑαυτὸν ἐκένωσεν, "emptied himself," in the text from Philippians quoted above. In its extreme form, this theory suggests that the Son of God, on becoming incarnate, laid aside his divine attributes, taking on our human infirmities in their stead, so that Christ was not conscious of his divinity until after the Resurrection. Its more moderate upholders, recognizing the in-

---

23 Phil. 2:6-8(S.).   24 James 1:17(S.).   25 2 Cor. 8:9.

compatibility of such an extreme view with the New Testament evidence, are content to say that the incarnate Word did not always enjoy the use of the divine attributes—more particularly those of omnipotence and omniscience—and accordingly, that it was only intermittently that he did not know himself to be God. This hypothesis was thought to be necessary in order to safeguard the reality of Christ's human nature and free will.

We shall note presently the Church's view of the problems this theory proposes to solve. Here it will be enough to remind ourselves that it conflicts, both with the picture of our Lord presented in the Gospels, and with the teaching of St Paul and St John. Jesus is nowhere shown as looking back upon his unique Sonship as something belonging only to a former state, still less as an honour yet to be achieved; it is an ever-present reality with him. His miracles are worked by his own power; there is no appeal for God's intervention, no summoning of the Father's aid; the divine omnipotence is Christ's personal possession *as man*. The *ex-inanitio*, the self-emptying, involved in the Incarnation means, not the relinquishing of anything pertaining to the Godhead, but that the Son of God set no store by the divine majesty and glory which belonged to him; he veiled them under the appearance "of a slave." We may also think of him as, so to speak, pouring himself out, like water from a vessel, in order to enrich others—a thought which may well have been in St Paul's mind when expounding this doctrine.

It is perhaps superfluous to remark that only God the Son, the Second Person of the Blessed Trinity, became incarnate; not the Father nor the Holy Spirit. It is true that the act of infinite power by which the Incarnation came about involved the Triune Godhead; for it is a necessary principle of the Church's theology that every act of God directed outside himself (*ad extra*) engages the whole Trinity; but in this case, the term of that act, the becoming "flesh," affected the Son alone. In consequence of God's being the infinite Creator, it follows that he contains within himself, according to the divine mode of being, all created things, including our human nature. This is what made it possible for him to assume that nature without adding to himself or undergoing change. At the moment of the Incarnation God received nothing; it was all self-giving. In the most sublimely mysterious act of which we have knowledge, God the Son embraced, with his own incommunicable personality, the humanity of Christ, uniting himself with it in a union than which nothing more intimate can be conceived—that of a single divine person. This movement of God's power was fittingly appropriated to the Holy Spirit; for the Jews always thought of his life-giving energy in terms of the divine Spirit. So, in the homestead at Nazareth, it had been foretold to Mary: "The Holy Ghost shall come upon thee, and the power of the Highest shall overshadow thee; and, therefore, the holy one who shall be born of thee shall be called Son of God." [26]

Everything that went to make up our Lord's humanity was assumed by God's only begotten Son into personal union with himself. Many of the Church Fathers, under the influence of Origen, held that the Word united the body to himself through the medium of the soul. For the soul is the highest principle in man, being that which is most characteristic of his nature; hence it must be most intimately involved in the Incarnation. There is a certain fittingness in this view, as St Thomas points out, since what is spiritual, and therefore more like to God, is better adapted to such a union.[27] The body was only capable of being, as it were, gathered to the Godhead, in so far as it was precisely a *human* body, that is, informed by an intellectual soul.[28] In this sense, by reason of its special aptitude, the soul may be said to be the *cause* of the body's being assumed by the Word. But this must be understood without prejudice to the fact that the body, being an essential part of human nature, was immediately united to the person of the Son at the first instant of the Incarnation.

It should be noted that this insistence that Christ's body is hypostatically united to the Word is not merely a matter

[26] Luke 1:35(S.).   [27] III, q. 4, art. 1.   [28] Q. 6, art. 1.

of theological speculation; it is implied in our Catholic faith. In the Apostles' Creed we profess our belief that God's only Son, Jesus Christ, "was crucified, dead and buried." Thus, during the entombment, our Lord's body was still personally one with the eternal Word; he who died and was buried was the Son of God. It was likewise the blood of God's Son which was shed for us on the Cross. Only so can we understand how it can be described as the price of our redemption: "... you were redeemed ... with the precious blood of Christ, as of an unblemished and spotless lamb." [29] It is the blood, not merely of a human body, but of God's only begotten Son which cleanses us from sin.[30]

According to the Creed, he who was "born of the Virgin Mary" had previously been "conceived by the Holy Ghost." From this it follows, as a truth of Catholic faith, that Christ's human nature was, from the first moment of its existence, hypostatically united to the Son of God. This union of the divine and human natures in a single person, which remained uninterrupted from Christ's human birth until the Ascension, now endures in heaven for ever. Our Lord might undergo dereliction on the Cross, through the withdrawal of the Father's protecting and sustaining hand; he enjoyed no immunity from physical and mental agony; but the union of his human nature with the Godhead could never be cancelled. Even when death had dissolved the elements of that nature, separating the body from the soul, these still maintained their unity with the Word, to be reintegrated by him in the glory of the Resurrection.

We shall find this mysterious fact less baffling if we remember that the hypostatic union was, for the human nature of Christ, a *grace*. That is to say, it was a supernatural gift of divine goodness which his humanity could not, in strict justice, either claim or merit.[31] This *grace of union,* to which there is no parallel in the whole sphere of God's dealings with man, is something *created,* in the sense that it began in time and posits a real relation in Christ's human

29 1 Pet. 1:18-19(S.).   30 Cf. 1 John 1:7.
31 St Thomas, III, q. 2, art. 11.

nature with respect to the Godhead.[32] With reference, however, to the hypostatic union, considered not in terms of relationship between humanity and divinity but in its ultimate foundation, we cannot speak of it as being created, since he who effects it is the uncreated person of God the Son. Hence the grace of union "is infinite, as the person of the Word is infinite." [33] Further—and this is what distinguishes the grace of union from all the graces we receive—it is a *substantial* grace. Whereas the sanctifying grace given to us, by which we become "partakers of the divine nature," [34] inheres in the soul as an accidental quality, the hypostatic union was not an accident of our Lord's human nature; it gave to that nature its *being* as a self-existing substance.[35] Consequently, his dignity and holiness are not something added to his humanity; they are of its very essence, making it holy with the holiness of God. The grace of union is thus the source of Christ's unique prerogatives as our Redeemer, of his mediatorship, his priesthood and his kingship. This was what made him, from the first moment of his conception in Mary's womb, Israel's Messiah; there then took place, in secret and in mystery, the Messianic anointing with divinity, to be publicly proclaimed and manifested by the Father at the Baptism: "Thou art my beloved Son; in Thee I am well pleased." [36]

That the hypostatic union should have suffered intermission, even for an instant, is inconceivable; for it would have meant the dissolution of our Lord's personality. We know that "God does not repent of the gifts he makes." [37] "What is given by God's grace," says St Thomas,[38] "is never recalled where there is no fault." If this is the case even with the grace of adoption whereby we are sanctified, how much more must it be so with the grace of union which constitutes the very person of Jesus. "Since, therefore, there was no sin in Christ, it was impossible that the union between his divinity and humanity (*caro*) should be broken." [39] The

---

32 St Thomas, III, q. 2, art. 7.   33 Q. 7, art. 11.   34 2 Pet. 1:4(S.).
35 St Thomas, *ibid.*, q. 2, art. 6.   36 Mark 1:11.
37 Rom. 11:29.   38 III, q. 50, art. 2.   39 *Ibid.*

Father might allow the agony on the Cross to rob his only
begotten Son of the divine consolation; but the Crucified
could not be other than he was—"the Lord of glory." [40] At
his darkest hour he was still the one of whom it had been
said: "He shall be great, and men will know him for the
Son of the most High; the Lord God will give him the throne
of his father David, and he shall reign over the house of
David eternally; his kingdom shall never have an end." [41]
"What Jesus Christ was yesterday, and is to-day, he remains
for ever." [42] That this should be so is the condition, not only
of his own glory, but of our redemption: "He, because he
continues for ever, holds a priesthood that does not pass to
another. And consequently he is able for all time to save
those who come to God through him, since he is always
living to intercede for them." [43]

The doctrine of the hypostatic union, in itself no more
than the theological expression of the unique personality
which the New Testament shows our Lord to have been,
was defined as of faith by the Church at the Council of
Ephesus in A.D. 431. It emerged, humanly speaking, from
the vigorous controversy conducted by St Cyril of Alexandria
against Nestorius. But the anti-Nestorian polemic over-
reached itself and, under the leadership of Eutyches, archi-
mandrite of a monastery near Constantinople, gave rise to
the heresy of Monophysitism (from the Greek words which
mean *one nature*). This aberration took various forms,
but fundamentally it lay in this, that while the union of
the human and divine natures in Christ was accepted, the
distinction between the two natures was denied. "Two natures before the Union," said Eutyches, "but, after it, One."
The Council of Chalcedon, solemnly approving Pope Leo's
"Dogmatic Letter to Flavian," upheld the real distinction
between the two natures, as persisting in the hypostatic
union itself,[44] and thus, concluding nearly four centuries of
controversy, finally formulated the revealed teaching on the
person of Jesus Christ.

[40] 1 Cor. 2:8(R-D.).   [41] Luke 1:32.   [42] Heb. 13:8.
[43] 7:24–25(S.).   [44] Denz., 148.

Monophysitism, like every heresy, served the purpose of throwing the true doctrine into sharper relief. Again, like most heresies, it can be seen as true in what it affirms, false in what it denies. Monophysitism holds that Jesus is the God-Man, but refuses to acknowledge that he is both God *and* man. It took the view that our Lord's human nature was *changed* into the divine nature, much in the way that a drop of wine thrown into the sea loses itself and becomes water. Accordingly, Christ could be said to be *from* two natures, but, in virtue of the hypostatic union, not *in* two natures—but in one only, namely, the divine, to which the external appearances of his human nature were, so to say, accidentally conjoined. From this it follows that our Lord's birth, life and death, have but little human significance, since he cannot be said to be "of the same substance with" ourselves. Little reflection is needed to convince us of the impossibility of reconciling this view with the teaching of the New Testament.

One argument by which the Monophysites defended their tenet, that the two natures in Christ had been fused together so as to form one divine nature, is especially interesting, because it is often used by the Fathers and can be understood in a right, as well as in a wrong, sense. It is said that the divinity and humanity form one thing in Christ, in the same way as the soul and the body do in man.[45] This analogy holds good in three important respects: First, our Lord's human and divine natures, like our body and soul, come together in the unity of a single subject or person. Secondly, just as our body and soul are two essentially distinct substances, capable of their characteristic activities, so likewise are Christ's humanity and divinity. Finally, in Christ the divine Word is the higher and dominating principle, as the soul is with reference to the body. The Word possessed the human nature as his own, as the soul possesses the body with which it is united. Our Lord's human nature received its supernatural perfection from the Word, somewhat in

---

[45] See the *Symbolum "Quicunque"* (better known as the "Athanasian" Creed); Denz., 39–40. Cf. St Thomas, III, q. 2, art. 1, ad 2.

the way that our body shares in, and is ennobled by, the spiritual life of the soul.

On two points, however, the parallel no longer applies: While our soul and body are *incomplete* substances, together forming one nature, the divinity and humanity are *complete*, and, throughout their union in Christ, remain two distinct natures and do not constitute a third. The rational soul plays an actualizing, formative role with reference to the material body; it is its substantial form. But this could never be said of the Word in relation to our Lord's humanity; for the reason that, if we are to avoid the absurdity of pantheism, the Creator can never be thought of as the informative principle of any creature. Lastly, soul and body make up real *parts* in the composite whole which we are. But—and here perhaps is the most elusive concept in the whole doctrine of the Incarnation—the divinity and humanity are not to be considered as component *parts* of the God-Man. The divinity cannot be a part; for that implies an imperfection, namely, the lack of its complementary part. Now, as we have already remarked, the divine nature in itself lacks nothing, and hence acquires nothing which it does not already possess in assuming human nature. Even the latter is not strictly speaking a part; both on account of the fact that it has no corresponding part proportioned to it, being infinitely transcended by the divine nature, and because it does not contribute to, but rather receives from, the personal being (*esse personale*) of the incarnate Word. At the same time we may say with truth, as will be touched on presently, that the person of Christ, in virtue of the hypostatic union, is *composed* of a human and a divine nature.[46]

Jesus Christ is God by his divine nature, man by his human nature. The great dogmatic texts,[47] which we have already examined, are inexplicable without this duality in oneness. The sacrifice of either element—the "one person" or the "two natures"—would mean that the central mystery

[46] Denz., 216.
[47] Notably John 1:14 and Phil. 2:6–8.

of the Redemption was no longer tenable. If our Lord's actions were not those of a single divine person, God received no adequate atonement for our sins. If Jesus had not, united with the Godhead, a humanity like ours, then it is not our human nature which is redeemed. Monophysitism, in whatever form proposed, is incompatible with the doctrine it strives to maintain, namely, the divinity of Christ. For the divine nature to be blended with the human would imply that it had lost its attributes of infinity and immutability. Any composition of the two natures, understood not as the hypostatic union, but as forming a third nature, destroys the distinction between what is infinite and what is finite. The attempt of Eutyches to preserve the reality of our Lord's human nature involved self-contradiction.[48] For if, at the moment of his conception in Mary's womb, his human nature was united to the divinity in such a way as to be changed into it, then he was no longer truly man.

The distinction between the two natures becomes clearer when we consider them in action. A subsequent attempt to reconcile Monophysitism with orthodoxy, on a basis of only one will (hence the name "Monothelitism") and one divine-human activity in Christ, could not but meet with condemnation,[49] as being patently in conflict with the evidence of Scripture. That our Lord had a human will distinct from the divine we know from his own words: "I came down from heaven, not to do my own will, but the will of him who sent me." [50] When the tension between Christ's antecedent human will and the divine will seemed near to breaking-point, during his agony in Gethsemane, he kept faithful to his Father's commission: ". . . as thy will is, not as mine is." [51] In this is disclosed to us, both the distinction between the divine and human will in Christ, and the free surrender of the latter to the former. In his prayer, "Abba, Father . . . take away this chalice from before me," our Lord gave expression to the natural desire of frail human nature

48 Eutyches, though devout and tenacious of what he held to be true, was no theologian. Pope Leo speaks of him, with justice, as "rash and unskilled" in such matters. Leo *Ep.* xxviii; *P.L.* 54, col. 757.

49 Denz., 291.   50 John 6:38(R-D.).   51 Mark 14:36.

to shrink from suffering; but in the words which follow, "only as thy will is, not as mine is," he placed everything in his Father's hands, by the rational *choice* which is the essence of free will in action. Christ's service of God was always free, not being determined from without; it was with full liberty that he became "obedient unto death, even the death of the cross." [52] But throughout all that this involved, the moral unity of the human and the divine, the perfect conformity of the lower to the higher, was preserved. "I cannot do anything on my own authority; I decide as I am bidden to decide, and my decision is never unjust, because I am consulting the will of him who sent me, not my own"; [53] "And he who sent me is with me; he has not left me alone, since what I do is always what pleases him." [54]

The active works of Christ, which have their source in the unique person of the Son of God, are shown to us, now as in accordance with his human nature, now with the divine. Thus at one moment he can say: "the Father is greater than I"; [55] at another: "I and the Father are one." [56] We see him as man, the greatest and last in the line of the Old Testament prophets: "Jerusalem, Jerusalem, still murdering the prophets and stoning the messengers that are sent to thee, how often have I been ready to gather thy children together, as a hen gathers her brood under her wings, and thou didst refuse it!" [57] Yet, through his divine nature, he can at choice perform deeds beyond the power of any prophet: "Just as the Father bids the dead rise up and gives them life, so the Son gives life to whomsoever he will." [58] When at prayer, he reveals his humanity's weakness and dependence before God: "Christ, during his earthly life, offered prayer and entreaty to the God who could save him from death, not without a piercing cry, not without tears; yet with such piety as won him a hearing." [59] According to his divinity, he is the object of men's prayers, sharing the omnipotence which can give them fulfilment: "... whatever

52 Phil. 2:8(S.).   53 John 5:30.   54 8:29.
55 14:28(R-D.).   56 10:30(R-D.).   57 Luke 13:34.
58 John 5:21.   59 Heb. 5:7.

you shall ask in my name, that I will do.... If you ask me anything in my name, that I will do." [60]

But to distinguish between the two natures is not to separate them. When the theologians, in their discussions on the Trinity, insist that the Father, Son and Holy Spirit are really distinct from one another, they are doing the very reverse of separating them; rather they are showing how they are at one with the divine nature, on account of their mutual relations with each other. Apart from this unity of the Three Persons in the Blessed Trinity, there is no more intimate union than that of the divine and human nature in Christ. Though distinct, as Creator and creature, they yet interpenetrate, and exist within, each other.[61] The active principle here, it need hardly be said, is the person of the Word, wholly divine in nature, and to be distinguished from God the Father only by virtue of his Sonship. The human nature plays a passive role; but it is so permeated by the divine, that it can be thought of as reciprocating in this mysterious compenetration. This may help us to understand how our Lord's actions, whether we think of them as according to his human, or according to his divine, nature are *personal* to him; that is to say, they are the deeds of the Son of God. Hence, when we ascribe some of his actions to *Christ as man,* others to *Christ as God,* language of this kind must not be taken as suggesting that the human and divine natures, while being admittedly distinctive mediums of his actions, are also two distinct sources from which they proceed; for this would conflict with the doctrine of the hypostatic union.

This point can be seen in its application to ourselves. All our deliberate actions engage our individual human nature; yet we do not attribute them to this. It is *you* and *I* who act; what we do is attributable to each of us as a *person.* So was it with our Lord; everything he freely chose to do, he did as the *person* of the incarnate Word. From this

---

[60] John 14:13–14(S.).
[61] This doctrine, of the "co-inherence" of the two natures in Christ, is known as the Christological—as distinct from the Trinitarian—*perichoresis.* It comes from the Greek Fathers, notably St Gregory of Nazianzus and St John Damascene.

emerges a principle, known in the technical language of theology as the *communicatio idiomatum*. By *idiomata* is understood the properties and actions of the two natures in Christ. The *communicatio* means that, in virtue of his being one person, the actions and properties of the two natures are interchangeable. We cannot of course equate "divinity" and "humanity," when used as abstract terms, but there is a sense in which we can and must do so when they refer to the concrete *person* (*hypostasis*) of the God-Man. St Thomas gives us the fundamental reason for this: "In the mystery of the Incarnation the divine nature is not the same as the human nature, but the hypostasis of each of the natures is the same." [62] So we find in Scripture, that what our Lord suffered according to his human nature is applicable to his Godhead: "... to rule the Church of *God,* which *he* has purchased with *his own* blood." [63]

Here it will be in place to pass briefly in review the supernatural prerogatives of Christ's humanity, which make his human nature the source and exemplary cause of all the graces mankind receives from God. "We were beholders of his glory, such glory as that of the Only Begotten of the Father, full of grace and truth ...; of his fulness we all received, and grace upon grace." [64] "He too is that head whose body is the Church; it begins with him, since his was the first birth out of death; thus in every way the primacy was to become his." [65] "... Christ, in whom lie hidden all the treasures of wisdom and knowledge." [66] "For in him resides bodily all the complete fulness of the Godhead; and you have your completion in union with him, who is the head of every principality and power." [67] Thus does the New Testament record our Lord's incomparable glory. The Catholic Church, in faithful witness to this revelation, teaches that his human nature was enriched with gifts from on high, infinitely transcending those of any other man.

The grace of the hypostatic union produced in Jesus Christ

[62] III, q. 16, art. 5.
[64] John 1:14, 16(S.).
[66] 2:2–3(W.).
[63] Acts 20:28(S.); cf. 1 John 3:16.
[65] Col. 1:18.
[67] VV. 9–10(S.).

the sanctity of the Godhead. To him, no less than to the eternal Father, can be applied the words of Isaiah's vision: "Holy, Holy, Holy, the Lord God of hosts, all the earth is full of his glory." [68] Even the evil spirits were compelled to acknowledge the fact: "I recognize thee for what thou art, the Holy One of God." [69] But, in addition to this uncreated sanctity, our Lord's human soul was made pleasing to God in the same way as ours; that is to say, by the infusion of sanctifying grace, the theological virtue of charity, and the gifts of the Holy Spirit. From the beginning he had these graces in all their fulness; there was no room for their increase, just as in him there is no evidence of any growth in holiness or moral stature. From first to last he stands before us, perfect: "Thou art my beloved Son; in thee I am well pleased." [70] Hence the entire sinlessness of Christ—"he has been through every trial, fashioned as we are, only sinless." [71] There was in him no trace of that original guilt and stain from which he came to redeem us. "You know well enough that when God revealed himself, it was to take away our sins; there is no sinfulness in him, and no one can dwell in him and be a sinner." [72] Actual sin in Christ is equally unthinkable; his actions were all of them holy in the sight of the Father: "What I do is always what pleases him." [73] So he could challenge the malevolence of his enemies: "Can any of you convict me of sin?" [74] At the hour of their seeming triumph, when Satan, "the Prince of this world," was allowed to have his way, our Lord remained untouched by evil: "One is coming, who has power over this world, but no hold over me." [75] He moved forward to the great sacrifice utterly blameless—"an unblemished and spotless lamb." [76]

For I would have you know how greatly I strive for you, . . . and for all those who have not seen my face in the flesh, that their hearts may be comforted and themselves be knit together in charity and [brought] to all the blessings of sure insight, to

68 Isa. 6:3.   69 Mark 1:24.   70 Vs. 11.   •
71 Heb. 4:15; cf. 7:26.   72 1 John 3:5–6.   73 John 8:29.
74 Vs. 46.   75 14:30.   76 1 Pet. 1:19(S.).

the full knowledge of the mystery of God, even Christ, in whom lie hidden all the treasures of wisdom and knowledge.[77]

St Paul, in explaining to the Colossians what is acquired through belief in Christ, at the same time tells us something of the boundless extent of our Lord's own knowledge. We shall see the practical importance of this when we come to speak of his role as Prophet.[78] Here it will be enough to recall the underlying theological principles without entering into any detailed analysis. In his divine nature the knowledge possessed by Jesus was of course co-extensive with that of the Godhead; but his human mind also enjoyed a unique enlightenment. He acquired by experience knowledge of the world around him, just as we do.[79] But always he had been "filled with wisdom."[80] In addition to this mode of knowledge, which he shares with us, he had that intuition into the nature of things which is, properly speaking, angelic rather than human. Such illumination befitted a human nature which, in virtue of the hypostatic union, takes rank, not only before all men, but far above the highest of the angels.

More than this, our Lord's mind was enlightened by the direct vision of God. Such is the explanation of the divine assurance behind everything he said. He could refrain from satisfying the undue curiosity of his disciples on a matter about which they had no right to enquire—"It is not for you to know the times and seasons which the Father has fixed by his own authority."[81] As touching a point which the Father had not charged him to reveal, he could even profess his ignorance.[82] But deep within his mind there was no absence of knowledge, whether of the past, present or future. In words and deeds alike there is no hesitancy, no uncertainty of touch; he lives always in the light of the vision of his Father: "... I have knowledge of him.... Yes, I have knowledge of him, and I am true to his word."[83] His human intelligence dwelt in heights never reached by any

[77] Col. 2:1–3(W.).   [78] § 18, pp. 224–30.   [79] Cf. Luke 2:52.
[80] Vs. 40.   [81] Acts 1:7.
[82] Cf. Mark 13:32; see also pp. 298 ff.   [83] John 8:55.

Old Testament prophet. "For the law was given by Moses: grace and truth came by Jesus Christ. No man hath seen God at any time: the only begotten son who is in the bosom of the Father, he hath declared him." [84]

We have already seen something of our Lord's miracle-working powers.[85] It should be noted that this gift of miracles was a permanent quality with him, even though there were occasions when, being confronted with hostility and unbelief, he was not disposed to make use of it.[86] But the people knew his secret "... so that all the multitude was eager to touch him, because power went out from him, and healed them all." [87] In this connection, the Fathers of the Church speak of our Lord's humanity as being the "instrument" of the Word. By this we are able to appreciate how Christ's human nature, though not of itself omnipotent, was the means most fittingly adapted for mediating divine power to men.[88] God works upon man as he is, his grace perfecting our nature as it now exists; thus it was fitting that he should effect the object of the Incarnation—the "recapitulation" of all things in Christ [89]—through the medium of a nature like ours, hypostatically united with himself. We must note also that this instrumental power of our Lord's humanity extends, not only to physical miracles and to conferring the miraculous gift upon others, but also to the interior operations of divine grace. "The Son of Man possesses authority upon earth to forgive sins." [90] "He that eateth my flesh and drinketh my blood hath everlasting life, and I will raise him up on the last day." [91] Thus we see the sacramental significance of our Lord's human nature; it is the sign and instrument of the grace of God so plentifully poured out upon us: "I have come so that they may have life, and have it more abundantly." [92]

Nevertheless, the supernatural prerogatives of Christ's humanity left it in all respects truly human. The Church gives no countenance to any docetic view, which would see in it

[84] John 1:17–18(R.-D.).   [85] § 7, pp. 78–82.   [86] Cf. Mark 6:5.
[87] Luke 6:19.   [88] St Thomas, III, q. 13, art. 2.
[89] Cf. Eph. 1:10.   [90] Matt. 9:6(S.).   [91] John 6:54(W.).
[92] 10:10.

no more than a veil for the divinity. It has been well said that he is the only perfect human being who has ever existed; in him the ideal of manhood was realized in all its completeness. The Son of God freely assumed *our* human nature—not as in its primitive innocence but in its fallen state. "For the law was powerless, because it was made ineffectual by the flesh. But God, by sending his own Son in the likeness of sinful flesh and in reparation for sin, condemned sin in the flesh...." [93] It is true that, in virtue of the hypostatic union, our Lord, unlike ourselves, enjoyed the vision of God, as well as immunity from original sin and its consequences of disordered concupiscence, ignorance and error; but he freely relinquished his right to exemption from those other human defects which derive from Adam's sin. There was nothing in him traceable to physical imperfection or moral weakness; yet he knew what it was to suffer hunger and thirst, fatigue [94] and vexation; [95] the fulness of his emotional life allowed him to show outward signs of affection; [96] he could experience joy,[97] as well as fear and sadness.[98] Finally, he submitted to the terrible reality of an agonizing death.

Nor were our Lord's physical and mental sufferings mitigated by the fact that, in the depths of his soul, he had before him the vision of God. As St Thomas explains, "By divine dispensation, the joy of contemplation was kept in Christ's mind, so as not to overflow into the sensitive powers, and thereby shut out sensible pain." [99] There was anguish of spirit also: "Christ's soul could apprehend things both as hurtful to himself, as were his sufferings and death, and as affecting others, such as the sin of his disciples and of the Jews who killed him. Hence, as there could be true pain in Christ, so could there be true sorrow." [100] In all this it should never be forgotten that our Lord underwent his sufferings freely; he was not constrained to endure them; they were the pledge of his love for the Father and for us. There was

[93] Rom. 8:3(S.).   [94] Cf. John 4:6–8.   [95] Cf. Mark 3:5.
[96] Cf. 9:36; 10:21.   [97] Cf. John 15:11.   [98] Cf. Mark 14:33–34.
[99] St Thomas, III, q. 15, art. 6.   [100] *Ibid.*

a sense in which they were involuntary, as being against all his human instincts; nevertheless, he *chose* them: "And thus Christ's death and passion were of themselves involuntary, and caused sorrow; although they were voluntary with respect to their end, namely, the redemption of the human race." [101] "The soul of Christ could have prevented these sufferings from coming upon him, especially if he had made use of the divine power; yet, of his own will, he freely submitted himself to these sufferings of body and soul." [102] How faithful is St Thomas to the teaching of Scripture here: "This my Father loves in me, that I am laying down my life, to take it up again afterwards. Nobody can rob me of it; I lay it down of my own accord. I am free to lay it down, free to take it up again; this is the charge which my Father has given me." [103]

It is an immense comfort for the believing Christian to realize that the metaphysics of the Incarnation—so necessary if we would even begin to appreciate the depths within depths of its mystery—serve to throw light upon, rather than to obscure, the Christ of the Gospels. He remains what we have seen him to be, the long-awaited Messiah, the fulfilment of Isaiah's prophecy of God's Suffering Servant. His passion and death, as the early Church so clearly understood, are the only answer to the problem of innocent suffering, the supreme example to us of how adversity should be borne. "If you do wrong and are punished for it, your patience is nothing to boast of; it is the patience of the innocent sufferer that wins credit in God's sight. Indeed, you are engaged to this by the call of Christ; he suffered for our sakes, and left you his own example; you were to follow in his footsteps." [104] "Wherefore, it behoved him in all things to be made like unto his brethren, that he might become a merciful and faithful high priest before God. For in that wherein he himself hath suffered and been tempted, he is able to succour them also that are tempted." [105]

Truly, then, Jesus Christ is our adorable Saviour. His

---

[101] St Thomas, III, q. 15, art. 6, ad 4. [102] Art. 4, ad 1. [103] John 10:17–18.
[104] 1 Pet. 2:20–21.   [105] Heb. 2:17–18(R-D.).

sacred humanity is itself worthy of the adoration to be paid
to God alone; not, however, as considered in distinction
from his divinity, but as hypostatically united with it. Accordingly, it is both more scriptural and more theological
to think in terms of devotion simply to our Lord himself,
rather than to his humanity—for reasons that should already
be clear. A spiritual life that is truly Catholic should always be based upon revealed dogma; and the fundamental
dogma of the Incarnation is that our Lord's human nature
is not a separate entity, but has been taken up into union
with God the Son, so as to form together with him one
divine person, that of the Word made flesh. We know that
Jesus, for all his selflessness and humility, required of men
the worship which is due only to God; so he expressly desired "that all may reverence the Son just as they reverence
the Father; to deny reverence to the Son is to deny reverence
to the Father who sent him." [106] If it was not until after
the Resurrection that the disciples fully recognized his majesty, then at least they paid fitting tribute: "When they saw
him there, they fell down to worship." [107] On Ascension Day,
"they bowed down to worship him, and went back full of
joy to Jerusalem." [108] In the Epistle to the Philippians, we
find St Paul rejoicing in the thought of the adoration due to
Christ: "... at the name of Jesus every knee should bend, of
beings in the heavens, on the earth and under the earth, and
every tongue should confess that Jesus Christ is Lord, to the
glory of God the Father." [109]

It is in complete harmony with the worship of our Lord's
adorable humanity, in the sense just explained, that there
should have arisen in the Church a particular devotion to
his Sacred Heart. For the heart is the symbol of Christ's love,
and was so presented in a private revelation to St Margaret
Mary: "Behold this Heart, burning with so great a love for
men." His heart was the chief organ of Christ's human nature, fountain-head of the precious blood so abundantly shed
for us. When, after his death on the Cross, it was pierced by

[106] John 5:23.
[108] Luke 24:52.
[107] Matt. 28:17; cf. John 20:28.
[109] Phil. 2:10–11(S.).

the lance, there flowed from it blood and water [110]—a figure of the sacraments of the Eucharist and Baptism. It should be remembered, however, that though his heart is in itself truly adorable, it is not to be thought of as an isolated physical organ, but rather, in the words of Pope Pius VI, "as the heart of Jesus, that is, the heart of the person of the Word, to whom it is inseparably united." [111] It is better, then, to consider the Sacred Heart in union with the whole interior life of the God-Man, of which it is, so to say, the generative force. Our Lord himself, in conformity with Old Testament usage,[112] gives to the word *heart* this more extended meaning. We are to love God with all our "heart"; [113] the disciples' "hearts" at the Last Supper are filled with grief; [114] later they will be glad.[115] Thus their divine Master must have regarded his own heart as the well-spring of affection, the seat of sorrow and joy, in a word, the source of his whole spiritual life, dedicated as this was to the Father's glory and the world's salvation. It is the living symbol of Christ's redemptive love.

"*Heart of Jesus, hypostatically united to the Word of God —Have mercy on us.*" This, the most theological petition in the Litany of the Sacred Heart, in reality underlies the whole. It is because a human heart has been assumed by the person of the Son of God, and can now be identified with him, just as our hearts are personally ours, that it is "infinite in majesty," "God's holy temple," "tabernacle of the Most High," and the rest. The Litany ends by recalling the words spoken by John the Baptist, when he first bore witness to the Messiah: "Behold, the Lamb of God, who takes away the sin of the world." [116] It is the same Lamb of God who now claims the adoration of the angelic hosts and the whole company of the redeemed:

And I saw, and heard a cry of many angels round about the Throne, and of the living beings and the ancients, and the num-

---

110 John 19:34.
112 Cf. Deut. 10:12; 11:16; 13:3; Prov. 2:2; 23:26.
113 Mark 12:30.
115 Vs. 22.

111 Denz., 1563.

114 John 16:6.
116 John 1:29(S.).

ber of them was myriads of myriads and thousands upon thousands, saying with a great voice: Worthy is the Lamb who was slain to receive power and wealth and wisdom and might and honour and glory and blessing! And every creature existing in the heavens and on the earth and below the earth, and on the sea and the things that are in it, I heard them all saying: To the Occupant of the Throne and to the Lamb, be the blessing and the honour and the glory and the dominion for ever and ever! And the four living beings cried, Amen. And the ancients fell down and worshipped.[117]

[117] Apoc. 5:11–14(S.).

§ 16. THE DIVINE PERSONALITY OF JESUS

Not a little light is thrown upon the personality of Jesus, by considering what theologians call the "fittingness" (*convenientia*) of the Incarnation. It should never be forgotten that the union of our Lord's divine and human natures in the person of the Word is a revealed mystery, whose content is completely beyond rational demonstration; even though the terms in which it is proposed to us by the Church can, within limits, be understood. St Thomas Aquinas, who was not prone to the use of superlatives, describes the Incarnation as "the miracle of miracles"; [1] it transcends human reason more than any other of God's works—*maxime rationem excedit;* "for no more wonderful deed of divine power can be conceived than that he who was truly God the Son should really become man." [2] It is "of all things the most marvellous"—*inter omnia mirabilissimum est*—and all the other wonders of our Faith are subordinated to it, as to their cause. Christian apologetics can go a considerable distance towards establishing the Divinity of Christ, but the inner mystery of the incarnate Word is accessible to faith alone; it demands the mind's surrender to God's revealing grace. We are involved in an obscurity which no processes of reasoning can remove, even while the believer knows that he is blinded with excess of light. He enters the night

[1] *De Potentia,* q. 6, art. 2, ad 9.
[2] *Contra Gentiles,* lib. 4, cap. 27.

of supernatural faith, albeit more sustaining to the soul than the clarities of reason; for, in the words of St John of the Cross, it is "the night more lovely than the dawn."

Nevertheless, to those surrounded by the infidelity of the modern world, it is encouraging to realize that there is an inherent suitability in the Incarnation, which should strengthen our faith and commend it to every rightly disposed mind.[3] How can one and the same person have two natures, one divine, the other human, infinitely distinct from one another? It would seem—so the rationalists of all ages have objected—that a God made man would be but a monstrosity, neither God nor man; or else, as Eutyches held, a mixed being, neither wholly divine nor wholly human. How is it possible for the Almighty God who governs the universe to be housed in a Virgin's womb, to become a little child? Certainly the union of divinity and humanity in Christ remains, as has just been said, an incomprehensible mystery to the believer; we shall understand it fully only in heaven. But even here on earth, in the light of two principles, which have the support of reason as well as faith, we can discern something of its outlines. We know that, in the nature of things, *God tends to communicate himself as much as possible to man,* and also that *Man tends to unite himself as much as possible to God.* Let us ponder, then, the mystery of the Incarnation with the help of these two principles.

The reason why God tends to communicate himself to man is because he is the sovereign Good; and, as St Thomas says, "it belongs to the essence of goodness to communicate itself to others."[4] What is essentially good is not content to be self-contained, it spreads abroad its riches; and the higher it is in the order of being, the fuller and more intimate is this self-communication.[5] The sun pours out its light and heat; the vegetable and animal creation give birth, from their own vitality, to others of the same species. At a higher level, the philosopher or poet communicates to the world

[3] See Garrigou-Lagrange, *Le Sauveur et son amour pour nous,* pp. 92–105; to which the present section is much indebted.
[4] III, q. 1, art. 1.
[5] Cf. *Contra Gentiles,* lib. 4, cap. 11, par. 1.

at large the conceptions of his own mind; the apostle strives to impart to all the zeal with which he is consumed. It is the same in the sphere of human affection; the friendships of the shallow-minded are, like themselves, light and superficial; but with deeper souls it is different—there is a heart-to-heart intimacy, a sharing of confidences, constant and generous self-giving. The good, then, is essentially communicative; and the more excellent it is, the more intimate and complete its self-abandonment to another.

God being the sovereign Good, it is highly fitting that he should pour himself out upon creatures in a way that accords with his nature, that is, with something of the divine plenitude and completeness. Plotinus and the neo-Platonists had a partial glimpse of this truth; but they overlooked the fact that God's self-communication to his creatures must be *free*. There is nothing in them which demands that they should have been created, or can determine him to act. He for his part, enjoying the infinite beatitude which is himself, can gain no increase, no essential enhancement of his glory, from his creatures. *Ipse solus est maxime liberalis;* "He alone is supremely free; because he does not act to gain something for himself (*propter suam utilitatem*), but out of the abundance of his goodness (*sed solum propter suam bonitatem*)." [6] In the beginning, it was with divine generosity and unrestricted freedom that "God created heaven and earth." [7] He gave to his creation existence, life and intelligence, impressing his own likeness upon it; [8] by a still greater act of self-communication, he raised both angels and men to "become partakers of the divine nature." [9] Was it possible for him to communicate himself yet more fully and intimately than this?

Why could not God give himself to us *in person?* This self-donation is what every lover strives to do for his beloved—even though the most intimate act of self-communication, that of the marriage union, falls short of the literal giving of one's own personality to another. But is the in-

---

6 St Thomas, I, q. 44, art. 4, ad 1.   7 Gen. 1:1.
8 Vs. 26.   9 2 Pet. 1:4(S.).

finite God so bound, as we are, within the limits of his own
selfhood, that such an act of generosity is impossible for him?
Why could not the divine Word so give himself to a privileged soul that the Word, together with this human soul
and body, should form a single *person,* a unique "I"? Thus
the Word would be "made flesh," [10] possessed alike of the
divine perfections and all that makes up our human nature.
Such a one would be able to say, "*I* am the way, the truth
and the life." [11] So would have been realized, in marvellous
fashion, the principle: God, the sovereign Good, tends to
communicate himself as much as possible to man. Good is
essentially communicative; the higher it is in the order of
being, the fuller and more intimate is its self-communication.
We reach here what may well be the highest level our minds
can achieve in contemplating the mystery of the Incarnation.

Let us turn now to its human side. It is often objected
by non-Catholic scholars and philosophers that, if our Lord
had not, as the Church teaches, a human personality, then
he cannot be considered to be truly man. This was in fact the
stumbling-block to Nestorius and his followers in the fifth
century; it remains perhaps the chief difficulty for the modern
mind in the acceptance of the Catholic Christology. Hence,
our contemporaries take refuge in the only possible alternatives—an adoptionist,[12] or else a completely humanitarian
Christianity. Some thinkers, under the influence of Leibnitz,
define human personality, not in terms of *substance,* but of
consciousness and *individual liberty.* On this view, it would
follow that, if our Lord was without a human personality,
then he would have not a human, but only a divine, consciousness and free will. In a word, he had not a complete
manhood; and further, not having human liberty, we cannot ascribe to him the power to merit and the virtue of
obedience. If, on the other hand, we maintain, as the Gospels

[10] John 1:14.   [11] 14:6(S.).
[12] *Adoptionism* is the notion that our Lord was, or conceived himself to
have been, adopted by the Father as "Son of God" at some point in his
earthly life. The moment usually pointed to for this is at the Baptism; when,
it is maintained, in contradiction to the New Testament evidence considered
as a whole, he first became aware of himself as the Messiah.

compel us to, that Christ had a fully human, as well as a divine, consciousness and liberty, then we must ascribe to him two personalities—intimately united with each other, no doubt, by knowledge and love; but still, two personalities and not one. So, in continuity with Nestorius, runs one of the commonest objections to the Church's teaching about our Lord. Its logical consequence is that Jesus is no more than the greatest of the saints; it can be admitted that he enjoyed the highest degree of intimacy with God ever given to man, so as to entitle him to be called the "Son of God"; but not that he himself was God. In brief, if the fundamental constitutent of personality is consciousness or freedom, then, since Christ had but one personality, there is no escape from the conclusion that he had likewise only a single consciousness and liberty; that is to say, he is no longer simultaneously God and man.

These difficulties have here been formulated with some force; not with a view to mere controversy, but because they preoccupy many sincere minds who profess allegiance to Christ, but cannot see their way to accepting the Catholic dogma of the hypostatic union. Let us, then, briefly re-examine our Lord's personality in the light of the foregoing objections. We shall necessarily be involved in considerations of some abstruseness, though the reader should be well re-paid for the effort of concentration demanded. It is too often forgotten that the apparent "technicalities" of theology are well within the reach of a quite normal intelligence, since they are in reality closely connected with common sense and everyday speech. In order to see how Jesus, without having a human personality—an "I" and a "me" applicable to him in the same sense as to us—can yet be fully man, and further, how his humanity, far from being diminished, is enhanced and glorified by the personality of the divine Word, we must recall to our minds the nature of personality in general. Not a little confusion has arisen on this point, with the result that the true significance of the words "I" and "me" as used in ordinary language has become obscured. If we ask ourselves, with St Thomas, what is the fundamental notion of "personality," and pass from the lower degrees of human personality to the highest example of all, we shall be enabled, in the light of faith, to form some idea of our Lord's personality. Thus we shall be able to discern what makes it immeasurably higher and more vital in its influence than that of a St John or a St Francis of Assisi.

Personality is something positive; it is that by which every reasonable being is an *independent subject,* able to say "I" and "me"; it is that whereby it enjoys self-mastery, is *sui juris.* We ascribe to personality a rational nature, actual existence, and the operations from which its activity proceeds. In this sense we say that Peter and Paul are two persons, each quite distinct from the other; each implies by the words "I" and "me" something that the other does not. Consequently the *person* is distinguishable—in a technical, but quite intelligible, phrase—as the *first subject of attribution* of all that pertains to it, and cannot itself be attributed to any other subject. We can say: "Peter is a man," "Peter exists," "Peter laughs"; but we cannot, speaking literally, attribute Peter to any other subject. He is himself the "first subject of attribution," existing and acting as a unique entity.[13] From this it follows that the human personality— namely, that by which every rational being is an independent subject, a whole to which we ascribe its nature, existence and operations—cannot fundamentally consist in anything which is attributed to it as a *part.* Our personality is not then formally constituted by our body, or even by our soul, that is, by either of the two parts of the nature attributed to us, still less by any of our powers or activities.

It should now be clear why the ultimate basis of personality cannot be consciousness. My awareness of myself presupposes, precisely, myself; it does not constitute me as a person, for I must exist before I can know myself. Neither can liberty provide the final explanation of personality; the exercise of free choice is what *manifests* personality on the psychological and moral plane. In other words, since we must *be* before we can act, liberty, like consciousness, is a function of an already existing person. Here we may note that what makes our personality is not our *existence*. Existence is a contingent attribute of the created person;[14] we none of us *are* our existence; we *have* it from God. He alone *is* his existence. "God said to Moses: *I am who am*. He said: Thus shalt thou say to the children of Israel: *He who is* hath sent me to you."[15] With this it is interesting to compare our Lord's striking words: "Believe me, before ever Abraham came to be, *I am*."[16] In Christ there was but one person, one unique existence.[17] He, unlike ourselves, could say, without further predicate or qualification: "*I am*." Personality, then, lies at a deeper level than the admittedly characteristically personal activities of consciousness and liberty. As has been said, it consists fundamentally in that which makes each of us an independent subject, to which we ascribe all that pertains to it. If then we can attribute to Jesus, *as to the same independent subject,* both a divine and human intelligence, and a divine and human liberty, we are still speaking of one person, and not two.

In this, the Catholic, position there is, let it be acknowledged, a mystery above our comprehension; but it is neither absurd nor unintelligible. Quite the contrary; as we can discover by reflecting on what makes for greatness in a human personality. It is recognized that, from the moral and psychological standpoint, we grow in stature in proportion as we unite ourselves intimately with God and efface our personalities before him. This union in effacement, far from implying an unworthy servitude, is our glorification.[18] Now it is possible to see the application of this principle in Christ himself, not merely from the moral and psychological standpoint, but in the ultimate ontological terms of what constitutes personality. If, as has been shown above, God tends to give himself as much as possible to man, the complementary aspect of this process is also true—the perfect man tends to unite himself as much as possible to God.

[14] Cf. St Thomas III, q. 17, art. 2, ad 1.   [15] Exod. 3:14.
[16] John 8:58. Note the other "*I am*" sayings in St John: 6:20; 8:24; 13:19; 18:5, 6; cf. Apoc. 1:8, 17.
[17] St Thomas, q. 17, art. 2.   [18] Cf. q. 2, art. 2, ad 2.

It is sometimes imagined that personality develops by man's becoming increasingly independent, both in his existence and in his actions, of all that is not himself, and in subjugating others to his own will. In this sense we regard such men as Napoleon and our modern dictators as outstanding personalities. But this is to confuse personality with egoism. It overlooks the fact that our personality consists, not in independence of all things, but in our capacity to rise above what is essentially inferior to ourselves. In extolling certain human personalities who have ignored the rights of God, their admirers fail to realize that man's independence of what is beneath him is in fact based upon his soul's close *dependence* upon what is above him; namely, a dependence upon the True and the Good and, in the last resort, whether or not this be consciously recognized, upon God, the source of all truth and goodness. If our mind transcends space and time and all that can be perceived by the senses, as it does, this is because it is made to know God, the supreme Truth. If likewise our liberty dominates all the sensible attractions of the material order, the reason is that our soul's desire hungers for the universal Good, and can only be satisfied, whether it knows it or not, with loving God above all things. From this emerges a highly important, though seldom remembered, principle: the full development of the personality consists in becoming increasingly independent of what is below us, and, at the same time, more and more closely dependent on the True and the Good, that is, on God.

The pseudo-personality, on the other hand, consists in a self-styled independence with regard to all things, including God, to whom obedience is refused. It is contemptuous of the so-called "passive" virtues of humility and patience, being itself rooted in insubordination and pride. Personality so conceived is realized in its ideal state in Satan, with his device: *I will not serve*. By a bitter but inevitable paradox, it is involved in the worst form of servitude—that of slavery to self. At the other extreme, true personality is realized in the saints, and above all, in Jesus Christ our Lord. The modern world would have been spared much tragic misconception about the development of personality if it had studied a little more closely the mystery of the Incarnation. There is grave need for a fresh recognition of the truth, that the human personality matures by effacing itself before God and being united, so far as this may be, with the divine personality. This is at length being acknowledged, amid much confused theorizing, by the experimental psychologists: "But whoever is unable to lose his life by the same token will never gain it." [19] Thus we are enabled faintly to catch a glimpse of how the human nature of Jesus was in no way diminished by being so intimately united to God as to enjoy, not a human, but a divine personality. At the first moment of the Incarnation, in the ontological depths of the God-Man, there was realized in a sublime degree the principle that human personality is enhanced by effacing itself before God. The manhood of Christ was so enveloped and permeated by the Godhead as to possess, not its own, but *his*, God's, personality.

This truth has its implications in the sphere of action, with reference to the free choices of the human will. We know that man is good, morally speaking, just in so far as his conduct is conformed to the nature of things, that is, to the dictates of conscience and the natural law. For the Christian, ethical goodness stands at a nobler level, at that of the correspondence of his personal liberty with the revealed will of God. Always there is demanded fidelity to what is higher than himself. It is the same in the order of intelligence: the man of genius is in some way inspired; he is mastered by ideas and images which come ultimately from God. Both moral and intellectual excellence presuppose an ideal, a vision, bigger than the self. This is even more true when it is a question of striving for the highest of all forms of human perfection—Christian holiness. The saints, in the ardour of their charity, are more outstanding personalities than the hero and the genius. Strength of personality may surely be measured by the depth and extent of its influence on men's lives. By this standard, the saints surpass in stature even the

[19] Jung, *The Integration of the Personality*, p. 304.

most striking notabilities of secular history. Their influence has not been limited to a single century or epoch; it extends to the whole Church, in a sphere transcending space and time. For nearly nineteen hundred years millions of souls have lived by the Epistles of St Paul, as if they were written but yesterday; while scarcely anyone, except for a handful of scholars, now reads the letters of Seneca. For fourteen centuries thousands of men and women have entered the cloister, inspired by the example and vowed to the Rule of St Benedict. No mere hero or genius has so powerfully affected mankind for good as St Augustine, St Bernard and St Teresa of Avila. By any criterion these were prodigious personalities. What, we may ask, is their secret?

Unquestionably it lies in the closeness of their union with God. In a sense they were dead to themselves, living solely for him. Only the saints have fully understood that the human personality finds its true development in dying to self, so that God may take complete charge of their lives. It is the paradox of the Gospel: "He who loves his life will lose it; he who is an enemy to his own life in this world will keep it, so as to live eternally." [20] So it is that sanctity brings with it a certain self-hatred, a detestation of the "I" —le moi haïssable of Pascal—with its pride and self-complacency. We find it revealed in the words of St John the Baptist: "He must become more and more, I must become less and less." [21] We see it exemplified in the work of St Thomas Aquinas, effacing himself before the great truths he is concerned to expound. This is the "higher impersonality" of the saints, which could never be confused with stoical apathy and the superior indifference of the philosopher. Souls of great holiness desire that God should become for them another self, an alter ego; they would have their own personality replaced, as it were, by his, so that they might be made more unreservedly his servants. They wish the adoptive sonship which they know to be theirs to be so realistically fulfilled, in the depths of the spirit, at the vital source of their thoughts and actions, that they may

[20] John 12:25; cf. Luke 17:33.   [21] John 3:30.

live with the life of God. Then they can make their own the boast of St Paul: "I am alive; or rather, not I; it is Christ that lives in me." [22] The full development of the human personality consists in losing itself in God.

And yet the saints, at the height of what the mystics have called the "transforming union," are still creatures distinct from God. They may have substituted God's thoughts for their own, his will for theirs, but they can never, ontologically speaking, be identified with him. Mary herself, Mother of the incarnate Word, even at the hour of her most intimate prayer, God's masterpiece though she was, remained a pure creature. At the summit of sanctity stands Jesus Christ himself. In him God's self-giving is, in the literal sense of the word, infinite. He gave himself *personally* to the humanity, so that the latter formed a single and unique *"I"* with the eternal Word. In Jesus, it is not simply that the thoughts and desires of God have been substituted for those of man, but, at the deepest roots of the intelligence and will, at the foundations of the soul itself, the divine person of the Word has assumed a created humanity. "For in him resides bodily all the complete fulness of the Godhead." [23] It is for this reason that he, and he alone, could say: *"I* am the way, the truth and the life." [24] It was as signifying an identity in nature that he could claim: *"I* and the Father are one." [25]

Our Lord's personality, being divine, was wholly distinct from that which gave individuality to his human nature. Though they are often confused, there is a profound difference between individuality and personality. The former is rooted in matter; the latter pertains to the spirit. Two men are distinct *individuals* because their human nature is received into different portions of matter, at this or that point in space and time; just as two drops of water, similar though they are, are precisely *two,* from the fact that the nature of water is received into distinct amounts of matter with their determined quantities. Thus our Lord's body was given its "individuality," just as ours is, by matter, which is the principle of individuation; it was in virtue of this that his body was *this* body rather than that, occupying one given portion of space rather than another. His soul was uniquely his in virtue of the mode of subsistence with which it was graced by its union with the Word. But his personality, as we have seen, is on an infinitely higher plane than his created body and soul. We remember that personality in a rational being is that by which it is an independent subject, *sui juris*. This holds good universally, not only of man, but of the angels and the persons in the Blessed Trinity. Each of the three divine persons is a distinct *"I,"* even while each possesses the same divine nature, wholly communicated by the Father to the Son, and by them to the Holy Spirit—so realizing within the Godhead the principle that the Good tends to communicate itself, and the higher it is the fuller and more intimate its self-giving. Hence the fundamental difference between individuality and personality. To give rein to one's individuality, with its roots in matter, is to emphasize the self at the expense of others, to become more and more the *egoist*. To develop the personality, with its foundations in spirit, tends, as we have seen, towards the losing of the self in God. The humanity of Christ had, as its ultimate selfhood, nothing less than the Godhead; it was possessed by the uncreated personality of the eternal Word. "Believe me, before ever Abraham came to be, *I am*." [26]

In this we have the explanation of the uniqueness with which our Lord used the first person singular—the *"I"* and the *"me."* The saints scarcely ever employ it save to accuse themselves of their sins, knowing that whatever good they have comes from God, that all they can claim as their own is egoism and self-love. But this is not the language of Jesus: "I am the resurrection and the life; he who believes in me, though he die, yet shall he live; and whoever lives and believes in me shall never die." [27] "I am the vine; you are the branches. He who abides in me, and I in him, he it is who bears much fruit; because apart from me you can produce

26 John 8:58.   27 11:25–26(S.).

nothing." [28] "He who loves father or mother more than me is not worthy of me; and he who loves son or daughter more than me is not worthy of me; and he who does not take his cross and follow me is not worthy of me. He who has found his life shall lose it; and he who has lost his life for my sake shall find it." [29] Such words as these could be spoken only by one who knew himself to be God.

Whence comes it that our Lord infinitely surpasses the greatest of the saints, for whom he is the model, the vital inspiration? It lies in this, that in his case, instead of a human personality, a human "*I*," the divine personality of the Word had been united to his human nature at the first instant of his conception in Mary's womb, and for ever. And withal his manhood remains perfectly intact; in truth, as St Thomas explains,[30] far from suffering diminution, it is enhanced and glorified. From its union with the Word it receives, as we have seen, an innate and uncreated sanctity. Somewhat in the way a human imagination is superior to that of the animals, in virtue of its union with the higher faculty of intelligence—as we can see by the imaginative work of the poet and the artist—so our Lord's humanity was uplifted by being united with the Word. Similarly, just as it is the highest dignity of the lower to serve the higher—of the imagination, for example, to be the instrument of the intellect—so was it the glorification of Christ's human nature, his adorable soul and body, to be wholly taken up, not only in the person, but in the designs and purposes of the Son of God. *Cui servire regnare est:* "to serve God is to rule as king." No creature has ever served him with such complete fidelity as the all-holy soul of our divine Redeemer.

[28] John 15:5(S.).   [29] Matt. 10:37–39(S.).   [30] III, q. 2, art. 2, ad 2.

CHAPTER IV

THE DIVINE REDEEMER

WE have seen that our Lord's disclosure of the mystery of his personality was a gradual process. At first implicitly, and only later with unmistakable clarity, did he show himself to be the Messiah and the unique Son of God. Even so, this revelation had been almost too much for the minds of his disciples; not until after the Resurrection and the Pentecostal outpouring of the Spirit was their faith fully confirmed, never afterwards to be shaken. It had been the same with their imperfect comprehension of their Master's life-work; its underlying purpose escaped them. They could never reconcile themselves to the thought that *the Son of Man must suffer*.[1] But not only had he clearly predicted his sufferings; he had supplied the key to their interpretation. They had a redemptive significance: "For the Son of Man himself came not to be served, but to serve, and to give his life a ransom for many (λύτρον ἀντὶ πολλῶν)."[2] To his enemies likewise he had made known the fateful outcome of his mission. In the parable of the unfaithful vine-dressers [3]—evil men who not only refuse to pay their dues to the absent owner of the vineyard but insult, maltreat and even murder the messengers he sends, to reach the climax of iniquity by murdering the heir to the vineyard, the beloved son of the owner—we have a figure of Israel's treatment of the prophets, God's messengers, which culminated in the rejection of her Messiah, the Son of God.

Our Lord did not fail to point the moral: "And now, what will the owner of the vineyard do? He will come and make an end of those vine-dressers, and give his vineyard to others. Why, have you not read this passage in the scriptures, The

---

[1] See p. 157 ff.   [2] Mark 10:45(S.).   [3] 12:1–12.

very stone which the builders rejected has become the chief stone at the corner; this is the Lord's doing, and it is marvellous in our eyes? [4] The "corner-stone," as the primitive Church clearly understood, is Christ the Redeemer.[5] "You crucified Jesus Christ, the Nazarene, and God raised him up from the dead.... He is that stone, rejected by you, the builders, and that has become the chief stone at the corner. Salvation is not to be found elsewhere; this alone of all names under heaven has been appointed to men as the one by which we must needs be saved." [6] It is God's will that all men should "be saved and come to the knowledge of the truth"; [7] but, for the achievement of this, man's final destiny, there exists but a single plan: "For there is one God, and there is one mediator between God and man, Christ Jesus, himself man, who gave himself a ransom for all (ἀντίλυτρον ὑπὲρ πάντων)." [8]

[4] Mark 12:9–11.
[5] Cf. Eph. 2:20; 1 Pet. 2:6.
[6] Acts 4:10–12.
[7] 1 Tim. 2:4(S.).
[8] VV. 5–6(S.). NOTE: The word λύτρον, meaning "ransom," appears in Mark 10:45 and its synonym, ἀντίλυτρον, in 1 Tim. 2:6; which is sufficient refutation, on textual grounds alone, of the view that the doctrine of the Redemption is Pauline rather than evangelical.

§ 17. THE ONE MEDIATOR

"Lord, said Thomas to him, we know not where thou art going, and how can we know the way? Jesus said to him, I am the way, the truth and the life; no one comes to the Father but by me." [1] So our Lord proclaimed himself to be the unique mediator between God and man. His mediatorship involved a threefold office: He is "the way," that is, the leader and guide, the ruler of those who would find the path to heaven; in a word, he is Christ the King. This leadership he exercised, not by any physical constraint, but by proclaiming God's truth: "What I was born for, what I came into the world for, is to bear witness of the truth." [2] He is the Master to whom all must listen,[3] the mouthpiece of God; and hence he is Christ the Prophet. He is greater

[1] John 14:5–6(S.).　　[2] John 18:37.　　[3] Mark 9:7.

than any of the prophets, however, for they were but witnesses to the truth: Jesus is more, he *is* "the truth." Finally, he is "the life": "I have come so that they may have life, and have it more abundantly." [4] And how was this to be? Not otherwise than by his death. "The time has come now for the Son of Man to achieve his glory. Believe me when I tell you this; a grain of wheat must fall into the ground and die, or else it remains nothing more than a grain of wheat; but if it dies, then it yields rich fruit." [5] In surrendering his life, Jesus is not only the willing victim, he is also the offerer, of his own sacrifice; [6] that is to say, he is Christ the Priest.

Christ as mediator thus embodied in his own person the three roles which the Jews had for centuries looked upon as the most significant of all—the king, the prophet and the priest. This triple office belonged to our Lord, in virtue of the hypostatic union, from the first moment of the Incarnation; even though it was only subsequently that it was fully exercised. The Baptism in the Jordan was the decisive moment for the beginning of the public ministry and the manifestation of his call as Israel's Messiah. In the chronological order, which we shall here follow, Jesus' work as prophet preceded his great priestly act on the Cross, while the latter was the indispensable preliminary to his entering upon his kingship. This was the heavenly consummation of his life's work. "Therefore, also, God highly exalted him, and bestowed upon him the name which is above every name; so that at the name of Jesus every knee should bend, of beings in the heavens, on the earth, and under the earth, and every tongue should confess that Jesus Christ is Lord, to the glory of God the Father." [7]

Our Lord's mediatorial act *par excellence* is that whereby he achieved our redemption on Calvary. But first we must recall that Christ is our *natural* mediator; from the fact that he is both God and man, and that his acts, as man, have their supreme value by reason of his human nature forming one person with the Son of God.

[4] John 10:10.   [5] 12:23–24.
[6] Cf. 10:18.   [7] Phil. 2:9–11(S.).

"Something is called an intermediary," St Thomas explains,[8] "when it exists between two extremes; for it is the function of an intermediary to act as a go-between (*extrema conjungere*). Hence we call someone a mediator when he performs this function of bringing together what has been separated. But he cannot do this unless, in some way, the nature of an intermediary belongs to him, namely, that he should stand between two extremes."

What is required, therefore, as the ontological basis of mediatorship between God and man, is that someone should be found in whose very *person* the divine and human extremes meet. No reflection is needed to see that this condition is verified in Christ, and in him alone.

So the Catholic Church has always taught. There is no release from sin "except through the merit of the one mediator, our Lord Jesus Christ, who has reconciled us to God in his blood, being 'made for us justification, sanctification and redemption.' " [9] This does not, however, preclude a subordinate mediatorship of intercession, such as is exercised by the faithful for one another, by the angels and saints and, above all, by the Mother of God. "Now to unite men to God effectively (*perfective*) belongs to Christ, through whom men are reconciled to God, according to the Second Epistle to the Corinthians, chapter 5, verse 19, 'God was in Christ, reconciling the world to himself.' Consequently, Christ alone is the perfect mediator between God and men, inasmuch as, by his death, he reconciled the human race to God. . . . However, nothing hinders certain others being called mediators, in some respects, between God and men; in so far as they co-operate, dispositively or ministerially, in uniting men to God." [10] Their function is simply to act as God's instruments, in preparing and adapting others to respond to the unique mediatorship of Christ. From the latter this lower form of mediation receives all its efficacy; hence it is but another expression of—rather than, as is some-

8 *In Sent.* 3, d. 19, q. 1, a. 5, sol. 2.
9 Council of Trent, Sess. 5, can. 3; Denz., 790.
10 St Thomas, III, q. 26, art. 1.

times falsely supposed, a derogation from—the work of the "one mediator." Moreover, it is wholly directed to the end that the benefits asked for should be acquired "from God, through his Son Jesus Christ our Lord, who only is our Redeemer and Saviour." [11] Thus, in gaining the intercession of our Lady and the saints, we are but honouring Christ, who "alone of all names under heaven has been appointed to men as the one by which we must needs be saved." [12]

It is "all men" whom God would save, through "Christ Jesus, himself man." [13] Accordingly our Mediator is Christ, *as man*. By definition, a mediator between God and man must be lower than God and higher than man. But only Christ as man differs from, and is inferior to, God; while, at the same time, even as sharing our humanity, in virtue of the hypostatic union and the plenitude of grace in his soul, he excels all men. Here we should note that Christ, subsisting in a divine and human nature whose respective operations are all attributable to him as a unique *person*, can do the deeds of both God and man. Hence, from this point of view, though from this alone, Catholic theologians speak of our Lord as being a double *moral* person. This enables us to understand how, notwithstanding the unity of Christ's *physical* person, he can mediate between men and himself as God. As man, he offers up the acts of the Mediator which, as God, he accepts—though always it should be borne in mind that what Christ does as man receives its perfect mediatorial value from the fact that his human nature is hypostatically united to the Godhead. "For we should not be made free by him, the one Mediator between God and men, the man Jesus Christ, unless he were also God." [14]

Christ carried out his office as Mediator by actions directed both to God and man. To anticipate what we are presently to examine in greater detail: He offered himself to God and, by the shedding of his blood, paid the price whereby men are released from sin and damnation. In order

[11] Trent, Sess. 25; Denz., 984.   [12] Acts 4:12.
[13] I Tim. 2:5(S.).
[14] St Augustine, *Enchiridion*, 108; *P.L.* 40, col. 282.

that we might be reconciled to God, he made perfect satisfaction for us. In his capacity as Head of the human race, our natural representative before God, he pleaded with him, in expiation, petition and intercession, and so gained for us God's grace and love. At the same time, as the Son of God, he represented God himself in this work of mediation, so that, by his own authority, he restored the bond of friendship between God and men. This last, the Atonement, is the fundamental aspect of his role as Mediator. With regard to man, Christ's mediatorship, as we have already seen, is exercised in virtue of his being personally the "Wisdom" of God and the divine "Word." Thus, where his forerunners could but offer faint hints of what was to come, he embodies the final revelation of God's truth, showing us, by word and example, the path of salvation. "God, having spoken of old to our forefathers through the prophets, by many degrees and in many ways, has at last in these days spoken to us by his Son." [15] Moreover, by his divine power, he guides us; for which purpose he founded the Church, as the kingdom of truth and grace. To the Church he has given the fulness of spiritual power and the effective instruments of the supernatural life. By these means the mediatorship of Jesus will reach its complete achievement—the eternal beatitude of those who have been redeemed by his precious blood.

Actions take their value from the status of the one who performs them. Accordingly, our Lord as man, simply by being what he is, can be said to mediate between God and the human race. For he is "the effulgence of God's glory and the very image of his substance." [16] From this it follows that, in Jesus, we have the ideal embodiment of the divine perfections and the best of all mediums for acquiring the knowledge and love of God. This is the underlying thought of the Preface for the Mass of Christmas: "For by the mystery of the Word made flesh, the light of thy glory has shone anew upon the eyes of our mind; so that, while we acknowledge him as God seen by men, we may be drawn by him

---

[15] Heb. 1:1(S.).   [16] Vs. 3(S.).

to the love of things unseen." Again, by his divine-human existence, he constitutes the prototype of all communion between God and man, the foundation and pledge of mankind's access to the Godhead. This was what led such Fathers of the Church as St Irenaeus, St Gregory of Nyssa and St Cyril of Alexandria to think that in the hypostatic union the Word took to himself in some "virtual" or "mystical" way the whole human race. It is the great theme of the *recapitulation in Christ*. "For he made known to us the mystery of his will, the free design which he had determined to carry out in the fulness of times, namely, to bring back all things both in the heavens and on the earth under the headship of the Christ." [17]

Nothing in Christ's work of mediatorship is more profitable for us to consider than his redemptive love. Its first object was his heavenly Father, whose only begotten Son he was; its second, us, his "brethren," [18] for whose sins he made atonement. The love of Jesus for the Father, in all its strength and tenderness, was his from the beginning. In this it was different from all human love, which only rises with difficulty above the surface attractions of the senses. It takes time before the child can pass, from its instinctive state of egoism and cupboard-love, to a generous and unselfish affection for even the members of its own family. Even more gradual is our approach to the love of God, who transcends all that can be seen and touched. It is true that the will has a natural inclination to love above all things the Author of nature,[19] in whom resides universal truth and goodness. This is what teaches us that "The eye is not filled with seeing, neither is the ear filled with hearing." [20] Thus we are slowly led on to make St Augustine's discovery that God alone can satisfy our desire: "Thou hast made us for thyself and our hearts are restless till they rest in Thee." [21] But how painfully we achieve, over and above these vague longings and aspirations, the really efficacious love of God! How re-

---

[17] Eph. 1:9–10(S.). [18] Rom. 8:29.
[19] Cf. St Thomas, I, q. 60, art. 5. [20] Eccles. 1:8.
[21] *Confessions*, I, 1; *P.L.* 32, col. 661.

luctantly our petty preoccupations yield to the disinterested desire for God's glory and the spread of his kingdom! Grudgingly, if at all, do we allow him to master our natural self-concern, to set right our disordered love for creatures, so that all our affections may become vivified and ennobled by his inspiration. Only in heaven will the human heart realize the absolute claims of Love.

With Jesus it was wholly otherwise. Always his soul was absorbed in God. Compared with this love, whose total expression is the creature's conformity to the divine will, the ceremonies and sacrifices of the Jewish Law were nothing worth.

"As Christ comes into the world, he says, No sacrifice, no offering was thy demand; thou hast endowed me, instead, with a body. Thou has not found any pleasure in burnt sacrifices, in sacrifices for sin. See then, I said, I am coming to fulfil what is written of me, where the book lies unrolled; to do thy will, O my God." [22]

This dedication in love flowed from the clear vision before his mind of his Father's infinite splendour and beauty. Such was the light which directed all his actions that he could do nothing from mere whim or caprice; waywardness was unthinkable in him. Adoration and thanksgiving, tokens of the reverential love for God, filled his soul; they were the heart of his religion: ". . . the time is coming, nay has already come, when true worshippers will worship the Father in spirit and in truth." [23] His Father's will, whether as ruling the universe, or as disclosing the divine secrets to his chosen ones, called forth his praise and gratitude. "Father, who art Lord of heaven and earth, I give thee praise that thou hast hidden all this from the wise and prudent, and revealed it to little children. Be it so, Father, since this finds favour in thy sight." [24] *Since this finds favour in thy sight;* from first to last, in every circumstance of his life, that was the only condition he ever laid down. It is the essence of man's love for God.

From the heights of the beatific vision the love of Christ

[22] Heb. 10:5-7.   [23] John 4:23.   [24] Matt. 11:25-26.

descends upon men's souls. Again we see that union of qualities so rarely found together, strength combined with tenderness. In us strength of character is often marred by arrogance, roughness, failure to perceive; while mere tenderness lacks vigour and can be touched with sentimentality. But the love of him, who would not "break a bruised reed, nor quench a smouldering wick," [25] was "strong as death"; it had the quality of which it is said that "Many waters cannot quench charity, neither can the floods drown it: if a man should give all the substance of his house for love, he shall despise it as nothing." [26] In this it is a reproach, as well as an encouragement, to ourselves. Our warmest affections sometimes scarcely reach below the surface. We delight in the congenial company of those who love us; but here it is as much our own pleasure as another's well-being that we seek. We wish our friends well; yet how deep is that wish? There is a simple test: how often do they form the subject of our prayer? Is it our first desire for them that they should gain eternal life? Most of us have to acknowledge also that the range of our affections is pitifully narrow. We have our circle of intimates; as for the rest, their concerns hardly touch us. To those who offend or injure us we respond, if not with equal hostility, at least with coldness and indifference.

How different was the merciful love of our Saviour! He met with ingratitude, contradiction, implacable hatred; yet he overwhelmed even the last in his redeeming prayer on the Cross: "Father, forgive them, for they know not what they do." [27] It is first of all the soul which is the object of Christ's love; he would have it attain to eternal life. He embraces each one of us as an individual, not merely as a member of the human race; "he calls by name the sheep which belong to him." [28] As the Shepherd of the flock, he is as much concerned for the one that is straying as for the ninety-nine who are safe.[29] The paupers and dispossessed have a special place in his affections. One of the signs that he is in truth

---

[25] Matt. 12:20(S.).   [26] Canticle 8:7.   [27] Luke 23:34(R-D.).
[28] John 10:3.   [29] Matt. 18:12-14.

the Messiah is that "the poor have the gospel preached to
them." [30] It is the same with the weary and faint-hearted;
whether they be sinners or not, all are invited: "Come to
me, all you who labour and are heavy laden, and I will give
you rest." [31] He had his preferences among the disciples, for
St John most of all; there was a particular warmth in his
encounters with Martha and Mary, a special mercy for the
good thief; but there was nothing selective in the all-
embracing character of his redeeming love. "He died for all,
so that the living should no longer live for themselves, but
for him who for their sakes died and rose again." [32]

Our Lord's reproaches to the scribes and Pharisees,
hardened in their opposition to him, was but a further evidence of the strength of his love for souls. His enemies stood
between him and the achievement of his Father's purpose;
hence he could not but denounce them. But he had not
failed to give them warning: "He therefore said to them
again, I am going away, and you shall seek me, and shall die
in your sin. Where I am going you cannot come." [33] Nor
had he left anything undone to win them over. "If you find
that I do not act like the Son of my Father, then put no trust
in me; but if I do, then let my actions convince you where
I cannot; so you will recognize and learn to believe that the
Father is in me, and I in him." [34] "If I had not done among
them the works that no other hath done, they would not
have sin; but now they have seen and they have hated both
me and my Father." [35] When he came to give the supreme
proof of his love, he chose to put it in these words: "This is
the greatest love a man can show, that he should lay down
his life for his friends." [36] But it was greater even than this;
it was not only for his friends that he laid down his life;
"while we were yet sinners, Christ died for us." [37] The love
of the Mediator reaches to the Father, to all the world, and
to the depths of each individual soul. So St Paul rejoices in

[30] Matt. 11:5.　　[31] Vs. 28(S.).　　[32] 2 Cor. 5:15(S.).
[33] John 8:21(S.).　　[34] 10:37–38.　　[35] 15:24(W.).
[36] Vs. 13.　　[37] Rom. 5:8(S.).

the thought that Jesus is personally *his* Saviour: "I live in
the faith of the Son of God, who loved me and gave himself
up for me." [38]

[38] Gal. 2:20(S.).

§ 18. THE PROPHETICAL OFFICE OF JESUS

Before approaching Christ's most significant act as our
Mediator, namely, the priestly sacrifice offered by him on
the Cross, it will be in place to consider the authority which
belonged to him as God's messenger. For what chiefly concerns us in his life-work is not the bare record of what he
achieved, but the interpretation which he himself gave to
that achievement. We need to be assured that, in attaching
a saving value to his death, in founding the Church upon
Peter and the apostles, he spoke and acted with the authority
of God. That this was in fact the case emerges from the
doctrine we have already examined; but it will throw further
light on the revelation which he embodied if we see it in
the perspective of his prophetical office. St John, in his account of the feast of Tabernacles, tells us of the impression
made by our Lord upon his hearers: "Some of the multitude,
on hearing these words, said, Beyond doubt this is the
prophet." [1] By this they meant the prophet like to Moses who
had been promised them.[2] That he was this and more is an
integral part of the Church's teaching. For Christ brought in
his own person the decisive revelation of God, to which the
Old Testament prophecy had been but the prelude: "God,
having spoken of old through the prophets, by many degrees
and in many ways, has at last in these days spoken to us by
his Son, whom he appointed heir of all things, and through
whom he made the worlds." [3]

The prophet is essentially the spokesman of God. If he
foretells the future, that is but a part of his prophetic role.[4]
Without enquiring into the nature of Old Testament prophecy generally, it may be said that the prophets were all of

[1] John 7:40.   [2] Deut. 18:15.   [3] Heb. 1:1-2(S.).
[4] Cf. St Thomas, IIa IIae, q. 171, Prologue.

them ministers of God's revelation; their function was to mediate the divine message to man. In this sense Moses, though he is often regarded as a law-giver rather than a prophet, was in fact the prototype of the prophets. "And there arose no more a prophet in Israel like unto Moses, whom the Lord knew face to face." [5] Moses was recognized as the mediator of the Old Law.[6] High amid the clouds, upon the summit of Mount Sinai, he had received the word of God. The people themselves were unable to bear the direct contact; they needed an intermediary. What was given to Moses in secret was a disclosure from God. It was not merely a law; it was also the institution of a covenant, the revealing presence of Yahweh, who willed to be near his people as their own God.

We may contrast the awe-inspiring scene on Sinai with that on another mountain side, when he who stands unique among the prophets, in all the approachableness of our humanity, gave a new code of laws to God's people and brought the old to perfection.[7] Again, how different from the flame and smoke and trumpet-sounds, which accompanied the giving of the ten commandments, was the quiet intimacy of the gathering in the upper room, when the Mediator of "the new covenant in my blood" [8] gave his disciples his own commandment, in which all that had gone before was summed up—"that you are to love one another; that your love for one another is to be like the love I have borne you." [9] Those present on that memorable night knew that their Master was armed with God's authority. Three of them, at the Transfiguration,[10] had heard, out of the cloud, the voice of the Father, ratifying his mission: "This is my beloved Son; to him, then, listen." [11]

The secret of our Lord's incomparable assurance, in everything he said and did, was his insight into the mind of God. All the prophets had this in some degree; but it came to them through "the word of the Lord," not as a vision of the

[5] Deut. 34:10.   [6] Cf. Deut. 5:5 and Gal. 3:19.
[7] See § 5, pp. 39–69.   [8] Luke 22:20(W.).   [9] John 13:34.
[10] See § 10, pp. 93–5.   [11] Mark 9:7.

source from which that word proceeds. Yet of Christ it could be said: "The Father loves the Son, and discloses to him all that he himself does." [12] The prophets derived their authority from on high; with Jesus it is vested in his own person: "I am the light of the world; he who follows me shall never walk in darkness, but shall have the light of life." [13] It was this quality in him, of being able to speak as if his message were a personal possession, which so struck his hearers; "... and they were amazed by his teaching, for he sat there teaching them like one who had authority, not like the scribes." [14] Even the agents of the Sanhedrin, sent to arrest him, testified to the same experience: "Nobody has ever spoken as this man speaks." [15]

The prophetical office of Jesus is for us, as for his first disciples, the basis of our acceptance of him as our Divine Master. He is our Mediator with God, not only in his redeeming death, but in his message; he brings a revelation on human destiny which is literally life-giving: "... the words I have been speaking to you are spirit, and life." [16] The reason being that, along with the acceptance of his words went the gift of grace, the stirring and uplifting of men's hearts which issued from the Word of God himself; "... to all who received him, he gave the right to become children of God, to those who believe in his name." [17] In the last resort the world has now no other teacher but Christ. All human instruction stands or falls by its conformity with his. "Nor are you to be called teachers; you have one teacher, Christ." [18] We have seen that he both entrusted his message to his chosen apostles and vested them with his own authority to proclaim it; [19] but they had nothing to teach save what he and the Holy Spirit would disclose to them, and no title to instruct others except in his name. Accordingly, we need not wonder that the Catholic Church regards it as her inviolable trust to preserve intact "the word of God, written or handed down." [20]

[12] John 5:20.   [13] John 8:12(S.); cf. 1:9.   [14] Mark 1:22.
[15] John 7:46.   [16] John 6:63.   [17] John 1:12(S.).
[18] Matt. 23:10.   [19] Matt. 10:27; 28:18–20.   [20] Denz., 1792.

After the coming of the Holy Spirit, we find St Peter trying to persuade the Jews that "Jesus Christ, who has been made known to you," [21] is the heaven-sent teacher whose message they must accept. "Thus, Moses said, the Lord your God will raise up for you a prophet like myself, from among your own brethren; to him, to every word of his, you must listen. It is ordained that every one who will not listen to the voice of that prophet shall be lost to his people." [22] And yet, in the main, this proclamation fell on deaf ears. The Jews would not receive Jesus as a successor to the prophets. There is a pathos, a note of lamentation, in his sigh: "Believe me, no prophet finds acceptance in his own country." [23] It is true that our Lord's teaching lacked the immediate political and social reference which characterized the message of the great Old Testament prophets; it was his other-worldliness which marked him off from them. His doctrine was quintessentially *religious;* even while it contained implicitly a political and social philosophy later to be worked out by his Church, in her role as the complement and fulfilment of Christ.[24]

Just as Israel could not rise to the heights of the Messianism of Jesus, so was she unable to grasp the sense in which he was a prophet. And the reason for his rejection is in each case fundamentally the same: his Messiahship was on a different plane from that of the popular expectations; it was likewise with his prophetical office. In the line of Old Testament prophecy, John the Baptist, by his position as the immediate precursor of God's kingdom, held the first place. "I tell you, among those born of women, there has not arisen one greater than John." [25] "But the testimony I have is greater than John's." [26] To the question of the Baptist: "Is it thy coming that was foretold . . . ?",[27] Jesus' answer had been a guarded but unmistakable "Yes." He speaks about his own mission in a way that is different from all the prophets. No prophet could claim *personal* authority; such authority as he had was derived from outside himself. His message was

---

[21] Acts 3:20.
[22] VV. 22–23; cf. Deut. 18:15.
[23] Luke 4:24.
[24] See pp. 315 ff.   [25] Matt. 11:11(S.).
[26] John 5:36.
[27] Matt. 11:3.

"Thus saith the Lord," and never "I say unto you." This was the essential difference. In Christ the kingdom of God has come; he has entered by his own right into the house of the "strong man," Satan, and plundered his goods.[28] Our Lord himself points to the unexampled power which he exercises as authenticating his mission; it is in virtue of this that he forgives sins; [29] not in the name of God—that would have aroused no opposition—but in his own name, appealing to the authority he knows to be his, which is likewise proved by a mighty work of healing. Hence he says plainly, what no one before him would have dared to say: "Blessed is he that shall not be scandalized in me." [30]

The prophetical office of Jesus is what raises him, as a witness to the mind of God, immeasurably above every mystic and religious genius in history. The difference between him and them is one not of degree but of kind. The mystic at the height of his experience sees only as in a mirror, dimly; the intuition of religious genius may unfold the implications of doctrinal and ethical truths hitherto undisclosed. But this is not the function of the prophet; least of all does it describe the knowledge of God communicated to us by Jesus Christ. He was not concerned with a revelation which, as it happened, no one had discovered before; but with truths which by their very nature could not have been attained by man at all, because their content is a divine mystery and lies outside the realm of human possibilities of knowledge. What he saw in the light of direct vision he imparted to others under the sanction of his own divine authority, at the same time giving them the grace of supernatural faith to enable them to receive it.

In this connection we may agree with Kierkegaard [31] in his contention that it is idle to attempt to reach the essence of Christianity, or form an adequate appreciation of its Author, merely on a basis of philosophical and aesthetic values. *Authority* is the decisive quality.

---

28 Matt. 12:28–29.   29 Matt. 9:6.   30 11:6(R-D.).
31 For an impression of Kierkegaard by the present writer, see the *Clergy Review*, Vol. 24, no. 12 (December 1944), pp. 535–41.

I have not got to listen to St Paul because he is clever, or even brilliantly clever; I am to bow before St Paul because he has divine authority; and in any case it remains St Paul's responsibility to see that he produces that impression, whether anybody bows before his authority or not. St Paul must not appeal to his cleverness, for in that case he is a fool; he must not enter into a purely aesthetic or philosophical discussion of the content of the doctrine, for in that case he is side-tracked. No, he must appeal to his divine authority and, while willing to lay down his life and everything, by that very means *prevent* any aesthetic impertinence and any direct philosophical approach to the form and content of the doctrine. St Paul has not to recommend himself and his doctrine with the help of beautiful similes; on the contrary, he should say to the individual: "Whether the comparison is beautiful or whether it is worn and threadbare is all one, you must realize that what I say was entrusted to me by a revelation, so that it is God himself or the Lord Jesus Christ who speaks, and you must not presumptuously set about criticizing the form. I cannot and dare not compel you to obey, but through your relation to God in your conscience I make you eternally responsible to God, eternally responsible for your relation to this doctrine, by having proclaimed it as revealed to me, and consequently proclaimed it with divine authority." [32]

This is forcefully and characteristically said; but surely no Catholic theologian would wish to dissent from the substance of it. Nor could he fail to subscribe to the following comment on a greater than St Paul:

Christ, as God-Man, is in possession of the specific quality of authority which eternity can never mediate, just as in all eternity Christ can never be put on the same level as an essential human equality. Christ taught, therefore, with authority. To ask whether Christ is profound is blasphemy, and is an attempt (whether conscious or not) to destroy him surreptitiously; for the question conceals a doubt concerning his authority, and this attempt to weigh him up is impertinent in its directness, behaving as though

[32] Kierkegaard's essay *On the Difference between a Genius and an Apostle* in "The Present Age" (translated by Alexander Dru), pp. 145-46. NOTE: In the New Testament there is a close relation between the idea of "apostle" and that of "prophet." Thus Christ speaks of *sending* "prophets" (Matt. 23:34); and he himself, while being *the* "prophet" (John 7:40), is also "the apostle" (Heb. 3:1).

he were being examined, instead of which it is to him that all
power is given in heaven and on earth.[33]

St John provides a moving commentary on the reason for
our Lord's rejection as a prophet. Jesus spoke a different
language from his hearers; nor would they allow him to interpret it for them. They could have understood, had they
taken him for their Master; but for this they would have
needed to open their hearts to the influence of his grace and
the gift of the Spirit. "He who comes from above is above
all men's reach; the man who belongs to earth talks the
language of earth, but one who comes from heaven must
needs be beyond the reach of all; he bears witness of things
he has seen and heard, and nobody accepts his witness. The
man who does accept his witness has declared, once for all,
that God cannot lie, since the words spoken by him whom
God has sent are God's own words; so boundless is the gift God
makes of his Spirit." [34] But Israel did not recognize, "and
that in this thy day, the things that are to thy peace." [35]
"Jerusalem, Jerusalem, still murdering the prophets, and
stoning the messengers that are sent to thee, how often have
I been ready to gather thy children together, as a hen gathers
her chickens under her wings; and thou didst refuse it. Behold your house is left to you, a house uninhabited." [36]

[33] Kierkegaard, *loc. cit.*, p. 154.   [34] John 3:31–34.
[35] Luke 19:42(R-D.).   [36] Matt. 23:37–38.

§ 19. OUR GREAT HIGH PRIEST

The ultimate purpose for which the Word became flesh
was to give honour to God. This our Lord made clear to
his disciples in his prayer after the Last Supper: "I have exalted thy glory on earth, by achieving the task which thou
gavest me to do; now, Father, do thou exalt me at thy own
side, in that glory which I had with thee before the world
began." [1] Nevertheless, so far as we are concerned, the dominating motive of the Incarnation was that man should be

[1] John 17:4–5.

redeemed from sin. Thus, in the Creed, we profess our belief in Jesus Christ, "who for us men and for our salvation came down from heaven." It was for our sakes that he was born upon earth. "For the Son of Man himself came not to be served, but to serve, and to give his life a ransom for many." [2] The Mediator, as St Thomas explains,[3] was to stand between God and his people, both to minister to them the things of heaven and, as their representative, to offer sacrifice and prayer to God. Now this is precisely the office of a priest. "The purpose for which any high priest is chosen from among his fellow-men, and made a representative of men in their dealing with God, is to offer gifts and sacrifices in expiation of their sins." [4]

One of the difficulties for the Jews, when presented with our Lord's teaching, had been that of reconciling his predictions of suffering and death with the Old Testament doctrine that the Messiah would abide for ever.[5] "We have heard out of the law that the Christ continues for ever. What then dost thou mean by saying that the Son of Man must be lifted up? Who is this Son of Man?" [6] The allusion here is to the thought expressed in the Messianic Psalm,[7] quoted by Jesus himself,[8] in which the following words occur: "The Lord hath sworn, and he will not repent: Thou art a priest for ever according to the order of Melchisedech." [9] The New Testament commentary on this verse is to be found in the Epistle to the Hebrews,[10] which is a veritable homily, in the form of a letter, on the priesthood of Christ. The object for which it was written was to restrain the waverers among the Jewish Christians from returning to the practice of the Old Testament sacrifice and ceremonial. Its underlying theme is the parallel between Judaism and Christianity, a parallel which is thrown into relief by the contrasting mediators of the two religions and their sacerdotal functions. "What the law contains is only the shadow of those blessings which

2 Mark 10:45(S.).   3 III, q. 22, art. 1.
4 Heb. 5:1.   5 Cf. Isa. 9:7; Ps. 88 (89) 4–5.
6 John 12:34(S.).   7 Ps. 109(110).
8 Mark 12:36.   9 Ps. 109(110):4.
10 Cf. Heb. 5:6, 10; 6:20; 7:15, 17, 21, etc.

were still to come, not the full expression of their reality. The same sacrifices are offered year after year without inter- mission, and still the worshippers can never reach, through the law, their full growth." [11] To return to it, therefore, would be to exchange the substance for the shadow, to pass from the full light of the Gospel into the twilight of the old order of things. The law of grace is better than the Mosaic dispensation because it is embodied in a religion which is changeless and eternal.

Jesus Christ, in his office as a holy mediator, is a priest after the manner of Melchisedech; he is also a high priest, being the antitype of Aaron, whom he replaces. Here we may note certain characteristics of the priesthood, which find their perfect realization in Jesus. First, there is the call and appointment to the priestly office by God—an event which coincided with the Incarnation. "So it is with Christ. He did not raise himself to the dignity of the high priesthood; it was God that raised him to it, when he said, Thou art my Son, I have begotten thee this day." [12] Secondly, the priest must be a member of the human race, one with ourselves. "Wherefore, it behoved him in all things to be made like unto his brethren, that he might become a merciful and faithful high priest before God, that he might be a propitia- tion for the sins of the people. For in that wherein he him- self hath suffered and been tempted, he is able to succour them also that are tempted." [13] Thirdly, the priest exists for the benefit of men: "... and now, his full achievements reached, he wins eternal salvation for all those who render obedience to him." [14] Finally—and this is the heart of the priestly office—he must offer sacrifice for sins; "... we have been sanctified through the offering of the body of Jesus Christ once for all." [15]

It should be remembered that, while the Epistle to the Hebrews here describes the essential characteristics of the priest, the comparisons between the Old Testament priest-

[11] Heb. 10:1.   [12] 5:5; Ps. 2:7.
[13] Heb. 2:17–18(R-D.); cf. 4:15; 5:2–3.
[14] 5:9.   [15] 10:10(S.); cf. 9:28.

hood and the unique priesthood of Christ are not all meant
to be taken literally. For instance, though Melchisedech
typifies the priest and Aaron the high priest, there is no
other distinction to be drawn between the two titles. The
name "high priest" does not imply a hierarchy of which
Christ is the head; it is merely the Hebrew high priest, whose
function has now been supplanted. The high priest's role
has as its background the impassable barrier placed between
man and the all-holy God by sin; his function is to take
men's place before God, "to offer gifts and sacrifices in expiation of their sins." [16] The priest is always man's representative with God; but in this case he represents a sinful
humanity. Hence his first task is to re-establish man's relations with God; this condition must be fulfilled before men
may venture to approach him; and only then through "the
one mediator between God and man, Christ Jesus, himself
man." [17] The Son of God was born on earth, therefore, in
order to wipe out sin; he became incarnate because God no
longer accepted the Aaronic sacrifices, and his purpose was
fulfilled when he had achieved expiation for sins.

The effectiveness of Christ's priesthood as contrasted with
that of the Old Testament, the depth and inwardness of the
new alliance between God and man as compared with that
made with Moses—"the type and shadow of what has its true
being in heaven" [18]—is shown in the following significant
passage:

As it is, he [Christ] has been entrusted with a more honourable
ministry, dispenser as he is of a nobler covenant, with nobler
promises for its sanction. There would have been no room for
this second covenant, if there had been no fault to find with the
first. But God, you see, does find fault; this is what he tells them:
Behold, says the Lord, a time is coming when I will ratify a new
covenant with the people of Israel, and with the people of Juda.
It will not be like the covenant which I made with their fathers,
on the day when I took them by the hand, to rescue them from
Egypt; that they should break my covenant, and I (says the Lord)
should abandon them. No, this is the covenant I will grant the

[16] Heb. 5:1.   [17] 1 Tim. 2:5(S.).   [18] Heb. 8:5.

people of Israel, the Lord says, when that time comes. I will implant my law in their innermost thoughts, engrave it in their hearts; I will be their God, and they shall be my people. There will be no need for neighbour to teach neighbour, or brother to teach brother, the knowledge of the Lord; all will know me, from the highest to the lowest. I will pardon their wrong-doing; I will not remember their sins any more. In speaking of a new covenant, he has superannuated the old. And before long the superannuated, the antiquated, must needs disappear.[19]

As it was by a divine ordinance that Aaron had been regularly invested with the high priesthood, an express call from God was needed to replace him. This was what was given to Jesus Christ. "He did not raise himself to the dignity of the high priesthood; it was God that raised him to it, when he said, *Thou art my Son. I have begotten thee this day.*" [20] Although he had been the Son of God from all eternity, these words of the Psalmist, italicized above, were addressed to him only at the moment when he assumed our human nature. In becoming man, by that very fact he was consecrated our great High Priest, and was thus made the accredited Mediator of the human race with God. The exclusive prerogative of Aaron was accordingly revoked. More than this, there is a change in the nature of the priesthood itself; it passed from the order of Aaron to that of Melchisedech. God ratified this transference with an oath: "The Lord hath sworn, and he will not repent: Thou art a priest for ever according to the order of Melchisedech." [21]

Melchisedech, the priest-king of Salem,[22] has a threefold significance with regard to Christ. The name Melchisedech connotes "king of righteousness" and king of Salem means "king of peace." [23] Now we have here two of the chief attributes of the Messiah, whose reign was to be one of righteousness and peace. Further, Melchisedech is both priest and king; it is the same with Christ, whose royalty is closely associated with his priesthood. Thus we find the ideal of the

19 Heb. 8:6–13; cf. Jer. 31:31–34.   20 Ps. 2:7; Heb. 5:5.
21 Ps. 109(110):4; Heb. 7:20–21; cf. 6:16–20.
22 Gen. 14:17–18.   23 Heb. 7:2.

priesthood, at the end of its historical development, brought back to its original conception. In the second place, what emerges from the incident recorded in Genesis [24] is that the posterity of Abraham, yet unborn, not excepting the priestly sons of Levi, virtually recognize the superiority of Melchisedech and, with greater reason, him of whom Melchisedech is only the figure, Christ. In him "another, like to Melchisedech, is set up as priest, who becomes such, not by a law of natural succession, but by virtue of an enduring life." [25] Finally, Melchisedech prefigures the eternal priest, for the reason that the genealogy, which was an essential qualification for the levitical priesthood, had no application to him. Nothing is known of his ancestry; "no name of father or mother, no pedigree, no date of birth or death." [26] Accordingly, he has the priesthood by personal right and not by inheritance. So it is that Jesus, the High Priest in the manner of Melchisedech, has the same privilege; his blood descent from Judah sets no obstacle in the way of his priesthood. Melchisedech "stands, eternally, a priest, the true figure of the Son of God." [27]

A further parallel has been noted by many of the Fathers: they have seen in the bread and wine offered by Melchisedech a symbol of the Eucharist. This is highly appropriate, but, as has often been pointed out, the author of the Epistle to the Hebrews could hardly dwell on this typical significance without digressing considerably from his principal theme. There is possibly an allusion to the Eucharist in the words: "We have an altar from which they who serve the tabernacle have no right to eat." [28] But the Epistle is concerned to demonstrate that Christ perfects the elect for ever by one sacrifice only, that any further sacrifice is therefore needless, and that the insufficiency of the ancient sacrifices is proved precisely from the need for their repetition. To have enlarged upon the Eucharistic sacrifice in this context might have had the appearance of compromising the author's main thesis.

---

[24] Gen. 14:17 ff. [25] Heb. 7:15–16(S.). [26] Vs. 3.
[27] Vs. 3. [28] 13:10(S.).

The Church, however, while preserving intact this all-important doctrine, has co-ordinated it with the other relevant parts of the Christian revelation.

Because, as the Apostle Paul testifies, there could be no final achievement under the Old Testament, on account of the inefficacy of the levitical priesthood, it was necessary (God the Father, in his mercy, so ordaining) that another priest should arise, *according to the order of Melchisedech* [Gen. 14:18; Ps. 109:4; Heb. 7:11], our Lord Jesus Christ, who should be able to complete his work *in those whom he sanctifies* [Heb. 10:14] and lead them to perfection. He, therefore, our God and Lord, was to gain for them an eternal redemption, *by offering himself once for all* to God the Father. Since, however, his priesthood was not to be put an end to by death [Heb. 7:24, 27], at the Last Supper, on the night he was betrayed, he left to his beloved spouse, the Church, a visible sacrifice, such as the nature of man requires. It was one whereby the bloody sacrifice on the Cross should be represented, and its memory preserved for all time [1 Cor. 11:23 ff], its salutary power being applied for the remission of daily sins. Hence Jesus, constituted *a priest according to the order of Melchisedech throughout all ages,* offered his body and blood, under the appearances of bread and wine, to God the Father. The same he handed to his apostles (so making them priests of the New Covenant) to be consumed by them. This rite they were to hand on, and the Lord commanded their successors in the priesthood to make the same offering, with the words: "Do this in remembrance of me" [Luke 22:19; 1 Cor. 11:24]. So the Catholic Church has always understood and taught. For, after Christ had celebrated the ancient Passover, which was a memorial of Israel's going forth from Egypt, he instituted the new Passover. This was to be the immolation of himself, under visible signs, by the Church through her priests. That is to say, a memorial of his own going forth from this world to the Father—the moment when, by the shedding of his blood, he redeemed us, *rescuing us from the power of darkness and transferring us to his kingdom* [Col. 1:13].[29]

We have seen that the essential function of the priest is to act as an intermediary between God and man. From this it follows that our Lord's priesthood is co-extensive with

[29] Council of Trent, Sess. 22, cap. 1; Denz., 938.

his mediatorship. Now he became our Mediator from the first moment of the Incarnation, by the grace of the hypostatic union; hence it is fundamentally this grace which makes him our great High Priest. The assumption of a human nature by the Word was equivalent to his call to the priesthood. To this there followed the infusion of sanctifying grace into his soul, whereby Christ was enabled to perform acts of satisfaction and merit on our behalf. As Head of his mystical Body, the Church, he could thus pass on to all its members the fruits of his priesthood. "Such was the high priest that suited our need, holy and guiltless and undefiled, not reckoned among us sinners, lifted high above all the heavens; one who has no need to do as those other priests did, offering a twofold sacrifice day by day, first for his own sins, then for those of the people. What he has done he has done once for all; and the offering was himself." [30]

If it was necessary that our High Priest should be one with us, so that he could share our weaknesses and temptations,[31] it was no less needful that he should himself be blameless in God's sight. The closer he has to approach God, in order to draw his brethren to him also, the more he needs to be holy. It is clear, as St Augustine teaches,[32] that the priesthood, that is, the mediatorship between God and man, gains in perfection according to the closeness of the priest's union with God; its efficacy is enhanced both in proportion to the correspondence between the victim offered and the interior sentiments of self-oblation on the part of him who offers it, and to the closeness of the priest's solidarity with the people on whose behalf the offering is made. We should have no difficulty in seeing how these principles find their ideal embodiment in the priesthood of Christ. Let us consider them in turn.

The more closely the priest is united to God, that is to say, the holier he is, the more the sacrifice, which is the priestly act *par excellence,* will be perfect. For the reason that the priest, in his role as mediator, is able to supply, by

30 Heb. 7:26–27.   31 Cf. 2:17; 4:15.
32 *De Trinitate,* lib. 4, cap. 14; *P.L.* 42, col. 901.

virtue of his sanctity, for the lack of adoration and thanksgiving, the defective acts of reparation, the half-hearted sup-
plications, on the part of the people. Now no creature is
more closely united to God than the sacred humanity of
Jesus Christ. Our Lord is not only absolutely free from all
original and personal sin and from every imperfection; he
is Holiness itself. This was why his priestly acts, proceeding
from his human intelligence and will, had an infinite value,
as belonging to the divine personality of the Son of God.
It is impossible to conceive of a priest more intimately and
indissolubly united to God. Moreover, our Lord, as Head of
the Church,[33] has received the plenitude of created grace,
a grace which overflows upon us—"For of his fulness we
all received, and grace upon grace."[34] There was likewise
given him the power to institute the sacraments, as the instruments of that grace, and to endow others with a share in
his own priesthood.[35] If sin still continues in the world, this
is not due to the insufficiency of Christ's sacrifice, but to
the fact that men are unwilling to receive its fruits. "Behold,
the Lamb of God, who takes away the sin of the world."[36]

The closer the union between priest and victim, the more
acceptable is the sacrifice. For the visible offering and immolation of the victim are but the symbols of the interior
oblation and self-immolation in the heart of the priest, the
inward attitude of soul which is the perfection of the virtue
of religion. Again, the purer and more precious the victim
in the sight of God, the more fully it is consumed in his
honour, by so much the greater is the sacrifice. Thus, under
the Jewish Law, the holocaust was regarded as the supreme
oblation, because the whole victim was consumed in God's
honour, as a sign of man's complete self-dedication to him.
But, in Christ, priest and victim coincide; the offering he
made to the Father was himself. How acceptable it was he
does not forbear to tell us: "This my Father loves in me,
that I am laying down my life, to take it up again after-

---

[33] Cf. St Thomas, III, q. 8, art. 1.   [34] John 1:16(S.).
[35] III, q. 64, art. 4; Suppl., q. 35, art. 2.
[36] John 1:29(S.).

wards. Nobody can rob me of it; I lay it down of my own
accord. I am free to lay it down, free to take it up again;
that is the charge which my Father has given me." [37] From
Christ's body, itself infinitely precious, being that of the Son
of God, torn with scourges and nailed to the Cross, all his
blood flowed out. The union between priest and victim
could not be more complete, since Jesus was a victim to the
depths of his soul; along with his bodily torments went the
anguish of the spirit, its sense of being utterly abandoned:
"My God, my God, why hast thou forsaken me?" [38] It was
the supreme immolation, the perfect holocaust, in atonement
for "the lust of the flesh, and the lust of the eyes, and the
vainglory of life." [39] Priest and Victim could not be more
wholly at one than in the sacrifice of Calvary.

Of the union between our great High Priest and his people
it will be more fitting to speak on a later page, in connection
with the mystical Body of Christ.[40] Here it will be enough
to recall that "Christ is the head of the Church, himself
being the saviour of his body." [41] For the moment we may
rest content with the significant words of the Epistle to the
Hebrews—"the very pith of our argument." "This high priest
of ours is one who has taken his seat in heaven, on the right
hand of that throne where God sits in majesty, ministering,
now, in the sanctuary, in that true tabernacle which the
Lord, not man, has set up." [42]

* * *

Sacrifice, in the religious sense, is prayer in action. In Biblical usage, whatever is done to signify man's self-dedication
to God can be described as a sacrifice; for example, a righteous life,[43] the offering of a lowly and contrite heart,[44] prayer
itself,[45] works of mercy, [46] the mortification of the flesh.[47]
All of which is well summed up by St Thomas, who is here
but repeating St Augustine: "Everything which is offered

---

[37] John 10:17–18.   [38] Mark 15:34.   [39] 1 John 2:16(S.).
[40] See § 24.   [41] Eph. 5:23(S.).   [42] Heb. 8:1–2.
[43] Ps. 4:6.   [44] Ps. 50(51):19.   [45] Ps. 140(141):2.
[46] Heb. 13:16.   [47] Rom. 12:1.

to God, so that man's spirit may be uplifted to him, may be called a sacrifice." [48] A mere external offering is valueless in God's sight; it has significance only as a symbol of inward dedication of heart. Nevertheless, sacrifice as a religious rite has always implied the oblation of some *visible* object to God, and its renouncement by him who-makes the offering. Where the visible object is a living thing, the sacrifice is normally a bloody one, involving the victim's death. It should further be noted, since this has bearing upon the Eucharist, that after a part of the object sacrificed had been consumed by fire or poured out in libation or destroyed in any way, the remainder was generally utilized for a sacred banquet. This was regarded as a natural complement to the sacrifice, a means whereby those taking part identified themselves with the offering and shared in its fruits.

That Christ in dying on the Cross offered a true and proper sacrifice is one of the chief themes of the New Testament. It emerges, not only from the Epistle to the Hebrews and the whole message of St Paul, but from our Lord's own words as recorded in the Gospels.[49] We have seen that his association of his Messiahship with the Suffering Servant of Isaiah is inexplicable except in terms of a redeeming sacrifice.[50] The familiar Pauline texts contain no new discovery or personal interpretation; their author has nothing to say apart from what he has himself been taught: "The chief message which I handed on to you, as it was handed on to me, was that Christ, as the scriptures had foretold, died for our sins." [51] Among the things "handed on" was the truth that "Christ our passover has been sacrificed," [52] that "he gave himself up on our behalf, a sacrifice breathing out fragrance as he offered it to God," [53] that "God has offered him to us as a means of reconciliation, in virtue of faith, ransoming us with his blood." [54] The language is that of the Old Law, but its application is to "the new covenant in my blood which is poured out for you." [55] "All the ancient sacrifices,"

---

[48] III, q. 22, art 2.   [49] Mark. 10:45; Matt. 26:28.
[50] See pp. 156 ff.   [51] 1 Cor. 15:3.   [52] 5:7(S.).
[53] Eph. 5:2.   [54] Rom. 3:25.   [55] Luke 22:20(S.).

says St Thomas, "were figures of that true sacrifice which Christ offered in dying for us." [56]

In our Lord's death all the conditions traditionally required to make a genuine sacrifice were fulfilled. The visible oblation, that is, the victim, and the priest, he who makes the offering, were embodied in Christ himself. "He who offers, and what he offers, are one and the same." [57] The sacrificial act was made externally manifest, namely, by bloodshed and the suffering of death. It was a holocaust, the perfect sacrifice, since it involved the Victim's destruction. Moreover, these externals were the signs of an inward dedication of heart, symbols of an unswerving obedience to the Father's will,[58] of filial devotion to God and a consuming love for men. "The world must be convinced that I love the Father, and act only as the Father has commanded me to act." [59] "This is the greatest love a man can show, that he should lay down his life for his friends." [60] Finally, all was done in fulfilment of the honour due to God; it was directed, as every religious act must be, solely to him. "I have exalted thy glory on earth, by achieving the task which thou gavest me to do." [61] With what assurance could he proclaim that it was finished: "Jesus said, crying with a loud voice, Father, into thy hands I commend my spirit; and yielded up his spirit as he said it." [62]

"As Christ comes into the world, he says . . . I am coming to fulfil what is written of me . . . ; to do thy will, O my God." [63] There is thus a very real sense in which, by reason of his eternal priesthood, the whole earthly life of Jesus was a sacrifice to God. This fact is all the more impressive when we remember that he foresaw what lay ahead of him, and, with complete single-mindedness and wholehearted self-dedication, co-ordinated the least significant of his actions with reference to the great plan of our redemption. It must be borne in mind, however, that, strictly understood, the redeeming sacrifice took place only on the Cross. This was the

[56] III, q. 47, art. 2, ad 1.
[57] St. Augustine, *De Trinitate*, lib. 4, cap. 14; *P.L.* 42, col. 901.
[58] Cf. Rom. 5:19; Phil. 2:8.   [59] John 14:31.   [60] 15:13.
[61] 17:4.   [62] Luke 23:46.   [63] Heb. 10:5-7.

supreme act of obedience which the Father had demanded of his Son, as the condition of man's reconciliation with him. Within the eternal counsels of the Godhead, the Son himself had wholly acquiesced in this requirement, in virtue of the identity of his divine will with that of the Father. Only thus could the sacrifices of the old Law be abrogated and the new covenant between God and man come into being. Accordingly, this is Christ's all-significant priestly act, his sacrifice *par excellence*. It was on account of this that "God highly exalted him, and bestowed upon him the name which is above every name; so that at the name of Jesus every knee should bend, of beings in the heavens, on the earth, and under the earth, and every tongue should confess that Jesus Christ is Lord, to the glory of God the Father." [64]

Nevertheless, as we have learned from the Epistle to the Hebrews,[65] Christ's priesthood, and with it his act of sacrifice, endures eternally: "Thou art a priest for ever." Just as, while on earth, our Lord was unceasingly offering himself to the Father, in virtue of his active obedience and charity, so likewise in heaven he may be said to continue his propitiatory sacrifice in acts of adoration, thanksgiving and intercession for us. Thus his sacrifice of expiation for our sins continues until the end of the world, in the sense that, through his mediation, its merits are ever being applied to our souls. Even when the time of full completion comes, "when he hands over the kingdom to God and the Father, when he abolishes all other sovereignty, authority and power," [66] the heart of our great High Priest will remain unchanged. His role of Mediator will be at an end; for, once their object has been achieved, there is no need for petitions and acts of expiation. But, at the head of the whole company of heaven, in the name of the human race redeemed by the shedding of his blood, our Lord will still give glory to God by his sacrifice of thanksgiving and praise. Meanwhile, for our comfort here on earth, "we have an advocate with the Father, Jesus Christ the Righteous One, and he is the expi-

[64] Phil. 2:9–11(S.).　　[65] Heb. 7:21, 24; 8:1–2.　[66] 1 Cor. 15:24(S.).

ation for our sins; and not for ours alone, but also for those
of the whole world." [67]

"And it is from him that you are in Christ Jesus, who was
made for us wisdom from God, as well as justification, sanctification and redemption; so that, as it is written, Let him
who boasts boast in the Lord." [68] "And when I came to you,
brethren," St Paul continues, "I did not come proclaiming
to you the evidence of God with lofty eloquence or learning;
for I determined to know nothing among you except Jesus
Christ, and him crucified." [69] In *Jesus Christ, and him crucified* lies the central mystery of the Redemption; to it we owe
the restoration of God's favour to us; by it we were released
from the slavery of sin and the fear of death; through it the
Devil's hold upon the world was broken. Such is the ultimate
significance of our Lord's own words: "For the Son of Man
himself came not to be served, but to serve and to give his life
a ransom for many"; [70] "for this is my blood, that of the new
covenant, which is poured out for many for the remission
of sins." [71] So the Catholic Church teaches, in complete conformity with Scripture: "Christ, in his own blood, has reconciled us to God." [72]

Elsewhere in the New Testament we find humanity's reconciliation with God ascribed to the death of Christ,[73] as also
the lesson that our redemption was won by the shedding of
his "precious blood." [74] But this is the truth which dominates
the mind of St Paul, and he is its divinely inspired exponent.
He saw men to be under the wrath of God, alienated from,
and at enmity with him, dead in sin.[75] And yet: "Enemies
of God, we were reconciled to him through his Son's death;
reconciled to him, we are surer than ever of finding salvation
through his Son's life." [76] This reconciliation meant the removal of sin,[77] together with the re-establishment and
renewal of the order of grace destroyed by Adam. "So that

[67] 1 John 2:1–2(S.).   [68] 1 Cor. 1:30–31(S.).   [69] 2:1–2(S.).
[70] Mark 10:45(S.).   [71] Matt. 26:28(S.).   [72] Denz., 790.
[73] Cf. 1 Pet. 2:24; 3:18; 1 John 1:7; 2:2; 4:9–10; Apoc. 1:5.
[74] 1 Pet. 1:19; cf. Apoc. 5:9.   [75] Eph. 2:12.
[76] Rom. 5:10; cf. Col. 1:20.   [77] Eph. 1:7.

whoever is in Christ is a new creature: the old things are passed away; behold, they have become new!" [78] Along with this went the conquest of sin and death, the abolition of the Mosaic Law, and hence the barrier between Jew and Gentile. "For he is our peace, who made both peoples one, and demolished in his flesh the partition-wall of enmity. He abrogated the law of precepts and decrees, so that from the two he might create in himself one new man, so making peace, and might reconcile them both in one body to God through the cross, killing by it that enmity." [79]

The Redemption involved also the defeat of the "prince of this world." In consequence of Adam's sin, God had permitted the Devil a certain power over mankind.[80] He had gained this right, in the words of St Bernard, "not by a lawful acquisition, but as basely usurped; nevertheless, it was justly allowed to him." [81] It was the prototype of the servitude into which man inevitably falls by committing sin. "Believe me when I tell you this; everyone who acts sinfully is the slave of sin." [82] From this thraldom, which brings in its train man's subjection to its chief agent, Satan, the death of Christ releases us. "Sentence is now being passed on this world; now is the time when the prince of this world is to be cast out." To which our Lord immediately adds: "Yes, if only I am lifted up from the earth, I will attract all men to myself." And St John interprets: "In saying this, he prophesied the death he was to die." [83]

* * *

Where is the sage, where the scribe, where the investigator of this age? Has not God made folly of the learning of the world? For since, notwithstanding the wisdom of God, the world did not discern God by its learning, it pleased God to save the believers by means of the folly of our preaching. For the Jews demand signs, and the Greeks search after learning, but we preach a crucified Christ—a stumbling-block to the Jews, and folly to the gentiles; but to those who are called, both Jews and

78 2 Cor. 5:17(S.); cf. Eph. 1:10. 79 Eph. 2:14–16(S.).
80 Cf. St Thomas, III, q. 48, art. 4. 81 Ep. 190, 5; P.L. 182, col. 1065.
82 John 8:34. 83 12:31–33.

Greeks, Christ the power of God and the wisdom of God. For what is foolish with God is wiser than men, and what is weak with God is stronger than men.[84]

St Paul here enunciates the divine paradox of the Redemption: God's wisdom declares itself in the folly of the Cross. Countless Christians, embodying this truth in their own lives, have been inspired to the heroic endurance of their trials, even to the voluntary embracement of suffering, by the memory of their crucified Redeemer.

The great theme of the imitation of Christ, founded on the example of his Passion, has its source in the New Testament.[85] St Paul himself could claim to be among those who bore in their bodies "the dying state of Jesus": [86] "Already I bear the scars of the Lord Jesus printed on my body." [87] So striking is this aspect of our Lord's redeeming death that some have thought the whole efficacy of his sacrifice lay precisely in this. It was a manifestation of love, designed to evoke a corresponding response in us. That this was indeed the case no Christian would wish to question; but to regard the Redemption as operating exclusively in this way [88] is to overlook the deeper implications of what was involved. Merely to view the matter thus is to reduce Christ's sacrifice to a human level, to sentimentalize it, above all, it is to ignore the essential gravity of sin. We have to remember, as the Church teaches, that Christ by dying on the Cross "merited for us justification and *made satisfaction for us to God the Father.*" [89]

Redemption is essentially the destruction of sin. There are as many aspects of redemption as there are of sin; if sin is a fall, redemption will be an uplifting; if sin is an infirmity, redemption will be a remedy; if sin is a debt, redemption will be its payment; if sin is a fault, redemption will be an expiation; if sin is a bondage, redemption will be a deliverance; if sin is an offence, redemption will be a satisfaction as regards man, a propitiation

---

[84] 1 Cor. 1:20–25(S.).   [85] 1 Pet. 2:21.
[86] 2 Cor. 4:10.   [87] Gal. 6:17.
[88] NOTE: This theory of the Redemption was held by Abelard; it was later revived, in heterodox circles, by Socinus and Ritschl.
[89] Denz., 799.

as regards God, and a mutual reconciliation between God and Man.[90]

If, therefore, God is to be propitiated and the sinner reconciled to him, a debt of satisfaction must be paid. This is the most deeply mysterious aspect of the Redemption—the fact, not only that Christ should suffer on our behalf, but that he should do so in obedience to the will of his heavenly Father. "He did not even spare his own Son, but gave him up for us all." [91]

How is the infliction of suffering upon the innocent, upon a "beloved Son," to be reconciled with God's justice and loving-kindness? Before approaching this difficult question, let us first recall the essential meaning of the word "redemption." It is "to buy back," and suggests the idea of a price paid, a *ransom* (λύτοον).[92] We remember that, in the Old Testament, Israel was the property, the private possession of Yahweh: "Because thou art a holy people to the Lord thy God. The Lord thy God hath chosen thee, to be his peculiar people of all the peoples that are upon the earth." [93] Thenceforth God could dispose of Israel at his pleasure; and he does in fact threaten to hand it over to its enemies.[94] As the event showed, he did indeed abandon his people in proportion to their infidelity to him; though this abandonment was never complete, being revocable on condition of repentance. Moreover God would redeem his people one day; this he was pledged to do, both in virtue of the covenant made with the posterity of Abraham and with the children of Israel, and in discharging his office as Redeemer. He would fulfil his self-imposed task of delivering his enslaved people and punishing their enemies.

Here it should be carefully noted that the commercial metaphor of "redemption" is not to be pressed too far. For example, there is no question of a price being paid to anyone but 'God himself. The theory evolved by some of the early

90 Prat, *La Théologie de Saint Paul*, II, 226 (E.T. p. 190).
91 Rom. 8:32.   92 Mark 10:45.
93 Deut. 7:6.   94 Cf. 32:30.

Fathers, that a ransom was given to the Devil, has little to be said for it. The enemies of Israel had no right of ownership over God's chosen people; hence they had no claim to compensation when Israel should be delievered from their hands. "For thus saith the Lord: You were sold gratis, and you shall be redeemed without money." [95] Turning now to the New Testament, we find a continuity of thought: "the Church of God" is something "which he has purchased with his own blood." [96] Speaking particularly of the Jews, St Paul says: "Christ ransomed us from the curse of the law by becoming a curse for us"; [97] and again: "God sent his Son, made from a woman, made under the law, in order that he might redeem those under the law, in order that we might receive our adoption as sons." [98]

In the New Testament the idea of "redemption" is more comprehensive than in the Old; it includes the entire work of our salvation, the remission of sins, sanctification and glorification.[99] The price paid was the Saviour's blood; [100] it gained for the Jews freedom from the burden of the law, and liberation for all who were the slaves of sin.[101] But here again there is no thought of a payment being made to the enemies of God's people. Christ is our "ransom" ($\lambda \acute{\upsilon} \tau \rho o \nu$), and it is well known that, in the Mosaic code, this word denotes the tax or the sacrifice required by God for the ransom of the first-born.[102] If the metaphor of purchase is to be pushed to its extreme limit, then it is to God himself that the price of our ransom is paid; for it is God whom the work of redemption appeases and renders propitious, and it is in relation to God alone that Christ "propitiates."

How, exactly, may he be said to have done this? The teaching of Scripture, that Christ died *for* us, was misinterpreted at the time of the Reformation in the theory of

---

95 Isa. 52:3.   96 Acts 20:28(S.).
97 Gal. 3:13(S.).   98 4:4-5(S.).
99 Cf. Col. 1:14; 1 Cor. 1:30; Rom. 8:23; Eph. 4:30.
100 Cf. 1 Cor. 6:20; 7:23.
101 Rom. 6:6, 17-20; 7:14; Tit. 3:3-5.
102 Num. 18:15; LXX.

redemption known as "penal substitution." It was imagined
that the Crucified had become the object of the Father's
wrath and punishment; that God persecuted his Son, pro-
ceeded against him with the full rigour of justice, regarded
him as an enemy deserving of all his vengeance; that he
delivered him over as a victim to the fury of his outraged
majesty and inflicted on him in some sense the punishment
of the damned. But this view of the matter is wholly repugnant to our ideas of the essential harmony between God's
justice and mercy. God may require suffering from the innocent, but he does not *punish* one who is personally guiltless. Whole groups, whether families, cities or nations, may
be allowed to suffer for the fault of one; but this happens
on account of their moral solidarity and not in virtue of the
theory of penal substitution. Christ did indeed endure a
suffering which he did not deserve; yet the substitution was
incomplete, since he who expiated our faults was the Head
of our family, and thus we expiate them in him and by him.
The fact that we are called upon to co-operate in his redemptive act points to our moral solidarity with him. He is the
Head, and we are the members of his mystical Body.[103]

St Thomas, in contrast with the subsequent exaggerations
of Luther and Calvin, throws into relief the chief motive of
our redemption, namely, God's love, which operates even
amid the agony inflicted on his only begotten Son. He tells us
that the Father surrendered his Son to the endurance of the
Cross, in decreeing his death for the world's salvation, by endowing him with charity, so inspiring him with the will to
die for us, and by not protecting him against his enemies.[104]
It is true that the Crucifixion is the terrible symbol of the divine justice. Yet the account against us was more than fully
paid; "the grace which came to us was out of all proportion
to the fault." [105] Christ, by the charity which inspired his
Passion, achieved something more pleasing to the Father than
the sum total of human iniquity is able to displease him. But
if it is the rigour of God's justice which first arrests our attention, when contemplating the awful scene on Calvary, it is

[103] See pp. 322 ff.   [104] III, q. 47, art. 3.   [105] Rom. 5:15.

consoling to remember that its place is secondary. The primacy, as in all God's dealings with his creatures, is held by love and mercy.

This principle is so important, and of such universal application, that it is well to recall its doctrinal foundations. With God, every act of justice is based upon a preceding work of mercy or gratuitous goodness. If he may be said to owe anything in justice to his creatures, it is in virtue of some previous gift to which they have no title; if, for example, he recompenses our merits, it is because he has given us the grace to merit, and more fundamentally still, because he first created us out of his sheer generosity. Divine mercy is thus the root-principle of all God's works; it characterizes the whole of his activity in our regard. Hence God's justice is subordinate to his mercy.[106] The well-known lines of Shakespeare are not merely poetical, they are theologically exact:

> And earthly power doth then show likest God's
> When mercy seasons justice.[107]

In Christ's passion and death, divine justice was appeased by the Righteous One, who bore the whole weight of human sin, by the Victim "wounded for our rebellions," [108] by the Word made flesh who died for us. But mercy triumphs over all: through his beloved Son, God the Father was reconciled with sinners; he now offers eternal life to every man, even to the most perverse, and glorifies the Redeemer by giving him the victory over the Devil, sin and death. More than the placating of God's offended justice, the Redemption was the merciful fulfilment of man's need. "Everything is for you, whether it be . . . the world, or life, or death, or the present, or the future; it is all for you, and you for Christ, and Christ for God." [109]

God the Father had willed for his Son the glory of the Redemption. His decree was that Christ, through the sacrifice

106 Cf. St Thomas, I, q. 21. art. 4.
107 *The Merchant of Venice*, Act 4, Sc. 1.
108 Isa. 53:5.   109 1 Cor. 3:22–23.

on the Cross, should merit his own exaltation; that is to say, the Resurrection and the state of heavenly glory.[110] Not that the Son of God needed to win such a prize for his own sake; it had been his by right from all eternity—"that glory which I had with thee before the world began."[111] Nevertheless, in his human nature, he could receive as a reward the splendour of an external triumph. This he achieved, in fulfilling his office as Head of the human race, so meriting these blessings for us, together with all the graces which prepare us for them. "Wretched man that I am!" exclaims St Paul, in memorable words, "Who will deliver me out of this body of death?" For him, as for us, there could be but one reply: "Thanks be to God, my deliverance is through Jesus Christ our Lord."[112] When we are tempted to fear the rigour of God's justice as exhibited in the Passion, "let us also, since we are encompassed by so great a cloud of witnesses, throw aside every encumbrance and the sin which so closely clings to us, and run with perseverance the race set before us, looking towards Jesus, the author and perfecter of our faith; who for the joy set before him endured the cross, despising shame, and is seated at the right hand of the throne of God."[113]

Here again, paraphrasing St Thomas,[114] we may recall the underlying principles. God's love for creatures is the cause of all the goodness to be found in them. Consequently, no one would be better than another unless he were more loved by God, that is, unless God willed for him a greater measure of goodness. Hence it is that God loves Jesus Christ, not only more than the whole human race, but more than all creatures taken together; for he has decreed for him a good higher than any other: "the name which is above every name."[115] The excellence of Christ, far from being diminished by God's handing him over to the humiliation of death for the world's salvation, is rather enhanced; since it was by this means that he became the glorious conqueror and all authority was given to him: "the government is upon his

---

110 Phil. 2:9–11; Heb. 2:9; cf. St. Thomas, III, q. 19, art. 3.
111 John 17:5.   112 Rom. 7:24–25(S.).   113 Heb. 12:1–2(S.).
114 I, q. 20, art. 4 and ad 1.   115 Phil. 2:9(S.).

shoulder; and his name shall be called, Wonderful, Counsellor, God the Mighty, the Father of the world to come, the Prince of Peace." [116]

The Father had honoured his incarnate Son by demanding of him the most heroic proof of love. Nor was the task he imposed on him without its human parallels. When we have to delegate a difficult and painful undertaking to another, we choose, in proportion to its importance, not someone to whom we are indifferent, but a valued and trusted friend. In warfare, a good general disposes, for the most critical and dangerous positions, not his worst troops but his best. It is the compliment he pays them. The standard-bearer of an army, who draws the enemy's concentrated fire, is appointed for his bravery; the respect and affection of the men he leads have won him his place of honour, even though it may involve his death. So was it with God the Father, who would not receive us back into his favour merely on sufferance; instead, he paid the tribute to fallen humanity of decreeing for it a just and adequate redemption. "He did not even spare his own Son, but gave him up for us all." [117]

> *Vexilla Regis prodeunt,*
> *Fulget Crucis mysterium.*
> *Quo carne carnis Conditor*
> *Suspensus est patibulo.*
>
> :
>
> Behold the Royal banners fly,
> The Cross's shining mystery,
> Where He in flesh, our flesh who made,
> Our sentence bore, our ransom paid.

We owe to the *Cur Deus Homo* of St Anselm what is perhaps the most consistently rational account of the economy of the Redemption. Briefly, his reasoning is as follows: Sin is an offence against God; but God's infinite wisdom and holiness cannot allow an offence against his honour to go unpunished. Consequently, the sinner remains a debtor to divine justice until the sin has been atoned for. Now no

[116] Isa. 9:6.   [117] Rom. 8:32.

created being, whether man or angel, can restore to God the
external glory which sin takes from him; for the act of every
finite being is by its nature finite, while sin, by affronting
God, acquires by this fact an infinite wickedness. Whence
follow the alternatives: either sinful man was irremediably
lost, or it was necessary that a God-Man should come to his
aid. But is is repugnant to the divine goodness to abandon
its plans of love and mercy. From this arises the necessity
for the incarnation of the Word; so that he may offer to God,
in the name of guilty humanity, a satisfaction equal to the
offence. By virtue of the hypostatic union, the divine person
of God's Son confers upon the acts of his human nature an
infinite value. Thus it came about that the redeeming death,
voluntarily accepted by Jesus as a supreme proof of filial
obedience for the purpose of restoring the honour due to
God, restored it with interest.

The lucidity and effectiveness of this argument can hardly
be denied; it is not surprising that it should be the one most
frequently met with in popular Catholic accounts of the Redemption. We should notice, however, that if pressed to its
logical conclusion, it presupposes the absolute necessity of
the Incarnation. This, for reasons which should by now be
clear,[118] is unacceptable. St Anselm's reasoning seems to demand precisely that adequate, and indeed superabundant,
redemption which we have in fact received. In other words,
it overlooks the fact that sin might have been forgiven and
remitted by means of an inadequate reparation; that it did
not so work out is due, not to the necessities of the case,
but to the wisdom and loving-kindness of God in choosing
freely to redeem us in the way he has. Moreover, the argument needs to be supplemented by other considerations, if
we are to understand how Christ merited for us. For personal
merit can no more be transferred than can personal guilt
or punishment. It is only in virtue of the moral solidarity
of the group that these things can be shared. As we have seen,
it was by reason of this principle that Christ, though personally innocent, by his natural kinship with us was able

118 See pp. 203, 332–34.

to take upon himself our guilt and punishment. So likewise, it is by his moral unity with us as Head of redeemed humanity, that is, his Church, that he was enabled to merit on our account.[119]

This fact of our solidarity with the Redeemer is the key to the doctrine of the mystical Body of Christ. It explains, not only how we share in the fruits of his sacrifice, but how we are enabled to co-operate with him in the work of redemption. Only thus can we understand, for example, the otherwise incomprehensible words of St Paul: "I rejoice now in my sufferings for your sake; I am filling up on my part the deficiency of the sufferings of the Christ in my flesh, for the sake of his body, which is the Church." [120] No one knew better than St Paul that he could claim nothing save what had come to him by gift; [121] and yet he ventures to offer something of his own! Not that we can, without God's grace, take even the first step towards the achievement of our redemption; but, having received it, we can then, with the divine help, co-operate in producing its richest fruits, in ourselves and others. All is summed up in these striking words to the Corinthians: "Christ never knew sin, and God made him into sin for us, so that in him we might be turned into the holiness of God." [122] To which we may add the illuminating comment of Père Prat: "Sin is not transferred from men to Christ, but it proceeds from men to embrace Christ as the representative of human nature; just as God's righteousness is not transferred from Christ to men, but proceeds from Christ to embrace men, when they, by filial adoption, are clothed with the divine nature." [123]

Considered in itself, the sacrifice of our great High Priest lacks nothing in completeness. But if we are to profit by it, we must respond to his call; salvation is reserved for those "who render obedience to him." [124] A merely passive acquiescence is not enough. "Bestir yourselves then, brethren, ever more eagerly, to ratify God's calling and choice of you

---

119 St Thomas, III, q. 48, art. 1.   120 Col. 1:24(S.); See p. 322.
121 Cf. 1 Cor. 4:7.   122 2 Cor. 5:21.
123 Prat, *op. cit.*, Vol. 2, p. 245 (E.T. p. 204).
124 Heb. 5:9.

by a life well lived." [125] The redeeming work of Christ is indeed unlimited in its efficacy. "A multitude will become acceptable to God through one man's obedience, just as a multitude, through one man's disobedience, became guilty." [126] God "wishes all men to be saved and to come to the knowledge of the truth." [127] Christ's sacrifice on Calvary pours out its saving grace upon all without exception; "we have an advocate with the Father, Jesus Christ, the Righteous One, and he is the expiation for our sins; and not for ours alone, but also for those of the whole world." [128] St Paul, who has revealed to us so much of the mystery of the Redemption, emphasizes its chief lesson: "He died for all, so that the living should no longer live for themselves, but for him who for their sakes died and rose again." [129]

[125] 2 Pet. 1:10.   [126] Rom. 5:19.   [127] 1 Tim. 2:4(S.).
[128] I John 2:1–2(S.).   [129] 2 Cor. 5:15(S.).

§ 20. Christ the King

"Knowing, then, that they meant to come and carry him off, so as to make a king of him, Jesus once again withdrew on to the hill side all alone." [1] With these words St John concludes the incident of the feeding of the five thousand. No other of Jesus' miracles evoked such popular enthusiasm as this. Yet it seemed that he had no wish to be acclaimed a king. Indeed, it may well have been that his refusal on this occasion to fall in with the wishes of the crowd marked the turning of the tide against him. Until then his mission in Galilee had enjoyed not a little success. But, following the events of the succeeding day, with the discourse on the Bread of Life, we read: "After this, many of his disciples went back to their old ways, and walked no more in his company." [2] He was indeed a king; but he would have men share his own understanding of his kingship, and not impose their own preconceptions upon it. Those preconceptions he had expressly repudiated at the outset of his ministry: "Once more, the devil took him to the top of an exceedingly

[1] John 6:15.   [2] Vs. 66.

high mountain, from which he showed him all the kingdoms of the world and the glory of them, and said, I will give thee all these if thou wilt fall down and worship me. Then Jesus said to him, Away with thee, Satan, it is written, Thou shalt worship the Lord thy God, and serve none but him." [3]

During his lifetime our Lord waived every claim to temporal sovereignty. For the time, the political and social order could be ignored; it was the tremendous urgency of God's kingdom which dominated his mind. He even refused to be appealed to as umpire in a merely human dispute: "Why, man, who has appointed me a judge to make awards between you?" [4] His judgement was reserved for another day, and for deeper issues, "when the Son of Man comes in his glory." [5] Then there would be no mistaking in what sense he was a king. [6] Yet, at his Messianic entry into Jerusalem he could accept from his followers a tribute to his kingship; had he forbidden it, "the stones would cry aloud." [7] So they saluted him: "Blessed is the king who comes in the name of the Lord; peace on earth, and glory in heaven above." [8] At least they could recognize the royalty which belonged to him as the Son of David. [9] But the scene before Pilate shows that his kingship was greater than David's. To Pilate's direct question: "Thou art a king, then?" Jesus had given a guarded reply. An unqualified "I am" would have been misunderstood. Instead, he left the query with the questioner and explained the meaning of his kingship: "What I was born for, what I came into the world for, is to bear witness of the truth. Whoever belongs to the truth, listens to my voice." [10]

Christ's royalty was concerned with "a kingdom of truth and life, a kingdom of holiness and grace, a kingdom of justice, love and peace." [11] His kingly power is unlimited

---

[3] Matt. 4:8–10.   [4] Luke 12:14.   [5] Matt. 25:31.
[6] Cf. VV. 34 and 40.   [7] Luke 19:40(S.).   [8] Vs. 38.
[9] Cf. Matt. 21:9.   [10] John 18:37; see p. 132.

[11] *Preface for the Mass of Christ the King.* The Feast of the Kingship of Christ was instituted by Pope Pius XI; see his Encyclical, *Quas primas; Acta Apostolicae Sedis,* 28 December 1925. This is the primary ecclesiastical document for the doctrine here expounded.

in its extent. In the Sermon on the Mount, with its authoritative interpretation of the divine law, and the code of conduct there laid down for the control of men's lives, our Lord comes before us as the supreme Legislator. His precepts were no mere administrative acts, applications of an already existing constitution to which he himself was subject; they were *his* commandments—"you must keep the commandments which I give you." [12] Moreover his authority, without being despotic, is absolute. With God's government of the universe, in which there is nothing arbitrary, whose wisdom reaches "from end to end mightily and ordereth all things sweetly," [13] there is no need for any division between the legislature and the judiciary. Christ is the judge of the observance of his own laws; "the Father, instead of passing judgement on any man himself, has left all judgement to the Son, so that all may reverence the Son just as they reverence the Father." [14] Thus would be fulfilled the prophecy made at the Annunciation to our Lady: "He shall be great, and men will know him for the Son of the most High; the Lord God will give him the throne of his father David, and he shall reign over the house of Jacob eternally; his kingdom shall never have an end." [15]

That God himself holds an undisputed kingship over all his creatures goes without saying; the point which now concerns us is the sense in which this is shared by Jesus Christ as the Redeemer. For it is Christ as man who is our King. The ultimate foundation of his royalty, as of his priesthood, is the hypostatic union. As we have already seen, the substantial union of our Lord's humanity to the person of the Word has conferred on it a dignity surpassing that of any other creature. This is the basis of his universal kingship. Nevertheless, his kingly rule is exercised in virtue of the sanctifying grace which adorns his human soul—a grace immeasurably greater than, but the same in quality as that which he gives to us. "For of his fulness we all received, and grace upon grace." [16]

12 John 14:15.   13 Wisd. 8:1.   14 John 5:22-23.
15 Luke 1:32-33.   16 John 1:16(S.).

The kingdom of Christ, as Pope Pius XI teaches, [17] "is chiefly spiritual and concerns above all the spiritual order." Christ's royalty, from this point of view, is but a function of the grace (*gratia capitalis*) whereby he rules the Church; but it is his by a different title.[18] Again, closely linked as are his priesthood and his kingship, on a basis of this same grace, they may yet be distinguished from one another. As Head of the mystical Body, Christ transmits his own life to its members; as King, he rules them. Strictly speaking, the work of sanctification, which belongs to our Redeemer as Head of the Church, is a function of his priesthood rather than of his kingship. It is thus that, within the depths of the soul, he brings the supernatural life to birth and makes us partakers of the divine nature.[19] This is his most vital task as the Mediator between God and man. It should be noted, however, that in his work of mediatorship he enjoys a true autonomy; he is a conscious and voluntary agent in our sanctification; "each of us has received his own special grace, dealt out to him by Christ's gift." [20]

It belongs to Christ, not only to give life to his mystical Body, but to organize the whole enterprise of our salvation; he has the right to draw whom he chooses to himself, to group the community of the faithful about him, to rule and govern them. Christ the King exercises his royal prerogative in dispensing graces to each according to his pleasure; for "on him all the body depends; it is organized and unified by each contact with the source which supplies it; and thus, each limb receiving the active power it needs, it achieves its natural growth, building itself up through charity." [21] As King, he proposes to the faithful both the end at which they are to aim and the means necessary to attain it. This he does, not merely by a moral exhortation disposing the soul to receive grace, but with the legislative authority and executive power of a supreme monarch. His place is at the head of the whole army of the faithful, inspiring it with his

---

[17] Encyclical, *Quas primas; A.A.S.*, Vol. 17, no. 15, p. 600.
[18] Cf. Héris, *Le Mystère du Christ*, pp. 148–83.
[19] 2 Pet. 1:4.   [20] Eph. 4:7.   [21] Vs. 16.

incomparable leadership, guiding it along the path marked out for salvation. Throughout the ages Christ the King will advance as a conqueror with the Church militant, until "the end, when he hands over the kingdom to God and the Father, when he abolishes all other sovereignty, authority and power." [22]

The kingdom of the Son of God, as Creator, is independent, inalienable and universal; it includes all rational beings, angels and men, good and bad. But the kingdom of Christ, as Redeemer, comprises only the elect. Even as man, everything is subject to him and he exercises his dominion over the whole universe—"All authority in heaven and on earth has been given to me." [23] Yet he reigns, strictly speaking, only in the saints. It is this kingdom, conquered by him, which he delivers up to him from whom he holds his mandate. He pays homage for it "to God and the Father," to him who is at the same time his God and his Father.[24] Moreover, the Son's handing over the kingdom to the Father does not at all imply his own loss or abandonment of it; for the corollary of this supposition would be the absurdity that God the Father loses or abandons his dominion over the universe when he delivers it to the Son.[25] In heaven Christ still remains "his Son, whom he appointed heir of all things, and through whom he made the worlds. He being the effulgence of God's glory and the very image of his substance, upholds the universe by God's powerful mandate. After effecting purification from sins, he seated himself at the right hand of the Majesty on high, having been made as much superior to the angels as he had inherited a more distinguished name than they." [26] Christ the King rules over us, not only by right of nature, but by an acquired right, since he has redeemed us with his precious blood. He is "crowned, now, with glory and honour because of the death he underwent." [27]

Essentially Christ's kingship "is directed, not to temporal

22 1 Cor. 15:24(S.).   23 Matt. 28:18.
24 Cf. Eph. 1:17; John 20:17.   25 Cf. Luke 10:22.
26 Heb. 1:2–5(S.).   27 Heb. 2:9.

things, but to the things that are eternal; for he rules to
this end, that he may guide men to everlasting life." [28]
But this power necessarily includes a rulership over all temporal things, inasmuch as these subserve his redemptive
purpose.[29] His temporal sovereignty, however, is not to be
limited to this indirect control. It is true that, while he was
on earth, our Lord concentrated on his chief work of bringing us salvation; but notwithstanding this, in virtue of the
hypostatic union, his power extends over the whole world
and to every department of men's lives. "It is a mischievous
error," writes Pius XI,[30] "to refuse to acknowledge that Christ
holds an *imperium* in civil affairs, since the absolute authority
over creatures, which he received from the Father, placed all
things under his control. Nevertheless, during his earthly
life, he wholly abstained from the exercise of this kind of
rulership. Moreover, just as he then disdained the ownership and administration of human things, so he left them,
and still leaves them, in the hands of their possessors."

> *Non eripit mortalia*
> *Qui regna dat caelestia.*[31]
> :
> He seeks not here an earthly throne
> Who comes to make all heaven our own.

If Christ does not claim to exercise direct control over the
political and social orders, the fact remains that he has the
right to do so. All men without exception, singly or collectively, baptized or unbaptized, whether they know it or
not, are subject to the empire of Christ the King.

Earthly rulers need fear no dispossession of their power
from the kingship of Christ. On condition that their government remains subject to his, they will find it reinforced.
"Every soul must be submissive to its lawful superiors; authority comes from God only, and all authorities that hold
sway are of his ordinance." [32] But the ease with which human

[28] St Thomas, *In Hebr.* 1, lect. 4.   [29] Cf. III, q. 59, art. 4.
[30] *Loc. cit.*
[31] *Epiphany Vesper Hymn*, quoted by Pius XI.
[32] Rom. 13:1.

power can be abused, its all but fatally corrupting influence on those who wield it, is proof that it can safely be held only by men who regard it as a trust from God. When politics are carried on without reference to the name of Christ, it is inevitable that the results should be disastrous. The enterprise of uniting the nations of the world in a common bond of fellowship, which is the greatest need of our time, is doomed in advance where there is no appeal to God, the source of all unity. To the "King of kings" [33] alone has been given the commission and the effective power "to bring together into one all God's children, scattered far and wide." [34]

That the denial of this truth should lead, sooner or later, to the persecution of those who uphold it is in the nature of things. Lust for domination is the quintessence of egoism; it brooks no rival. So it is that Christ's kingdom will be persecuted until the end of the world. Evidence of just such a clash between human and divine interests is not lacking in our own day. The cry of the Mexican martyrs, "Long live Christ the King," is the heraldic device of the Church militant. It is her title of appeal, over the heads of all earthly rulers, to a higher power than theirs. Nor can it fail to ring painfully in the ears of the dictator and political despot. We remember that it was this same appeal, voiced in a memorable phrase, which led St Thomas More to his death. He claimed to be "the King's good servant, but God's first."

More's words are in striking contrast to the usual speech from the scaffold in Tudor times. The words of Thomas Cromwell are normal: "I am by the Law condemned to die; I have offended my prince, for the which I ask him heartily forgiveness"; the victim admits the supremacy of the State which is demanding his head. More's words are the most weighty and the most haughty ever spoken on the scaffold. Dante could not have bettered them: "The King's good servant, but God's first." [35]

33 Apoc. 17:14; 19:16.   34 John 11:52.
35 R. W. Chambers, *Thomas More*, p. 350.

CHAPTER V

CONSEQUENCES OF THE INCARNATION

It seems convenient to group under this heading, not indeed the whole vast range of effects which flow from the Word's becoming flesh, but the two chief consequences in which all the rest may be said to be included: the gift of the Holy Spirit to the faithful and the unique position held by Mary, the Mother of God, in their regard. In his divine nature, the Son of God always bears the same relationship to the Holy Spirit, the third person of the Blessed Trinity, eternally proceeding from the Father and the Son. But, as man, he received an abundant outpouring of the same Spirit, which, in turn, he promised to give to those who believed in him. By the Spirit they were to live, when Christ's visible presence had been withdrawn from them; so it is that the Holy Spirit is the vivifying principle, the "soul," of his mystical Body, the Church. Moreover, it was part of the divine purpose that the Incarnation should take place through the instrumentality of a privileged member of the human race, the Blessed Virgin Mary. She was to be the Mother of the incarnate Word; consequently she would have both a more intimate relationship with, and a more potent influence upon, him than could be enjoyed by any other creature. We are now concerned to examine these two aspects of the mystery of our redemption.

§ 21. The Spirit of Jesus Christ

"Where the Lord's spirit is, there is freedom." [1] We shall see presently that the Spirit by which the Church lives is

---

[1] 2 Cor. 3:17. Note: The meaning of "spirit" here is almost certainly not the person of the Holy Spirit, but the "spirit" of the new, as opposed to the

not some vague "influence," or "atmosphere," inspired by the memory of Christ; though this is what is commonly implied by the phrase, "the spirit of Christianity." Such language, if somewhat nebulous, has its value, as St Paul's words suggest; but it can only be rightly understood in connection with the living personality of the Holy Spirit; for the Christian "spirit" is precisely the result of the workings of his grace. It is worth our while, however, to strive to appreciate something of what it means, as it was certainly our Lord's intention to bring to birth just such a spirit in us. "Take my yoke upon yourselves and learn from me; I am gentle and humble of heart." [2] The imitation of Christ—to live, as we say, in his spirit—is the ideal of every Christian. "Follow my example, then," writes St Paul, "as I follow the example of Christ." [3] Accordingly, it will be in place to recall the impression our Lord makes upon us, judged simply as an historical character.

But as soon as this has been said, we are at once obliged to admit that the life and character of Jesus lend themselves only partially to such an approach. A consistent historical account, from the point of view of scientific study, is an impossible task; the reason being that the hidden unity of his life, which is itself the key to the full understanding of his human history, namely, the person of the God-Man, is, as we have seen, not human and historical at all. [4] The Incarnation is a fact of history, in that it took place at a definite point in time; but he who became incarnate, God's only begotten Son, remains eternally above the temporal sequence of events. This is why, as Brunner has pointed out, Christ is always a disturbing factor to the secular historian; not on account of any absence of data, which is indeed abundant, but because he cannot be fitted

---

"letter" of the old, Law—what St Thomas calls "the law of Christ understood spiritually, not written down in words, but as impressed by faith upon the heart." Cf. Prat's note, *Dominus autem Spiritus est; op. cit.,* II, 522–29 (E.T. pp. 435–41).

[2] Matt. 11:29.   [3] 1 Cor. 11:1.

[4] Emil Brunner (*The Mediator,* pp. 355–76) has some penetrating observations to make on this point; though we must part company with him on a number of issues.

into any existing historical category. Such an historian is aware of his embarrassment, without, however, being able to explain it. The truth is that the historical appearance of Jesus is itself determined by the mystery of his divine personality; and it is just this which presents the historian, as such, with an insoluble problem. Only one who has entered, through faith, into something of the viewpoint of Jesus himself, can even begin to understand his significance.

We notice that the Gospels never attempt to *describe* our Lord; they simply recount what he said and did, leaving the reader to form his own judgement. There is no piling up of laudatory epithets, no effort to win our admiration on extraneous grounds; we are presented simply with his words and deeds. "Moral greatness," it has been finely said, "is always self-evident." Never was a principle more fully realized than here. Jesus is shown to us in many different and extraordinary situations; in each of them he manifests not only an entire self-possession, but a complete adequacy to what is demanded, an inimitable originality which never leaves him at a loss. This is what gives to his figure an aspect of regal repose and dignity, a loftiness of spirit, a sense of mastery over the world of nature, which would be almost inhuman if, at the same time, we were not made aware of an immense passion, an intense energy of will and feeling. There have been some who have reproached our Lord with being one-sided. The charge may be accepted if by "one-sided" is meant that he subordinated everything to the "one thing necessary." To be wholly given over to a cause, and that the highest and most exacting, must always appear one-sided to the humanitarian moralist. There is an entirely different scale of values from any merely human ethic behind the words: "My meat is to do the will of him who sent me, and to accomplish the task he gave me." [5]

It has been pointed out that the beautiful phrase in which Goethe, with a touch of hyperbole, praised Schiller, seems almost banal when it is applied to Jesus: "Far behind him, remote and insignificant, lay that which holds the rest of

[5] John 4:34.

us in thrall—all that is common and low." The temptations
of Satan, searching though they were, had, in the event,
glanced off him like blunted arrows. There is in him no
opposition between his self-affirmation in proclaiming the
Father's cause and his complete self-effacement in its service.
Even the conflict in Gethsemane reveals no warfare within;
it was the struggle of his human will with the conviction
that the way of complete failure is the one which is ordered
by God, and therefore absolutely necessary. Of self-assertion
for its own sake there is none. Yet in Christ selflessness is
coupled with an intense positive energy and will. He is not
at all the detached, philosophical "spectator of all time and
all existence." He moves forward with his eyes fixed on the
goal, making decision after decision in the light of the great
objective. Blended with complete repose, we find in the
rhythm of his life the spirit of a breathless race towards
its final achievement. "There is a baptism I must needs
be baptized with, and how impatient am I for its accomplish-
ment!" [6] Thus his selflessness is combined with a royal sovereign will, which the Roman centurion recognized as something akin to his own military authority.[7]

Of this harmony of opposites—the *coincidentia opposi-
torum*—which is so strikingly exemplified in Jesus Christ,
perhaps the highest instance is that of the gravity of his
moral judgements and of infinite forgiving love. He is at
once the implacable destroyer of resistance against his Father
—no one ever attacked the religious leaders of his day with
more severity—and a friend of sinners and outcasts. He manifested the wrath of God more powerfully than John the
Baptist or any of the prophets before him; but the element
which was new in Israel was his active compassion for the
non-observers of the Law. This unconditional, unlimited
friendship with bad people was unintelligible to those who
saw it; it was this in particular which gained him the enmity
of the scribes and Pharisees. They thought such an attitude
"lax," because it laid down no conditions at all. What it did
show was that our Lord was not afraid of being misunder-

6 Luke 12:50.   7 Cf. 7:2 ff.

stood, that he knew himself as one into whose soul evil could make no entry, that it had no affinity with his spirit in any direction or at any point. He knew that in his own life he embodied the truth that in the Gospel the Law is fulfilled as well as abrogated.

Another instance of this "harmony of opposites" is his nearness to men and yet his remoteness from them. His complete humanity is revealed, for example, in his attitude towards children. He has been well called "the discoverer of the child." The child strikes us as possessing human nature in its purest state, unmoulded, undetermined by such acquired habits as differentiate the mature man from his fellows. Hence, for our Lord, the child, with its simplicity and candour and open-heartedness, is the living model of what man's attitude to God should be. The disciples, in their well-meant efforts to save their Master's time and strength, thought they knew the difference between what was important and what was unimportant; so they tried to keep the children away from him.[8] Yet he always had time and strength to give to these, his "little ones." [9] Again, what a wealth of sympathetic understanding for the smallest things in life, for the humble occupations of ordinary folk, is revealed in the parables! All those who defend the cause of the common man and the life close to nature, in the village and on the farm, can rightly appeal to Jesus for their support. He lived, a man among men, with nothing of the doctrinaire in his approach to their problems. He is not an "intellectual" or "progressive," straining to reform the social conditions of his day—though here, it should be remembered that they were very different conditions from those of our modern industrial society. There is nothing in his language of rabbinical sterility and learned abstraction, no attempt to bury natural life and feeling beneath a weight of pedantic theory.

And yet, with all this, he is completely detached from the world and its ways. During his public ministry, this detachment extends to his own Mother and near relatives,[10]

[8] Mark 10:13-16; cf. 9:35-37.   [9] 9:42.   [10] Mark 3:31-35.

and he bids his disciples follow his example.[11] His famous words—"Render to Caesar the things that are Caesar's, and to God the things that are God's" [12]—show him as neither a nationalist patriot nor a collaborator with the Roman occupying power. He is a partisan of no cause except God's, and lives a stranger in this world. He has no profession, and he draws his disciples away from all that was naturally nearest and dearest to them. He is without property or income; he has no home. He preaches detachment, but not stern asceticism; he can bear the reproach: "Here is a glutton; he loves wine." [13] Himself a celibate, he praises the celibacy of elect souls; [14] yet he consorts with women in unembarrassed freedom. He would be their guest, and allow them to wait on him.[15] He condemns the love of riches [16] without attacking inequality of possessions. He respects the accepted customs of his people, but breaks through them if by so doing he can help any man in need. All human experience is his, yet it never claims him, never draws him out of himself. He stands firmly on the ground in a real world, with none of its interests alien to him, even while there is nothing in them which absorbs him. He has not been disinherited, torn up by the roots, and yet he has no inheritance and no roots anywhere.

We notice further that he makes no break with the moral and religious traditions of Judaism. The Old Testament scriptures are for him the revelation of God. The Law is to be fulfilled down to its minutest detail.[17] The Temple, with its sacrificial worship, was for him the "house of prayer." [18] He respects the synagogue also, where he teaches in the manner of the Rabbis. And yet, he sets over against all this the message embodied in his person, as being of unparalleled importance. "Heaven and earth shall pass away, but my words shall not pass away." [19] He knew that the vital ferment in his teaching was incompatible with the maintenance of the existing order; there was an incongruity

---

11 Matt. 10:37.   12 Mark 12:17(W.)   13 Matt. 11:19.
14 19:12.   15 Luke 10:38–42.   16 Mark 10:21 ff.
17 Matt. 5:17–19.   18 21:13.   19 Mark 13:31(R-D.).

in sewing new cloth on to a worn-out garment, in pouring new wine into old wine-skins.[20] We can only faintly imagine the effect on a devout Jew of his words: *You have heard that it was said to the men of old. . . . But I tell you . . .* It has been remarked that if he had been a man of the type of Socrates, the contemporary of the Sophists, this would not have been extraordinary. But he was himself a teacher of the Torah; he was a member of the synagogue, born subject to the Law.[21]

At his trial he was falsely charged with aiming at the destruction of the Temple; [22] though in fact he had come to supplant the Jerusalem Temple and what it stood for. His enemies were right in seeing in Jesus a menace to their very existence. His intense concentration on the ultimate things in religion, his every word, threatened their status of power and privilege. It arose from the nature of the case that he, who was neither the one nor the other, should be condemned as an iconoclast and revolutionary. By a supreme irony his condemnation lay not with the State and civil order, but with the representatives of religion, of the Jewish religion and the Law. For they alone understood that if he prevailed it would mean the downfall of many in Israel.[23]

When we consider the character of Jesus in relation to what he taught, we can detect no discrepancy between precept and practice. His teaching is embodied in himself. What we invariably find in even the best of men—the lack of correspondence between their desires and their achievements, between their ideals and their deeds, between their knowledge and their obedience—is not discoverable in any way in him. His manner of demanding the highest, so imperatively and yet so naturally, shows that he takes it for granted that he belongs to a different order from his followers. But this, while evoking our admiration, raises a question of great practical importance to every Christian, namely, the value of our Lord's life considered precisely as an example to our-

[20] Matt. 9:16–17.   [21] Gal. 4:4.
[22] Cf. Mark 14:58 and John 2:19–21.   [23] Cf. Luke 2:34.

selves. Perhaps, half unconsciously, even the sincere believer feels tempted to interpose some such objection as this: Christ, by the very fact that he was God, is more than man. The truth of his complete humanity is inescapable, and yet, at the same time, he impresses us as being almost superhuman, betraying no sense of error, moral weakness or insufficiency. But here is what takes from the force of his example. For this to be effective, so that we may gain inspiration and courage from him, he should be no more than a man—a human being like ourselves, with no greater resources to draw upon than we have, and no exemptions from our common frailties.[24]

It is interesting to remember that St Augustine, in the fifth century, had to deal with just this objection; for it had been raised by his Pelagian antagonist, Julian of Eclanum.[25] Augustine replied with some searching counter-questions: Did Christians really want a Christ who started merely from the common level of human sinfulness? And further, if we are to be quite logical, should we not find the most encouraging Christ to be one who began life with the most evilly disposed nature to tame and the most unruly passions to subdue? These questions have only to be asked for us to feel their destructiveness. The thought of a Christ who is entirely on our own level is intolerable. It is true that, if it is merely a matter of example, we are in fact most encouraged by a person not essentially different from ourselves, having no advantages not available to us. But what emerges from the Gospels is that our Lord did not appeal to his disciples, at least in the first place, as an example they could follow. They felt him to be in some mysterious sense above them—teaching and working with an awe-inspiring power—drawing them with a tremendous proclamation from on high—claiming, controlling, saving, judging.

24 This point is ably discussed by Charles Gore, *The Reconstruction of Belief*, p. 469 ff; though his work as a whole, admirable in many respects, is spoiled by its unresolved rationalism and an over-anxiety to accommodate Christ to the "modern mind"—whose mood, incidentally, has changed since the time it was written!

25 Cf. St Augustine, *c. Julian, op. imperfect.*, iv, cc. 48–57; *P.L.* 45, col. 1366–1373.

Christ our Lord is indeed our supreme example—"I have been setting you an example, which will teach you in your turn to do what I have done for you." [26] "He suffered for our sakes, and left you his own example; you were to follow in his footsteps." [27] But what we notice is that this example only became effective after his death, with the sending of the Holy Spirit. This was the means whereby the influence of Christ would be perpetuated through the ages. By the power of the Spirit of Jesus men were to be enabled to live in the "Christian spirit." While our Lord was living as a man among men, it appears that neither his teaching nor his example had any lasting effect on his first disciples. The magnetism of his personal presence proved irresistible; but his followers failed under the strain he put upon them; at the hour of his seeming defeat, they deserted him. He was altogether too high for them, too unworldly. It was only in the revived faith of the Resurrection, confirmed by the outpouring of the Spirit at Pentecost—his Father's Spirit and his own—that they realized the force of his example. Then they knew that Christ was their living Lord in heaven, inspiring, guiding, governing and enriching them with an inward divine power. Thus it was—and this is a remarkable fact—that Jesus was never looked upon by the early Church as a departed hero, a "lost leader," from whose memory alone his disciples might draw their inspiration. They knew that he was alive, moulding them to his own example by his Spirit; they knew that it was only "in Christ" that they could follow Christ.

But all this had been possible only for the reason that he was something more than man, that he was now, as he had always been, far above his followers, one to whom it would have been madness to think themselves equal. It was because he was God, because, as man, he had risen from the dead and ascended to the Father, that he could have access to their inmost souls, to remake them, and dwell "through faith" [28] in their hearts. So our Lord had promised on the night before he died:

26 John 13:15.   27 1 Pet. 2:21.   28 Eph. 3:17.

I have still many things to say to you, but you cannot bear them now. But when he, the Spirit of truth, comes, he shall guide you into all the truth; for he shall not speak from himself, but whatever he will hear he shall speak, and shall announce to you the events which are still to come. He shall glorify me; for he shall receive of what is mine; and shall announce it to you. All that the Father has is mine; that is why I said, He receives of what is mine, and shall announce it to you.[29]

Just as the disciples could not follow their Master then, but would follow him afterwards,[30] so was it with the deeper implications of his teaching—"you cannot bear them now." They were as yet no more than children in the Faith; they could scarcely grasp the import of his ministry, still less anticipate the significance of his passion and death.

From this we learn that if we would enter into the mind of Christ, we must not confine our attention to what he did and said while he was on earth. Then he kept his teaching, so far as might be, within the mental grasp of his immediate hearers. Even so, much of it was above their heads; but those with good will could assimilate enough to form the basis for later instruction—by "the Spirit of truth." This they would receive from the inspired apostles, themselves the instruments of Christ's further revelation—a revelation to be preserved for all time by his Spirit-guided Church. The truth which the Spirit will disclose refers to Christ, who is himself "the truth." [31] Men will be led through the Holy Spirit to an ever fuller understanding of Jesus. It is not his message—"he shall not speak from himself"— but the Lord's own message, which he in his turn has received from the Father,[32] that he will deliver. The Spirit coming from the Son comes also from the Father.[33] "All that the Father has is mine." [34] The Son receives it from the Father that the Spirit should proceed from him, just as he does from the Father. The Father and the Son are thus the

[29] John 16:12–15(S.).   [30] Cf. 13:36.   [31] 14:6.
[32] Cf. John 7:16–17.   [33] 15:26.   [34] 16:15(S.).

single source for the procession of the Holy Spirit.[35] The Spirit's coming will bring honour to Christ because he "shall announce"—that is, make plain—"to you the events which are still to come"; [36] namely, our Lord's passion, death, resurrection and ascension.

These momentous happenings must first become history before their meaning could be expounded. For the present— "you cannot bear them now." But in the light of Pentecost all would be changed; then they would understand. So it proved; the apostolic preaching, in the power of the Spirit, mainly concerned those events which, at the Last Supper, were "still to come." We remember what they were: "Christ never knew sin, and God made him into sin for us, so that in him we might be turned into the holiness of God." [37] "God has offered him to us as a means of reconciliation (ἱλαστήριον), in virtue of faith, ransoming us with his blood." [38] "We were buried therefore with him by baptism into death; so that, as Christ rose from the dead in the glory of the Father, thus we also might walk in newness of life." [39] "How rich God is in mercy, with what an excess of love he loved us! Our sins had made dead men of us, and he, in giving life to Christ, gave life to us too; it is his grace that has saved you; raised us up too, enthroned us

[35] NOTE: This is the meaning of the famous *Filioque* clause in our present Nicene Creed.

[36] John 16:13(S.).   [37] 2 Cor. 5:21.

[38] Rom. 3:25. NOTE: Rom. 3:24–25 is a key-text in the doctrine of the Redemption. Fr. Spencer's version gives a more literal rendering of the operative words: "They are justified freely by his grace, by means of the redemption which is in Christ Jesus; whom God has put forward as a propitiation (ἱλαστήριον) in his blood through faith." There seems no grounds for taking the all-important word, ἱλαστήριον, to mean "Mercy Seat" as Temple does (*Readings in St John's Gospel*, II, p. 291;—a work which no one can read without lasting indebtedness), following Origen, Ritschl and others. For St Paul it signifies a "means of expiation" or "of propitiation," or perhaps both. The ideas of *expiation* and *propitiation* are in fact closely related, for God is appeased or made propitious only in so far as sin is expiated, and the one redeeming act produces at the same time this double result. When ἱλαστήριον is connected with "in his blood," the meaning is unmistakably *sacrificial*, as Deissmann concedes. Hence Jesus Christ is here represented as a victim of expiation, or propitiation. See Prat, *op. cit.*, I, pp. 504–7 (E.T. pp. 429–32).

[39] Rom. 6:4(S.).

above the heavens, in Christ Jesus." [40] "Having therefore, brethren, freedom of entrance into the sanctuary by the blood of Jesus, by the pathway which he dedicated for us—a new-made and living pathway through the veil, that is, his flesh—and having a great priest over the house of God, let us approach with a true heart in full assurance of faith, our hearts being sprinkled from a bad conscience, and our bodies washed with pure water." [41]

These were the things which the disciples were unable to bear at the Last Supper. How could it have been otherwise? But when the events to which these declarations refer had taken place, then, under the guidance of Christ's Spirit, they would be able to interpret them aright. For such is the function of the Holy Spirit's coming—to interpret Christ. And not only this, but to give us Christ over again, in a way more accessible to us. In the words of St Epiphanius, "Christ is sent by the Father and the Holy Spirit is also sent; Christ speaks in the saints, the Holy Spirit speaks also; Christ heals and the Holy Spirit likewise heals; Christ sanctifies and so does the Holy Spirit." [42]

Nothing in St Paul is clearer than the intimate union between the Son and the Holy Spirit in their joint work of sanctification. Grace, the *charismata*,[43] filial adoption, good works, salvation, eternal glory; in a word, all the manifestations of the divine life are referred sometimes to Christ, sometimes to the Holy Spirit. Thus, "we live by the Spirit" and yet Christ is "our life." [44] The Holy Spirit is the dispenser of all the *charismata*, nevertheless these are "Christ's gifts." [45] It is through Jesus Christ that we receive the adoption of sons; while, at the same time, the Holy Spirit is the Spirit of adoption.[46] "Those who follow the leading of the Spirit are all God's sons." [47] The dead will rise again by "a

---

40 Eph. 2:4–6.   41 Heb. 10:19–22(S.).
42 *Ancoratus*, 68; *P.G.* 43, col. 140.
43 NOTE: These divine favours are not what we now call sanctifying grace, but gifts bestowed to enable their recipients to perform various functions in the Church; see 1 Cor. 12:28–30.
44 Gal. 5:25 and Col. 3:4; cf. Phil. 1:21.
45 1 Cor. 12:11 and Eph. 4:7.   46 Gal. 4:5–6.
47 Rom. 8:14.

man," Christ; and yet God will raise us up through "his Spirit who dwells in you." [48] For St Paul, to be *in Christ* is virtually one with being *in the Spirit*.[49]

It would be an error, however, to conclude from this, as some have done, that Christ and the Spirit are identical. There are no grounds for the view that the Spirit merely signifies a mode of Christ's activity, still less for the manifest absurdity that, after the Resurrection, he was completely transformed into the Spirit. It will be remembered that, neither in St Paul nor in St John, is the pre-existent Christ identified with the Holy Spirit. Nowhere in the New Testament is there suggested an identity between the Spirit and Christ before his death. Christ as Saviour is never identified with the Spirit in the work of redemption. Only after the Resurrection and Ascension, in the glorified Christ, do we reach a point of identity between him and the Spirit; and even this is not in Christ's physical, personal life at the right hand of the Father, but in his mystical life in the bosom of the Church. In other words, the glorified Christ and the Holy Spirit, who appear everywhere else as two distinct persons, seem to be identified with each other in their work of sanctifying souls. Here, indeed, their sphere of influence is the same and their fields of action blend; for Christ is the Head, or, under a somewhat different figure, the organism of his mystical Body, the soul of which is the Holy Spirit. Now, just as in ordinary language, almost all vital phenomena can be referred equally to the head or to the soul, so may we with equal correctness, attribute the Church's divine vitality to Christ or to the Holy Spirit.

Moreover, as Père Prat has pointed out,[50] there exists a deeper reason for the identity of Christ's and the Spirit's influence on the life of the Church. Christ as man possessed the fulness of the Spirit, and after his redemptive work was accomplished, he was to cause the Spirit to be poured out

[48] 1 Cor. 15:21 and Rom. 8:11.
[49] Compare the following texts: 1 Cor. 6:11 and Gal. 2:17; 1 Cor. 6:11 and 1:2; Eph. 2:22 and 2:21; 1:13 and 4:30; Rom. 14:17 and Phil. 4:4; Rom. 14:17 and 5:1.
[50] Prat, *op. cit.*, II, p. 354 (E.T. p. 293).

upon us. At the Resurrection he became, both for himself and for us, a quickening spirit: for himself, since the grace in which his soul abounded overflowed into his body and spiritualized it; [51] for us, because he endowed us lavishly with all the gifts of the Holy Spirit and the Holy Spirit himself. Henceforth we live in faith and grace by the Son and also by the Spirit; or, to be more precise, by the Spirit as sent by the Son; whence arises an identity of operations without confusion of persons. Thus, in the process by which we are adopted as sons of God, the privilege of sonship comes to us from the Son, who causes us to be accepted by God as his brothers, Christ himself being "the first-born among many brethren." [52] To this state God has called us, namely, "into the fellowship of his Son." [53] At the same time, the Holy Spirit is the "Spirit of adoption," and those to whom he comes "are all God's sons." [54] Hence, simultaneously, the Father adopts us as his sons by giving us his Spirit, and Christ, the only begotten Son, adopts us as his brothers by sending us his Spirit. "A man cannot belong to Christ unless he has the Spirit of Christ." [55] The Holy Spirit is the witness, the messenger, the agent, and the pledge of our divine sonship.

From this it will be seen that we can hardly ever begin to grasp the significance of our Lord's life-work until we appreciate the relationship and active interpenetration between him and the Holy Spirit. It was so ordained that Christ had to rise from the dead before he could become himself a life-giving spirit and send his Spirit upon us. We recall St John's comment on his Master's words at the feast of Tabernacles: "Now he said this in reference to the Spirit whom those who believed in him were to receive; for the Spirit had not yet been given, because Jesus had not yet been glorified." [56] We learn also something of the nature of the mystical Body,[57] which is not a simple metaphor or a mere moral entity, but a supernatural organism, receiving

51 1 Cor. 15:44.   52 Rom. 8:29(S.).   53 1 Cor. 1:9.
54 Rom. 8:14–15.   55 Vs. 9.   56 John 7:39(S.).
57 See § 24, pp. 318–21.

at the same time a vital influx from its Head, Christ, and from its soul, the Holy Spirit. The glorified Christ, who is the unique Son of God, in union with the adopted sons of God, his "brethren," together form his "Body"—a unity of Head and members which St Augustine was later to call the "whole Christ," *Christus totus*.[58] This is the Church, the society of the redeemed, in the lives of whose members should be reflected the spirit of Jesus Christ. Such was to be the effect of the gift of the Holy Spirit. "To prove that you are sons, God has sent out the Spirit of his Son into your hearts, crying out in us, Abba, Father. No longer, then, art thou a slave, thou art a son; and because thou art a son, thou hast the son's right of inheritance." [59]

[58] *Enarr. in Ps.* XVII, 51, and XC, 11,1; *P.L.* 36, col. 154 and 37, col. 1159.
[59] Gal. 4:6–7.

§ 22. THE ROLE OF THE MOTHER OF GOD

"When the sixth month came, God sent the angel Gabriel to a city of Galilee called Nazareth, where a virgin dwelt, betrothed to a man of David's lineage; his name was Joseph, and the virgin's name was Mary. Into her presence the angel came, and said, Hail, thou who art full of grace; the Lord is with thee." [1] St Bernard of Clairvaux provides the most fitting commentary on this scene of the Annunciation:

The angel awaits an answer, for it is time to return to God who sent him. And we, too, Lady, await the word of pity, we who are piteously oppressed by the sentence of damnation. Here thou art offered the price of our salvation; if thou wilt consent, then immediately we shall be freed. We have all been made in God's eternal Word, and behold, we die; in thy brief reply we are to be made anew, that we may be recalled to life. Adam, shut out from paradise with all his unhappy progeny, tearfully supplicates that reply of thee, O loving Virgin. Abraham and David entreat it also, and those other Fathers, ancestors of thine, who alike dwell in the valley of the shadow of death. The whole world, prostrate at thy knees, waits for thy consent; and not without reason, since upon thy lips hangs the consolation of the

[1] Luke 1:26–28.

wretched, the redemption of the captive, the freedom of the condemned; in brief the salvation of Adam's children, of the whole human race. O Virgin, give quickly thy reply. O Lady, speak the word which earth, hell, and even heaven await.[2]

Almighty God, in the boundless freedom which marks all his actions with reference to creatures, need not have chosen Mary to be the Mother of the Word, nor made her the freely consenting instrument of the Incarnation. But this, in fact, was what he did. Not that the plan of our redemption thereby became uncertain, as being made dependent on a creature's will; for the human will is no less subject to God's power than is the rest of his creation. "As the divisions of waters, so the heart of the king is in the hand of the Lord; whithersoever he will he shall turn it." [3] "If it is God's intention that the man whose heart he moves shall obtain grace," says St Thomas, "then he infallibly obtains it." [4] Under the movement of divine grace then, Mary freely consented to become the Mother of him who was "the Son of the most High," to whom "the Lord God" would give "the throne of his father David," that he might "reign over the house of Jacob eternally," whose "kingdom" should "never have an end." [5] But in her motherhood nothing of her virginity would be lost; it was to be kept for ever afterwards in sacred trust. Her Child's birth was to come about, "not of blood, nor of the will of the flesh, nor of the will of man, but of God." [6] So the angel explained to her: "The Holy Spirit will come upon thee, and the power of the most High will overshadow thee." [7] "And Mary said, Behold the handmaid of the Lord; let it be unto me according to thy word." [8] Such was her act of acceptance of God's will, her surrender to all his designs for her in the work of our redemption; it is the key-note of her life, the expression of the sublime dignity of Mary.

Hail, thou who art full of grace! So from the first moment of her conception she had always been. Her Son was indeed

2 Hom. IV *super: Missus est; P.L.* 183, col. 83.
3 Prov. 21:1.   4 Ia IIae, q. 112, art. 3.   5 Luke 1:32.
6 John 1:13(R-D.).   7 Luke 1:35.   8 Vs. 38.

for her, as for the rest of mankind, the Redeemer; it is God her "Saviour" whom she salutes in the Magnificat, "because he has looked graciously upon the lowliness of his hand-maid." [9] With prophetic insight she could say in humble triumph, "Behold, from this day forward all generations shall count me blessed"; yet, again, it was "because he who is mighty, he whose name is holy, has wrought for me his wonders." [10] Among those wonders was the manner in which, even at that moment, she had been redeemed. Our Lady's birth, unlike her Son's, had been that of a normal child. She was the daughter of her parents, in the long line of human generation which reaches back to Adam. By that very fact she was under the doom of our race. In Adam all had sinned—"all alike were guilty men." [11] Mary, by her complete kinship with us, had contracted the common debt we owe to God; even for her the price had to be paid. And by whom? There is only one answer to that question: for our Lady, as for us, redemption had come through Jesus Christ her Son. To all humanity, not excepting Mary, St Peter's words apply: "Salvation is not to be found elsewhere; this alone of all names under heaven has been appointed to men as the one by which we must needs be saved." [12]

On the other hand, Mary was called from eternity to be the Mother of the Saviour. God the Father, with a love of predilection, had chosen her from among all women to pro-vide a human body for the incarnate Word. Only the Father and the Virgin Mother would be able to say to Jesus, "My Son." With this destiny in view, it is hardly to be thought of that he would have allowed her who was to be so highly privileged, to inherit the guilt of original sin. It was un-fitting that she, who was to be the Mother of the Author of grace, should herself ever have lacked this gift. So in fact it proved. He whose wisdom reaches "from end to end mightily and ordereth all things sweetly" [13] found a way, without ab-solving even Mary from the debt of original sin, to preserve her from all contact from its guilt and stain. She was to re-

9 Luke 1:46–48.   10 Vs. 49.   11 Rom. 5:12.
12 Acts 4:12.   13 Wisd. 8:1.

ceive a unique redemption. For the rest of us Christ's redemptive sacrifice was an act of reparation for, and liberation from, sin; for our Lady it was a complete preservation from it. Such is the Immaculate Conception. At the moment of her soul's infusion into her body, when, by the laws of a nature vitiated through Adam's sin she should have contracted its guilt, God exempted her from it—in view of the foreseen merits of his Son, and hers. Thus she who was in truth the second Eve, from whom the new human race would take its origin, was conceived and born justified from sin by the gift of that divine inheritance which she would pass on to her children.

Our Lady's preservative redemption is one of the treasures of Catholic dogma. It was defined by Pope Pius IX in 1854.[14] We shall better appreciate its significance if we remember that not only is Jesus Christ the Saviour of Mary, but that he exercised his redemptive mission in her regard more fully than in any other creature. It was fitting that her soul, which was to share most intimately in his saving work, should in the first place be the recipient of a unique and sovereign redemption. Now redemption in its most perfect form would be, not simply the uplifting of the soul from a state of sin, but its complete preservation from it. Just as, in our own case, when God keeps us from falling into mortal sin, he sustains the life of grace more effectively than when he heals us from the wounds of a sin into which we have already fallen, so we find that Christ's redemption was applied in all its fulness to his immaculate Mother, not merely uplifting her from our sinful condition, but wholly protecting her from it. The Immaculate Conception is thus the outstanding proof of the uniqueness of Christ's love for his Mother. For God gives grace to a creature in proportion to his love for it; grace is, in fact, the result of his love.[15] Hence, God's love for Mary was greater than that for any other creature, with the exception of the sacred humanity of our Lord himself.

The grace in Mary's soul was the generative principle of

[14] Denz., 1641. [15] St Thomas, Ia IIae, q. 110, art. 1.

all her abundant merits, which themselves progressively increased in accordance with the unceasing fidelity to God's
will that characterized her whole life. Nevertheless, it would
be incorrect to think of her as having merited the Incarnation itself. The theological reason for this is that the source
of merit cannot itself be merited; it cannot produce itself
any more than a first cause can be the effect which it produces. Now our Lady's merits derive from the future merits
of her Son; on these they are dependent, not merely as a
final cause, but as a moral efficient cause foreseen and willed
by God. It is true that, on the basis of the divine favours
freely bestowed on her, she may be said to have merited to
become the Mother of the incarnate Word. Indeed we rejoice in this thought as it is expressed in the beautiful
Easter prayer:

> O Queen of Heaven rejoice, alleluia,
> For he whom thou didst merit to bear, alleluia,
> Hath arisen, as he said, alleluia,
> Pray for us to God, alleluia.

How this is to be understood is explained with admirable
precision by St Thomas: "The Blessed Virgin is said to have
merited to bear the Lord of all things, not because she merited that he should become incarnate, but because, in virtue
of the grace given to her, she merited that degree of purity
and holiness whereby she might fittingly (congrue) become
the Mother of God." [16]

"God sent his Son, made from a woman, made under the
law, in order that he might redeem those under the law." [17]
Miraculous as were the conception and virginal birth of
Jesus Christ, the Child's gestation in our Lady's womb was
entirely normal. Mary, like every mother, gave of her own
substance to form the human body of her Son. "And behold, thou shalt conceive in thy womb, and shalt bear a son,
and shalt call him Jesus." [18] The long-awaited Messiah had
for his Mother "Mary." [19] The Wise Men from the East had

---

[16] III, q. 2, art. 11, ad 3.   [17] Gal. 4:4(S.).
[18] Luke 1:31.   [19] Matt. 1:18.

found the Child at Bethlehem "with Mary his mother." [20] Mary is the Mother of Jesus Christ; but Jesus Christ is God; therefore Mary is the Mother of God. This argument, brief as it is, contains the whole theology of the divine mother-hood. Its conclusion flows as a logical necessity from the fact that in Christ there is but one person, that of God's Son, who had assumed our human nature. Mary is not the Mother of the Godhead; nor, of course, was she the Mother of the Word before the Incarnation; but she bore in her womb, and gave birth to, him who was God. She is the "God-bearer" (θεοτόκος, *Deipara, Dei Genitrix*) who mothered the only begotten Son "according to his humanity"—a humanity already assumed by the divine Word, so as to form one person with him. But, just as a normal mother is not said merely to be the mother of her child's body but of all that makes him to be the unique personality he is, so was it with Mary; she is truly the Mother of God. Such is the teaching of the Catholic Church, enunciated at the Council of Ephesus in 431 [21] and reaffirmed at the Councils of Chalcedon, 451, [22] and Constantinople, 553. [23] This truth forms an essential part of the doctrine of the Incarnation. History has shown that the denial of Mary's title to be the Mother of God inevitably brings with it the rejection of the Church's teaching about Christ.

It is perhaps unnecessary to point out that Mary does not bear the same relation to her divine Son as does God the Father. From the Father he is born before all time; from Mary he was born at a definite point in history. Consequently we may speak of two relations of sonship (*filiatio*); [24] one eternal, by which the Father generates his Son according to his divine nature; the other temporal, whereby Mary gave birth to him in time according to his human nature. But the term of both the Father's and Mary's relationship to the Son is one and the same, namely, the person of the Word. Whence it must follow, since the hypostatic union

[20] Matt. 2:11; cf. vv. 13, 14.   [21] Denz. 113.   [22] No. 148.
[23] No. 218.   [24] St Thomas, III, q. 35, art. 5.

can never be broken, that our Lady's role as the Mother of God remains throughout all ages.

Let us consider for a moment the unique prerogatives of Mary. We know that, by reason of the grace of divine mother-hood, she stands closer to God than any of the angels or saints. We know also that, as a consequence of the Immaculate Conception, she was freed from the initial clouding of the mind and feebleness of will which are the results of Adam's sin passed on to us. She comes before us, God's masterpiece, of all pure creatures the fairest, the noblest and the best. Yet, like her Son, she could be tempted to sin, she could suffer, and she was subject to death. Moreover, unlike him, she could increase in virtue; there was room in her for advancement in God's grace. Her act of self-abandon-ment to the divine will—"Let it be unto me according to thy word" [25]—would gain in depth and reality throughout her life until, as a reward for her flawless fidelity, she achieved the highest degree of merit ever gained by a crea-ture. For it should be remembered that Mary, like her children, lived by faith and not by sight. She did not have before her eyes the vision of God; hence, for her under-standing of the secret of her Child's person and mission, she was dependent on whatever God should choose to dis-close to her. That she had received a fuller revelation of, and had herself a deeper insight into, the mystery of our redemption than any of our Lord's apostles and disciples is certain. Nevertheless, as the New Testament clearly shows,[26] the contemplative soul of Mary could ponder over the as yet hidden implications of what had been revealed to her.

Catholic piety delights to dwell on our Lord's boyhood years at Nazareth, while "the child grew, and became strong, being filled with wisdom." [27] We strive to reconstruct in imagination the fascinating picture of Mary and Joseph with the youthful Jesus, as he "lived there in subjection to them." [28] Our fancy runs on how he would have learned the carpenter's trade from his foster-father, mixing with others of

25 Luke 1:38.   26 Cf. 2:19, 51.
27 Vs. 40(S.).   28 Vs. 51.

his age, to all appearances in no way different from them. Unquestionably he was more intelligent, more thoughtful, more preoccupied with religion than his companions. This emerges from the impression he made on the Rabbis in the Temple: "All his hearers were in amazement at his quick understanding and at the answers he gave." [29] But if the life of the Holy Family is hidden from us, it was not at all hidden from their neighbours at Nazareth; as we might have expected, there was no "keeping themselves to themselves." In fact the Nazarenes knew, or thought they knew, all about them.[30] Of this we can be certain, that Mary looked after his every need, gave him his first lessons, and cherished him with all the affection of the most perfect of mothers. How charming is the thought that he must have been not unlike her in appearance! People would doubtless have remarked on it; and she in her turn would proudly claim, as mothers do—though in this case with absolute truth—that no woman ever had such a son. More significant still is what must have been his attitude of loving reverence towards her—the "Blessed among women," whom from all eternity the Son of God had chosen to be the one he would speak of as "My mother."

But if Jesus allowed Mary all the rights of a mother over

[29] Luke 2:47.

[30] "How did he come by this wisdom, and these strange powers? Is not this the carpenter's son, whose mother is called Mary, and his brethren James and Joseph and Simon and Judas? And do not his sisters, all of them, live near us? How is it that all this has come to him? And they had no confidence in him."—Matt. 13:54-57. NOTE: This text raises the question of the "brethren" and "sisters" of Jesus (cf. Mark 6:3; Luke 4:22; John 6:42) and of the putative fatherhood of St Joseph, which again involves that of our Lady's perpetual virginity. For a discussion of this and comprehensive bibliographies see Lebreton, *The Life and Teaching of Jesus Christ our Lord*, I, 32-37; also Lagrange, *Évangile selon Saint Marc*, pp. 72-89. Here it must suffice to quote the latter scholar's remark on Luke 4:22—"Luke makes the people of Nazareth say: 'Is not this the son of Joseph?' As these people knew nothing of the mystery on which Luke has written at length, they could not have spoken in any other fashion. Thus they merely bear witness to what was outwardly apparent and about which there was no difference of opinion, for Mary was really married to Joseph. But what about the brothers and sisters? According to the significance of the Greek terms used, they are indeed brothers and sisters; but the Semitic terms represented by the Greek can without any question be used of cousins or even more distant relations.... The whole group simply designates relations (cf. 1 Cor. 9:5)." Lagrange, *L'Évangile de Jésus-Christ*, pp. 193-94 (E.T. I, pp. 204-5).

her child, he was at the same time teaching her a still deeper lesson. The theologians are surely right in their conjecture that his chief work, during those first thirty years, was the sanctification of the souls of Mary and Joseph, above all, the preparation of his Mother for the part she was to play in his redeeming mission. This finds support in the one incident in the hidden life disclosed to us, the loss and finding of the boy Jesus when he was twelve years old. Let us recall the scene: Mary and Joseph—the latter being clearly regarded at Nazareth, as he must have been alluded to in the little family circle, as Jesus' "father" [31]—having missed the Child on the homeward journey, returned to Jerusalem and at length discovered him in the Temple. "Seeing him there, they were full of wonder, and his mother said to him, My Son, why hast thou treated us so? Think, what anguish of mind thy father and I have endured, searching for thee. But he asked them, What reason had you to search for me? Could you not tell that I must needs be in the place which belongs to my Father?" [32] Where else should they have expected to find him but in the Temple, his Father's house? But St Luke adds: "These words which he spoke to them were beyond their understanding." [33] It appears that, even to Mary, the full implications of the angel's message—that her child should be the "Son of God" [34]—were not yet made clear. [35]

During the years that followed, "his mother kept in her heart the memory of all this." [36] What is thus thrown into relief is the greatness of Mary's faith and her complete docility to God's will. These are the two characteristics which make her the supreme model, after Christ, for every Christian. If it was true of her divine Son that "he learned obedi-

[31] Luke 2:48. St Luke, unlike many of our contemporaries, can have seen no inconsistency between the virginal birth and the putative fatherhood of St Joseph.

[32] VV. 48–49.   [33] Vs. 50.   [34] 1:35.

[35] For a persuasive interpretation of this whole incident, see Father E. F. Sutcliffe. S. J., "Our Lady's Knowledge of the Divinity of Christ," *Irish Ecclesiastical Record,* December 1945 and August 1946; also *The Month,* no. 180 (1944), pp. 347–350.

[36] Luke 2:51.

ence by the things he suffered," [37] how much more true must it be of her. We should never forget that Mary, as befitted the Mother of Jesus Christ, was cast in the heroic mould. We are right in thinking of her as the embodiment of gentleness and human sympathy. In so far as these qualities can be transferred by heredity, surely we may suppose that, under God, Jesus had inherited something of these very dispositions from her. But the Godhead in him, which for all his accessibility made him a transcendent and awe-inspiring figure, was lacking to her. It is just this which, so to say, places her so completely on our side, makes her the ideal mediator between our sinful selves and Jesus Christ. Nevertheless, we should be on our guard against investing her with an aura of sentimentality which has its origin, not in the scriptural accounts, but in notions of womanhood deriving from Western romanticism. We shall be nearer to the truth, and to the Jewish *milieu* of which Mary is the perfect product, in applying to her the famous description of the "valiant woman" to be found in the Book of Proverbs:

Who shall find a valiant woman? Far and from the uttermost coasts is the price of her.... She hath girded her loins with strength, and hath strengthened her arms.... She hath put out her hand to strong things, and her fingers have taken hold of the spindle.... Strength and beauty are her clothing, and she shall laugh in the latter day. She hath opened her mouth to wisdom, and the law of clemency is on her tongue.... Favour is deceitful, and beauty is vain; the woman that feareth the Lord, she shall be praised.[38]

This is the explanation of the extreme reticence, even austerity, which marks the attitude of Jesus to Mary throughout the public ministry. Thus there is no record of his addressing her by the familiar name of "Mother"; always it is the distant, but in the Jewish and Greek idiom wholly respectful, "Woman." The marriage feast at Cana [39] is proof, even then, of the power of her intercession with him; but this was not to reach its full realization until the time of

[37] Heb. 5:8(S.).   [38] Prov. 31:10, 17, 19, 25, 26, 30.
[39] John 2:1–11.

their common sacrifice is over. Our Lord himself, while abandoning the security of a home and the joys of motherly affection, is at the same time guarding her against any "possessiveness" over him—to which, surely, like every mother, she must have been tempted. He was preparing her for a more universal motherhood. So we find him brushing aside a fulsome compliment to his Mother based on their merely physical relationship—"Blessed is the womb that bore thee, the breast which thou hast sucked" [40]—and recalling the speaker to what should be the real grounds for her enthusiasm: "Shall we not say, Blessed are those who hear the word of God, and keep it?" [41] No one had heard and kept the word of God more faithfully than Mary; but we are taught that it was less by her physical motherhood of the incarnate Word than by her humble obedience that she merits our praise. The *Fiat*—"Let it be unto me according to thy word"—which dominated her whole life, discloses the most vital of all relations between Mary and her Son. Already, as St Augustine says, "she had conceived him in her soul before conceiving him in her womb." [42]

These thoughts find striking confirmation in the words of Pope Pius XII. Among the elements which went to form Mary's sacrifice on Golgotha, offered in union with her Son's, was "the holocaust of her maternal rights and motherly love." [43] Now, just as Christ's sacrifice had, in a sense, begun from the first moment of the Incarnation—"As Christ comes into the world, he says, ... See, ... I am coming ... to do thy will, O my God" [44]—so, at the same instant, had Mary's: "Behold the handmaid of the Lord; let it be unto me according to thy word." [45] This parallelism continued unbroken until our Redeemer uttered his triumphant cry on the Cross—"It is finished." [46] This is why we may fittingly call Mary our "Co-redemptrix"; for the offering of our great High Priest was accompanied by her surrender of him to God. It was his will as the new Adam "to give his life a

[40] Luke 11:27.   [41] Vs. 28.
[42] *Serm.*, 215, 4; *P.L.* 38, col. 1074; cf. St Thomas, III, q. 30, art. 1.
[43] Encycl. *Myst. Corp. Christi*; *A.A.S.*, vol. 35, no. 7, p. 247.
[44] Heb. 10:5-7.   [45] Luke 1:38.   [46] John 19:30(W.).

ransom for many"; [47] therefore it was hers, as the second Eve, to share in his immolation. She stood at the foot of the Cross, not in rebellious protestation at its injustice, but accepting with him its hideous torments, and accepting them for the same reason—the redemption of the world.

Not that our Lady could contribute to the price of our redemption; for that price had to be paid even for her; it had purchased the Immaculate Conception, "through the foreseen merits of Jesus Christ, the Saviour of the human race." [48] The payment of the price—what theologians call *objective* redemption—could be accomplished by Christ alone, in virtue of his being the "one mediator between God and man." [49] No one but the Head is "the Saviour of his body." [50] This is the sense in which Pius XII speaks of the mystical Body, of which Mary is a member, as being unable to co-operate in its own redemption: "Dying on the Cross, he bestowed upon his Church the boundless treasure of the Redemption without any co-operation on her part." [51] Mary's immense merits could not enhance her Son's; for these were infinite, and were the source and cause of hers. There was, however, a very real sense in which Mary could co-operate in the Redemption, namely, in the distribution of its fruits. As the most perfect member of Christ's mystical Body, the Church, there apply to her in an eminent degree the words with which the Pope continues: "But in the distribution of that treasure, he not only shares this work of sanctification with his spotless Bride, but he wills it to arise in a certain manner out of her labour." Our Lady, by her co-operation with divine grace, merited that the fruits of Christ's unique redemptive act should be applied to her own soul and to the souls of others.

Thus Mary is Co-redemptrix, not in the order of achievement as having paid our ransom, but in the order of application as interceding with God that the benefits of the Redemption may be bestowed upon us. She reigns now in heaven, as Pius XII teaches, to make intercession with her

---

47 Mark 10:45(S.).   48 Denz., 1641.   49 1 Tim. 2:5(S.).
50 Eph. 5:23(S.).   51 *Loc. cit.*, p. 213.

Son, "so that from that august Head abundance of grace may flow in a steady stream into all the members of his mystical Body." [52] Mary co-operated in the Redemption essentially in the same way as the rest of the saints and even we ourselves co-operate; that is, by the willing union of her heart with, and her acceptance of, Christ's sacrifice. But because of her unique relation to the Redeemer, because she was physically present with him at the supreme moment, because she had been given to the human race in the person of St John [53] as the new "mother of all the living," [54] the honour of her co-redemptive activity belongs to no other creature. Just as the saints and even the individual faithful, having been made members of Christ's mystical Body by his redeeming act, can merit its further fruits for themselves and others by co-operating with the Head, so too, though in an immeasurably higher degree, was it the case with Mary. This is the sense in which the Pope explains her role as Queen of Martyrs; our Lady "by bearing with courageous and confident heart her immense weight of sorrows, more than all Christians 'filled up those things that are wanting to the sufferings of Christ for his Body which is the Church.' " [55]

This is why our Lady's intercession is always requested first among the saints, for she is their Queen. Thus, in the prayer of expiation which Pius XI ordered to be recited publicly on the Feast of the Sacred Heart, her intercessory merits are associated with those of the saints and the other members of the mystical Body: "We invoke the sacrifice which once upon the Cross thou didst offer to thy Father, and which day by day thou dost renew upon the altar. And we join therewith the acts of expiation of the Virgin Mother, of all the saints, and of the devout faithful." [56] Likewise, in the Canon of the Mass (*Communicantes*) we call upon God to grant that, through the merits and prayers of our Lady and the saints, "we may be guarded by thy protecting help. Through the same Christ our Lord." As the Mass adds

---

[52] Pius XII, *loc. cit.*, p. 248.   [53] John 19:27, § 24, pp. 322 ff.
[54] Gen. 3:20.   [55] *Loc. cit.* p. 248; quoting Col. 1:24
[56] *A.A.S.*, Vol. 20, no. 6, June 1928, p. 179.

nothing essential to the sacrifice of Calvary and differs from it only in the manner of its offering,[57] being no more than its true representation and the application of its fruits, it follows that the intercessory prayers we invoke concern not the essence of Christ's redemptive act, as achieved by him alone, but the application of the boundless graces which flow from it. We ask that, through the prayers of the Blessed Virgin and the saints, we may share yet more fully in the benefits gained for us by the one Mediator between God and man.

Just as the will behind Christ's sacrifice remains for ever unrevoked, so is it with the sacrificial dispositions in Mary's immaculate heart. What power and dignity must be recognized in her, when we remember that it was in correspondence with her prayers that God sent the Holy Spirit at Pentecost! "So too it was she who, by her most powerful intercession, brought it about that the Spirit of the Divine Redeemer, already given on the Cross, should be conferred at Pentecost upon the new-born Church, with his wonderful gifts." [58] Not that the giving of the Spirit, any more than the Incarnation itself, was thereby made contingent on a creature's will. But it was fitting that the divine initiative should be seconded by Mary's intercession. For we pray, as St Thomas explains,[59] not in order to change God's decree, but to obtain from him what he has designed from all eternity to give to us in fulfilment of our prayer.

Though our Lady herself was the chief recipient of the visible mission of the Spirit at Pentecost, we should remember that he had dwelt invisibly with her from the time of the Immaculate Conception. "Her most holy soul, more than the soul of all God's creatures together, was filled with the divine Spirit of Jesus Christ. She, representing the whole of humanity, gave her consent to 'a spiritual marriage between the Son of God and human nature.' [60] " [61] At the moment Christ's sacrifice was accomplished on the Cross, Mary's universal motherhood came into being; he had given her to his disciples throughout all ages, to play that role with them

---

[57] Denz., 940.   [58] Pius XII, loc. cit.; cf. Acts 1:14.
[59] IIa IIae, q. 83, art. 2.   [60] III, q. 30, art. 1.   [61] Pius XII, ibid., p. 247.

she had so faithfully discharged with him. "Upon the mystical Body of Christ, born from the pierced Heart of our Saviour, she bestowed that same maternal care and eager charity with which she had fostered and nurtured the suckling infant Jesus in the cradle." [62]

Mary, like her Son, was to suffer the penalty of Adam's sin, the experience of death. She did not share the personal triumph of our Lord's resurrection; though even here there was a certain kinship with him. Her body, like his, was not allowed to see corruption; it was fitting that the sentence passed upon our first parents—"dust thou art, and unto dust thou shalt return" [63]—should be suspended in her favour. God restored her to life in her marvellous Assumption, transporting her body and soul into heaven, there to reign as Queen above the highest of the seraphim and the whole company of the redeemed. "She has attained a summit of glory," says Pope Leo XIII, "such as no other, whether man or angel, can ever reach, because in merit of virtue none can be compared with her." [64] As Queen she does not share Christ's kingly power and authority; for she has none of the three titles to royalty which we have seen to be his prerogatives: that based on the hypostatic union, that which is his as Head of the Church, and that which he has won for himself as our unique Redeemer. But in subordination to him, as Co-redemptrix and Mediatrix of the graces he chooses to bestow, she enjoys a regal authority over all his creatures. Moreover, through the medium of the beatific vision, the needs and petitions of each of her children are revealed to her, so that she has the full knowledge needful for her role as universal Mother.

God's joy in Mary is second only to the pleasure he takes in contemplating the sacred humanity of his Son. As all graces are given to us by means of that humanity, what could be more fitting than that they should also be given in response to the intercession of our Lady? Such is in fact the teaching of the Church. As the second Eve, her interest in

[62] Pius XII, *loc. cit.*, p. 248.   [63] Gen. 3:19.
[64] *Magnae Dei Matris;* Allocutiones ..., V, p. 113.

her spiritual children is as vast in its extent as that of the new Adam. Just as Christ is "always living to intercede" [65] for us, so does she, in correspondence with his will, stand before the throne of God in supplication for those same graces. If God's generosity is not honoured by a request for his gifts by his heedless creatures, if men are too uninterested in their own salvation to plead for themselves, that breach of reverence and good faith is atoned for by the worshipping heart, the motherly solicitude, of Mary. So great is the power of our Lady's intercession that theologians do not hesitate to ascribe to her a certain omnipotence. She cannot, of course, share the active power which belongs to Almighty God alone, but, as her supplication corresponds, on a creaturely level, with the administration of his graces, we may attribute to her a "suppliant omnipotence." This is her due, as St Thomas explains, in virtue of the closeness of her soul's union with God: "The greater the charity of the saints in heaven, the more they pray for wayfarers on earth, since the latter can be helped by their prayers; and the more closely they are united to God, the more efficacious are their prayers; for the divine order is such that the lower beings receive an overflow of the excellence of the higher, even as the air receives the brightness of the sun." [66] But none of the saints can approach Mary's degree of charity; hence she is a more powerful intercessor than any of them.

Our Lady obtains grace for us by her intercession; but she is not the source of grace, since this is Christ's inalienable prerogative. "The Blessed Virgin gives (redundavit) grace to us; in such a way, however, that she can in no sense be considered the author of grace." [67] Nor even is she its instrument, as are the sacraments. Mary does not share the unique grace (gratia capitalis) which belong to Christ as the Head of the Church. Moreover the idea of a sacrament—a physical instrument of grace effecting what it signifies—is clearly inapplicable to our Lady. Here it should be noted that her role as Co-redemptrix and Mediatrix of graces derives from

---

65 Heb. 7:25(S.).   66 IIa IIae, q. 83, art. 11.
67 St Thomas, In Joan., 1, lect. 10.

God's absolutely free decree; it is ordained by him, and inserted, so to say, within the total economy of grace, according to his designs. Now the sacramental system is essential to that economy; whence it follows that those graces which God wills to give us expressly by means of the sacraments do not call for, though they do not necessarily preclude, Mary's direct intercession.

"Let it be unto me according to thy word." [68] In heaven our Lady's self-abandonment to God remains; indeed it has reached its consummation; she follows always the order of things laid down by him. When, for example, God has decided that we shall merit grace by the performance of some good work, Mary does not intercede for it, so that we may be none the worse off for our neglect of duty. That could have no place in her who must so often have prayed: "Thy kingdom come; Thy will be done on earth as it is in heaven." Though even in such matters as these, our Lady's intercession is at hand to help us; she prays that we may receive actual graces to make our reception of the sacraments more fruitful, and likewise that we may be given the strength to fulfil our obligations to God. From no element in the divine economy of grace may her influence be excluded. Seeing that it was by her free consent that Christ came into the world and that her motherly care now extends to all the members of his mystical Body, we may say that, under her divine Son, every grace that is given to men since the moment of her Assumption, each blessing and gift which helps us on our way to God, is dispensed to us—even though unsought and unacknowledged—as pleaded for by the suppliantly omnipotent intercession of the Blessed Virgin Mary.

What good cause have we then to seek our Lady's prayers —*now, and at the hour of our death*! Christ himself is always directly accessible to us; but when we feel moved to approach him through Mary, we are not thereby deserting the one for the other. The very fact that we are so inspired suggests that this is how he wills it to be. There is greater pleasure and more fittingness in granting favours that are asked for than in bestowing them unsought. This is why God

[68] Luke 1:38.

has appointed Mary to be Mediatrix of his graces—so that he shall always be asked. And asked by one whose will, after his only begotten Son's, he is most desirous to fulfil. The marriage feast at Cana is a proof of the power of her intercession; it seems, to our human eyes, that the divine plan was almost interfered with at the request of Mary. Catholics always delight to remember that Jesus' first miracle, which aroused the faith of his earliest disciples,[69] was worked at the intercession of his Mother. At a greater marriage, "the wedding-feast of the Lamb," [70] her triple role of Co-redemptrix, Reparatrix and Mediatrix of graces will be at an end; to her in particular can then most fittingly be applied the tribute which St John pays to the whole company of the blessed: "His bride has clothed herself in readiness for it; hers it is to wear linen of shining white; the merits of the saints are her linen." [71] The guests will meet her as their hostess and Queen, to learn at last how much it is due to her intercession that they find themselves, in the beautiful phrase of Dante, "in the heaven of humility, where Mary is." [72]

[69] John 2:11.   [70] Apoc. 19:7.
[71] Vs. 8.   [72] Vita Nuova, 35.

CHAPTER VI

THE INCARNATION THROUGH THE AGES

"WHAT Jesus Christ was yesterday, and is to-day, he remains for ever." [1] After the Word had become flesh, humanity and divinity were never again to be separated from one another. Not only would their indissoluble union be maintained in Christ's own person; but the reconciliation between God and man that he had effected was to be continued in his followers throughout the ages. Christ's earthly role of prophet, priest and king had passed to his Spirit-guided Church, even while he would still uphold it, though now invisibly, as the Head of his mystical Body. The Church's prophetical office is discharged in her authoritative and infallible witness to God's revelation. This function is in its turn subordinate to the spiritual rulership and sanctifying mission with which our Lord likewise empowered his Church. These are what give us the deepest insight into the way in which the Incarnation prolongs itself in history. The first is clearly realized in the kingdom of God, itself closely connected with the kingship of Christ; it is thus that God's monarchic rule comes, as it were, vertically downwards upon mankind. The second is co-extensive with the Church as the mystical Body of Christ; to continue the spatial metaphor, it is the horizontal—or, to be more exact, the social—aspect of the kingdom. Here is fulfilled all that is involved in the work of our great High Priest. In the mystical Body we see the Incarnation diffused through space and time; though with differences from its unique prototype in Christ which it will be our task to discriminate. An attempt to elucidate these two aspects of the central Christian mystery should throw further light upon our theme.

[1] Heb. 13:8.

§ 23. THE KINGDOM OF GOD

At the outset it should be noted that the New Testament teaching on the kingdom of God (or *of heaven*—a reverential periphrasis; the terms are synonymous) is by no means simple. Only a careful exegesis of the texts can yield the complete picture. But as this is beyond our present scope, we must be content with outlining its main features. Our Lord's message, as recorded in the Synoptic Gospels, clearly presupposes that the Messianic age would see the realization of the kingdom. It is true that the writings of the Jewish Rabbis, all of them subsequent to the Gospel, relate the kingdom to the "yoke of the Law," rather than to the Messianic hopes; but this view of the matter may well have been intended as a counter-criticism to the Christians, who held from the first that their expectations of the kingdom were fulfilled in the Messiah.[1] In any case, we are left in no doubt as to Jesus' own mind on the point; nor is there any evidence that the evangelical doctrine on the kingdom of God raised, to begin with, any objection on the grounds of principle.

There is a sense in which it is true to say that our Lord did not preach himself; he proclaimed a message from God his Father. He brought the glad tidings which the Father sends to men, namely, that the time is fulfilled and the kingdom is at hand. So at least is he presented to us in the Synoptic Gospels, particularly during that phase of his ministry which is characterized by the parabolic teaching.[2] Though how closely his message is bound up with the acceptance of his own person we have already seen. "You have one teacher, Christ"; [3] even while it was left to St John to record what was implied in this: "Whoever has seen me, has seen the Father." [4] Christ is one with the Father to whom he testifies; hence there is no difference of viewpoint between the bearer of the message and him from whom he comes. "The Son cannot do anything at his own pleasure,

---

[1] Cf. Lagrange, *Le Messianisme chez les Juifs*, pp. 148–157; Prat, *op cit.*, II, 458–59 (E.T. pp. 376–77).

[2] See § 6, pp. 69-78.   [3] Matt. 23:10.   [4] John 14:9.

he can only do what he sees his Father doing; what the Father does is what the Son does in his turn." [5]

John the Baptist had preached to the people the urgent need for a change of heart, if they were to be ready to receive the kingdom when it came. "The appointed time has come, he said, and the kingdom of God is near at hand; repent and believe the gospel." [6] In this respect, at least, we find our Lord in continuity with, and as the fulfilment of, the message of the Baptist. Throughout his ministry it is the kingdom which dominates his thought. To the disciples, as to the multitudes, he speaks of little else. "So Jesus went about the whole of Galilee, teaching in their synagogues, preaching the gospel of the kingdom." [7] "But he told them, I must preach the gospel of God's kingdom to the other cities too; it is for this that I was sent." [8] He gives the same commission to his chosen disciples—"And preach as you go, telling them, The kingdom of heaven is at hand." [9] The vital importance for all men of submitting themselves to the kingdom never leaves his mind. "This gospel of the kingdom must first be preached all over the world, so that all nations may hear the truth; only after that will the end come." [10] Finally, after the Resurrection, our Lord, when appearing to his disciples, is still "telling them about the kingdom of God." [11]

Christ's teaching on the kingdom can be appreciated only against the background of the Old Testament development of this doctrine, from which, in its verbal expression, it largely derives. He took from this all its loftiest and most spiritual elements, more particularly as these were set in relief by the great Hebrew prophets, and gave them a new setting in relation to his own person. As we have seen, it was this harking back to the message of the prophets, so much neglected in the political and materialistic conceptions of contemporary Pharisaism, which occasioned much of the hostility and misunderstanding he experienced at the hands

[5] John 5:19.   [6] Mark 1:15.   [7] Matt. 4:23.
[8] Luke 4:43.   [9] Matt. 10:7.   [10] Matt. 24:14.
[11] Acts 1:3.

of the religious leaders of his day. Though it must also be remembered—and this intensified the conflict with those who would not admit him as Master—that his own teaching on the kingdom contained radically new elements, of transcendence and universality, incompatible with the maintenance of the old order. We recall his point about the futility of patching a worn-out garment with new cloth, the idleness of pouring newly fermenting wine into old wine-skins.[12]

The notion of the "kingdom [perhaps, more accurately, the *rule*] of God" foreshadowed in the prophetical writings may be said, at the risk of undue simplification, to contain three chief elements: (1) a kingdom that was national and at the same time universal—reigning over Israel as his chosen people, Yahweh was to extend his kingdom so as to subjugate the Gentiles; (2) a spiritual kingdom, in which the moral qualities of justice and peace were to flourish; (3) an eschatological kingdom, in the sense that its perfection was to come after a judgement in which the wicked were to be separated from the righteous. In continuity with and as a development of this, our Lord announces a kingdom that is to be (1) no longer national, but universal, embracing all peoples and all times; (2) interior and spiritual, yet at the same time visible and social; (3) present here and now, but also future and eschatological, looking forward to a time when the good shall be separated from the bad.

The scriptural imagery in which the kingdom is portrayed is frequently suggestive of the pomp and circumstance of earthly kingship. Indeed it could hardly be otherwise, in view of the exalted place held by King David in Jewish history and legend. Nor is this notion repudiated by Jesus; but the fundamental conception of it is the rule or dominion of God, with the absolute primacy of the divine will that this implies, God and man being respectively what they are. The Greek word βασιλεία may mean both "kingship" and "realm," and the synoptists appear to use it now in one sense, now in another; but it is important to notice that these closely related ideas merge in the more fundamental one just

12 Cf. Matt. 9:16–17.

mentioned, namely, God's unlimited mastery and lordship as manifested in nature and providence.

Our Lord's teaching presents the kingdom of God under a number of aspects; it contains subtleties and shades of thought which cannot be reduced to a single formula. He speaks of the "mystery [or secret] of the kingdom." [13] It is a *heavenly* kingdom which is suggested in the Beatitudes.[14] "Be glad and rejoice, because your reward will be abundant in heaven." [15] The *realm* of God, something into which one enters, and not simply his kingship, is indicated, for instance, in the following: "And I tell you, that if your justice does not give fuller measure than the justice of the scribes and Pharisees, you shall not enter into the kingdom of heaven." [16] Entry into it is the equivalent of being "saved." [17] Moreover, the state of soul needful for making entrance is the product, not of nature, but of grace; a spiritual rebirth is demanded.[18] Again, the kingdom has a supra-mundane and eschatological aspect; the just are received into it at the end of the world.[19] The way into this kingdom, in which an eternal banquet is enjoyed,[20] is through the resurrection,[21] and at the time of Christ's final coming, the Parousia. After a solemn judgement,[22] Jesus will drink anew the fruit of the vine with his own.[23] The risen just will there lead the lives of angels; [24] they will shine like the sun [25] and enjoy perfect felicity.[26]

Thus the βασιλεία τοῦ Θεοῦ, considered as a divine realm, culminates in the transcendent and eschatological reign of God over the elect in heaven; which is the kingdom as described in the apocalypses and rabbinical literature. Nevertheless God's kingdom is already, at least in part, realized on earth: "But if, when I cast out devils, I do it through God's power, then it must be that the kingdom of God has suddenly appeared among you." [27] The true believers in Jesus are already "in the kingdom." [28] No doubt it does not yet

[13] Mark 4:11.
[14] Matt. 5:3-10.
[15] 5:12 (S.).
[16] Vs. 20.
[17] Cf. Mark 10:23-26.
[18] John 3:5.
[19] Matt. 13:37-43.
[20] 8:11.
[21] Mark 12:25.
[22] Matt. 25:31-46.
[23] Mark 14:25.
[24] Matt. 22:30.
[25] 13:43.
[26] 5:3 ff.
[27] Luke 11:20.
[28] Luke 7:28.

exist in its full splendour; men cannot point to it: "See, it is here, or, See, it is there." [29] But the same verse shows that, in some sense, God's kingdom has now come: "the kingdom of God is here, within you." Yet the *Thy kingdom come* of the Lord's prayer tells us that its fruition is still to be looked for in the future. What is suggested—and this is confirmed by the lesson of the parables—is that the coming of the kingdom means the progressive development of the kingdom already in being. Furthermore, it is to include the Gentiles, many of whom will be called to it to the exclusion of the chosen people. "And this I tell you, that there are many who will come from the east and from the west, and will take their places in the kingdom of God with Abraham and Isaac and Jacob, while the kingdom's own sons are cast into the darkness without, where there will be weeping, and gnashing of teeth." [30]

Mention must now be made of our Lord's eschatological teaching; [31] it bears upon the coming of the Son of Man "with power." Having depicted in apocalyptic language the terrors of that time, he immediately goes on to say: "Believe me, this generation will not have passed, before all this is accomplished. Though heaven and earth should pass away, my words will stand. But as for that day and that hour you speak of, they are known to nobody, not even to the angels in heaven, not even to the Son; only the Father knows them." [32] The discourse in which these words occur had been occasioned by our Lord's prophecy of the coming destruction of the Temple at Jerusalem; [33] for the disciples had asked him, "Tell us, when will this be?" [34] He used the oppor-

---

[29] Luke 17:21.   [30] Matt. 8:11–12.

[31] NOTE: This highly complex subject can only adequately be treated by a detailed exegesis of the texts. These fall into five groups: (a) Matt. 10:21–23; (b) Matt. 16:27–28; Mark 8:38, 9:1; Luke 9:26–27; (c) Matt. 23:34–36; Luke 11:49–51; (d) what is known as the *Synoptic Apocalypse*, Matt. 24:1–44; Mark 13; Luke 21:5–36; (e) Matt. 26:63–65; Mark 14:61–63; Luke 22:66–71. See M.-J. Lagrange's separate commentaries on the Synoptic Gospels, *in loc.*, and his *L'Évangile de Jésus-Christ*, pp. 473–92 (E.T. II, 170–89); Grandmaison, *Jésus Christ*, II, 280–312 (E.T. III, 61–96), where the texts are reproduced; Lebreton, *Life and Teaching of Jesus Christ*, II, 185–212.

[32] Mark 13:30–32. In connection with our Lord's professed ignorance of the *Parousia*, see Lebreton, *Histoire du Dogme de la Trinité*, I, 559–90.

[33] Mark 13:1–2.   [34] Vs. 4.

tunity, not only to foretell the signs that would herald that particular event, but to enlarge upon the final consummation of this present order of things, when they would see "the Son of Man coming upon the clouds, with great power and glory." [35]

Here it should be noted that Jesus is speaking of two matters quite distinct from one another. That this is so emerges, as Lagrange points out, even from the text of St Mark, who was writing for the benefit of Jews, whom the current apocalyptic literature had familiarized with such sudden leaps from earth to heaven; though the distinction is admittedly clearer in St Luke, who bears in mind that his Gentile readers have no such advantage to aid their understanding. The forthcoming destruction of the Temple is left wrapped in symbolism, but only as regards the main occurrence. This cataclysm is accomplished in earthly conditions, in circumstances of themselves quite natural, and men are able to seek safety in flight. The scene of the final catastrophe, on the other hand, though it also takes place on earth, is set amid preternatural wonders: false Christs will arise, "the sun will be darkened, and the moon will refuse her light; the stars will be falling from heaven, and the powers that are in heaven will rock." [36] The prophetic vision, here as in so many instances, bridges the time-interval between the two events; nevertheless, that interval as an historic sequence remains. What is first described does not spell the end of all things; no matter how sudden its coming might be, it was still possible to escape from it. But such flight would be senseless if there were nothing to follow. The first event, then, was to be of some duration, in its consequences at least; there would be nothing instantaneous about it. But instantaneity, unheralded suddenness, was precisely the characteristic of the Son of Man's coming: "when the Son of Man comes, it will be like the lightning that springs up from the east and flashes across to the west." [37]

The moral of this teaching, which was not lost upon the early Christians and should not be lost upon us, is inescap-

[35] Mark 13:26.   [36] VV. 24-25.   [37] Matt. 24:27.

able: "Be on the watch, then, since you do not know when the master of the house is coming, at twilight, or midnight, or cockcrow, or dawn; if not, he may come suddenly, and find you asleep. And what I say to you, I say to all, Watch." [38] No matter how long the time of waiting for Christ's coming, by contrast with the eternal duration of God's kingdom, it will be short; hence his disciples must ever hold themselves in readiness. Their attitude should never be one of heedlessness, but filled with a sense of urgency and eager expectation. Instead of counting on a length of years in which we may leisurely make our peace with God, we are invited to apply to our situation here and now the message of the Apocalypse: "And he who gives this warning says, Indeed I am coming soon"; and to make our own the response: "Be it so, then; come, Lord Jesus." [39] This is the real lesson enforced by Christ's profession of ignorance as to the date of his coming. He, whose knowledge was universal and infallible, willed notwithstanding to tell his disciples that he did not know the "great day." He would have them to understand that his Father wished it to remain his own inscrutable secret. Then they, and those to whom they would hand on his message, could the better appreciate the only point which concerned them: *What I say to you, I say to all, Watch.*

Within the general framework of this eschatology, it seems that there were to be several παρουσίαι, or "comings," of the kingdom and the Son of Man "with power"—the Resurrection was certainly one of these—before the final coming at the Last Judgment. The close interconnection between the eschatological discourses and the predictions of the fall of Jerusalem warrant the interpretation that the kingdom's coming "with power" points to a particular development of the already existing kingdom of God on earth, a development bound up with the disappearance of the Jewish nation. God's kingship is concerned chiefly with his holding sway over men's hearts; but, as we have already seen,[40] the kingdom, or realm, of God appears under the form of a "Church,"

---

[38] Mark 13:35–36.   [39] Apoc. 22:20.   [40] Matt. 16:18–19.

that is, a visible and organized society. So considered, it is opposed to, and impregnable by, the forces of evil. A special authority with reference to it is deputed to the chief of the apostles, Simon Peter; he is its rock-foundation, he holds the "keys of the kingdom," being armed with the Lord's assurance that his executive acts on earth will be ratified in heaven.

This close relationship between the kingdom and Christ's Church emphasizes the still more intimate connection between it and his own person. Jesus clearly shows himself to be not only the founder of the kingdom, but the possessor of it; it is *his* kingdom, as well as the Father's, and he is the Lord and Ruler over it.[41] It is thus closely linked with the Old Testament theocracy, with God's kingship over a chosen people and its exercise through visible representatives. Typically, though imperfectly, adumbrated in the descendants of David, it is now definitively realized in the Messianic King, in virtue of his being wholly at one with God.[42] The new theocracy has Christ for its living embodiment; he is the prototype of the new status as sons of God which men are able to acquire through him. Hence, in the deepest sense, the kingdom of God may be said to have existed on earth from the first moment of the Incarnation.

The building up of the kingdom is measured by men's union with Jesus; in faith and love, in obedience and submission to his rule—which is the same thing as doing the Father's will—in the ever-deepening reality of their vital contact with him, as of branches with their parent vine. Whence there follows the "transvaluation of all values" involved in the very nature of the kingdom. Christ's sovereignty was exercised, not by violence and earthly power, but by lowliness, by service and deeds of mercy, above all, by the invincible witness to truth in the face of a hostile world and at the price of bitter suffering. So likewise is his kingdom to be ruled; not by compulsion and tyranny, but by patient and steadfast testifying to the Gospel and the all-

[41] Matt. 13:41; 16:28; 20:21; 25:34.   [42] Matt. 11:27; John 10:30.

conquering influence of love over hearts freely submitted to
its sway.

As soon as the idea of the kingdom had been realized in
the Church, the formula, "the kingdom of God," passes to
a subordinate position. It appears occasionally in the early
apostolic preaching, where it is synonymous with the Christian Gospel, as in that of St Paul recorded in the Acts,[43]
and very frequently in his Epistles, but it does not hold
the dominating place given to it in the Synoptic Gospels.
The reason for this is twofold: first, in Christ the kingdom
had come, and his life-work clearly implied other truths
which, though they could be included within, were nevertheless distinguishable from, the notion of a kingdom. Secondly, the conception of God's kingship, or for that matter,
of kingship in any form, had not the same significance for
the Gentiles as it had for the Jews. Moreover, it was especially
calculated to offend the susceptibilities of the Roman authorities, who would not fail to see in it political implications. Hence it was natural for St Paul to lay stress on those
aspects of the kingdom which did not suggest a conflict
with imperial Rome; he sees the kingdom as identified with
the spirit of Christianity, the essence of the Gospel.[44] In
particular, it is an eschatological kingdom, having its consummation in eternal glory; [45] though he also recognizes it
as the Church Militant here on earth, or joined with the
Church Triumphant as it will be in its final state.[46] In general, the kingdom denotes the life everlasting which the
just will enjoy, reigning with Christ. For in St Paul, as in
the Gospels, the kingship belongs to Christ, at least until
he places it in the hands of God, his Father.[47]

Christ, as we have already seen, will always be our King,
to reign over his Kingdom-Church; just as he is always the
Head of his mystical Body and High Priest of the religious
society which he has founded. From this point of view his
kingship will never end. But he is also the Head of the

[43] Acts 19:8; 28:23, 31.   [44] Rom. 14:17; 1 Cor. 4:20.
[45] 1 Cor. 6:9–10; 15:50; Gal. 5:21; Eph. 5:5; 2 Thess. 1:5.
[46] 1 Cor. 15:24; Col. 1:13; 4:11; 1 Thess. 2:12; Acts 20:25.
[47] 1 Cor. 15:24.

Church Militant, charged to vindicate God's honour, to lead to victory those who march under his banner, and to punish rebels and subdue them. This temporary viceroyalty, which Christ holds as man, ceases with the functions which constitute it; the mandate of a commander-in-chief expires at the moment when there are no more battles to be fought or hostile forces to be overthrown. Christ's rulership must continue "until he has put all his enemies under his feet;" [48] then he will deliver it to the Father, to whom, as man, he will himself be subject. Such will be the full realization of God's kingdom: the reign of the elect in heaven, under Christ their King—"so that God may be all in all." [49]

Not all, it seems, are to enjoy that blessed day, but only those who, while on earth, have been of the company, "thanking God our Father for making us fit to share the light which saints inherit, for rescuing us from the power of darkness, and transferring us to the kingdom of his beloved Son." [50] God's saving will, universal as it is, still respects the liberty of man; the Redemption, which is offered to all, is not forced upon any, and Christ, the sole Mediator, associates with his victory only those who accept his mediation and are united to him in love. Hence the crucial importance of men's submitting themselves to God's Kingdom-Church on earth. Christ's Messianic kingdom had been embodied in his Church; that is, an organized religious society, so patently visible to men's eyes that they could appeal to its authority.[51] This is the early Christian community whose corporate life is described in the Acts,[52] whose members were persecuted,[53] to which St Paul alludes as "the Church of God, which he has purchased with his own blood." [54] In his Epistles, which were written at an earlier date than the Acts, he uses the word "church" over sixty times, now in its local, now in its universal sense. He owned himself the least of the apostles, "since there was a time when I persecuted the church of God." [55] To discover how much

---

[48] 1 Cor. 15:25. [49] Vs. 28. [50] Col. 1:12–13.
[51] Matt. 18:17. [52] Cf. Acts 2:42; 4:34–35. [53] 12:1.
[54] 20:28(S.). Note the close connection of ideas with the "kingdom of God," vs. 25. [55] 1 Cor. 15:9; cf. Gal. 1:13.

the Church meant to St Paul, we have only to read the Epistle to the Ephesians.[56]

Such was the community of believers which was recognized, within the lifetime of men who had known the apostles, under the name of the "Catholic Church." St Ignatius of Antioch, who died not later than the year 117, could write: "Wheresoever Christ Jesus is, there is the Catholic Church." [57] With the growth and development of this divine institution we are not here directly concerned, except in so far as it bears on our present theme. At this point a question of some moment calls for discussion. To what extent do the Church and the kingdom of God coincide, in all the fulness with which the latter notion is revealed to us in Scripture? Not a little misunderstanding and confusion have arisen on this point. It is sometimes said that the Catholic Church claims to identify herself absolutely with the kingdom of God, and to draw the inferences which would logically follow from this position. St Augustine in his famous treatise *On the City of God* has been credited with originating this doctrine.[58] His works certainly had an immense influence on the subsequent history of Europe; his *Soliloquia* were translated by King Alfred into Anglo-Saxon, and Charlemagne had had the *De Civitate Dei* read to him at meals. Its ideals were the inspiration of the Holy Roman Empire; and the Papacy, from Gregory VII to Innocent III, embodied them in practice.[59]

[56] Eph. 1:22–23; 3:10; vs. 21; 5:23–32.

[57] *Smyrnaeans*, viii, 2; *P.G.* 5, col. 713.

[58] "But Augustine gave a much stronger hold than his predecessors to the conception that the Church is the kingdom of God, and by the manner in which in his "Divine Comedy," the *De Civitate Dei,* he contrasted the Church with the State, far more than by his own expressed views, he roused the conviction that the empirical Catholic Church *sans phrase* was the kingdom of God, and the independent State that of the devil."—Harnack, *History of Dogma* E.T. V, p. 151.

[59] A misreading of the Catholic position is evident in the writings of Reinhold Niebuhr, whose powers of historical generalization are prone to operate independently of the data: "All Catholic errors in overestimating the sinlessness of the redeemed reach their culmination, or at least their most vivid and striking expression, in the doctrine of the church. Here the reservations of Augustine are forgotten; and the church is unreservedly identified with the Kingdom of God. It is the *societas perfecta*".—*The Nature and Destiny of Man*, vol. 2, p. 148.

It is true that an unqualified identification of God's kingdom with the Church has in fact been made. We find St
Augustine himself replying to a Roman correspondent, who
seems to have written him a letter based on this assumption; [60] nor is Augustine here concerned to correct it. But
this over-simplified view finds no support in the main thesis
of the *De Civitate Dei*. It will be remembered that the work
was occasioned by the fall of Rome under Alaric and his
Goths in A.D. 410, with the wave of universal horror which
passed over the Roman world at the news of the city's sack.
St Augustine explains his reasons for writing: "The pagans
endeavoured to connect the overthrow of Rome with the
Christian religion.... Wherefore I determined to write a
treatise, *On the City of God,* in order to refute the mistakes
of some and the blasphemies of others." [61] The first ten
books are directed to this object; the last twelve to what was
later to be called a "philosophy of history," summarized in
the famous sentence: "Two loves made two cities—the earthly,
built up by the love of self to the contempt of God, and
the heavenly, built up by the love of God to the contempt
of self." [62] In the light of this principle Augustine reads the
whole story of the human race; for these two cities have
been running their course from the beginning of time, not
rigidly separated but mingling together, and will so move
forward through the ages until they are parted at the Last
Judgement.

From this it follows that the earthly and heavenly cities
cannot be identified *tout court* respectively with the State
and the Church. Nor does St Augustine make any consistent attempt to do so, convinced though he is that the
heavenly city is in fact represented by the Church, and that
the State, as alienated from God, is of the Devil. The two
antitheses—the heavenly and the earthly city, on the one
hand, and the Church and State on the other—do not in
fact coincide.[63] The earthly city is not the State. For all the

---

[60] *Ep.* 36, 17; *P.L.* 33, col. 143-44.
[61] *Retract.,* 2, 43, *P.L.* 32, col. 647-48.
[62] *De Civ. Dei,* 14, 28; *P.L.* 41, col. 436.
[63] Cf. Étienne Gilson, *Introduction à l'étude de Saint Augustin,* pp. 233-35.

members of this city will finally be lost; but the future elect
are necessarily part of the State, whose members they are
and in which they live. Hence it is a mistake to confuse the
earthly city—which, according to Augustine himself, is a
mystical entity—with this or that concrete city, as it exists in
space and time. Conversely, surprising as this may sound,
the Church is not the city of God; since this city is the society of all the elect, past, present and future. But we know
that there were men elected to salvation before the Church
of Christ was founded, and that there are others, perhaps
even among its present persecutors, who will eventually submit to its discipline, as having been elected by God. Moreover
we have grounds for believing that, even within the Church,
there are men who will not finally be saved. In other words,
the members of the two cities are mixed together in this
world, and will so remain, until they are separated at the
Last Judgement—*perplexae quippe sunt istae duae civitates
in hoc saeculo, invicemque permixtae, donec ultimo judicio
dirimantur.*[64] In St Augustine's thought, consistently with his
rigorous doctrine of predestination, there is a mutually exclusive opposition between the divine society of the elect and
the diabolical society of the reprobate; but this antithesis
cannot strictly be applied to the position of the Church over
against the State.

St Augustine does indeed teach that the Church is the
heavenly kingdom of Christ.[65] So it must be, since Christ has
promised to be with his Church "until the consummation of
the world." [66] This kingdom, however, is not the city of
God; for the reason that in it the tares are allowed to grow
together with the wheat till their separation at the harvest.[67]
The Church is in truth God's kingdom, but not, in Augustine's terminology, his *city*. The State, in itself, is simply a
human society unconnected with a supernatural end, organized apart from God. Accordingly, if a man is no more
than a citizen of the State, he is thereby excluded from
the heavenly city. On the other hand, although the Church

64 *De Civ. Dei*, 1, 35; *P.L.* 41, col. 46.
65 *Ibid.*, 20, 9, 1; col. 672–73.   66 Matt. 28:20.
67 Cf. Matt. 13:36–43.

is not the city of God, it is the one human institution which works for its construction. The Church is expressly willed, founded and assisted by God to recruit the elect for his heavenly kingdom. Whence it follows that, in principle, its members will be the future citizens of that kingdom. The vigorous statement of this truth is what led St Augustine occasionally to over-simplify history, reducing it to the sharpest antitheses: two cities—Babylon and Jerusalem; with two peoples—the reprobate and the elect; and two kings—the Devil and Christ.[68]

The upshot of this, in the simplest terms, is that the Catholic Church is the kingdom of God *on earth;* it is God's kingdom realized, not in its ideal form, but as modified by mundane and imperfect elements. "The kingdom of heaven and the Church founded upon Peter are not wholly identical. For the Church founded upon Peter belongs to this world and this life, since it is founded upon Peter, a mortal and terrestrial man, who will bind and loose 'on earth.' But the kingdom of heaven will exist when time is at an end, and for all eternity." [69] The qualification of the Church, as being God's kingdom *on earth,* is of primary importance, though it is sometimes overlooked by Catholic writers. To apply to the Church in its present state the praises reserved by St Paul for God's kingdom as consummated in heaven is unscriptural and untheological. Historically, it is the standpoint, so warmly repudiated by St Augustine, not of the Catholic Fathers, but of Pelagius.[70] In this sense we may agree with Reinhold Niebuhr that, "The deification of the church is spiritually dangerous, however conceived". St Thomas, commenting on the words of the Epistle to the Ephesians, describing "the Church in all its beauty, no stain, no wrinkle, no such disfigurement," [71] observes as follows: "This is the final end, to which we are led by Christ's passion; hence it will be our state in heaven, not as we are on

---

[68] Cf. *Enarr. in Ps.* 61, 6; *P.L.* 36, col. 733; *Enarr. in Ps.* 86, 6; *P.L.* 37, col. 1106.

[69] Schultes, *De Ecclesia Catholica,* pp. 41–42.

[70] *De gestis Pelagii,* cap. 12; *P.L.* 44, col. 336–37.

[71] Eph. 5:27.

earth, in which condition: 'Sin is with us; if we deny that, we are cheating ourselves.' [72] " [73] The kingdom of God on earth is indeed, even now, the *holy* Catholic Church, visibly distinguishable as such by the holiness of its doctrine, the means of grace to be found within the fold and the heroic sanctity of so many of its members. But among the faithful we must frankly acknowledge "the lamentable tendency of individuals towards evil, a tendency which her divine Founder suffers to exist even in the higher members of his mystical Body, for the testing of the virtue of both flock and pastors, and for the greater merit of the Christian faith in all." [74]

There is thus thrown into relief what we have seen to be a primary feature of the scriptural teaching, namely, the eschatological aspect of the kingdom of God. The Church Militant must be merged in the Church Triumphant before God's rule over the faithful is fully established. God, as Creator and Lord, dominates the whole earth; but his kingdom, as proclaimed by Jesus Christ, exists only as the Church, because there alone are his true subjects, proving their allegiance in faith and love and the whole-hearted acceptance of his Gospel. But even within the Church the kingdom may be said to be realized in varying degrees of completeness. Christ the King rules every part of it, but he only *reigns* in those who give their loyalty to him in grace and charity. All the Church's members are under the rule of the kingdom, but it takes possession of their hearts proportionately to the measure of their surrender to it. This, surely, is the meaning of the words of the Our Father: "Thy kingdom come. ..." We pray that God's external kingdom may be extended throughout the world, but also that our own submission to its claims may one day become unconditional, that the barriers of self-will may be broken down so that Christ may reign not only over us but in us.

Within the Kingdom-Church the Incarnation is continued through the ages. As God's kingdom was embodied in Christ at his first coming, so now is it realized in his Church. But

[72] 1 John 1:8.   [73] III, q. 8, art. 3, ad 2.
[74] Pius XII, Encycl. *Myst. Corp. Christi; A.A.S.,* vol. 35, no. 7, p. 225.

the Redemption, whereby he established it among men, has still to achieve its full effects. So long as sin or any of its results remain, Christ's victory is incomplete; all his enemies are not yet beneath his feet. Not until his own triumph over sin and death is reproduced in his followers, the members of his mystical Body, will Satan's kingdom at length be utterly vanquished. Only our own resurrection, our personal conquest of death, will cancel finally the dire results of Adam's sin, and so bring into being the kingdom of God in its full splendour.

For as in Adam all die, so also in the Christ shall all be made alive. But each in his own order; namely, Christ, the first-fruits; then those who are Christ's at his coming; then the end, when he hands over the kingdom to God and the Father, when he abolishes all other sovereignty, authority and power.... And when all things have been subjected to him, then the Son himself shall be subject to him who subjected all things to him, that God may be all in all.[75]

[75] 1 Cor. 15:22-24, 28(S.).

§ 24. THE MYSTICAL BODY OF CHRIST

The thoughts with which we have just been occupied call, as their natural complement, for a consideration of the Church as the mystical Body of Christ.[1] The revelation of this truth had dominated the mind of St Paul from the moment of his dramatic vision on the road to Damascus. "He fell to the ground, and heard a voice saying to him, Saul, Saul, why dost thou persecute me? Who art thou, Lord? he asked. And he said, I am Jesus, whom Saul persecutes." [2] To persecute the Christians was to persecute Christ! It was thus, by a direct personal encounter with the risen Lord, that St

[1] Pope Pius XII's Encyclical, *Mystici Corporis Christi,* is an authoritative exposition of the nature of Christ's mystical Body, "especially those aspects of it which concern the Church militant" (p. 193). Accordingly, it is a primary ecclesiastical document for much that is said in the present section. The reference "p." denotes the page number in the Latin version published in *A.A.S.,* vol. 35, no. 7 (20 Julii 1943). The Encyclical has been translated by Canon G. D. Smith, and is published by the Catholic Truth Society, London.

[2] Acts 9:4-5.

Paul received a disclosure never afterwards to be forgotten—
Christ and the Christian community were inseparably united.
God the Father had decred that his Son's life-work, achieved
on the Cross, should reach its complete fulfilment in the
Church. "And he subjected all things under his feet, and
has made him supreme head of the Church, which is his
body, the complement (πλήρωμα) of him who in all things is
made complete by means of us all." [3] The Church is the
counterpart of Christ. We can no more think of him without
his Church than we can think of a head without a trunk, or
of an organism without organs through which to function.
Christ apart from the Church would be an incomplete being,
a Messiah without the Israel of God; he would have no fulfilment as Redeemer, since the grace which is his for the
purpose of passing on to others (*gratia capitalis*) would remain inactive; he would have no fulfilment as the second
Adam, for he is this only by his solidarity with regenerated
humanity; he would be without fulfilment even as Christ,
for, in this office, he is not simply a single divine person but
a collective personality. Hence Christ "in all things is made
complete by means of us all,"—by the members of the ecclesiastical hierarchy as Head of the Church, and by the least
of the faithful as Saviour and Sanctifier.

It was in God's design that St Paul should be the instrument for revealing to us the boundless implications of
Christ's Church as his mystical Body:

> With what grace God gives me (and he gives it in all the
> effectiveness of his power), I am a minister of that gospel; on
> me, least as I am of all the saints, he has bestowed this privilege,
> of making known to the Gentiles the unfathomable riches of
> Christ, of publishing to the world the plan of this mystery, kept
> hidden from the beginning of time in the all-creating mind of
> God. The principalities and powers of heaven are to see, now,
> made manifest in the Church, the subtlety of God's wisdom;
> such is his eternal purpose, centred in Christ Jesus our Lord,
> who gives us all our confidence, bids us come forward, embold-
> ened by our faith in him.[4]

[3] Eph. 1:22–23(S.).   [4] 3:7–12.

This was one of those overwhelming truths which our Lord's disciples could not have been expected to grasp before the Resurrection. It was to this revelation he had referred at the Last Supper: "I have still many things to say to you, but you cannot bear them now. But when he, the Spirit of truth, comes, he shall guide you into all the truth." [5] Nevertheless, the doctrine is found implicitly in our Lord's own words, where he identifies himself with his disciples and especially with his Church. We remember his attitude towards the children: what we do to them will be reckoned as done to himself and to the Father. "Whoever welcomes such a child as this in my name, welcomes me; and whoever welcomes me, welcomes, not me, but him that sent me." [6] At the Last Judgement, reward or punishment will be assigned to us, not with reference to what we may suppose to have been our service to God, but as this is tested by our practical conduct towards others. "Believe me, when you did it to one of the least of my brethren here, you did it to me." [7] "Believe me, when you refused it to one of the least of my brethren here, you refused it to me." [8]

We have seen also, from the allegory of the vine and the branches,[9] how intimate was to be the communion between Christ and his disciples. Christ is the true vine; yet the vine and its branches live the same life, are nourished by the same sap, and work together in the production of the same fruit. They form one being and share in each other's activity. Clearly, it is only by the difference in the similitude used that St John's doctrine is to be distinguished from that of St Paul on the mystical Body. The *vine-stock* corresponds to the *body* and the branches to the *members*. Indeed, as regards the essential point, there is almost an identity of language; where St John records our Lord as saying "in me," St Paul employs his characteristic phrase "in Christ Jesus." [10]

---

5 John 16:12–13(S.).   6 Mark 9:37.   7 Matt. 25:40.
8 Vs. 45.   9 John 15:1–11; see p. 118.
10 This phrase, or its equivalents, occurs 164 times in the Epistles. See Deissmann's tables, reproduced in Prat, *op. cit.*, II, 476 (E.T. p. 391). The contention of many scholars that the phrase "in Christ Jesus" *always* refers to the mystical Christ will hardly hold in view of Phil. 2:5!

312 THE CHRIST OF CATHOLICISM

But Paul's formula adds something to John's; with the latter the union of the faithful with Jesus is a personal one. St Paul does not ignore this aspect of it,[11] but it is not the point which he is concerned to stress. St John thinks of our being *in Jesus* or *in Jesus Christ;* whereas, for St Paul, it is *in Christ* or *in Christ Jesus.* This shows that what he is chiefly considering is not the individual person of Jesus, but rather his office as the Messiah, his quality as the second Adam; that is to say, his representative character. In other words, his thought dwells on the "mystical" Christ, and the formula *in Christ Jesus* relates to his "body," which is the Church.[12]

Consider how St Paul describes the Christian's being incorporated in Christ:

Are you ignorant that all of us who were baptized into Christ Jesus were baptized into his death? We were buried therefore with him by baptism into death; so that, as Christ rose from the dead in the glory of the Father, thus we also might walk in newness of life.[13] ... For you all are sons of God in Christ Jesus through faith. For as many of you as were baptized into Christ did put on Christ. There can be neither Jew nor Greek, there can be neither slave nor free man, there can be no male and female; for you all are one in Christ Jesus.[14]

In its original meaning *to baptize* meant *to plunge into the water;* hence St Paul here has in mind the external rite of immersion and emersion, which are themselves efficacious symbols of death and a new life. By baptism we are plunged into Christ, grafted upon Christ, incorporated in Christ, identified with Christ. The mystical Christ is now the element in which we move, the whole of which we are a part.

[11] Cf. 2 Cor. 13:5; Gal. 2:20-21.

[12] NOTE: The word *mystical* as connected with Christ's "body" does not occur in St Paul. It was its obvious appropriateness, as a means of distinguishing the Church from Christ's physical body, that led to its later usage. The phrase "mystical body" seems first to have been used by the Fathers as a description of the Eucharist; not until the thirteenth century do we find it employed, as in our present context, as being the equivalent of the Pauline "Body of Christ." Cf. Bishop Myers, *The Mystical Body of Christ,* pp. 27-28.

[13] Rom. 6:3-4(S.).   [14] Gal. 3:26-28(S.).

Just as Adam's sin brought death upon us by reason of our solidarity with him, so, in virtue of the same principle, do we gain newness of life in Christ.

"For since by a man came death, by a man also came the resurrection of the dead; for as in Adam all die, so also in the Christ shall all be made alive." [15] Adam and Christ respectively represent the whole human race. All men are in Adam and all are in Christ—*In Adam Christus et Christus in Adam* [16]—,although in a very different way. In the words of St Cyril of Alexandria, "All die in Adam because, on account of his transgression, human nature was condemned in him; thus all shall be justified in Christ because, thanks to his redemptive act, human nature is once more blessed in him." [17] The phrase "in Christ Jesus," understood in its full meaning, refers to Christ the Saviour, the second Adam, a title which belonged to him from the moment he inaugurated our redemption on the Cross. Thenceforth we suffer and die with him, we rise from the dead and, finally, reign with him. In him we are predestined, called, justified and elected; consequently it is in him that we obtain all heavenly blessings, grace, filial adoption, sanctification and eternal life. Such are the implications of our being "in Christ Jesus."

It should be remembered, however, that St Paul's doctrine on the mystical Body is expressed in metaphorical rather than literal terms. St Thomas points out in this connection that when we are using metaphors, that is, describing one thing in terms of another, we must not expect our comparison to hold good in every respect.[18] Pope Pius XII, alluding to the union between the members of the Body and its Head, has reproved those who fail to make the necessary distinctions "between the several meanings of physical, moral, and mystical body, with the result that they introduce a perverse explanation of this union." [19] Though Christ, together with the Church, may be said to form "one mystical person," [20] we must avoid any notion of the faithful being so

<hr>

[15] 1 Cor. 15:21–22(S.).
[16] St Augustine, *In Psalm.* 101, *sermo* 1, 5; *P.L.* 37, col. 1296.
[17] St Cyril, *Fragm. in* 1 Cor. 15:22; *P.G.* 74, col. 901.
[18] III, q. 8, art. 1, ad 2. [19] P. 234. [20] P. 226.

united to Christ as to constitute one *physical* personality with him. Such a conception is as repugnant to reason as it is to faith; moreover, it would nullify much of the doctrine expounded in the preceding pages. Its logical consequence would be the ascribing of divine qualities to human beings, and conversely, the attribution to Christ of human frailty and error. As the faithful guardian of the traditional doctrine, the Pope insists that "any explanation of this mystical union is to be rejected if it makes the faithful in any way pass beyond the order of created things and so trespass upon the divine sphere, that even one single attribute of the eternal God could be predicated of them in the proper sense."[21] If the distinction between creature and Creator is not obliterated even in the incarnate Word himself, how much less must this be so in the members of his mystical Body!

Pius XII also draws our attention to the fact that, although St Paul unites Christ with the members of his body in the most intimate of unions, he yet contrasts one with the other as being parties to a marriage.[22] Nor are these warnings directed simply to the preservation of dogmatic truth; they have practical implications of great importance. Speculative error always brings with it repercussions in the sphere of moral conduct. Thus, in placing too much stress on the "divinization" of man effected by grace, or in misconceiving the nature of the Christ-life within us, we can be led into a form of quietism; we shall be tempted to underestimate the need for the use of our native energies in responding to God's grace. This is, in fact, to travesty the doctrine of the mystical Body; as we shall see presently when we come to speak of the co-operation demanded of its members.

For the moment it will be in place to recall the balanced outlook of St Augustine. No one has stressed more emphatically than he the identification of the Church with Christ— *homines sancti et fideles fiunt cum homine Christo unus Christus.*[23] Yet Augustine is also the Doctor of Grace; and

21 P. 231.   22 P. 234; cf. Eph. 5:22–23.
23 *De pecc. merit. et remiss.,* I, 31, 60; *P.L.* 44, col. 144–45.

here his whole teaching is based upon the absolute distinction between God and his creatures.[24] We are utterly dependent upon God for any good we have or can do; at the same time, we must co-operate with him to the fulness of our powers: *Qui ergo fecit te sine te, non te justificat sine te. Ergo fecit nescientem, justificat volentem.*[25]

It is likewise St Augustine [26] who insists on a further truth, about which Pope Pius XII finds it necessary to remind the faithful; namely, "that in these matters all things are to be held common to the Blessed Trinity, so far as the same relate to God as the supreme efficient cause." [27] In other words, we must remember that the grace by which we are made members of Christ's Body comes to us from the Father, Son and Holy Spirit operating together, and not simply from Christ alone. The doctrine of the mystical Body is a revealed truth, accessible only to supernatural faith; its content can in some degree be analysed, but it cannot be fully explained by human reason. We shall fall into error if we seek to apply St Paul's anthropomorphic analogy of head and members too rigidly to the relations between Christ and his Church. "We are dealing with a hidden mystery which during our exile on earth can never be completely unveiled, never altogether understood, nor adequately expressed in human language." [28]

Bearing these cautions in mind, we may now return to our principal theme. The Church as his mystical Body is the "fulness" ($\pi\lambda\acute{\eta}\varrho\omega\mu\alpha$) of Christ.[29] But the Church is not filled directly with the Godhead. Between pure deity and redeemed humanity stands the "one mediator between God and man, Christ Jesus, himself man." [30] What fills us is the divine-human life of Christ together with his love. St Paul would have us gain "the love of Christ which surpasses knowledge: to the end that you may be filled with all the plenitude of

[24] For an outline of St Augustine's doctrine on Grace by the present writer, see *Eastern Churches Quarterly*, Jan.–Mar. 1946, pp. 228–47.
[25] *Sermo* 169, 11; *P.L.* 38, col. 923.
[26] *De Trinitate,* I, 4; *P.L.* 42, col. 824, II, 7, 12; col. 853.
[27] P. 231.   [28] *Ibid.*
[29] Eph. 1:23.   [30] 1 Tim. 2:5(S.).

God." [31] There is thus a double sense in which the Church is the fulness of Christ; first, because the mystical Body is like a vessel into which the fulness of Christ is poured. He fills it with himself. Secondly, for the reason that Christ's fulness cannot be manifested among men without a human vessel to contain it. As Christ is the Mediator of God's fulness, so the Church is the mediator of Christ's fulness. Just as the Church is empty without Christ, so is Christ unfulfilled in himself, and inaccessible to us without the Church. The Church is the household of God and the family of redeemed humanity. From this point of view, God himself would be incomplete without the Church; for he would be a heavenly Father without a family. His beloved Son would still be the first-born of the Father, but he would not be "the first-born among many brethren." [32]

Man is nothing apart from God; but God has freely willed to make man indispensable to the carrying out of the divine plan. From the call of Abraham onwards a chosen people had been the instrument through which God's purpose was fulfilled. We cannot think of the Messiah without Israel, of the Word becoming flesh without the co-operation of the Virgin Mother, of Christ without the Church, of his fulness without the mystical Body. There can be no saving knowledge of God among men except through a holy community in which they can see God's love in some way reflected, and no habitation of God among men without a human temple which he can make his dwelling-place. "The same God who bade light shine out of darkness has kindled a light in our hearts, whose shining is to make known his glory as he has revealed it in the features of Jesus Christ." [33] The Church is needed so that God may display before the world the riches that are his in Christ. Yet here we are reminded that we have nothing of which we ourselves can boast; all comes from God. "We have a treasure, then, in our keeping, but its shell is of perishable earthenware; it must be God, and not anything in ourselves, that gives it its sovereign power." [34]

[31] Eph. 3:19(S.).   [32] Rom. 8:29(S.).   [33] 2 Cor. 4:6.   [34] 2 Cor. 4:7.

We have already dwelt at some length on the various aspects of Christ's headship of the Church.[35] We noted that it is based fundamentally on the uncreated grace of the hypostatic union, by which Christ is the unique Mediator between God and man, and that it operates through the fulness of created grace (*gratia capitalis*) in his human soul, which belongs to him precisely in virtue of his being Head of the Church. It is of this that St John speaks when he says: "For of his fulness we all received, and grace upon grace." [36] We have also noticed how Christ delegated his authority to Peter and the apostles, and through them to their successors, so giving to his mystical Body a constitution and visible juridical structure. In this we find but another instance of the principle that God requires man's co-operation in the furtherance of his providential designs. Christ's fulness, which has been poured into his mystical Body, includes his three roles as prophet, priest and king. Without the Church these could no longer be fulfilled; hence they receive their complement and completion in the doctrinal magisterium, the sacrificial and sanctifying mission, and the ruling authority vested in the ministers of the Catholic Church.

St Paul speaks of Christ being the Head of the Church as the husband is the head of the wife.[37] It is the familiar scriptural image of Christ as the Bridegroom with the Church as his bride.[38] What is pointed to is the principle that the fellowship of the mystical Body and its oneness with Christ are modified by the dependence of the members upon the Head. As the Bridegroom, Christ is the "saviour" of the Church, which is now subject to him.[39] The head preserves the body from harm; the brain controls the limbs and protects them against accidents. Likewise the Head of the Church saves his members from the disintegration sin would cause apart from his saving grace. It has been pointed out that St Paul's language here [40] is coloured by that of the story

---

35 Cf. Pius XII, pp. 213–17.
36 John 1:16(S.).
37 Eph. 5:23.
38 Cf. Pius XII, p. 210.
39 Eph. 5:23–24.
40 VV. 30–31.

of Adam and Eve recorded in Genesis; [41] the pair were to become "one flesh." Now in the Old Testament we find that Yahweh has the part of the bridegroom in correspondence with Israel, his bride.[42] The title of bridegroom, which in this sense belongs to God alone, our Lord claims for himself; [43] in one of the parables, which describes the eschatological crisis, he depicts the kingdom of heaven as a marriage feast which God has prepared for his Son.[44] No one else can share Christ's prerogative as Bridegroom.[45] When we recall the words used by our Lord concerning the marriage union —"and the two shall become one flesh" [46]—in conjunction with St Paul's statement that they contain a "mystery" applicable to Christ and his Church,[47] it seems that the inspired account of the institution of the sacrament of matrimony contains a much higher significance than is suggested by its literal meaning. The "one flesh" in which husband and wife are united symbolizes the "one flesh" that unites Christ and the Church in virtue of the Incarnation.[48]

On an earlier page we considered the virtual equivalence of the Pauline formulas *in Christ* and *in the Spirit*.[49] Christ is the Head of the Church, its "soul" is the Holy Spirit.[50] The Church, taking its birth from the Saviour's death on the Cross, was confirmed in newness of life by the outpouring of the Spirit at Pentecost.[51] "Do you not understand that you are God's temple, and that God's Spirit has his dwelling in you? If anybody desecrates the temple of God, God will bring him to ruin. It is a holy thing, this temple of God which is nothing other than yourselves." [52] The Spirit is given, not only to the Church collectively, but to each of

---

[41] Gen. 2:20–25; 3:20.
[42] Cf. Hos. 1–3; Isa. 54:1–8; Ezek. 16, etc.
[43] Mark 2:19.   [44] Matt. 22:1–14.
[45] John 3:29; 2 Cor. 11:2–3.   [46] Mark 10:8(S.).
[47] Eph. 5:32.
[48] Cf. L. S. Thornton, *The Common Life in the Body of Christ*, pp. 222–26. NOTE: This is an admirable contribution by an Anglican scholar to our understanding of the scriptural teaching on the mystical Body; though it is conspicuously lacking in one particular, viz., an account of how Christ's fulness is achieved in the hierarchic structure of the Church.
[49] See p. 273.   [50] Pius XII, pp. 218–20.
[51] Acts 2:1–4.   [52] 1 Cor. 3:16–17.

its individual members; their very bodies are holy because of the Spirit's presence within them. "Surely you know that your bodies are the shrines of the Holy Spirit, who dwells in you. And he is God's gift to you, so that you are no longer your own masters. A great price was paid to ransom you; glorify God by making your bodies the shrines of his presence." [53] The Church is the temple of God; he dwells in it, since it is now fit to be inhabited by him, being the society redeemed by his Son. The mystical Body is God's tabernacle [54] by contrast with the heathendom and apostasy which surround it.

As the soul by its presence ennobles the human body, vivifies it by its contact and moves it by its activity, so does the Holy Spirit animate Christ's mystical Body. He is the divine guest of the Church and of each of its members; proceeding as he does from the Father and the Son, he is yet, in a very special sense, the "Spirit of Christ" or the "Spirit of the Son"; [55] for Christ's sacrificial death was the condition of our receiving the Spirit. Christ merited for us this most precious of God's gifts; in Christ alone the Spirit dwells without measure; [56] to the members of his mystical Body he is given according to the measure of Christ's gift.[57] But for all he is the sole agent and motive power of the life of grace.[58] The Holy Spirit is God's creative love; self-giving therefore is his chief characteristic; he gives himself together with his gifts.

The love with which Christ loves us is made manifest by the gift of his Spirit, and at the same time by an infusion of sanctifying grace, which is an effect of the Spirit's presence within us. This gift of grace is what unites us to, and enables us to correspond with, the Holy Spirit himself, who is its source; "the love of God has been poured out in our hearts by the Holy Spirit, whom we have received." [59] Accordingly, the charity and grace within our souls, which are distinct from the Spirit, are finite and hence are susceptible of in-

---

[53] 1 Cor. 6:19–20. [54] Cf. John 1:14.
[55] Rom. 8:9; 2 Cor. 3:17; Gal. 4:6. [56] John 3:34.
[57] Eph. 4:7. [58] Rom. 8:9. [59] 5:5.

definite increase. We have received the Spirit wholly, for he is indivisible; but we have been given only a portion of the blessings God intends for us. This is why St Paul sometimes speaks of our having received "the first fruits" [60] or "the pledge" [61] of the Spirit. Christ himself is in us through his Spirit; together they perform their saving work upon us, so that "any divine effect produced in our souls by the Holy Spirit must be said to be produced in us also by Christ." [62]

The object of the Spirit's coming is to produce in the members of the mystical Body an ever-increasing correspondence with their Head, that is, to fashion us in the likeness of Christ. "The Spirit we have been speaking of is the Lord; and where the Lord's spirit is, there is freedom. It is given to us, all alike, to catch the glory of the Lord as in a mirror, with faces unveiled; and so we become transfigured into the same likeness, borrowing glory from that glory, as the Spirit of the Lord enables us." [63] This indicates the term of the process, as it will be in heaven; but even now the whole Church, as well as its individual members, is intended to reflect an ever more faithful image of the Saviour. "We are to follow the truth, in a spirit of charity, and so grow up, in everything, into a due proportion with Christ, who is our head. On him all the body depends; it is organized and unified by each contact with the source which supplies it; and thus, each limb receiving the active power it needs, it achieves its natural growth, building itself up through charity." [64]

Students of St Paul often remind us that the apostle is but little concerned with our Lord's earthly life; it is the risen and glorified Lord who dominates his mind. Yet no one was more insistent than St Paul on the need for the imitation of Christ. Since an ounce of practice is worth a pound of precept, he does not hesitate to point to himself as a model of how it may be done. "Follow my example, then, as I follow the example of Christ." [65] The Pauline teaching suggests an

[60] Rom. 8:23.   [61] 2 Cor. 1:22; 5:5; cf. Eph. 1:14.
[62] Pius XII, p. 230. NOTE: For the manner in which the persons of the Blessed Trinity dwell within the soul, see the present writer's *The Love of God*, pp. 205–22.
[63] 2 Cor. 3:17–18.   [64] Eph. 4:15–16.
[65] 1 Cor. 11:1; cf. 2 Thess. 3:7.

important lesson, which is sometimes forgotten: the imitation of Christ does not consist in doing precisely what he
did, but in responding to the dictates of his Spirit in all
the circumstances of our lives. Our Lord lived in first-century
Palestine, amid conditions quite different from ours; his
vocation to teach, to heal, to save, was also different, even
though many of his followers are called to take their share
in this. But essentially his life was unique; the saints have
loved to base their lives on a literal imitation of his; yet
not even they can reproduce it.

Let us consider some of the very practical maxims which
the idea suggests to St Paul, all of them within the range of
every disciple of Christ: "You must never act in a spirit of
factiousness, or of ambition; each of you must have the humility to think others better than himself, and study the
welfare of others, not his own." [66] "Rejoice with those who
rejoice, mourn with the mourner. Live in harmony of mind,
falling in with the opinions of the common folk, instead of
following conceited thoughts; never give yourselves airs of
wisdom." [67] "Each of us ought to give way to his neighbour,
where it serves a good purpose by building up his faith." [68]
"It is more blessed to give than to receive." [69] In uphold-
ing the principles of truth, we must at the same time take
account of the weaknesses, mental as well as physical
and moral, of others. St Paul is ready to anathematize
false doctrine in every form, whether it be that of the ag-
gressive Judaizers in Antioch, Jerusalem and Galatia, or the
Manichean dogmatizers at Colossae; but he will not trouble
the mentally confused with sterile theorizing or oppress the
scrupulous with nice points of observance. It is well worth
sacrificing an exact application of principles for the greater
good of maintaining peace and unity among the brethren.
Charity, while never taking refuge in what is merely expedi-
ent, is yet capable of infinite adaptability. "To the weak I
became weak, so that I might gain the weak. I am become
all things to all men, so that I may at all events save some." [70]

[66] Phil. 2:3–4.   [67] Rom. 12:15–16.   [68] 15:2.
[69] Acts 20:35.   [70] 1 Cor. 9:22(S.).

There is, however, a sense in which the mystical Body as
a whole does reproduce a faithful image of Christ's earthly
life. Indeed it is the Church's function, as his fulness, that
she should do so. "Christ intends the whole Body of the
Church, as well as each of its members, to be like himself.
This likeness is clearly seen when, following in the footsteps
of her divine Founder, she teaches, governs and offers the
divine sacrifice. Again, when she practises the evangelical
counsels she portrays in herself the poverty, the obedience
and the virginity of the Redeemer. And again, the manifold
Orders and Institutes in the Church—so many jewels with
which she is adorned—show forth Christ in various aspects
of his life: contemplating on the mountain, preaching to
the people, healing the sick, bringing sinners to repentance,
and doing good to all. No wonder, then, that during her existence on this earth she resembles Christ also in suffering
persecutions, insults and tribulations." [71] The Church has
inherited the representative role of Israel's Messiah, who was
God's suffering Servant; hence the Church herself, being
made a partaker in Christ's sacrificial life, fulfils the prophecy
of Isaiah [72] with which our Lord identified himself. "And
Jahweh was pleased to crush him with suffering; though his
own life be made a sin-offering, he shall see a seed that shall
have length of days, and the purpose of Jahweh shall prosper
in his hand." [73]

This is the explanation of St Paul's mysterious saying that
he makes up, on his own account, for what is lacking to
Christ's sufferings: "I rejoice now in my sufferings for your
sake; I am filling up on my part the deficiency of the sufferings of the Christ in my flesh, for the sake of his body, which
is the Church." [74] At first sight it might seem that Christ's
passion was here regarded as insufficient, as though his mediatorial work had been left unfulfilled. If this were really
true, then nothing St Paul or anyone else could do or suffer
would make any difference; we should have been left un-
redeemed. Moreover the whole context of these words for-

[71] Pius XII, pp. 214–15.   [72] Isa. 52:13—53:12.
[73] 53:10(Kissane).   [74] Col. 1:24(S.); cf. Pius XII, p. 245.

bids such an interpretation; for St Paul is countering the argument of those who say that other mediators are needed; whereas Christ alone has "all the fulness" and only he can reconcile the world to God. "For it was the pleasure of the Father that all the fulness should dwell in him; and that through him he should reconcile to himself all things, whether things that are on the earth or things that are in the heavens, making peace by the blood of his cross." [75]

The key to St Paul's meaning lies in the contrast between *"my* [i.e. Paul's] flesh" [76] and *"his* [i.e. Christ's] flesh." The sufferings "in his body of flesh" [77] sufficed to reconcile the whole creation to God.[78] But, since Christ and his mystical Body form one organism, there is an identity of life between him and his members; hence the latter share in, and re-produce, his sufferings. Not only the salvation we derive from them, but the sufferings themselves "overflow upon us." [79] This explains St Paul's joy in his afflictions as "the prisoner of Christ Jesus"; [80] they form a part of his mystical identity with Christ; in accepting them he is, as it were, complementing Christ's passion "for the sake of his body, which is the Church." [81] From this point of view a certain measure of the sufferings of Christ remains to be completed; the members of the mystical Body contribute towards this end by the unity of their sufferings with its Head. This is the process known as "co-redemption" which, as we have seen, received its ideal embodiment in our Lady's co-opera-tion with the unique redemptive mission of her Son.[82] So it is that Christ's sufferings are a spiritual treasure that enriches the Church; to partake of them is to partake of Christ's ful-ness; [83] they are a necessary part of the "whole Christ."

"A man's body is all one, though it has a number of dif-ferent organs; and all this multitude of organs goes to make up one body; so it is with Christ . . . And you are Christ's body, organs of it depending upon each other." [84] St Paul's

---

[75] Col. 1:19–20(S.).   [76] Vs. 24.   [77] Vs. 22(S.).
[78] Vs. 20.   [79] 2 Cor. 1:5(S.).   [80] Eph. 3:1(S.).
[81] Col. 1:24(S.).   [82] Cf. Pius XII, p. 248; see *supra*, pp. 285–7.
[83] Cf. 2 Cor. 4:14–18.
[84] 1 Cor. 12:12, 27; cf. Pius XII, pp. 212–13.

comparison of the mystical Body to a human body should be understood rather as a parable than an allegory. In other words, he is illustrating the likeness between the two on a broad principle of similarity, not entering into the details of the mystical anatomy. We are not meant to ask what the various subordinate organs signify: the ears, the eyes, the feet, the hands and the rest. The essential point is that the diversity of organs in a human body is not only an element of its beauty, it is a condition of its life. This unity in variety does not arise, in the members of the mystical Body, from the fact that they are Christians, since in this respect there is no difference between them; nor is it due to the diversity of natural characteristics, although these, when perfected by grace, can form a contributory factor. Its source lies in those gratuitous gifts which the Holy Spirit grants to the faithful for the common good of the Church: the apostolate, prophecy, discourses marked by wisdom and learning, discernment of spirits, power to heal the sick and to work miracles, aptitude for administration, teaching, helping the poor, consoling the afflicted and performing other works of mercy. Moreover, this diversity is also manifested in the respective functions of the ecclesiastical hierarchy, and in the inequality, which the difference in their co-operation with the various calls of grace produces, among the members of the Church.

What is emphasized here is the supernatural counterpart of the truism that man is by nature a social being. If each of the body's organs could instinctively attract everything to itself, the whole organism would quickly perish. It is the same with the social body; hence nature warns us against selfishness. We learn by experience that no man is sufficient to himself, that each member of society has his own contribution to make, that those who are intrinsically the least honourable are often treated with the greatest honour, that the general health depends upon the proper working of the whole, and that the welfare of all is bound up with the good condition of each. But we must not stop short at such obvious considerations as these; St Paul furnishes us with the true formula of Christian altruism—all must live and act together *"in Christ."* "Each of us has one body, with many different parts, and not all these parts have the same function; just so we, though many in number, form one body in Christ, and each acts as the counterpart of another." [85] The other members of the Body are not strangers to us; they are part of us; they work for us just as we work for them; we need their help and we owe them ours.

Community of life is thus the nerve and sinews, the very life-blood, of the mystical Body. The individual member does not live by his own life, but by the life of the Body. Hence he must be united, not only to the Head, from whom the living influx flows, but also to the other members, each of whom, in his own sphere, transmits that life to him. Separated from the Head, the member inevitably dies; isolated from the other members, he leads only a precarious and impoverished life. It is from the Head that the whole Body draws its nourishment and, as a compact structure, grows up unto God.[86] In this context we may notice the characteristically Pauline emphasis in the exposition of a truth held in common with St John. We have already remarked on the evident kinship of thought between the mystical Body and the similitude of the Vine and its branches.[87] In both instances the supernatural life is compared to the growth of a living being, a growth deriving from an internal source and wholly dependent upon its union with the centre of life. But in St John the branches draw their sap from the vine-stock to which they are directly joined; while in St Paul the members, united to the Head by the other members, reciprocally give and receive the flow of life with reference to each other. The first considers primarily the individual life of believers, while St Paul's standpoint is that of the communal life of the Church. But in St John and St Paul alike the agent of the supernatural life is Christ and the Holy Spirit.

The foregoing consideration on the Church as the fulness and complement of Christ, together with their practical

[85] Rom. 12:4-5. [86] Col. 2:19. [87] John 15:1-11.

bearing upon the co-operation demanded of the members of the mystical Body, are admirably summed up in the words of Pope Pius XII. Not only does Christ fulfil himself through his Vicar on earth, the successor of St Peter, "but also while he himself is invisibly ruling the Church, our Saviour desires to be helped by the members of his mystical Body in furthering the work of the Redemption. This is not on account of any need or insufficiency in him, but rather because he has so ordained it for the greater honour of his spotless Bride. Dying on the Cross, he bestowed upon his Church the boundless treasure of the Redemption without any co-operation on her part; but in the distribution of that treasure, he not only shares this work of sanctification with his spotless Bride, but wills it to arise in a certain measure out of her labour. This is truly a tremendous mystery, upon which we can never meditate enough: that the salvation of many souls depends upon the prayers and voluntary mortifications offered for that intention by the members of the mystical Body of Jesus Christ, and upon the co-operation which pastors and faithful, and especially fathers and mothers of families, must give to our divine Saviour." [88]

The union of the mystical Body reaches its culminating point in the Eucharist, which is the divinely efficacious symbol of the Church's sacrificial life.[89] "We have a cup that we bless; is not this cup we bless a participation in Christ's blood? Is not the bread we break a participation in Christ's body? The one bread makes us one body, though we are many in number; the same bread is shared by all." [90] Here we may note that the Greek word translated by "participation" is κοινωνία, from which we get our "communion." For the Jews, as for the ancient peoples generally, to eat food offered in sacrifice was to share in that sacrifice. The religious banquets held in honour of the heathen gods were a form of ritual worship; [91] this is the context of St Paul's words to the Christians at Corinth, for they were not yet immune from these idolatrous practices. In their case such indulgence

[88] P. 213.   [89] Cf. *ibid.*, pp. 232–33.
[90] 1 Cor. 10:16–17.   [91] Cf. Judges 9:27.

amounted to an apostasy from Christ. But St Paul concedes that there is truth in the idea itself—"do not those who eat their sacrifices associate themselves with the altar of sacrifice?" [92] The heathen worship was perverse, not necessarily in itself, but because it was directed to a wrong object, paying tribute to a false god. Yet the underlying principle was applicable to the Christians: to eat food that had been sacrificed to the true God implied a recognition of him and his lordship; it promoted fellowship with him in a common life.

The Jewish Christians were to understand that even their own Old Testament sacrifices, and in particular that of the passover meal, had undergone a complete transformation. Jesus, their Lord, who had offered himself as a sacrificial victim on the Cross, was the true Paschal Lamb. So sacrificed, he had become their passover food. In partaking of this food they performed an act of worship to God; further, they gained a share in his life. Now the Christian conception of life may be summed up in the word "communion." The life which we share with one another is not that of a human community; it is wholly drawn from a divine source, and is mediated to us as we are linked together in our joint-participation in Christ. This is the significance of St Paul's use of the word κοινωνία in the passage quoted in the preceding paragraph. Thus the Eucharist is not primarily an individual act of communion between the Christian and his divine Redeemer, even though a fruitful reception of the Blessed Sacrament does in fact always involve this. What makes the Eucharist pre-eminently the sacrament of Christ's mystical Body [93] is that it is the rite whereby the whole communal life of the Church, as a participation in Christ, is corporately manifested in its full significance and reality. To "go to Holy Communion" is for us our highest privilege, but we should always remember that it is this because we are fellow-guests at a heavenly banquet, united with one another in charity. We participate jointly with our fellow-communicants

[92] 1 Cor. 10:18.
[93] So St Thomas: "The reality (res) of this Sacrament is the unity of the mystical Body"; III, q. 73, art. 3.

in the life of Christ as that life is imparted to the Church.

But the life of Christ is essentially sacrificial. It was offered once for all on Calvary, an offering which is renewed daily on our Catholic altars in a sacramental representation. What we offer in the Mass is Christ's body and blood; the body representing his complete personality, the blood his vital energy. Now the "whole Christ" is the corporate personality in which we are all included, the mystical Body of which we are members. In baptism we were united with Christ's death and resurrection; thereafter the life which was renewed in him is reproduced in us. What began in baptism is being nourished continually through the sacrament of the Eucharist. The process of growth implies that we are increasing in stature to the likeness of Christ's resurrection. By this means we are being conformed to the image of God's Son, so that the initial grace we received at baptism attains finally to full fruition in the state of glory. Thus the sacrifice offered by Christ, the Head, is continued and fulfilled in his members; both sacramentally in the Mass, whose full symbolism is only completed by our joint-participation in Holy Communion; and in concrete actuality, by offering our own bodies, that is, our whole personalities,[94] in dedication to God, together with the expenditure of our vital energies— of which the symbol is "blood" [95]—in his service.

For Christ our Lord willed that this wonderful and inestimable union, in which we are joined with one another and with our divine Head, should find a special manifestation before the eyes of the faithful in the Eucharistic Sacrifice. Herein the ministers at the altar represent not only our Saviour, but also the whole mystical Body and each one of its members; in this sacrifice the faithful are associated in the common prayer and supplication and, through the hands of the priest, whose voice alone renders the immaculate Lamb present on the altar, they themselves offer to the eternal Father this most pleasing Victim of praise and propitiation for the needs of the whole Church. And as the divine Redeemer, when he was dying on the Cross, offered himself as the Head of the whole human race to the eternal Father, so in

[94] Cf. Rom. 12:1.   [95] Heb. 12:4.

this "clean oblation" [96] he offers to the heavenly Father, not only himself as the Head of the Church, but in himself also his mystical members; for he encloses them all, the weakest and frailest among them, most lovingly in his Heart.

Moreover, the Sacrament of the Eucharist, while also presenting a vivid and marvellous picture of the unity of the Church—since the bread to be consecrated results from the kneading together of many grains of wheat [97]—gives to us the very Author of supernatural grace, from whom we are enabled to draw that Spirit of charity which bids us live not our own life, but the life of Christ, and whereby we love the Redeemer himself in all the members of his mystical Body.[98]

It is thus that the incarnate Word, and his redeeming work, live on through the ages. The Church, his mystical Body, will faithfully reproduce his sacrificial life, proclaiming to the world the death of the Lord "until he comes." [99] As yet the Body is still growing and gathering strength; then it will have attained to full stature, the complete "fulness of Christ." At the end of the Apocalypse we are told that the Lord's coming will be soon. Whatever be the appointed day, its approach will not be long in comparison with eternity. Until it dawns the Church, the Body of Christ, which is also his Bride, looks forward to it as to the consummation of a marriage. "Be it so, then; come, Lord Jesus." [100]

[96] Mal. 1:11. [97] *Didache*, 9, 4. [98] Pius XII, pp. 232-33.
[99] 1 Cor. 11:26. [100] Apoc. 22:20.

CHAPTER VII

CONCLUSION

§ 25. LOOKING BEFORE AND AFTER

BY way of rounding off the meditative study on which we have been engaged, we shall examine briefly the general setting and background to the Incarnation. This should throw further light on the mystery itself and open up a yet wider vista on the "unfathomable riches of Christ." [1] Two aspects of the Word's becoming flesh at once present themselves to our minds: on the one hand, the eternal fact of the Son of God's pre-existence "in the bosom of the Father," [2] and on the other, the historical event of his entry into the world of space and time. That Jesus of Nazareth, unlike any other man, had a "pre-history" is of course a fundamental truth of our Catholic faith; were this not so his Incarnation would be unintelligible, indeed, an impossibility. Nor does the New Testament reveal the slightest ambiguity on the point. St Paul's is the earliest record we have of the Christian belief positively in writing; for, as will be remembered, his Epistles were written before the Synoptic Gospels and antedate St John by some forty years. Let us recall his most characteristic statements.

"Though he was divine by nature, he did not consider his being on an equality with God a thing to be grasped; but on the contrary he emptied himself, took the nature of a slave, and was made like to men." [3] "He is the image of the invisible God, the first-born of all creation. For in him were created all things in the heavens and on the earth, things visible and invisible, whether thrones or dominations or principalities or powers—all were created through him and

[1] Eph. 3:8.   [2] John 1:18.   [3] Phil. 2:6–7(S.).

for him. And he himself exists before all things, and in him all things hold together." [4] "For the grace of God has appeared to save all men, instructing us that, renouncing worldly lusts, we should live soberly, uprightly and religiously in the present world, awaiting the blessed hope and manifestation of the glory of our great God and Saviour Jesus Christ; who gave himself for us that he might redeem us from all iniquity, and purify for himself a special people of his own, zealous for noble works." [5] "God, having spoken of old to our forefathers through the prophets, by many degrees and in many ways, has at last in these days spoken to us by his Son, whom he appointed heir of all things, and through whom he made the worlds. He being the effulgence of God's glory and the very image of his substance, upholds the universe by God's powerful mandate." [6]

At a certain moment in history "God sent his Son, made from a woman, made under the law, in order that he might redeem those under the law, in order that we might receive our adoption as sons." [7] Christ came into the world,[8] he appeared in the flesh; [9] being rich, he became poor, that through his poverty we might be made rich.[10] "Therefore, also, God highly exalted him, and bestowed on him the name which is above every name; so that at the name of Jesus every knee should bend, of beings in the heavens, on the earth, and under the earth, and every tongue should confess that Jesus Christ is Lord, to the glory of God the Father." [11] Thus we can distinguish three states or phases in the life of Christ: the eternal pre-existence of the Son with the Father; his historical appearance on earth at the appointed hour; and the glorious exaltation of the risen Lord.

How closely all this conforms to the thought of St John: "In the beginning was the Word, and the Word was with God, and the Word was God." [12] "And the Word became flesh, and dwelt among us." [13] Then the sorrowful commen-

[4] Col. 1:15–17(S.).
[5] Tit. 2:11–14(S.).
[6] Heb. 1:1–2(S.).
[7] Gal. 4:4–5(S.).
[8] 1 Tim. 1:15.
[9] 3:16.
[10] 2 Cor. 8:9.
[11] Phil. 2:9–11(S.).
[12] John. 1:1(S.).
[13] Vs. 14(S.).

tary on the reception given to the Son of God: "He was in the world, and the world was made through him, yet the world knew him not. He came into his own possession, and his own people received him not." [14] Only when he had been raised on the Cross would he be enabled to break down the resistance of human pride: "Yes, if only I am lifted up from the earth, I will attract all men to myself." [15] Afterwards, when he had risen from the dead, he would send his Spirit to convince the world of the wrongness of its judgement.[16] Then, in the glory of the Resurrection, men would understand that "Jesus is the Christ, the Son of God, and so believing find life through his name." [17]

All that we have seen in the preceding pages has pointed to the harmony and beauty of God's redeeming plan. Some thinkers have been so struck with this aspect of the mystery, as to see it arising by an inevitable necessity from the nature of things, God and man being respectively what they are. But, as we have insisted more than once, the Incarnation embodies a revealed truth accessible only to supernatural faith. Its content is beyond the capacity of our reason to master; the data it provides form an object eminently worthy of theological investigation, and still more profitably, of prayerful contemplation; but they cannot be reached by a process of demonstration from observable facts. We are here concerned with "the secret that had been hidden from all the ages and generations of the past," [18] which God has now at last disclosed to his chosen ones. The Christian, in the light of faith, has an absolute conviction of its truth. This, however, is due, not to the probative force of the arguments which may have prepared the way for belief, but to the fact that, in his case, as with St Peter, the Father has revealed it to him.[19]

Nevertheless, merely on the basis of historical evidence and rational consistency, a Catholic theologian may confidently challenge his critics to produce as coherent an account of Jesus Christ as the one offered by the Church. He may

---

[14] John 1:10–11(S.).   [15] 12:32.   [16] John 16:7–11.
[17] 20:31.   [18] Col. 1:26.   [19] Matt. 16:17.

even make so bold as to affirm that, granted the truth of the New Testament, there is no alternative account that can survive the test of serious examination. It is interesting to remember that, despite the fact that the Incarnation cannot be logically demonstrated, St Thomas Aquinas held that its inherent fittingness [20] made it, relatively speaking, inevitable.[21] On the assumption that God chose to redeem us in the most effective of all ways, we may say that there was a conditional necessity for his doing precisely what he has done. Nothing accords better with our human aspirations than the figure of the Son of God made man; he provides us by his very existence with the ultimate explanation of life, stimulating us to good, protecting us from evil, gathering us together in the final enjoyment of his own beatitude.

His coming was not necessary for the perfection of the created universe; that could have been achieved by man's being directed to the service of God within the limits of his natural capacities.[22] What called out for the Incarnation, from mankind's point of view, was not any natural need for such a fulfilment, but our abject and sinful state. God's only begotten Son became incarnate in order to redeem us. So we profess in the Creed—*Qui propter nos homines, et propter nostram salutem, descendit de caelis.* From Adam's sin which, considered in itself, was our greatest misfortune, it was God's design not only to reclaim us, but to raise us to a dignity surpassing that of our first parents—to make us "heirs of God, sharing the inheritance of Christ." [23] Such is the divine power to draw good out of evil; for God never permits evil unless he intends to draw therefrom a more than countervailing good. No wonder, then, that the Church, in her Easter Liturgy, can presume almost to make light of Adam's fall, since it was the occasion of our being offered a destiny beyond man's highest hopes. *O felix cupa, quae talem ac tantum meruit habere redemptorem!*

What is thus brought home to us is that God's redeeming plan, to which the Incarnation was the prelude, far from

20 Cf. III, q. 1, art. 1.   21 Art. 2.
22 Art. 3, ad 2.   23 Rom. 8:17.

being due to any compelling necessity, arose from the completely free exercise of the divine mercy. "How rich God is
in mercy, with what an excess of love he has loved us! Our
sins had made dead men of us, and he, in giving life to
Christ, gave life to us too; it is his grace that has saved
you." [24] The process of salvation had its origin in God's unrestricted choice; he was constrained by nothing outside
himself, whether in man's nature or in his good works. "Has
he not saved us, and called us to a vocation of holiness? It
was not because of anything we had done; we owe it to his
own design, to the grace lavished on us, long ages ago, in
Christ Jesus." [25] In a word, it was from out of the abundance
of God's love and pity, as moved by no other motive, that he
made the supreme gesture which is the Incarnation. It is
summed up by St John, in what is surely the most pregnant
single sentence in all literature: "For God so loved the
world, that he gave his only begotten Son, in order that
whoever believes in him should not perish, but possess eternal
life." [26]

The Son of God came upon earth "in the fulness of the
times"; [27] that is to say, after a series of historical periods
succeeding one another in accordance with a plan determined in advance, just as the regular cycle of the seasons
brings in turn the buds, the flowers, and finally the fruit.
Man comes to maturity only by passing through childhood
and youth. So God adapts himself to this harmonious natural
arrangement; he allows the human race to reach its majority,
"the fulness of the time," [28] before opening out before it its
final destiny.[29] He determined to lead man to his ultimate
goal by four successive stages: the law of nature, the time of
the promises, the period of the Covenant, and the era of
Grace. Such is the idea of human progress made known to
us through divine revelation; it is directed throughout its
course by God's controlling hand. Some have called it a
philosophy of history; but, as Père Prat acutely remarks, it

[24] Eph. 2:4–5.   [25] 2 Tim. 1:9.   [26] John 3:16(S.).
[27] Eph. 1:10.   [28] Gal. 4:4.
[29] See the whole passage on the role of the schoolmaster, guardians and
trustees: 3:23, 4:7.

could be more justly named a "theology of providence."

The religious story of mankind began with the creation of Adam and Eve; it opens on a note of tragedy. Adam, through disobedience, lost the divine friendship which he had enjoyed in his original state; he was thereby made subject to an inclination to evil and incurred the penalty of death. Yet, ignorant and perverse as pagan man subsequently became, he could still perceive something of God's attributes as mirrored in the sensible world; [30] in the light of the eternal law, his conscience still retained knowledge of how to serve him. That this was so was in reality due to divine providence; it was to be the preliminary stage in man's journey back to God.[31] By virtue of the same providence God keeps Gentile and Jew alike under the dominion of sin. He proposes to show mercy to both; [32] for he remains the God, not only of the Jews, but also of the Gentiles; [33] he intends to draw profit from their misery, and even from their wickedness, and lift them out of the abyss.[34]

The preparation of the Gentiles for faith was chiefly negative; but the spread of Christianity in the Graeco-Roman world proved by the event that it had not been ineffective. Men had learned to despise the absurd and indecent assembly of gods which formed the object of the popular cults. Licentiousness had brought in its train a feeling of satiety and despair. The confused philosophies of the day were lacking in vital power and could not give to the ordinary folk a satisfactory explanation of life. With this there had come to birth in the souls of many an aspiration towards a nobler religious ideal, an awakening of conscience, a vague sense of the need for salvation. Such were the intimations, coming in the last resort from "the unknown God," [35] which prepared the way for the heralds of the Gospel.

But between the state of nature and the *régime* of the Law was inserted the age of promise. St Paul dates this from the time of Abraham, since he is its personification, though in

30 Rom. 1:20.   31 Acts 17:26–27.
32 Rom. 11:32; Gal. 3:22.   33 Rom. 3:29.
34 5:20–21.   35 Acts 17:23.

fact it goes back to the first announcement of the Redeemer,[36] and the hope subsequently given to Noah after
the flood.[37] St Paul habitually regards the promise as a function of the Jewish Law, even while he has no doubts as to
the superiority of the former over the latter. This appears
from the contrast between them: the promise is a testament,
absolute in character; the Law is a contract, hedged about
with conditions. Consequently, the promise is immutable,
but the Law can be abrogated at will; the promise pledges
God's fidelity irrevocably; by the Law it is pledged only
in proportion to the fidelity of the other contracting party,
the Jewish people. Now by the promise is to be understood
the whole of the gracious prospects for the future revealed
to Abraham, the father of the faithful, prospects affecting
both him and his race. These include the possession of the
Promised Land,[38] a progeny more numerous than the stars
of heaven and the grains of sand in the desert,[39] and finally,
being the most significant of all, a blessing to be inherited by
all the nations of the earth. At the same time, the inheritance
of the promise is limited by God's free election. Thus it does
not extend to all the children of Abraham; it passes first to
Isaac, with the exclusion of Ishmael, and then to Jacob, with
the exclusion of Esau.[40] It is not the carnal, but the spiritual,
posterity of Abraham who are the inheritors of the promised
blessings.

The promise made to Abraham was universal, since all
nations were to be blessed in him.[41] The world-wide exten-
sion of Abraham's blessings takes effect as a response to faith;
those who share the faith of the father of the faithful are
the true sons of Abraham.[42] Moreover, the promise is collective, for it concerns not each of Abraham's descendants,
but his race, his seed.[43] This collectivity is in its turn realized
in union with Christ, who is the unique source of the
blessings. Abraham's true heirs, therefore, are not the Jews,
as such, but the Christians; for they form with Christ one

---

[36] Gen. 3:15.   [37] 9:8 ff.   [38] Gen. 12:7.
[39] 15:5; 22:17.   [40] Rom. 9:6–13.   [41] Gal. 3:8.
[42] Cf. Matt. 3:9.   [43] Gal. 3:16.

and the same mystical person and are thus the spiritual lineage of Abraham. Hence the promise has three characteristics which liken it to the Gospel. It is universal, it is based upon faith, and it is dependent upon grace. The promise is the Gospel seen in anticipation; the Gospel is the promise realized.

What then is the function of the Jewish Law? Is it a step forwards or backwards from the point of view of human progress? [44] There are two points on which the Jews have no advantage over the Gentiles: both alike are under the dominion of sin, both need to be made righteous through faith. And yet: "Of what use is it, then, to be a Jew? What value was there in circumcision? Much, I answer, in every respect; chiefly because the Jews had the words of God entrusted to them." [45] They were the recipients of God's revelation to a unique degree, gaining thereby a light to the mind and a strengthening of the will of which no other people could boast. Nor was this all; the Jews bear a name chosen by God himself—they are *Israelites*. As the elect of God, they are his adopted children; they have the glory of Yahweh dwelling with them. As Israelites, they are the heirs of the patriarchs and inherit the covenant made between God and the holy men of the past. The Jews possess a divine Law transmitted to them by angels; they perform a ritual worship prescribed by God himself; they are still in a special sense the repositories of the promises—for included in these is the promise that from their race the Messiah shall be born. To the Jews belongs the glory of the patriarchs, as it were by family inheritance. Finally, as a climax of honour, they are kinsmen by race of the Messiah, Jesus Christ, the God-Man. It is thus that St Paul sums up the prerogatives of the Jews: "They are Israelites, adopted as God's sons; the visible presence, and the covenant, and the giving of the law, and the Temple worship, and the promises, are their inheritance; the patriarchs belong to them, and theirs is the human stock from which Christ came; Christ, who rules as God over all things, blessed for ever. Amen." [46]

[44] Gal. 3:19.   [45] Rom. 3:1-2.   [46] 9:4-5.

St Paul would not have been a true disciple of his Master if he had regarded the Jewish Law otherwise than as just, noble, holy, spiritual, and given by God. On this point he never wavered. But the truth that filled his mind was that the Law could not bring salvation; in itself it was powerless to make men pleasing to God, even though it could prepare the way for these blessings. A law might have been given possessing this efficacy; in that case "it would have been for the law to bring us justification." [47] But this in fact was not God's design; it was not his intention that man should be able to take credit for his own salvation merely by the observance of the Law.[48] Now if the Law in itself justified, man could boast of his righteousness as of a personal achievement; this being so, he would have no need for redemption, and Christ's death would have been "needless." [49] Nevertheless, the observance of the Law was meant to lead on to justification, even though, for the achievement of this, something needed to be superadded, namely grace. The Jews, in failing to observe the Law, were plunged yet further into sin; so that the Law was being proved ineffectual for its original purpose. God had allowed the Law to be productive of sin in order that its inefficacy might be realized and the need for grace manifested. "The law intervened, only to amplify our fault; but, as our fault was amplified, grace has been more amply bestowed than ever." [50]

The Law was powerless to hold back the invasion of sin and the flood of evil.[51] But God had maintained it to protect the Jews from dangerous contacts with heathendom and as a preparatory discipline until the coming of Christ. If this function was chiefly negative, it was nevertheless invaluable in preserving belief in the one true God and in his unique revelation.[52] The divinely given Law contained within itself the seeds of its own decay; from its dissolution there was to arise a new and higher Law, which would bring the old to perfection. Our Lord himself had taught that on the love of

47 Gal. 3:21.
49 Gal. 2:21.
51 8:3.

48 6:14; Rom. 3:27; 4:2; Eph. 2:8–9.
50 Rom. 5:20.
52 Gal. 3:23–24.

God above all things, and of one's neighbour as oneself, "all the law and the prophets depend." [53] St Paul was to repeat after him: "Love therefore is the fulfilling of the law." [54]

With the coming of the new dispensation the Law was doomed. When the human race had reached its maturity, when the moment fixed by God for its emancipation had come,[55] when the hour he had appointed for the fulfilment of the promise made to the father of the faithful should strike, when Christ, whose coming the Law subserved, should appear, and when the system of grace, with which it is incompatible, should come into being, then the *régime* of the Law would be supplanted for ever. "But in fact scripture represents us all under the bondage of sin; it was faith in Jesus Christ that was to impart the promised blessing to all those who believe in him. Until faith came, we were all being kept in bondage to the law, waiting for the faith that was one day to be revealed. So that the law was our tutor, bringing us to Christ, to find in faith our justification. When faith comes, then we are no longer under the rule of a tutor; through faith you are all now God's sons in Christ Jesus." [56]

The onward march of humanity, considered from the ultimate viewpoint, has Christ for its term. The world itself, that collective entity which remains as yet outside the Christian fold, can know no real progress except as an approach to him. The world, which at the beginning of history sin had invaded,[57] which still vainly boasts of its wisdom,[58] which is compelled to own itself subject to the divine Law,[59] over which the saints will one day sit in judgement,[60] is the world with which God strives so that he may reconcile it to himself in Christ.[61] Human learning and philosophy, which the world laboriously acquires and of which it is so proud, compared to the saving knowledge of Christ, are no more than schoolroom tasks, an alphabet taught to children. This is what St Paul means by "worldly rudiments"—*"the elements*

[53] Matt. 22:40.
[54] Rom. 13:10(R-D.).
[55] Gal. 4:4.
[56] 3:22–26.
[57] Rom. 5:12.
[58] 1 Cor. 1:20.
[59] Rom. 3:19.
[60] 1 Cor. 6:2.
[61] 2 Cor. 5:19.

of the world" (τὰ στοιχεῖα τοῦ κόσμου) [62] They provided an elementary education, from which the Christian, having reached maturity, has emerged and to which he must never return.

See to it that there is no one to victimize you by his philosophy and shallow deceit, according to worldly rudiments, and not according to Christ. . . . If you have died with Christ from these worldly rudiments, why, as though living according to the world, should you be bound by such decrees as, Handle not this, Taste not this, Touch not this, about things which are all to perish in the using? Rules like these are in conformity with the precepts and doctrines of men, which indeed have a show of wisdom in would-be religion, humility of deportment, and bodily austerity, but are not of any value against indulgence of the flesh.[63]

The "weak and beggarly elements" [64] that mankind has now outgrown refer directly to the Mosaic Law and the traditions superimposed on the Code of Sinai by the Rabbis, but they include also the religious customs of the Gentiles. St Paul may also have been warning the Jewish Christians against the syncretism with pagan cults from which they were by no means immune.[65] The "elements of the world" have become identified with merely human traditions and are opposed to the doctrine of Christ. With his coming their sanction had been withdrawn and the life had gone out of them; by his death they were nailed to the Cross.[66] The Christian is now dead to the Law; [67] for to observe the Law has in his case no value, except as ministering to false piety and self-esteem.[68] "God forbid that I should make a display of anything, except the cross of our Lord Jesus Christ, through which the world stands crucified to me, and I to the world." [69] The "fulness of the times"—the measure of time being regarded as a kind of receiver, which is continually

[62] Col. 2:8, 20; cf. Gal. 4:3.   [63] Col. 2:8, 20–23(S.).
[64] Gal. 4:9(S.).
[65] Cf. Guignebert, *The Jewish World in the Time of Jesus*, p. 243.
[66] Col. 2:14.   [67] Gal. 2:19.
[68] Gal. 6:13; Col. 2:22–23.   [69] Gal. 6:14.

filled by the addition of successive moments—had come, the
moment when God had decided to bring all things to a head
in Christ: ἀνακεφαλαιώσασθαι τὰ πάντα ἐν τῷ Χριστῷ. [70] Human progress is not to be measured by the mere sequence of
events, on the assumption that what is latest is also what is
best. It depends upon the free decree of God, who because
he is timeless and almighty can break through the temporal
order and fix *this* as its culminating point. So in fact he has
done: "It was his loving design, centred in Christ, to give
history its fulfilment by resuming everything in him, all that
is in heaven, all that is on earth, summed up in him." [71]

Not only the Old Testament Law, but the natural wisdom
of Greece and Rome and all that is of value in every civilization before or since, find their completion in "the mystery
of God, which is Christ, in whom lie hidden all the treasures
of wisdom and knowledge." [72] Thus the Incarnation remains
the dominating factor throughout all history. It is not that
men are thereby called upon to live in the past, centring
their thoughts upon an event which took place in first-
century Palestine. They will indeed be well repaid in ac-
quainting themselves with the temporal setting of that event;
but the Incarnation looks forwards as well as backwards. In
the incarnate Word human history is focused upon an eternal
point, which is therefore contemporary with all the ages.
This is implicit in what we have seen, both of the manner
in which man's nature has been assumed by the Son of God
into a personal union with himself, so as never afterwards
to be separated from him, and of the way in which the Incarnation is continued in the Church, as being herself the
complement, the "fulness," of Christ. Hence it follows that
the work of re-establishing all things in Christ must likewise
continue as an integral part of his redeeming mission. Mankind as a whole, and indeed the entire creation, is summed
up, "recapitulated," in Christ. Such are the implications of
St Paul's words quoted above.[73]

[70] Eph. 1:10. This is the scriptural source for the doctrine of the *recapitulation in Christ*. The Vulgate has *instaurare omnia in Christo;* which the
Rheims-Douay Version renders: "to re-establish all things in Christ."
[71] Eph. 1:9–10.   [72] Col. 2:2–3(W.).   [73] Eph. 1:10.

This doctrine of the "recapitulation in Christ" presents one of the most fruitful aspects of the mystery of the incarnate Word. A brief outline of what it suggests will form a fitting conclusion to our present study. It is interesting to recall that the theology of "recapitulation" was first clearly formulated by St Irenaeus (who was born in or near Smyrna in Asia Minor somewhere between A.D. 135 and 140); he exercised great influence as Bishop of Lyons. Among those from whom he had learned his Christianity was St Polycarp, who had spoken with those who had seen the Lord and was himself a disciple of St John the Evangelist. Irenaeus thus moved in the apostolic circles for whose benefit St Paul had written the Epistle to the Ephesians. He had acquired from them a pious regard for the Catholic rule of faith and a collection of historical traditions and principles.[74] In order to combat the errors of Gnosticism, he wrote a work in five books entitled *Against the Heresies;* this is our source for the doctrine of "recapitulation in Christ." [75]

What St Irenaeus was concerned to maintain against the Gnostic dogma of an essential opposition between matter and spirit, together with its conception of a number of intermediaries between God and man, was that the Creator of the world and the supreme God are one and the same; and further, that Christianity is real redemption, a redemption which only Christ could effect. These principles are so obviously scriptural, and have entered so completely into the Catholic tradition, that they may seem to us truisms. But they were by no means truisms in the world of Irenaeus. The Gnostic heretics who, but for their antinomianism, might be described as a Puritan intelligentsia, believed that the universe contained a vicious combination of opposing elements; accordingly they regarded Christ's redeeming work as the separation of what was unnaturally united. Irenaeus, on the contrary, began with the idea of the absolute causality of God the Creator, and was therefore convinced of the good-

[74] Cf. Harnack, *History of Dogma*, II, 238, n. 1.
[75] The following are the most important passages: *Adv. Haereses*, iii, 16, 6; *P.G.* 7, col. 925–26; 18, 1 col. 932; 18, 7, col. 937–38; 21, 10, col. 954–55; 22, 2–3, col. 956–58.

ness of all creation. He saw that the Gnostic dualism was based on a denial of this; hence, while agreeing that there were in the world faulty estrangements and separations, he drew from the evidence a very different conclusion. He taught that the Redemption is the reunion of things unnaturally separated; this, in a word, is the "recapitulation in Christ." Whence it follows that the central point in history is not the Logos of Greek philosophy, taken over by the Gnostics, but the divine Logos who had become flesh, Christ the incarnate God.

Thus there is one God and Father, as we have shown, and one Christ Jesus our Lord, who comes throughout the entire economy and recapitulates all things in himself. But in all things he is also man, fashioned by God; therefore he recapitulates man in himself. The invisible has become visible, the incomprehensible has become comprehensible, and the impassible passible; and the Word has become man, recapitulating all things in himself. Thus, just as he is the first among heavenly and spiritual and invisible things, so also is he first among visible and corporeal things. He takes the primacy upon himself, and by making himself the Head of the Church, he draws all things to himself at the appointed time.[76]

Christ is the Head of a new race, the first-fruits of regenerated humanity. It was therefore necessary that he should recapitulate in his own person the different stages of an ordinary human life, so that man's whole nature might be united to God. Hence the second Adam "did not evade any condition of humanity, nor exempt himself from the law which was his own ordinance for the human race." [77] Infancy, childhood, boyhood, youth, manhood, all these he passed through, both as an example to us and that he might dedicate them for ever to God. Thus, after experiencing every phase of a normal human life, "he yielded himself to death, that in all things he might have the pre-eminence, existing before all and going before all." [78] In Christ, the new Adam, all mankind gains the victory over sin. "For it behoved him

[76] *Adv. Haereses,* iii, 16, 6; col. 925–26.   [77] ii, 22, 4; col. 784.
[78] *Ibid.*

who was to destroy sin and redeem man, subject to the
penalty of death, that he should himself be made the same
thing that man was—man who had been enslaved by sin and
held by death; in order that sin might be destroyed by man,
and man might go forth from death. . . . God recapitulated
in himself the ancient formation of man, that he might kill
sin, deprive death of its power, and give life to humanity." [79]

Christ is thus the consummation of all that has gone before; he comprises humanity in himself as its true representative, along with all its spiritual and material elements. He
assumes human nature in its completeness as it had been left
by the Fall, sin only excluded. He passes through each successive stage of human life in order to consecrate it afresh
to God. As Mediator between God and man, he presents it,
according to the truth of its original idea, to the Father.
He brings it back into harmony with God's first design for
it; as the archetype of manhood, he restores it in his own
person to its initial wholeness and purity. He "joins the end
to the beginning." In him, not only humanity but all the
material and spiritual creation is summed up, gathered into a
unity of which he is the representative. Thus "recapitulation
in Christ" implies the recombination of elements which had
been disintegrated by the Fall, the restoration of man and
his universe to their original truth and unity.

This comprehensive view of the significance of Jesus
Christ, modified in certain of its details, has become part
of the heritage of Catholic Christianity. To form the complete picture it requires to be filled in with the doctrine
we have already examined; but in itself it presents an aspect
of the Incarnation which seems to have a particular relevance to the needs of our own time. When so many are at
a loss to discover a meaning for their existence, it should be
encouraging to find that the incarnate Word brings them
not only eternal salvation but a coherent philosophy of life.
We cannot live simply at a rational level, still less on a basis
of mere sensation; intellect and senses alike call for their
fulfilment, the latter in subordination to the former. Ulti-

[79] Irenaeus, *Adv. Haereses,* iii, 18, 7; col. 938.

mately they can achieve this only in the harmonious unity of the Word made flesh. Those of our progressive-minded contemporaries who imagine that they can transcend institutional Christianity, to reach a "mystical" communion with the Absolute without reference to the humanity of Christ, are deceived when they think themselves enlightened; in reality they have a closer kinship with the absurdities and superstitions of the early Gnostics—the "intellectuals" of the first and second centuries—than with the great religious thinkers of the past. To the mind which relies on reason alone, now as in St Paul's day, the Cross of Christ must always appear "folly"; [80] to those who live in the light of faith, possessors of the true *gnosis*,[81] it remains "the power of God and the wisdom of God." [82]

To this truth the central Christian tradition bears faithful witness. *Instaurare omnia in Christo*—"to restore all things in Christ"—was the motto chosen for himself by one of the saintliest of the modern Popes.[83] Christ's visible representative on earth proclaims the age-long mission of his Church—to make known to the world, in season and out of season, "the unfathomable riches of Christ." [84] "Salvation is not to be found elsewhere; this alone of all the names under heaven has been appointed to men as the one by which we must needs be saved." [85] To which may be added the words of the Epistle to the Hebrews announcing the theme we have attempted to expound: "What Jesus Christ was yesterday, and is to-day, he remains for ever." [86]

[80] 1 Cor. 1:23. [81] Cf. 1:5; 2 Cor. 4:6. [82] 1 Cor. 1:24.
[83] Pius X, *Analecta Ecclesiastica*, 1903, p. 376. [84] Eph. 3:8.
[85] Acts 4:12.
[86] Heb. 13:8. NOTE: The relevance of this conclusion to the predicament of the modern world finds support in a memorable passage from one of the most distinguished of contemporary historians: "In our war-ridden generation, in which the lately brilliant prospects of a neo-pagan dominant minority have been rapidly growing dim, the sap of life is visibly flowing once again through all the branches of our Western Christendom; and this spectacle suggests that perhaps, after all, the next chapter of our Western history may not follow the lines of the final chapter of Hellenic history. Instead of seeing some new church spring from the ploughed-up soil of an internal proletariat in order to serve as an executor and residuary legatee of a civilization that has broken down and gone into disintegration, we may yet live to see a civilization that has tried and failed to stand alone being saved, in spite of itself, from a fatal fall by being caught up in the arms

of an ancestral church which it has vainly striven to push away and keep at arm's length. In that event a tottering civilization which has shamefully succumbed to the intoxication of a showy victory over physical nature, and has applied the spoils to laying up treasure for itself without being rich towards God, may be reprieved from the sentence—which it has passed upon itself—of treading out the tragic path of κόρος – ὕβρις – ἄτη; or, to translate this Hellenic language into a Christian imagery, an apostate Western Christendom may be given to be born again as a *Respublica Christiana* which was its own earlier and better ideal of what it should strive to be."—
Arnold J. Toynbee: *A Study of History* (Abridgement of volumes I–VI by D. C. Somervell; Oxford University Press 1946), p. 403.

APPENDIX

SOURCES

BIBLIOGRAPHICAL NOTE

KEY TO REFERENCES

THE SOURCES

The primary source for the foregoing study is the proclamation concerning Jesus Christ upheld by the Catholic Church. This is contained in "the word of God, written or handed down"; [1] that is to say, in (a) Holy Scripture and (b) the divinely guarded Tradition.

a) Our chief document has necessarily been the Bible, and in particular, the New Testament. With the exception of an occasional phrase, as rendered by the author, the texts quoted are drawn from four approved Catholic translations: *The New Testament Newly Translated into English* by Mgr Ronald Knox [2] and the Rheims-Douay Version (which, unless otherwise stated, is the source for the Old Testament quotations), both based in principle upon the Vulgate Latin; [3] *The New*

[1] Denz., 1792.

[2] Apart from the isolated words and phrases mentioned above, all citations are from this version unless otherwise stated. Where another version is quoted, this has been indicated by the appropriate initial letters; see Key to References below.

[3] The position held by the Vulgate in the Catholic Church, which is often misunderstood, has recently been clarified by Pope Pius XII: "As for the decree of the Council of Trent requiring the Vulgate to be the Latin version 'which all should use as authentic,' this, as everybody knows, concerns only the Latin Church and her public use of the Scripture, and obviously in no way derogates from the authority and value of the original texts. For the subject of discussion at that time was not the original texts, but the Latin versions then circulating, among which the Council rightly decreed preference to be given to that version which 'has been approved by long use in the Church for so many centuries.' Hence this pre-eminent authority, or *authenticity,* of the Vulgate was determined by the Council not primarily on critical grounds, but rather by reason of its legitimate use in the Church through the course of so many centuries, a use which proves this version, as understood by the Church, to be entirely immune from any error in matters of faith and morals; so that, by the very witness and approval of the Church, it may safely and without danger of error be cited in discussions, lectures and sermons. Its authenticity is therefore more properly called *juridical* than *critical.* Consequently the said authority of the Vulgate in matters of doctrine in no way forbids—indeed to-day it almost requires—this same doctrine to be proved and corroborated also by means of the original texts; nor does it forbid the aid of these texts to be generally invoked, in order to make clearer and explain better the true meaning of Holy Writ. Nor, finally, does this same decree of the Council of Trent prohibit the making of translations into the vernacular, and what is more,

Testament of the late Father F. A. Spencer and *The West-minster Version of the Sacred Scriptures,* being translations directly from the Greek. It may be well to anticipate the charge of mere eclecticism by stating the principles underlying the selection from these versions: In texts of primary dogmatic or exegetical importance, the most literal rendering of the Greek has been adhered to; in other passages, where the sense seems to be made more intelligible by a translation less verbally exact, choice has been made accordingly. In certain memorable passages from the Gospels, it was thought preferable to avoid departing from the more familiar Biblical phraseology. Only in subordination to these guiding principles have such considerations as aptness to context, and felicity of phrasing, been allowed to play their part.

b) The traditional Christian teaching on the Incarnation was formulated, as to its substance, at the early Oecumenical Councils. The relevant documents can conveniently be found in Denzinger's well known *Enchiridion Symbolorum.* (The abbreviation Denz. in the foot-notes is followed by the appropriate marginal number.) Other ecclesiastical and authoritative documents are either referred to in full, or the contracted form, where it is not self-explanatory, is explained in the Key to References below. As witnesses to the Tradition, the Catholic Fathers are cited according to the standard edition of Migne's *Patrologia.* The doctrinal exposition, when not confined within the limits of strictly Biblical theology, draws chiefly upon St Thomas Aquinas. Unless otherwise stated, all references are to his *Summa Theologica.*

The secondary sources are indicated in the following Bibliographical Note. No complete bibliography to a work of this kind, each section of which has an exhaustive bibliography of its own, could be compiled within reasonable limits. What follows therefore is no more than the expression of conscious indebtedness; it is not so much a course of reading recommended to the student

---

from the original texts themselves, for the use and benefit of the faithful and for the easier understanding of the word of God, as we know to have been done in many places laudably and with the approval of the authority of the Church."—Encycl., *Divino afflante Spiritu,* 30 Sept. 1943. *A.A.S.* XXXV, pp. 309–10. The Encyclical has been translated by Canon G. D. Smith, and is published by the Catholic Truth Society, London, as a pamphlet entitled, *Stand by the Bible.*

—though a number of the works cited obviously fall within that category—as a tribute of thanks to the authors concerned.

BIBLIOGRAPHICAL NOTE

The titles of foreign works followed by (E. T.) indicate that an English translation is available. Where such works have been consulted only in translation, the English title alone is given. The use made of the labours of Anglican and non-Catholic scholars generally (indicated with an asterisk *) is both explained and duly acknowledged in the Preface.

Adam, Karl. *The Son of God.* London 1934.

Allo, E. B. *Le Scandale de Jésus.* Paris 1927.

Arendzen, J. P. *Whom do You Say?.* London 1927.

———. *Men and Manners in the Days of Christ.* London 1928.

*Barth, Karl. *The Doctrine of the Word of God.* Edinburgh 1936.

Billot, L. *De Verbo Incarnato.* 7th edition. Rome 1927.

*Brunner, Emil. *The Mediator.* London 1934.

Chapman, John. *The Four Gospels.* London 1944.

*Charles, R. H. *The Apocrypha and Pseudepigrapha of the Old Testament.* 2 vols. Oxford 1913.

Dawson, Christopher. *The Making of Europe.* London 1932.

*Deissman, Adolf. *Paul—A Study in Social and Religious History.* London 1926.

Dieckmann, Hermannus. *De Ecclesia.* 2 vols. Freiburg 1925.

Diekamp, Franciscus. *Tractatus de Redemptione per Jesum Christum.* Paris 1933.

*Dodd, C. H. *The Parables of the Kingdom.* London 1936.

Duchesne, Louis. *The Early History of the Christian Church.* 3 vols. London 1909–24.

Felder, Hilarin. *Christ and the Critics.* 2 vols. London 1924.

Festugière, A. J. *L'Idéal Religieux des Grecs et L'Évangile.* Paris, 1932.

Fillion, L.-Cl. *Vie de N.-S. Jésus-Christ.* 3 vols. Paris 1925.

*Findlay, J. Alexander. *The Gospel according to St. Luke—A Commentary.* London 1937.

Gardeil, A. *Le Donné révélé et la théologie.* Juvisy, Seine-et-Oise 1909.

Garrigou-Lagrange, R. *Le Sens Commun—la Philosophie de l'être et les formules dogmatiques.* Paris 1922.

Garrigou-Lagrange, R. *De Revelatione per Ecclesiam Catholicam Proposita.* 2 vols. 3rd edition. Rome 1929-31.

——. *Le Sauveur et son amour pour nous.* Juvisy, Seine-et-Oise 1933.

Gilson, Étienne. *Introduction à l'étude de Saint Augustin.* Paris 1929

Goodier, Alban. *The Public Life of Our Lord Jesus Christ.* 2 vols. London 1930.

——. *The Passion and Death of Our Lord Jesus Christ.* London 1933.

*Gore, Charles. *The Reconstruction of Belief.* London 1926.

Grandmaison, Léonce de. *Jésus Christ—sa personne, son message, ses preuves.* (E. T.) 2 vols. Paris 1928.

*Guignebert, Ch. A. H. *The Jewish World in the Time of Jesus.* London 1939.

*Harnack, Adolf. *History of Dogma.* 7 vols. London & Edinburgh 1894–97.

——. *What is Christianity?* 3rd revised edition. London & New York 1904.

Hefele, Charles Joseph. *A History of the Church Councils,* 5 vols. Edinburgh 1894–96.

Héris, Ch.-V. *Le Mystère du Christ.* Paris 1928.

*Hoskyns, Edwyn [and *Davey, Noel]. *The Riddle of the New Testament.* Revised edition. London 1936.

——. [edited by Davey, Noel] *The Fourth Gospel.* 2 vols. London 1940.

*Kidd, B. J. *A History of the Church to* A.D. *461.* 3 vols. Oxford 1922.

*Kierkegaard, S. *The Present Age,* containing the essay "On the Difference between a Genius and an Apostle." London & New York 1940.

Kissane, Edward J. *The Book of Isaiah,* 2 vols. Dublin 1941–43.

*Klausner, Joseph. *Jesus of Nazareth—his Life, Times and Teaching.* London 1925.

Lagrange, M.-J. *Le Messianisme chez les Juifs.* Paris 1909.

——. *Le Judaïsme avant Jésus-Christ.* Paris 1931.

——. *Évangile selon Saint Matthieu.* Paris 1923.

——. *Évangile selon Saint Marc.* Paris 1911.

——. *Évangile selon Saint Luc.* Paris 1921.

——. *Évangile selon Saint Jean.* Paris 1925.

Lagrange, M.-J. *Synopsis Evangelica*. (E. T.) Paris 1926.
———. *L'Évangile de Jésus-Christ*. (E. T.) Paris 1929.
La Taille, M. de. *Mysterium Fidei*. (E. T.) Paris 1921.
Lattey, Cuthbert. *The Psalter—in the Westminster Version of the Sacred Scriptures*. London 1944.
Lebreton, Jules. *Histoire du Dogme de la Trinité des origines au Concile de Nicée*. (E. T.) 2 vols. Paris 1927–28.
———. *The Life and Teaching of Jesus Christ Our Lord*. 2 vols. London 1935.
——— [and Zeiller, Jacques]. *The History of the Primitive Church*, 3 vols. London 1942–46.
Lemonnyer, Fr. *The Theology of the New Testament*. London 1929.
Lepin, M. *L'Idée du Sacrifice de la Messe*. Paris 1926.
*Major, H. D. A., *Manson, T. W., *Wright, C. J., *The Mission and Message of Jesus—An Exposition of the Gospels in the Light of Modern Research*. London 1940.
*Mascall, E. L. *Christ, the Christian and the Church*, London 1946.
Masure, Eugene. *The Christian Sacrifice*. London 1944.
Mersch, Emile. *Le Corps Mystique du Christ*. (E. T.) 2 vols. Brussels 1936.
Myers, Edward. *The Mystical Body of Christ*. London 1930.
*Niebuhr, Reinhold. *The Nature and Destiny of Man*. 2 vols. London 1941-43.
*Oesterley, W. O. E. *The Jews and Judaism during the Greek Period—The Background of Christianity*. London 1941.
Ollivier, M.-J. *The Parables of Our Lord*. Dublin 1927.
*Ottley, Robert L. *The Doctrine of the Incarnation*. 7th edition. London 1929.
*Otto, Rudolf. *The Kingdom of God and the Son of Man*. Revised edition. London 1943.
Penido, M. T.-L. *Le Rôle de l'Analogie en Théologie Dogmatique*. Paris 1931.
Prat, F. *La Théologie de Saint Paul*. (E. T.) 2 vols. 3rd edition. Paris, 1925–27.
*Prestige, G. L. *God in Patristic Thought*. London & Toronto 1936.
Rivière, J. *The Doctrine of the Atonement*, 2 vols. London 1909.

Robert, A. and Trictot, A. *Initiation Biblique.* Paris, Tournai, Rome 1939.

*Sanday, W. *Outlines of the Life of Christ.* 2nd revised edition. Edinburgh 1906.

Schultes, R.-M. *De Ecclesia Catholica.* Paris 1931.

Smith, George D. *Mary's Part in our Redemption.* London 1938.

Sturzo, Luigi. *Church and State.* London 1939.

*Temple, William. *Readings in St. John's Gospel.* 2 vols. London 1939–40.

*Thornton, L. S. *The Common Life in the Body of Christ.* London 1942.

Tixeront, J. *History of Dogmas.* 3 vols. St Louis, Mo. 1910–16.

———. *Précis de Patrologie.* 6th edition. Paris 1923.

Vonier, Anscar. *The Personality of Christ.* London 1915.

———. *Christ the King of Glory.* London 1932.

Vosté, J.-M. *Commentarius in Epistulam ad Ephesios.* 2nd edition. Rome & Paris 1932.

KEY TO REFERENCES

The following abbreviations have been used for purposes of reference:

A.A.S.: *Acta Apostolicae Sedis.*

col.: column (in Migne's *Patrologia*).

D.A.F.C.: *Dictionnaire Apologétique de la Foi Catholique.*

Denz.: Denzinger-Bannwart-Umberg: *Enchiridion Symbolorum Definitionum et Declarationum de rebus fidei et morum.*

D.T.C.: *Dictionnaire de Théologie Catholique.*

E. T.: English Translation

H.D.B.: *Hastings: *A Dictionary of the Bible.*

LXX: *Septuagint;* the ancient Greek version of the Old Testament.

P.G.: *Patrologia Graeca* (ed. Migne).

P.L.: *Patrologia Latina* (ed. Migne).

R-D.: Rheims-Douay Version of the Bible.

S.: Spencer, F. A.: *The New Testament* (translated from the Greek).[1]

vs.: verse.

vv.: verses.

W.:*Westminster Version of the Sacred Scriptures.*

[1] By permission of the Macmillan Company, publishers.

NOTE: *a*) When the Vulgate numeration of the Psalms differs from the Hebrew, the Vulgate is given first, followed by the Hebrew in brackets; e.g., Ps. 109 (110):1.

b) In references to the *Summa Theologica*, the Roman numerals indicate the Part, q. the number of the Question, art. the Article, and ad the reply to an objection. Thus III, q. 8, art. 1, ad 2 signifies the reply to the second objection in the first Article of the eighth Question in the third Part. The *Summa* has only three parts; but the second Part is itself divided into two—hence the numeration Ia IIae and IIa IIae. Once this is understood, an apparently complicated system of reference becomes easy to manage.

INDEXES

I.

INDEX TO BIBLICAL PASSAGES

II.

Index to Subjects : Persons : Places

Aaron, 232

Abraham, 207, 212, 235, 246, 275, 316, 335, 336

Adam, 34, 197, 243, 277, 278, 309, 313, 318, 333, 335. *See also* Jesus Christ

Adoption, 272, 274

Adoptionism, 21, 182, 204 n.

Adoration, 200, 221

Adversus Haereses of St Irenaeus, 342

Advocate, 120. *See also* Holy Spirit

Agony, in Gethsemane, 126–7, 190, 264; on the Cross, 136–38, 197,

Allegory, 71, 118, 324

Alliance, 233

Almsgiving, 60

Analogy of being, 12

Angels, 37, 108, 200, 258, 337

Animals, 213

Anna, 27

Annas, 128

Annunciation, the, 25, 256, 275–6. *See also* Mary, the Blessed Virgin

Anointed, the Lord's, 151. *See also* Messiah

Anointing, 151, 186

Anthropomorphism, 13

Antinomianism, 342

Antioch, 321

Anti-Semitism, 76

Anxiety, 64

Apocalypse, Synoptic, 298 n.

Apocalypses, Jewish, 155

Apologetics, 19, 82, 201

Apostasy, 62, 76, 319, 327

Apostle, significance of, 229 n.

Apostles, 32, 33, 40, 74, 84, 143, 226, 304, 317

Apostolic See, the, viii.

Arabia, 27

Aramaic, 137, 150, 154, 171

Arians, 7, 10

Artist, the, 213

Ascension, the, 6, 146, 148, 185, 199, 273

Asceticism, 63, 266

Assumption, the, 289, 291. *See also* Mary, the Blessed Virgin

Atonement, 147, 190, 219 (*see also* Redemption); Day of, 62

Attributes, the divine, 182, 314

Augustus, Emperor, 23

Authority, 228, 229; of Christ, 145, 191, 224, 226, 229, 250, 256; of apostles, 84, 226, 229. *See also* Ecclesiastical Magisterium, Church

Babylon, 307

Baptism, 33, 89, 147, 200, 312, 328; of Jesus, 30–34, 165, 186, 216

Barabbas, 134

Bartimaeus, 100

βασιλεία, 296, 297

Beatitudes, 42–52, 68. *See also* Sermon on the Mount

Being, concept of, 13, 14. *See also* Analogy

Belief, baptismal profession of, 7; verbal profession of, 67. *See also* Faith

Bethany, 100

Bethesda, pool of, 166

Bethlehem, 23, 24, 27, 28, 178, 280

Bethsaida, 96

Betrayal of Jesus, 101, 104, 106–08, 127, 131

Biology, 11

Bishops at Chalcedon, 8

Blessed Sacrament. *See* Eucharist

Blood, 173, 185, 217, 242, 243, 247, 328; of new Covenant, 103, 109, 225, 236, 240

Body, 188, 189, 206, 328; Christ's human, 184; mystical, of Christ, 89, 90, 114, 118, 146, 237, 239, 253, 261, 274, 286, 287, 291, 293, 302, 309–29 *passim.*

Bread, the living, 109, 254. *See also* Eucharist

Brethren, 316

Bride, 90, 326, 329

Bridegroom, 318

Caesar, 100, 135

Caesarea Philippi, 85, 145, 150, 161

East, wise men from, 27, 279
Easter, 140, 147, 333
Ecclesiastical magisterium, 7, 8, 12
Education, Jewish, 29
Egoism, 212
Egypt, 28, 117
ἐκκλησία, 86 n.
Elect, the, 258
Elias, 93, 95
Emmaus, 142, 157
Empire, Holy Roman, 304
Enchiridion of St Augustine, 218 n.
Encyclicals, Papal: *Divino afflante Spiritu*, v, 18 n., 350 n.; *Mystici Corporis Christi*, 285 n., 286, 287, 288, 308, 309–329 *passim.; Quas primas*, 255 n., 257 n.
Enoch apocalypse, 155
Entombment of Jesus, 139
Ephesus, St Paul at, 6; Council of (A.D. 431), 8, 187, 280
Ephraim, 28
Epiphany, 33, 259 n.
Esau, 336
Eschatology, 297, 298 ff., 308
esse personale, 189
Essence, 180
Eucharist, 65, 89, 200, 235, 240, 326 ff.; institution of, 108–111
Europe, history of, 9
Eutychianism. *See* Monophysitism
Evangelists, 16, 103. *See also* Gospel
Evil, 47, 49, 62, 265
Evolution, 169
Exaltation of Christ, 148, 242, 331
Example of Christ, 268 ff.
exinanitio, 183
Existence, 181, 206, 207
Exodus, Book of, 103
Expiation, 219, 233, 242, 271 n.
Ezekiel, Book of, 56, 154
Ezra apocalypse, 155

Faith, 66, 109, 114, 201, 271, 336; Catholic, 8, 185. *See also* Rule of Faith
Fall, the, 335. *See also* Adam, Sin
Family, Holy, 27, 29
Fasting, 60, 62
Fathers of the Church, 7, 71, 184, 196, 235, 307; ante-Nicene, 6; as witnesses, 350
Feet, washing of, 104 ff.
Fideism, 12 n.
Filioque clause, 271 n.
Five thousand, feeding of, 79, 254
Flesh, 109, 179, 183, 204, 230, 318, 345

Forgiveness, 46, 62, 65, 68, 96, 137
Form-criticism, 16, 1⁻
Freedom. *See* Liberty
Friendship of Jesus, 264
"Fulness of Christ," 238, 310, 315 ff., 341

Gabriel, 275
Galatia, 321
Galileans, 113
Galilee, 29, 81, 113, 141, 144, 254, 295
Genius, 209, 228
Gentiles, 97, 100, 152, 302, 337, 340
Germany, nineteenth-century, 3
Gethsemane, 126, 264
Gifts, sacrificial, 233
Glory, 94; light of, 140
Gnosis, the true, 345
Gnosticism, 10, 168, 342 ff.
God, Fatherhood of, 3, 61; immutability of, 179; self-communication of, 202 ff., 212; the living, 172
God the Father, 165, 173, 182, 183, 185, 245, 248 ff., 294
Godhead. *See* Deity, Divinity
God-Man, the, 174–201
Golden Rule, the, 66
Golgatha, 136, 285. *See also* Calvary
Good, the, 208
Gospels, sources behind, 16, 22; Synoptic, vi, 146, 154, 162, 294, 302, 330
Goths, 305
Grace, 118, 196, 255, 289, 291, 319; St Augustine's doctrine of, 315 n.; sanctifying, 186, 194. *See also* Hypostatic Union
gratia capitalis, 257, 290, 310, 317
Greece, 341
Greeks, 11, 90, 97, 171, 244

Hades, Christ's descent into, 139–40
Hallel, the hymn, 103
Headship of the Church, Christ's, 257, 310, 317 ff., 325. *See also gratia capitalis*, Jesus Christ
Healing, 81, 228
Heart, hardening of, 77; purity of, 47. *See also* Sacred Heart
Hell, gates of, 86
Heresy, 188
Herod, King, 23, 27, 28
Herod Antipas, 98, 133
Heroism, 59
Hierarchy of priesthood, 233; ecclesiastical, 310

High Priest, 128, 129, 130, 153. *See also* Jesus Christ
Holiness, 42, 209; of Christ, 186, 194
Holy Spirit, 98, 117, 143, 149, 183, 185, 192, 226, 261, 276, 318; as Giver of truth 16, 120; as proving the world wrong, 120–3; as "soul" of the Church, 275, 318; in relation to Christ, 269–75
Humanitarianism, 47, 50, 204
Humanity, 174–213 *passim*, 233, 339
Humility, 43, 105, 199
Hypocrisy, 59–60
Hypostasis, 180, 193
Hypostatic Union, 180 ff., 209, 211

I am sayings in St. John, 207 n.
ἱλαστήριον, 271
Imitation of Christ, 245, 262, 321, 322
Immaculate Conception, 26, 278. *See also* Mary, the Blessed Virgin
Immolation, 111, 238
Immortality, 124, 146, 172
Incarnation, the, 166, 341; *a priori* reasoning with reference to, 21; and the chosen people, 26; Catholic doctrine of, 4, 21 (*see also* Chalcedon); considered as a theophany, 21; fittingness of, 201, 333; metaphysics of, 198; motive for, 230, 333; mystery of, 14, 201, 332; "necessity" for, 252, 333; sum and substance of, 25; temporal setting for, 341
in Christ, 269, 273, 318, 325
in Christ Jesus, 133
in the Spirit, 273, 318
Incommunicability, 181
Incorporation in Christ, 312
Independence, 208
Individual, 181
Individuality, 211
Individuation, 212
Infallibility. *See* Church
Innocent, suffering of the, 246
Innocents, massacre of the, 28
Inspiration of the Gospels, 16
Intelligence, divine and human in Christ, 207
Intercession, 217, 218, 242, 286 ff.
Interim-ethic, 3
Intermediary, 217. *See also* Mediator, Mediatorship
Isaac, 298, 336
Ishmael, 336
Israel, 150, 216, 227, 310; apostasy of, not irrevocable, 76; consolation of,

27; deliverance of, 103; house of, 86; King of, 136; lost sheep of house of, 89; vineyard of, 164
Israelites, concern of, for temporal well-being, 172; privileges of, 337

Jacob, 298, 336
Jairus, 79
James, St, son of Zebedee, 99, 126
Jericho, 30, 99, 156
Jerusalem, 26, 28, 30, 101 ff., 144, 147, 255, 307
Jesus Christ, Our Lord and Saviour [PART I. *Incidents in the life of*; PART II. *Points of doctrine concerning*; PART III. *Teaching of*; PART IV. *Titles and Offices of*]
    I. *Incidents in the life of*: pre-existence with the Father, 123, 330; birth at Bethlehem, 23–26; presentation in the Temple, 26; visited by the wise men, 27; flight into Egypt, 28; boyhood, 29; the hidden life, 282; loss and finding in the Temple, 29, 283; Baptism, 30–4; temptations, 34–9; at marriage feast of Cana, 292; ministry of healing, 79 ff.; calling of disciples, 83; choosing the Apostles, 40, 83 ff.; preliminary teaching, 40; conflict with the Pharisees, 40; preaching, 39–69; the parables, 69–78; founding of the Church on Simon Peter, 85 ff.; prophecy of the Passion, 91; Transfiguration, 93 ff.; end of the Galilean ministry, 96; at Feast of Tabernacles, 96; with Martha and Mary, 97, 266; at Jericho, 99; Holy Week, 101; end of the public ministry, 101; at the Last Supper, 103–26; in Gethsemane, 126–8; before Annas and Caiaphas, 128; denied by Peter, 129; before the Sanhedrin, 129; found deserving of death, 130; before Pilate, 131; sentenced to death, 136; crucified, 137; words from the Cross, 137 ff.; dereliction, 137; death, 138; burial, 139; descent into Hades, 139–40; appears alive to Mary Magdalen, 141; to two disciples, 142; to the Apostles, 142; institutes sacrament of Penance, 143; appears to Thomas, 143; in Galilee, 144; makes Peter shepherd of the flock, 145; other appearances, 145; at Jerusalem, 147; ascends into Heaven, 148; exalta-

Jesus Christ (continued)
    tion at right hand of the Father,
    148
    II. *Points of doctrine concerning:*
    character, 174 ff., 262 ff.; consub-
    stantial with the Father, 176; con-
    substantial with us, 175; "one per-
    son, two natures," 176; Chalce-
    donian definition, 175–77; the
    "Word made flesh," 167–174, 179;
    the Hypostatic Union, 180; the
    exinanitio (self-emptying), 182 ff.;
    he alone became incarnate, 183; as-
    sumed a real human body, 184; a
    "grace," 185; the Hypostatic Union
    unending, 186; source of his unique
    prerogatives, 186; the manner in
    which the divine and human na-
    tures are united, 187 ff.; two wills,
    190; acts according to the divine
    and human natures, 191; all his
    acts *personal* to him, 192; the
    communicatio idiomatum, 193; his
    holiness, 194; his knowledge, 195,
    300; possessed the beatific vision,
    197, 225; his power, 196; his com-
    plete manhood, 196; immunity
    from sin, 197; capacity to suffer,
    197; his freedom, 197; adorability,
    198; his Sacred Heart, 199; relation
    to the Holy Spirit, 270 ff.; relation
    to the Blessed Virgin Mary, 275 ff.;
    his "finality," 174, 341 ff.
    III. *Teaching of:* The Beatitudes,
    42; on meekness and patience, 43;
    consolation to the sorrowful, 44; on
    hungering and thirsting after right-
    eousness, 45; on mercy and for-
    giveness, 46; on purity of heart, 47;
    on peacemakers, 48; on suffering,
    49; the reversal of human values,
    52; on the salt of the earth, 52; at-
    titude to the Law and the proph-
    ets, 53 ff.; on the scribes, 55; use of
    Old Testament scripture, 56; the
    need for a change of heart, 57; on
    marriage, 57; on truth-telling, 58;
    on bearing with injuries, 58; on the
    meaning of the word "neighbour,"
    59, 97; on purity of motives, 60;
    on prayer, 61 f.; the Our Father,
    61 f.; on fasting, 62; on riches and
    worldly cares, 63; on serving two
    masters, 64; on trusting in God's
    providence, 64; on judging others,
    65; on prudence, 65; on the treat-
    ment of others, 66; "By their fruits

you shall know them," 67; on lip-
service, 67; his manner of teaching,
68; on the kingdom of God, 295 ff.;
on the service of others, 104 ff.; on
humility, 105; on the Eucharist,
109 ff.; the "new commandment,"
111; on faith, 114; on praying in
his name, 115, 123; on the love of
God, 115; on peace, 116; on the
True Vine, 118; "no longer servants but friends," 118; on mutual
charity, 119; on being hated for his
sake, 119; on the work of the Holy
Spirit, 120 ff., 270 ff.; "Take courage; I have overcome the world,"
124; on eternal life, 124; his prayer
to the Father, 125–6; his claim to
be Messiah and Son of God, 130
(*see also* Messiah, Son of God); on
his kingship, 131 ff. (*see also* Kingdom of God, Kingship of Christ);
on the source of all human authority, 135; on the Last Things and
the need for being ever on the
watch, 298 ff.
    IV. *Titles and Offices of:* Adam,
the second, 34, 313, 343; Head of
the Church, 257, 310, 317 ff., 325;
High Priest, 232 ff.; King, 254–260;
Law-giver, 42, 256; Lord, 150, 153,
154; Master, 42, 149; Mediator,
215–24; Messiah, 91, 151–61; Prince
of Peace, 26; Prophet, 224–30; Redeemer, 213, 214–60; Saviour, viii,
24, 111, 198; Shepherd, the good,
87; Son of David, 152, 153; Son of
God, 130 n., 135, 161–67; Son of
Man, 154 ff.; Victim, 89
John the Baptist, St, 30, 62, 95, 141,
    154, 174, 210, 227, 264, 295
John the son of Zebedee, St, 93, 99,
    126, 144
Jordan, the river, 30, 216
Joseph, foster-father of Jesus, 23, 25,
    27, 28, 29, 282 n., 283
Joseph of Arimathea, 83, 139
Journey to Jerusalem, Lucan, 96 ff.
Joy, 119, 122
Judah, 235
Judea, 26
Judas Iscariot, 100, 101, 104 ff., 127,
    131, 135
Judgment, 99, 167. *See also* Escha-
    tology
Justice, 43, 45, 65; divine, 25; and
    mercy, 248 ff.
Justification, 217, 243

Philip, St, Apostle, 114
Philippi, 6
Philosopher, the, 202
philosophia perennis, 12
Philosophical schools, Greek, 11
Philosophy, Cartesian, 9; critically realist, 14; Greek, 11, 343; of life, 344; rôle of, in Catholicism, 12–15
Physics, 11
Piety, 60, 63
Pilate, Pontius, 128, 131 ff., 139, 255
Platonism, 168
πλήρωμα, 310, 315
Poet, the, 202, 213
Popes, modern, 18, 345
Poverty, 42–3
Power, 259
Prayer, 61 ff., 328; Christ's, 32, 127; at Last Supper, 125–6; See also Lord's Prayer
Predestination, 306
Pre-existence of Christ, 123, 166, 273, 330
Prerogatives of Christ's humanity, 193 ff.
Presence, the Real, 110. See Eucharist
Presentation, the, 26. See Mary, the Blessed Virgin
Pride, 38, 50
Priest, High. See High Priest
Priesthood, Aaronic, 233 f.; Levitical, 235; of Christ, 232–255
Priests, Apostles made, 111
Primacy of Church, visible, 85 ff., 112, 145, 149, 301, 307, 326; See also Peter, St
Proclamation, 227, 349
Progress, 334, 337, 339
Projection, psychological, 47
Prologue of St John's Gospel, 167 ff., 173
Promises, the, 335 ff.
Prophecy, 30, 56
Prophet, Christ as, 224–30; official garb of, 30. See also John the Baptist, St
Prophets, 56, 74, 82, 93, 142, 295; false, 67
Propitiation, 242, 246, 247, 271 n., 328
Protestantism, Liberal, 4
Protevangelium, the, 35, 336
Providence, 61, 64; theology of, 335
Prudence, 65
Psalter, Hebrew, 355
Psychologists, 9, 209
Publican, 99. See also Tax-gatherers

Rabbis, 56, 58, 69, 77, 86, 151, 156, 266
Rachel, 28
Ransom, 62, 158, 214, 231, 247
Rationalism, 16
Rationalists, 177, 202; French, 3
Recapitulation in Christ, 220, 341 ff.
Reconciliation, 217, 219, 243, 246, 339
Redeemer, the, 214–60; See also Jesus Christ
Redemption, 147, 245, 246, 247, 251, 252, 254; objective, 286; theories of, 245 n., 248
Reformation, the, 247
Regina caeli, the hymn, 279
Relatives of Jesus, 282 n.
Religion, of Israel, 48; of Jesus, 52, 68; philosophy of, 12; virtue of, 238
Remission of sins, 110
Remnant, doctrine of, 74
Reparation, 238, 252
Repentance, 246
Representative, 233
Research, historical, and Christ, 19; modern, 15
Resurrection, the, of Christ, 140-49; of mankind, 297, 309
Revelation, 14, 201, 332
Riches, 43, 62, 63
Righteous One, the, 242, 254
Righteousness, 45, 46, 121. See also Holiness, Justice, Justification
Romans, the, 5, 92
Rome, 135, 302, 305, 341
Royalty, 234, 255, 256
Rule of faith, 6, 7, 8

Sabbath, 54, 81, 98, 163
Sacraments, 89, 200, 291. See also Baptism, Eucharist, Penance
Sacred Heart of Jesus, 199, 329; Feast of the, 287; Litany of the, 200
Sacrifice, 239 ff.
Sadducees, 100, 102
Saints, the, 205, 209, 211, 212, 213, 287
Salt of the earth, 52–3
Salvation, 200, 345. See also Redemption
Samaria, 152
Samaritan, the good. See Parables
Sanctification, 243, 313
Sanctity. See Holiness
Sanhedrin, 99, 100, 128, 129, 226, 228
Satan, 35, 36, 81, 116, 122, 194, 208, 243, 244, 247, 264
Satisfaction 219, 245

III.

Index to Authors and Non-Biblical Names

Abelard, 245 n.
Alaric, 305
Alfred, King, 304
Allo, E. B., 78 n.
Anselm, St, 251, 252
Aquinas, Thomas, St. *See* Thomas Aquinas
Arendzen, J. P., 102 n., 176
Aristotle, 10, 13
Athanasius, St, 7, 10, 180
Augustine, St, vii, 71 n., 75 n., 83, 180, 210, 218 n., 220, 237, 239, 241 n., 268, 275, 285, 304, 305, 306, 307, 313 n., 314, 315

Bacon, Francis, 133 n.
Barth, K., 4, 12 n.
Baur, F. C., 3
Benedict, St, 210
Benoit, P., 17 n.
Bernard, J. H., 78 n.
Bernard of Clairvaux, St, 210, 244, 275
Boethius, 180, 181
Bouquet, A. C., 12 n.
Bousset, W., 168 n.
Brunner, E., 4, 262
Bultmann, R., 17 n.
Buzy, D., 75 n.

Cadoux, C. J., 17 n.
Caird, E., 9 n.
Callan, C. J., ix
Calvin, 248
Celsus, 162
Chambers, R. W., 260 n.
Charlemagne, 304
Charles, R. H., 155 n.
Crashaw, Richard, 24 n.
Cromwell, Thomas, 260
Cyprian, St, 6
Cyril of Alexandria, St, 8, 10, 113, 187, 220, 313

Dante, 260, 292
Deissmann, A., 271 n., 311 n.

Descartes, 9, 10
Dibelius, M., 17 n.
Dieckmann, H., 84 n.
Dodd, C. H., 71 n., 73 n.
Driver, S. R., 154 n.
Dru, A., ix, 229 n.

Eliot, T. S., 38 n.
Epiphanius, St, 272
Eutyches, 8, 187, 190, 202

Francis of Assisi, St, 43, 206
Fuller, R. C., ix

Gardeil, A., 9 n.
Garrigou-Lagrange, R., 9 n., 181 n., 202 n.
Gilson, E., 9 n., 306 n.
Goethe, 263
Gore, C., 268 n.
Grandmaison, L. de, 76, 77 n., 78 n., 79 n., 298 n.
Gregory VII, Pope St, 304
Gregory of Nazianzus, St, 192 n.
Gregory of Nyssa, St, 220
Guignebert, C., 340 n.

Hananiah, Rabbi, 163
Harnack, A., 3, 10, 11, 168, 304 n., 342 n.
Hefele, C. J., 8 n.
Hegel, 9 n., 10
Héris, C. V., 257 n.

Ignatius of Antioch, St, 90 n., 304
Illingworth, J. R., 175 n.
Innocent III, Pope, 304
Irenaeus, St, 6, 220, 342, 344 n.

Jerome, St, v, 86 n.
John Damascene, St, 192 n.
John of the Cross, St, 202
Josephus, 30
Julian of Eclanum, 268
Jung, C. G., 209 n.

380